The Essential Elements
of the Detective Story,
1820–1891

The Essential Elements of the Detective Story, 1820–1891

LeRoy Lad Panek *and*
Mary M. Bendel-Simso

McFarland & Company, Inc., Publishers
Jefferson, North Carolina

RECENT WORKS OF INTEREST AND FROM MCFARLAND
Early American Detective Stories: An Anthology, edited by LeRoy Lad Panek and Mary M. Bendel-Simso (2008; softcover 2014); *After Sherlock Holmes: The Evolution of British and American Detective Stories, 1891–1914*, by LeRoy Lad Panek (2014); *Before Sherlock Holmes: How Magazines and Newspapers Invented the Detective Story*, by LeRoy Lad Panek (2011); *The Origins of the American Detective Story*, by LeRoy Lad Panek (2006); *Reading Early Hammett: A Critical Study of the Fiction Prior to* The Maltese Falcon, by LeRoy Lad Panek (2004); *The American Police Novel: A History*, by LeRoy Lad Panek (2003)

LIBRARY OF CONGRESS CATALOGUING-IN-PUBLICATION DATA

Names: Panek, LeRoy, author. | Bendel-Simso, Mary M., 1965– author.
Title: The essential elements of the detective story, 1820–1891 / LeRoy Lad Panek and Mary M. Bendel-Simso.
Description: Jefferson, North Carolina : McFarland & Company, Inc., Publishers, 2017. | Includes bibliographical references and index.
Identifiers: LCCN 2017000240 | ISBN 9781476666990 (softcover : acid free paper) ∞
Subjects: LCSH: Detective and mystery stories—History and criticism. | Fiction—19th century—History and criticism.
Classification: LCC PN3448.D4 P356 2017 | DDC 809.3/872—dc23
LC record available at https://lccn.loc.gov/2017000240

BRITISH LIBRARY CATALOGUING DATA ARE AVAILABLE

ISBN (print) 978-1-4766-6699-0
ISBN (ebook) 978-1-4766-2811-0

© 2017 LeRoy Lad Panek and Mary M. Bendel-Simso. All rights reserved

No part of this book may be reproduced or transmitted in any form or by any means, electronic or mechanical, including photocopying or recording, or by any information storage and retrieval system, without permission in writing from the publisher.

Front cover image of Gun Shot Argument, magnifying glass and newspaper border © 2017 Roman Stoliarchuk/benoitb/iStock

Printed in the United States of America

McFarland & Company, Inc., Publishers
  Box 611, Jefferson, North Carolina 28640
  www.mcfarlandpub.com

For Penelope Taylor

TABLE OF CONTENTS

Introduction	1
1. Setting	7
2. Law and Lawyers	38
3. Physicians and Forensics	66
4. Women and Detectives	97
5. Crime and Criminals	137
6. Detectives and Their Stories	170
Afterword	215
Appendix: Women Writers	223
Bibliography	225
Index	233

Introduction

More than a decade ago, while looking for historical material about detectives in old issues of the *New York Times* and *Washington Post* online we found something we were not looking for. Sure there were news pieces about detectives in the 19th-century papers, but there were also pieces that were clearly fiction, pieces that were detective stories—from the 1830s onward. That was at a time when digitizing and online publishing of historical newspapers by private enterprises, states' historical societies, universities, and the Library of Congress' *Chronicling America* project were just beginning. These hitherto unavailable resources now provide access to an immense amount of information about a lot of things—literally millions of pages of magazines and newspapers printed in cities, towns, and even hamlets from Maine to California beginning in the 1830s. We started to look for detective stories in them. Then we also started looking at the books and magazines found on Google Books, various online periodical databases, and volume after volume of family story papers in library archives. We found that the total amount of new material available to anyone interested in popular fiction in 19th-century America was enormous and was becoming even more enormously enormous every year. We decided to start collecting the detective stories we found. But there were some problems. The first was to decide what was a detective story and what wasn't. Many of the stories we have discovered were labeled as detective stories in their original publications, so they weren't a problem. But some weren't. Many of those were about the actions of characters specifically called detectives, so they were easy. And then there were stories in which someone not called "a detective" (a lawyer, a physician, an amateur) does what detectives do—solves real or imagined crime problems. These were somewhat more problematic. Since we were dealing with very early popular literature, some of it from before the word *detective* was coined or current, we decided to err on the side of generosity. Incidentally we had to contend with the fact that current OCR programs cannot always distinguish between f's and t's in some old newsprint and include the word *defective* in searches for the word *detective*, and the necessity of sorting imaginary from real detectives in newspapers in which the word *story* can be used for news as well as for fiction. The excitement of discovering the first few detective stories in 19th-century papers led us to decide to catalog and eventually publish online every detective story printed in the United States before 1891, the date dictated by the publication of the first Sherlock Holmes short story and the beginning of what really turns out to be the rebirth of the detective story. We called our project The Westminster Detective Library and it can be found at https://wdl.mcdaniel.edu. Setting aside serial fiction (which also had a role to play in the history of the detective story), our first notion was that we would find maybe a hundred short stories. We reached five hundred. Then the total became a thousand. Now we are not sure where it will end. We are still looking for—and finding—new stories to read, catalog, and put on the waiting list for processing and publishing online. We have put out of our minds for the time being that searchable databases exist for historical English and even Australian newspapers—and the fact that we know that they contain detective stories. Limiting ourselves to American short stories is daunting enough for now.

One of the things we are doing in the pages below is taking a look at what we have collected so far and what it says about detective stories during what amounted to their formative years. There doubtless remain a trove of undiscovered stores; yet we still reckon that we have a pretty solid sample of 19th-century short detective fiction—well over 1,300 stories. That sample, we believe, reveals a great deal about both detective stories and 19th-century fiction in America. To a far lesser extent, it also says something about the detective story in Britain and France.

The basic discovery that we have made is that newspapers played a vital role in the creation and development of the detective story. The 19th-century newspapers that are sources of the majority of the pieces we have collected were a lot different from the newspapers some people still remember. First of all, most towns in the U.S. had their own paper, like Orion Clemens' *Western Union* in Hannibal, Missouri, where his brother, Mark Twain, worked. Indeed, one sign of being a town instead of a settlement or crossroads was having a newspaper. The year Tombstone, Arizona, became an official town its first paper, *The Tombstone Epitaph*, began publishing. Towns had papers with their names attached to the words *gazette, news, reporter, citizen, sentinel, herald, bulletin*, and *press*. Some attached a political party to the town's name, and some editor-publishers opted for something more colorful—thus *The Sedalia Weekly Bazoo, White Cloud Chief, The Raftman's Journal, Catoctin Clarion, Alpena Argus, The Arizona Kicker, The Branding Iron*, and *The Ellensburg Dawn*. Although lots

Introduction 3

of towns had newspapers, before the telegraph system fully developed there was precious little news to print from outside the local community. Of course there were always advertisements—advertisements which take up more space than the copy in some papers. Most importantly for us, mid–19th-century newspapers published fiction, a lot of it. Through the 1860s it is not unusual to find that the whole first page of the typical town newspaper in every section of the country consisted of a short story, with a poem and a local-interest piece thrown in. To date, no one has undertaken a comprehensive study of this mountain of fiction. That being said, even a brief survey shows three recurring types of fiction in mid-century American newspaper fiction: love stories, ghost stories, and detective stories. Many papers even added a separate headline (i.e., "A Ghost Story") or inserted the genre of the story in the title of stories like "Human Bones: A Modern Ghost Story" in *The Preble County Democrat* (December 23, 1858); "Love, Its Sunshine and Shadow" in *Vermont Phœnix* (June 2, 1855), and the word *detective* in the titles of many of the stories we discuss below. Those three types of fiction form a pattern that surely needs much more scrutiny and one which no doubt says something about the development of popular fiction and its audience. But here we are only concerned with detective stories. Finding and reading them presents a more than generous set of issues, conundrums, and problems.

We have already touched on availability: although we have found a very significant number of detective stories in rescued 19th-century papers, periodicals, and story papers, it is entirely likely that there are others that have not and perhaps will not be found. The near certainty of missing resources (and of unknown originals) adds to the considerable number of knotty editorial problems which do not come as single spies. First of all, plagiarism ruled 19th-century journalism. If an editor-publisher found a story he or she liked in a magazine or another paper—or even just needed copy for the day's or week's edition, it was cut out and reprinted. It happened with "The French Detective: The Little Affair." Atypically, we know that it was first published in *Ballou's Monthly* on October 1866. Then, two years later, it went viral. On November 7, 1868, it appeared as "The French Detective" in the *St. Joseph Herald*; ten days later both *The Lincoln County Herald* and the *Fayette County Herald* ran the same story; *The Fayetteville Observer* published it on November 26, *The Democrat* printed it on December 1, and in Irasburg, Vermont, the *Orleans Independent Standard* printed it on December 8, 1868. And who knows where else? Stealing stories from abroad was just as popular as nibbling from American publications: titles were often printed in the U.S. within weeks of their publication in London or Paris. Much to his dismay, American papers ripped off Dickens's stories and used his name without permission or royalties. The same thing happened with the detective pieces extracted from *Chambers' Edinburg Journal*. It's not that American printers were the only freebooters in the English-speaking world. "The Coiners of Kansas," for example, a story that circulated in American papers in 1880 appeared in the *Darling Downs Gazette* published in Toowoomba, Queensland, Australia, on December 23, 1881. And in 1887 "A Foot-Light Flash. A Detective's Story" by *The New York Ledger*'s Sylvanus Cobb, Jr., appeared in New Zealand's *Tuapeka Times*. But that is a whole other voyage of exploration.

While citing sources for stories stolen from England (without paying for them) added a whiff of respectability to magazines and newspapers, some stolen goods were edited to pass as American originals—the 1863 volume *Strange Stories of a Detective; or The Curiosities of Crime* does this to Ward and Lock's London published *The Detective's Note-Book* (1860). The widespread practice of pilfering texts also brings up the possibility that some of the many stories about French detectives published in American papers and magazines might have been translations of French originals. The real giveaway in this regard is fact that Gaboriau's "Une Disparition" from *Le Petit Vieux des Batignolles* (Paris 1876) turns up as the anonymous "The Jandidier Mystery" in the *Freeport Daily Bulletin* on December 3, 1877, and in New York State in the *Franklin Gazette* four days later. While story papers and magazines usually gave writers byline credit, the practice was not routinely followed by newspapers until late in the period. Without writers' names and dealing with an era when publishers acknowledged sources only when it served their purposes, knowing which of a number of versions represents the original becomes vexing. Thus, "Saved by a Mark: A Detective Story" and "Tried for Murder" published in late 1872 and early 1873 are essentially the same story—except one is more than 100 words longer. Was it editing to shorten it, or rewriting it to make it longer? Given questions like these, while we have usually quoted and cited the earliest versions of stories that we have found, it is with the knowledge that some of them may not be the original versions.

There is, however, enough whining connected with trying to assemble 19th-detective stories to occupy a whole college of bibliographers. Why, one might ask, collect and read 1,300-plus short detective stories in the first place? The first answer is that they represent a robust literary movement that began before Poe's tales of ratiocination. This movement had a definite connection with contemporary developments in Anglo-American jurisprudence and went back and forth between England, France, and America for more than half a century before the creation of Sherlock Holmes. Unlike Poe's stories that were directed at intellectuals or the dime novels written for boys, the stories in magazines, newspapers and story papers were meant for and read by a wide class of readers: whole families. And they were not Eastern or Southern or Western stories—the same stories appeared from coast to coast and even in the Indian territories. The big questions are (1) are they any good? and (2) how does one deal with so many stories? The answer to the first question is, not many of them: while in general 19th-century short detective stories escape from trenchant melodrama and overt didacticism (which in itself is a point worth making), most, *but not all*, are humdrum, scarcely mediocre entertainment. Right now we are not about singling out the original, inventive, clever, well-written stories—even though some will get passing mention below. Writing about them is another project. Before us we have the remains of the first question nagging at the second one: how to deal with so many stories if some or most of them are humdrum, scarcely mediocre entertainment? Our view has been that while it is easy and maybe even sometimes necessary to dismiss one story written by an untalented anonymous writer, it is necessary and important to take notice when the same or similar kind of story is told twenty, fifty, or seventy times, in different places, and over a period of years. We are interested, therefore, in aggregates.

Looking at and asking questions about detective fiction published in 19th-century America yields some tantalizing suggestions about the origins and fundamental nature of the genre. But at the present they need to remain hypotheses, because given the enormity of just the American material by itself we have not had world enough or time to take on British or French periodical literature which may, and in the case of Britain probably does, contain hundreds of yet to be identified detective stories printed in magazines and newspapers before *The Strand* discovered Sherlock Holmes.

Because the material we have been looking at hasn't been seen or read for a century and a half—and has never been discussed—the following chapters are, roughly speaking, hybrids: part introduction, part classification, part description, part sample, part history, part analysis. What we are trying to do is isolate and discuss some of the fundamentals of the detective story as it began and grew in 19th-century America. We have tried to cram all of those objectives into chapters which are about setting, characters, and meaning in 19th-century short detective fiction. Since almost all of our primary material is obscure and some of it will not be online by the time of publication, we have quoted generously. All of the newspaper, story paper, and magazine fiction to which we refer is (or eventually will be) available in The Westminster Detective Library (https://wdl.mcdaniel.edu). We apologize ahead of time for the awkward intrusiveness of some of our in text citations which have been made necessary by the fact that we deal with multiple stories with the same or similar titles and different origins. Above all it is our hope that readers will come away with new perspectives on detective fiction, the history of the genre, and 19th-century literature (popular and otherwise) in the U.S. And we also hope that they will visit The Westminster Detective Library to draw their own conclusions.

We would like to thank McDaniel College and our student assistants for their support. Sally Jones, Lisa Russell, Rhonda Stricklett, and Jordan Sly have been generous, helpful, and timely in answering barrages of questions and chasing elusive resources and deserve our thanks. We are also grateful to Greg William for his patience and advice. Most of all, our thanks to Chris, Paul, Flannery, and Izzy.

1

Setting

> It will give you no interesting sidelights on archeology, there will be no beautiful descriptions of scenery, no treating of economic problems, no racial reflections, no history—Agatha Christie, *Come, Tell Me How You Live*

In the 19th century, American writers and readers together created the detective story. But they did not create the story about the detective. In the beginning, stories from France and then from England whetted the new nation's appetite for reading about the lives and works of the new profession invented overseas. Here's how and when stories about detectives came to the United States.

A Digression on Imports

Until the mid–1850s very few stories about detectives published in the United States actually took place in America. The earliest stories about detectives to arrive in the country were imported from France. This is not terribly surprising given that, for the first part of the century, Philadelphia was the center of publishing in the U.S., and with Napoleon's exiled elder brother, Joseph-Napoléon Bonaparte, and other exiles, as well as the richest man in the U.S., former Frenchman Stephen Girard, in residence, the city had a decidedly Gallic flavor. The earliest of these stories about detectives recounted the exploits of actual French detective Eugène François Vidocq (1775–1857). "Vidocq and the Sexton" appeared in the *Philadelphia Album and Ladies Literary Gazette* (February 20, 1830). Four years later, in 1834, Cary and Hart of Philadelphia, one of the nation's premiere publishers, printed the first American translation of Vidocq's memoir, *Memoirs of Vidocq: Principal Agent of the French Police Until 1827*. Four years after that actor-writer-publisher William Edwin Burton printed a series of nine stories ("Unpublished Passages in the life of Vidocq, The French Minister of Police") in his *Gentleman's Magazine* from September 1838 to May 1839. A number of East Coast newspapers picked up Burton's Vidocq stories and reprinted them in 1839. And then in 1841 Burton's former editor, Edgar Allan Poe, used Paris as the setting for "Murders in the Rue Morgue"; in 1843 he used it again for "The Mystery of Marie Roget," and finally for "The Purloined Letter" in 1844. Stories about Vidocq continued to be published sporadically for the rest of the century, including "Spirits Utilized: Two thieves Captured Through Information Given by the Spirit of Vidocq" (*The Bismarck Weekly Tribune*, November 13, 1875), and a surge of popularity for French detectives occurred after Émile Gaboriau's works appeared in the late 1860s; but after mid-century Paris and its environs lost their preeminence as the setting of choice for fiction about detectives printed in the United States.

While he was publishing stories about Vidocq, British born William Edwin Burton wrote two stories about detectives for his *Gentleman's Magazine*. One of them, "The Cork Leg" (March 1838), takes place in France. Set in London, the other story, "The Secret Cell" (September and October 1837), was the first of what was going to be a British invasion. Beginning in 1849 one of Britain's most popular magazines, *Chambers' Edinburgh Journal*, began to publish a series of stories about a plainclothes English policeman (i.e., a detective) called "Recollections of a Police-Officer." *Chambers'* published the first of these "Police-Officer" stories, which came to be titled "The Gambler's Revenge," on July 28, 1849. Almost as fast as a copy of the magazine could cross the Atlantic, the story began to appear in American newspapers: on September 4, 1849, it appeared in *The Boston Daily Atlas*; on October 10, 1849 in *The Tioga Eagle*; and on November 16, 1849, in *The Oshkosh True Democrat*. In 1852 New York City publishers Cornish and Lamport gathered all of the *Recollections* stories together and issued them as *Recollections of a Policeman*—the first (albeit unauthorized) collection of detective stories to be published as a book. Individual stories from the "Recollections of a Police-Officer" series continued to be reprinted in American newspapers for the next decade. After *Chambers'* began its series of stories about detectives, Charles Dickens turned his attention to detectives and began publishing stories about them in his magazine *Household Words*. They, too, were pirated by American publishers: "The Butcher's Story—A Detective Police Party," published in London on August 10, 1850, appeared two months later in the *Brooklyn Eagle*. Perhaps the most illuminating of the transatlantic passage of texts appeared in New York publisher Dick & Fitzgerald's collection of short stories *Strange Stories of a Detective; or The Curiosities of Crime* (1863). It begins with an "autobiographical" introduction by the author:

I continued in this until the new police was established. Well, I joined the force, and you have no idea what a difference there was between the new system and the old, or rather, between system and no system. There was a good deal of animosity against us for a long while, and all sorts of opprobrious epithets were bestowed upon us. They called us Mayor's Pups, and dear knows what.

This simply added a superficial disguise to cover the transparent plagiarism from Ward and Lock's *The Detective's Note-book* (1860):

> I continued in this until the new police was established *by Sir Robert Peel, and I must not omit to pay my tribute of admiration to the genius of that enlightened statesman, who was far in advance of his time.* Well, I joined the force, and you have no idea what a difference there was between the new system and the old, or rather, between system and no system. There was a good deal of animosity against us for a. long while, and all sorts of opprobrious epithets were bestowed upon us [our italics].

Throughout the nineteenth century American book publishers, as well as magazines and newspapers, routinely turned to *Chambers'* for stories about detectives. In the 1850s, for example, Harper Brothers caught the detective bug from *Chambers'*. In its first year *Harper's New Monthly Magazine* published two stories from *Chambers'* "The Recollections of a Police-Officer" series ("Villainy Outwitted" [November 1850] and "The Robber's Revenge" [January 1851]). And then, in 1852 *Harper's* published five crime/detective stories. All of them—including "Crime Detected: An Anecdote of the Paris Police" by Henry Mills Alden (May 1852) and "A Reminiscence of a Bow-Street Officer" (September 1852)—take place abroad. In spite of an occasional French incursion, British sources dominated the piracy market in the last half of the 19th century. *Chambers' Edinburgh Journal*, to be sure, was the stand-out favorite with stories such as "A Great Jewel Robbery" (August 1869), "A Queer Clue" (October 1877), and "A Mysterious Valise" (July 1885) being cribbed. Detective tales from Dickens' magazines *Household Words* and *All the Year Round* crop up in U.S. publications through the 1880s. "A Bank Note in Two Halves" (September 1879) and "In Answer to an Advertisement" (February 1887), among others, came from *Cassell's Magazine*. Stories from *Bentley's Miscellany*, *Once A Week*, *The Cornhill Magazine*, *The London Paper*, *London Society*, *The London Referee*, *The London Truth*, and *The London World* also provided detective stories for readers of American magazines and newspapers.

On Setting: A Brief Survey

Although "Vidocq and the Sexton" in 1830 provides readers a time-frame (after 1814) and mentions several French place names, all the detective story in it actually requires is a nondescript place in which the treasure is hidden and another undefined place for the villain to be uncovered. That it takes place in France makes no real difference. Although "Marie Laurent" (the first of the Vidocq stories run in *Burton's Gentleman's Magazine*) takes place in Paris and opens with "One night, as I was going my rounds with some of my men...," in the way of setting, the detective interest only requires a wealthy person's residence which has no particular connection with Paris or France. Likewise, "The Strange Discovery," the fifth of Burton's Vidocq pieces (January 1839), superficially takes place in Paris, but requires only a bedroom in a hotel with space enough for two beds in order to convey the essence of its crime and detection story. The Vidocq stories, then, are all about Vidocq; the setting really doesn't matter much—it's the characters (actually only Vidocq) that make them French.

Shortly before he undertook to print the nine Vidocq stories in the series "Unpublished Passages in the Life of Vidocq, The French Minister of Police" in his *Gentleman's Magazine*, William Burton published his own story about detecting, "The Secret Cell," in 1837. It's a much longer piece than the Vidocq exploits, running in two issues of the magazine, and has a lot more character drawing, dialog, and action. Burton adds plenty of local color with place names ("Joe walked rapidly towards Shoreditch Church. I was within a hundred feet of him when the early Cambridge coach dashed down the Kingsland Road") and even local dialect ("The waiter declared that 'nothin' of a four-veel natur, 'cept a vaggin and a nearse' had passed"). He even hints at the beginning of the piece that the following narrative would become an exposé in the same vein as the urban mysteries and misery stories begun by Eugène Sue five years later:

> About eight years ago, I was the humble means of unraveling a curious piece of villainy that occurred in one of the suburbs of London; it is well worth recording, in exemplification of that portion of "Life" which is constantly passing in the holes and corners of the Great Metropolis.

While Burton's introduction of the police and his detective is unarguably English, nevertheless the precise descriptions of the thoroughfares, inns, and the monastery do nothing to serve the detective plot. All they do is add gothic touches to embellish the detective's search, and, as far as that goes, they could be anywhere as long as they are lonely thoroughfares, dark inns, and a portentous monastery. The heroes do search said monastery for the "secret cell," but Burton provides no detail and supposes that from reading Gothic fiction like *The Monk* his readers would assume that secret cells were standard appurtenances of all monasteries. There is no surprise. In short, "The Secret Cell" is too literary to be a real detective story. The same generalized treatment of setting can be seen in Burton's other story, "The Cork Leg" (March 1838), except that in that story the abundant detail about goings-on in post–Napoleonic France serve as surrounding for the story's central puzzle of how to identify the man with an artificial limb in a group of people who wish to shield him. Neither the dueling-field of Paris nor the chateau where characters engage in funny walks has detail beyond the absolute minimum. In effect "The Cork Leg" is a three-act farce.

Shortly after the spate of stories about detectives in *Burton's Gentleman's Magazine*, Poe had a go at the evolving form and revolutionized, maybe even invented, the detective story—or one type of detective story at least. Part of that had to do with his approach to setting. Prior to Poe, setting was on its own: it had little or no connection with the essentials of the detective story—i.e., the plot. While the Vidocq stories take place in France, what happens in them could happen to a detective anywhere. Poe, on the other hand, made the setting an integral part of the narrative. This can be seen if one reverse engineers "The Murders in the Rue Morgue." Take away (or change) all of the street names and the darkened mansion, forget about Dupin's odd habits, drop the deduction demonstration about the actor, and delete the mistaken accusation of Le Bon, and even move it to another city—like, say, Philadelphia, or any a city cosmopolitan enough that it could be plausible to overhear the speech of a Frenchman, Spaniard, Italian, Englishman, German, and Russian. The elements of setting that remain are the essentials of Poe's story: (1) an apartment with specified interior including a chimney and windows; (2) at least one flight of stairs leading to the apartment; and (3) an apartment in a building with a lightning rod. The "locked room" detective story in "The Murders in the Rue Morgue," therefore, relies on the scene of the crime, one of the new focuses that Poe brought to the form. And so in "The Mystery of Marie Roget" there has to be the river, and in "The Purloined Letter" there must be Minister D—'s apartment and furniture. While the particular city doesn't matter much in the Dupin tales—his Paris, in fact, has Philadelphia and then New York in their background—they are all decidedly metropolitan. But the setting and intention of "Thou Art the Man!" differ from the earlier stories. While in his Dupin stories Poe focuses readers' attention on enigmatic evidence, in "Thou Art the Man!" he gives readers very little to go on before springing his jack-in-the-box surprise. Of course, "Thou Art the Man!" does not take place in France and the decoding of the Rattleborough enigma very clearly takes place in small-town U.S.A. Indeed, one of Poe's aims in "Thou Art the Man!" is to define the small town and its denizens as an assembly of credulous nincompoops. To this end he amps up the circumstantial evidence motif which he used with the accusation and arrest of Le Bon in "The Murders in the Morgue" and has a Rattleborough jury condemn a patently innocent man to death:

Mr. Pennifeather, amid the loud execrations of all Rattleborough, was brought to trial at the next Criminal Sessions; when the chain of circumstantial evidence, [...] was considered so unbroken and so thoroughly conclusive, that the jury, without leaving their seats, returned an immediate verdict of *"Guilty of Murder in the First Degree"* [*Godey's Lady's Book*, November 1844].

Admittedly the denouement takes place at a banquet up at the big house, but what matters there is only that the gathering provides an audience for the narrator. In "Thou art the Man!" Poe gave his readers characters drawn in the broadest strokes, and a setting done with the same brush. "Thou Art the Man!" centers on the macabre surprise ending, but to make that work he chose the smalltown setting, and the pattern of the circumstantial-evidence story—a tradition of crime/justice fiction which, as he knew, had had and would continue to have a defining influence on detective fiction for the rest of the century. In the development of the detective story that makes a difference; and while Burton had toyed with conventional treatments of setting, it was Poe who made setting important, even necessary.

Small Towns and Circumstantial Evidence

When Poe published "The Murders in the Rue Morgue" in 1841, Paris had a population of 935,261 and greater London had a population of almost two million. In contrast, New York had a population of 515,547 and Philadelphia's was 93,665. Indeed, the 1850 census listed only ten cities in the country (with New York at the top) with a population of more than 50,000—that year Cleveland's population was 17,034, Memphis 8,841, and Indianapolis 8,091. Also there were only thirty-one states in 1850, with much of the country frontier territory. So in 1841 the United States was largely made up of small towns and sparsely settled spaces. For American readers, therefore, stories about crimes and police detectives in far-off Paris or London contained exotic allure, an element that also attached to New York when detectives from the metropolis became regular characters in fiction late in the 1850s. From early in the century, however, a kind of fiction featuring crime and increasingly detection made more direct contact with the experience of smalltown readers in America than tales of crime in London or Paris or even New York—the circumstantial evidence story.

Originally written to showcase and protest an inflexible system of justice and draconian punishments in England, stories centered on the dangers of circumstantial evidence began at the start of the nineteenth century. Writers based these stories on the difference between direct, or eyewitness evidence, and indirect, inferential, circumstantial evidence and the tragic errors caused by dependence on the latter. There will be a lot more about these stories in the chapter on law and lawyers. British tales about circumstantial evidence placed blame for injustice on antiquated laws and harsh, inflexible judges. American stories about circumstantial evidence, on the other hand, placed far more stress on the traditional ingredients of tragedy, being in the wrong place at the wrong time. In short they placed more emphasis on setting. Like Poe's "Thou Art the Man!" they emphasized some qualities taken by writers as emblematic of small towns in the United States.

Before the late 1850s, almost all crime/detective stories set in the United States take place in small towns. "Mr. Snicker's Misadventure" enunciates the somewhat paradoxical prevailing attitudes about cities and towns before the Civil War:

> Uncle Isaac Snickers, citizen of Gossippee, a charming little village some ways back in Connecticut, had finally made up his mind that it was high time for him to go to New York. He had been once, when he was a boy in a satinet jacket and bone buttons, and never since. From that day forward to this very important one of his resolution, he had kept himself quite at home, while the great metropolis had gone on growing like a monstrous giant, as it is [*Ballou's Dollar Monthly Magazine*, January 1856].

After an encounter with crime and a detective on his way to the city, Mr. Snickers makes a beeline back to Gossippee. There was for him, as for story paper readers, no place like home. And those small towns is where detective stories set in the United States began. Even after the war, the enormously popular *The New York Ledger* continued to favor detective stories set in small towns, often small towns surrounded by wild nature. Early on the atmosphere of wild places and small towns served as the setting for stories about detection. There is nature-gothic in the setting of "The Blasted Tree" in *The Casket* of 1827 which begins on a virtual Walpurgis night imagined by inhabitants of an isolated village:

> It was a night in which the fancy of an honest German could not fail to conjure up a thousand phantoms his shrieking ghosts cried from the crevices of every sapless tree; his witches rode on the pale moon-beams, in the distant and scarcely perceptible mist that spread a thin veil over the beautiful stars; and the wandering spirits of departed friends peeped, like premature resurrectionists from behind every thicket.

Even before Poe's Rattlebourough in "Thou Art the Man!," the American frontier appeared as setting in stories about crime and justice. "Circumstantial Evidence" recounts a tragic misinterpretation of evidence, but begins by setting this pastoral scene:

> Beneath the magnificent sycamores which bordered a lovely stream in the southwest part of Kentucky, a company of emigrants had pitched their encampment for the night. The tents were set up, the night-fire threw its gleams upon the water, the weary horses were feeding,

the evening repast was over, and preparations were made for repose. The party consisted of three brothers with their families, who were wending their way to the new lands of the distant Missouri [*The Illinois Free Trader*, November 27, 1840].

This bit of the exotic frontier, however, serves as stark contrast to the miscarriage of justice that takes place in the small town where the travelers settle.

While naming small towns "Rattlebourough" (i.e., "rattlebrained") and "Gossippee" makes light of their insular, provincial nature, in many stories of the period the use of the small town as setting carries with it a darker message, a message about the fragile nature of justice. As in "Thou Art the Man!," unsophisticated juries know nothing of intricacies of the law and can be easily manipulated for ill and for good:

> I worked hard to get a jury of ignorant men, who had more heart than brain who, if they could not fathom the depths of argument, or follow the labyrinthine mazes of the law could feel for a young fellow in a bad fix, [...] I tried that game once in a murder case and a weeping wife and sister made a jury render a verdict against law, evidence and the judge's charge, and saved a fellow that ought to have been hung as high as Haman ["A Lawyer's Adventure," *Bradford Reporter*, July 16, 1857].

Citizens of small communities in popular fiction in the nineteenth century often have a disturbingly simplistic view of the processes of the law: "I am afraid there is little chance for you, then, for juries in this county, to my certain knowledge, have an awful proclivity toward verdicts of guilty, and they will hang you on the slightest possible evidence" ("An Alibi," *Harper's New Monthly Magazine*, September 1856). Even several decades later this characterization of smalltown setting remained a part of popular fiction about crime:

> "Has she been indicted?"
> "Yes, at the last court; she was indicted and we would have lynched her; yes, sir, we came near stringing her up."
> "We must give her a fair trial before we hang her," I remarked.
> "We don't object to that. Everybody says that she is guilty; and she is guilty, and must be hung, that's all there is to it [...]" ["Circumstantial Evidence," *The News and Herald*, March 1, 1883].

With threats and the reality of lynching occasionally arising in popular crime fiction, the very nature of the small town setting unleashes the worst parts of human nature which lead to frightening miscarriages of justice. Thus

> The tribunal of pubic opinion had pronounced against him the sentence of conviction; and even his friends, as the excitement of the party struggle subsided, became cold in his defense and wavering in their belief of his innocence. Conscious that the eye of suspicion was open, and satisfied that nothing short of a public investigation could restore him to honor, the unhappy young man surrendered himself to the civil authority, and demanded a trial. Ah! little did he know the malignity of man, or the fatal energy of popular delusion! He reflected not that when the public mind is imbued with prejudice, even truth itself

ceases to be mighty. Many believed him guilty, and those who, during the canvass, had industriously circulated the report, now labored with untiring diligence to collect and accumulate the evidence which should sustain their previous assertions. But arrayed in the panoply of innocence he stood firm, and confident of acquittal. [...]

As the trial proceeded the confidence of his friends diminished, and those who doubted became confirmed in the belief of the prisoner's guilt. Trifles light as air became confirmations strong as proofs of Holy Writ, to the jealous minds of the audience, and one fact was linked to the other in curious coincidence, until the chain of corroborating circumstances seemed irresistibly conclusive ["Circumstantial Evidence," *The Illinois Free Trader*, November 27, 1840].

Some of these stories in which small towns are a major part of the problem depend upon divine intervention for resolution: a death-bed confession, news from out of town, and other similar devices free the innocent and identify the guilty. As the innocent victim in these circumstantial evidence stories is often an outsider, so, increasingly, is the hero an alien who untangles the mess concocted by time, space, and public prejudice. Sometimes this hero is a lawyer who rides with the court as it travels its circuit and volunteers his services to help innocence prevail. But increasingly after mid-century that outsider is a detective.

Ah, Wilderness

As in small towns, in wild and unsettled places it wasn't the setting that was the problem, it was the people. The Old World had its own small towns as well as the occasional tract of forest. Traveling in wild, unknown places has always been creepy and dangerous. The New World, too, had landscapes as spooky as those in the brothers Grimm, and sometimes detectives travel in them:

I looked about me, and became alarmed at the density of the forest. The sighing of the wind, the rustling of a bush, the hooting of an owl, startled me. In the thick shades of almost every tree, I imagined a wild beast ready to spring upon me, and behind the tree's monstrous trunks, I expected some hideous animal to dash furiously at me. I carried my revolver ready, for any emergency, and loosened my heavy knife in its scabbard. But little did I imagine that, having passed the dangers of the woods, those of a more fearful and awful character awaited me ["The Robbers' Roost," *White Cloud Kansas Chief*, January 25, 1872].

In traditional stories, finding refuge during a storm in the middle of the forest was always chancy—it was where bandits convened, hosts robbed and murdered their guests, and guests robbed and murdered their hosts. This is the sort of thing that turns up in stories like "The Dead Man's Inn" (*The New York Ledger*, May 3, 1856). While American forests and unsettled, wild places provided inspiration and challenges for writers from Thoreau to Cooper as well as settlers moving West, they could also be far more threatening and dangerous than unsettled places in the Old World. The wilderness wasn't all Daniel Boone and Natty Bumppo. It was a refuge for crime:

> At this time Mountain Kentucky was in a state of anarchy. Law and order were but little regarded, and the woods were filled with armed men engaged in those terrible family feuds which have made the dark and bloody ground famous ["The Romance of Cracker's Neck," *The Bee*, June 10, 1882];

and

> The state [Virginia] was at that time fairly overrun with outlaws of all classes. Bushwackers, highwaymen, counterfeiters and "moonshiners" nestled in all the countryside among the mountains and far from towns and cities upon lonesome roads, while gamblers and desperadoes swarmed in and about the settlements ["The Silver Bullet," *The Sandusky Daily Register*, June 30, 1891].

And by one account things were worse in the West:

> At that time, as all know who are conversant with the history of the "Lone Star," the whole country was filled with outlaws and desperadoes of every description, from the common gambler and thief, down to the highway robber and cold-blooded assassin. In every settlement of note they could be found by scores, and sometimes by hundreds; and in many places they formed by far the largest portion of the population ["Arresting a Murderer," *The New York Ledger*, June 17, 1865].

One of the most often reprinted stories about an American detective, "The Coiners of Kansas," begins with a setting full of bad people and then outlines one of the roles for the detective in America:

> The large floating population and the wilderness of the border country rendered the task of unearthing the coiners a hard one, but after several seasons of persistent and stealthy work, the United States Detective Service became satisfied as to the location of at least one gang of the "Sharps"; and Jack Densmore, an experienced agent, was instructed to visit the State (Kansas), ingratiate himself with the counterfeiters, and learn of their haunts and habits [*The Weekly Register*, November 10, 1880].

In stories like these, bad people pollute unsettled and wild places and make them very dangerous. It was not, however, the detective's job to cleanse these places. That romantic theme was left for western stories to promulgate. In detective stories, the hero's goal is to navigate a dangerous environment, not change it. The detective, after all, is on a job, not on a mission or crusade:

> For two years previous to my start, a man known as Bill Gibbs had been outlawed in Arkansas. He was a robber and murderer, had a price set upon his head, and had taken refuge in the Boston mountains, and from his lair defied all authority of law. He was a terror to a large district and the plan to get rid of him was discussed and arranged like an ordinary business transaction ["Gunning for Outlaws," *The Pullman Herald*, August 10, 1889].

This category of detective story often moves from city to country and depends upon the hero's ability to blend in with the environment—in this case playing the role of a criminal rather than wearing the false beard and moustache used in the city. Rather than problem solving, they show off the detective's quick wit, along with cleverness and guile, and they also center on his or her bravery and chutzpah: "Crime was frequent, and the life of a United States officer was a series of stirring adventures involving great danger, and demanding as great tact and personal bravery" ("The Silver Bullet," *The Sandusky Daily Register*, June 30, 1891).

Another Bit of Literary History

Although pieces from *Chambers'* "Recollections of a Police-Officer" series were reprinted in magazines and newspapers, and lawyer stories about circumstantial evidence were a staple of popular fiction since the beginning of the century, detectives, *per se*, did not appear in stories set in America until "Mr. Snicker's Misadventure" in *Ballou's Dollar Monthly* (January 1856) in which hayseed Uncle Isaac is falsely accused of a crime on his trip to New York and is saved because "there was another officer—a sly detective—in the crowd, unnoticed, but watching every face that passed him." But no problem-solving comes into the narrative; the detective knows who committed the robbery on the ferry because he knows how criminals look and act. Another very early instance of a detective doing his job in the U.S. appeared in the first edition of Harper Brothers' newest magazine, *Harper's Weekly*. In "A Police-Officer's Seven Thousand Miles' Chase," the detective, once again, knows the identity of the criminal:

> A few months since information was brought to me, by the officers connected with several Ohio banks, of the mysterious disappearance of one of their customers, named B—. His residence was some thirty miles distant from the village of U—, at another county town, and consequently some days elapsed before the creditors at U— were advised of his flight [*Harper's Weekly*, January 3, 1857].

And the title lets readers know that they are in for a chase narrative and a bit of a travelogue.

Six months later *Harper's Weekly* added a new dimension to the American detective story in "How Bob Bolter's Prisoner Escaped" (July 25, 1857). First of all, it is a reminiscence—akin to the Police-Officer stories from *Chambers' Edinburgh Journal* which *Harper's* had printed. Like Dickens' police pieces, however, it has a slightly more genial, familiar tone. Thus "How Bob Bolter's Prisoner Escaped" begins with

> *Bob Bolter* (as he has been familiarly termed in the Police Department for many years—he is now a resigned member, choosing neither to wear the red nor the white rose of the Plantagenet Commissioners) loves to take a quiet "drop" into my easy chair in the little study, and with a Romano cigar in one corner of his mouth, play narrator from the other side.

And then the story shifts to the streets of New York City. Mentioning roses and Plantagenet Commissioners alludes to the police "Civil War" of 1857 when the city had two police forces—one the city's and one appointed by the state to clean up the corruption of the old NYPD. And it exempts the hero from the chaos of the real world of politics-infused policing. Bob's story begins between the NYPD headquarters and the city's jail: "Just by Pearl Street in Centre, as we were going to the Tombs […]." The substance of the plot lies not in mystery or surprise or scene painting but in describing (1) the techniques of professional criminals and (2) the procedures of the police in detecting and arresting them. The uniqueness of "Bob Bolter" lies both in its focus on professional police procedure and in its story-telling. The tale has two settings, one present, cozy and convivial, and the other professional and exciting. This two-setting framework would go on to inform the detective story up to the 221B Baker Street stories and beyond.

Harper Brothers, collectively or singly, realized that they were on to something with Bob Bolter and over the next year and a half they made the recollections of a police officer (or notebook) form imported from England into a standard vehicle for the American detective story. Thus they published "The Button: An Experience of a New York Detective, Related by Himself" in *Harper's Weekly* (October 16, 1858); "T4FG2G: A Detective Experience" in *Harper's Weekly* (December 4, 1858); and "The Costly Kiss: A New York Detective Experience" in *Harper's New Monthly Magazine* (April 1859). "The Button" and "The Costly Kiss" use New York City as a backdrop for telling readers a tale about specialized police knowledge and routine and its practical application in catching a particular criminal. The narrator of "The Button," for instance, begins his story with

> I expect you've no idea how scientifically burglars do their work sometimes. It's a regular trade; I don't know but you might call it one of the arts and sciences. Folks generally think a burglar is a rough-looking villain, with a horrid face and bushy eyebrows, who breaks into any house or store where he thinks there's anything worth taking, and kills everybody that makes any resistance. Just let me show you a burglar (turning to the Rogues' Gallery), one of the best of them. There, that fellow, number 203; you wouldn't think *he* was a rascal; he looks more like an Episcopal minister, doesn't he? Now that fellow had as nice a kit of tools as you'd care to see. His "skeletons," with movable wards, were made with a polish on 'em. Give him a chance and he'd open any lock in town. He never "weeded" a place till he knew just where he was to go and what he was to do. If it was a store, he'd have been through it carefully, under the pretext of buying goods, or finding some Mr. Jones or other among the clerks. He'd find just the right time for his job, if he waited weeks. I suppose he *might*,

possibly, quiet anybody that disturbed him, if it was really necessary, and he had a large "swag," but he would avoid the risk of a murder from principle.

I was going to tell you of some smart work there was done some years ago by three men, down in Maiden Lane and thereabouts.

"The Button" showcases detectives' patience and determination in identifying warehouse robbers, and in "The Costly Kiss" a detective follows the money to track down an embezzler. Along with sharing the city story form's innovation of centering on a professional detective and the detection and pursuit of career criminals, "T4FG2G: A Detective Experience" reconnects the detective story with Poe by focusing on presenting and solving what appears to be a bizarre problem.

Shortly after *Harper's* published detective stories set in New York, Maturin Ballou began introducing nominal city detectives in stories in his story paper and then in his magazine. First there was "The Robbery of Plate," in which

> The man's features seemed familiar to me, and I soon recognized him as a noted detective officer, who lived in Philadelphia. He had succeeded some two years before in bringing some famous counterfeiters to justice [*Flag of Our Union*, December 1859].

In the first few paragraphs of this story the writer manages to mention the detective's cases in Trenton, New Jersey, and Doylestown, Pennsylvania, before introducing the report of a robbery on Vine Street in Philadelphia. Two years later, this time in his *Monthly*, Ballou went on to introduce the character of the "city detective," but the term "city" was not connected to setting but rather used to attract both urban and rural readers. Just because he is called a New York detective doesn't mean that the detective detects in New York. Thus the first of what became the New York Detective stories, "The Masked Robbers," begins with

> Some six or eight years ago I received a requisition from the mayor of a small town in the interior of the State of New York, to visit that place for the purpose of discovering the perpetrators of various highway robberies which had been committed in the neighborhood. I soon reached my destination, and found Elliotsville, the name of the town in question, consisted but of one long, straggling street, containing the usual number of stores, taverns, etc., which are to be found in all country places. The neighborhood, however, was very pretty, and I was not surprised to learn that in summer time it was the favorite place of resort for the dwellers of cities.

After "The Masked Robbers: A Leaf from a Detective's Note-Book" (April 1862), Ballou continued the same character in "The Mysterious Advertisement" (July 1862), where the narrator is formally identified as "A New York Detective." Among the other stories about detective James Brampton, the name attached to said "New York Detective," "The Bowie Knife Sheath" takes place in Athens, New York (population 2,791 in 1860), "Stabbed in the Back" takes place in "a small town in the extreme western portion of the State," and "The Silver Pin" takes place in Washington, D.C. While Ballou had run a short series about a French detective, labeling his hero with the New York title gave him his second, and most successful, series detective. From August 1862 to January 1863 he printed nine more stories authored by "A New York Detective." In 1865 publisher Dick & Fitzgerald snatched up Ballou's New York Detective stories, added a few more, and printed them as *Leaves from the Notebook of a New York Detective*, a book into which newspaper and magazine editors across the country would dip for detective stories for years to come. For Dick & Fitzgerald this was the continuation of a theme, for they had issued a collection of partly (or mostly) pirated detective stories, under the title of *Strange Stories of a Detective; or The Curiosities of Crime*, supposedly by "A Retired Member of the Detective Police," some of which actually take place in New York. Indeed, there is some evidence that the label "New York Detective" became a sales feature for detective stories, for in the 1880s a number of Australian newspapers printed (probably reprinted) detective stories using the byline "A New York Detective" even though some of the tales do not take place in the U.S.: "A Detective Outwitted" from Queensland's *Darling Downs Gazette* (November 21, 1885), for example, clearly takes place in London and the hero reports to Scotland Yard although the story is attributed to "A New York Detective."

The Naked City

By the 1860s, for a variety of reasons, cities, or at least the names of cities, became increasingly important for detective stories. While New York remained the most popular draw, and Boston, Chicago, and New Orleans came in a distant tie for second, most of the major cities of the country became the nominal setting of detective stories. For example, from Baltimore there was "The Broken Cent" (*Leaves from the Notebook of a New York Detective*); from Cleveland there was "A Detective's Story" (*Decatur Daily Republican*, December 2, 1887); from Detroit there was "Detected by Peculiar Habits" (*Sandusky Daily Register*, October 28, 1889); from Denver "A Detective's Story" (*Rocky Mountain News*, September 23, 1880); from Philadelphia "A Moustache, and What Came of It" (*The Columbia Spy*, October 1, 1870); from San Francisco "Wicked Ah Hee" (*Frank Leslie's Popular Monthly*, July 1877); and from St. Louis "A Detective's Story" (*St. Louis Globe-Democrat*, December 3, 1876).

Indeed, advertising a detective story by including a location in its title became a minor trend in publishing over the last part of the century. This led to titles such as

"A Detective's Story of New York Life" (*Fayetteville Observer*, February 24, 1870);

"Catching a Ghost: A Philadelphia Detective's Story" (*The Bee*, January 27, 1883);

"The Burke Diamond Case, An Omaha Detective Story, Showing the Trails and Disappointment of Detective Work" (*Omaha World Herald*, September 3, 1899);

"The Detective: A Story of New Orleans" (*New York Fireside Companion*, June 29, 1869); and

"The Murderer's Ordeal: A California Story" (*The New York Ledger*, August 10, 1861).

If the city's name does not appear in the title, it sometimes occurs in the first line of the story. Thus "A Detective's Yarn" in *The Golden Era* (October 19, 1862) begins with "I am a New York Detective." In May 1865 "I had been eight years on the special detective force in Philadelphia when that trouble about Joe Myers turned up" opens "The Pigot Murder" in *Harper's New Monthly Magazine*.

Imported stories, however, had a real advantage in that new American cities had little in the way of identity and few universally recognized landmarks while Paris had Versailles, the Louvre, Notre Dame and L'Arc de Triomphe; and London had the Tower, Buckingham Palace, Saint Paul's, and Big Ben. And, of course, for American readers foreign cities had the distinction of being inhabited by foreigners who had unique customs, character, and funny names. Written before the effect of the industrial expansion caused by the Civil War and the rush of new ethnic immigrants in the last quarter of the century, beyond the city's name and the mention of a few street names, one American city is pretty much like another in 19th-century detective fiction. Some writers in fact chose to use the urban setting, but opted to locate their hunt-and-chase stories in generic rather than real cities, a decision abetted by the tradition on using blanks to simulate realism:

> He made no objection to this, and, having examined the register, informed me that the name of the person to whom it had last been transferred was Clarence Allerton, who then resided at No. 204 B— Street, in this city, and was a man of large wealth ["The Blue Diamond," *Frank Leslie's Pleasant Hours*, August 1872].

The only American city to rise above the generic in 19th-century detective fiction is New York. The city, to be sure, was the most populous in the country and, after mid-century, the center of publishing. But it was not those things, or the location, architecture, cuisine, climate, or ethnic or racial make-up that made New York stand out. New York had class, and Broadway was the place to be:

I was walking one day quietly down Broadway, thinking that I would buy a present for my wife, for the following day was her birthday, and she and I have always kept up the good old fashion of making each other presents on these occasions ["The Lottery Ticket," *Ballou's Dollar Monthly Magazine*, October 1862];

At length, at nightfall, I made up my mind to stroll through the town, to look at the shops on Broadway by gas light, to drop in at the theatre, to give up the whole evening to enjoyment ["The Scratch of a Pin," *The New York Ledger*, January 25, 1862];

and

I followed them to a French coffee shop in Broadway, then kept by Palmo, who started the first opera house in New York, and waited till they had refreshed themselves ["The Confidential Clerk," *Strange Stories of a Detective; or The Curiosities of Crime*, New York: Dick & Fitzgerald, 1863].

Although still in its infancy, Wall Street had banks:

The next day, as soon as I had breakfasted, I proceeded immediately to the Bank of America, situated in Wall Street. The bank had just opened ["The Bowie Knife Sheath," *Leaves from the Note-Book of a New York Detective,* Dick & Fitzgerald, 1865].

Readers across the country knew about Fifth Avenue—it meant money and class. Take this slice from period stories:

At this time my mother was the only near relative I had living, and she was the housekeeper at Colonel Lester's, one of the first families, residing on Fifth Avenue ["The Scarlet Ribbon: A Detective's Story," *Ballou's Monthly Magazine*, December 1866];

[...] she has furnished a splendid residence in Fifth avenue, and gives extensive *fetes* nearly every week ["A Detective's Story," *Gleason's Monthly Companion*, January 1879];

and

She gave a whoop of "murder" that raised his hair and startled every one in the station. The idea of murder in the aristocratic mansion of Mr. Samuel Morton, on Fifth avenue [...] ["The Fatal Potato," *The Franklin Gazette*, October 18, 1889].

And the furnishings of every one of those mansions reflected the wealth of their owners, and especially their wives and daughters. In practical terms that meant collections of curious rarities, valuable jewelry, and soirees to show them off. They all show up in detective stories set in New York. Indeed, the accoutrements of wealth, especially jewelry, formed the identity both of New York and then most other cities in 19th-century detective fiction.

The city as setting manifested itself in two different kinds of plots, one of which was peripatetic and the other based on narrowing the setting's focus. Peripatetic stories are basically hunt-and-chase stories in which a city's geography replaces the countryside and serves as the site map for hunt-and-chase stories. One early example is "The Costly Kiss" in *Harper's*, which takes the hero all over New York City in his attempt to identify an embezzler. As readers became more familiar with New York, "The Man with Big Whiskers" (*The Plain Dealer*, June, 3, 1871) takes readers on an even more extensive tour of following the narrator from Sullivan Street to Booker Street to Grove Street to Courtland Street to Canal Street to Broadway to Ann Street to Leonard Street and even over to Staten Island. From this trek even readers unfamiliar with New York City realize the extent and complexity of the city and appreciate the detective's knowledge both of his or her environment and of the criminal's hypothetical destination. Additionally, this kind of plot also showcases the stamina, determination and dedication necessary to follow the clue and navigate a maze of streets.

CSI

While some writers used cities as sign posts in their hunt-and-chase stories, others chose to center their plots on finding and interpreting evidence whether it was in a city, small town, or countryside. This all began with "The Murders in the Rue Morgue" in which a stroll in the city led to a building, which led to a staircase, which led to the crime scene that Dupin interprets to the readers' wonder and delight. By the 1860s detective stories reemerged in which the scene of the crime gained new importance. Their plots stressed two different kinds of evidence, people or things. In the former, while the scene of the crime is important, the detective's investigation depends upon discovering who was present when the crime was committed—i.e., who was where. In these the theme of the alibi loomed large. Thus there were stories like "An Alibi" (*Harper's New Monthly Magazine*, September 1856), "The Fourfold Alibi" (*The Prairie Farmer*, May 31, 1873), and "An Alibi, Being False It Could Not Withstand Investigation" (*The Reno Evening Gazette*, August 8, 1889). In these stories the detective's job usually entails understanding who was where by discovering who was lying and who was telling the truth.

Stories in which finding the truth depends on finding or interpreting things center on the detective's close examination of physical objects. In "The Walker Street Tragedy," for example, the detective's search of an entire house ends with this bit of discovery and reasoning:

> The reader will bear in mind that the house was a very old one, and consequently the doors had shrunk a good deal. This was specially the case with the one opening into Miss Alford's room. In fact a piece of list had been nailed along the bottom of it to keep out the cold air. I was first attracted by a single spot of blood on the outside of the piece of list. I thought it very strange it should be there, and stooping down I turned it up. I found there was a space of more than an inch between the bottom of the door and the floor. I then turned up the carpet in the room, and found a long scratch on the boards, extending from the door to where the dagger was found concealed. The whole truth flashed on me in a moment; the

murderer after committing the deed had thrust the dagger under the door and pushed it with a stick as far as he could under the carpet ["The Walker Street Tragedy," *Leaves from the Notebook of a New York Detective*, Dick & Fitzgerald, 1865].

The focus on setting and the emphasis on close observation stresses the detective's alertness, visual acuity, and ability to sort truth from lies, but, more importantly, it changes the detective from one who follows a known antagonist to one who interprets the environment in order to identify the unknown antagonist. Ironically, in an age in which inference was the whipping boy of so many writers in their stories about the misuse of circumstantial evidence, in these stories the ability to infer the truth from a crime scene became one of the prime attributes of the detective hero. This is the case, perhaps, because of science. This variety of detective story embodies fictional precedents of what would eventually be embodied in Locard's Exchange Principle—that humans inevitably leave a trace of their presence wherever they go. Thus a criminal can be betrayed by the nails in a boot:

> We were about to quit the apartment, when my eyes suddenly alighted on several faint but peculiar marks upon the floor, which had hitherto escaped my notice, and which, to a superficial observer, might have been allowed to pass unnoticed, but as I had always been accustomed to give one parting and scrutinizing glance previous to quitting a scene of this description, I halted, and casting my eyes close to the marks that had attracted my attention, I saw distinct bloody impressions of the nails of a man's boot or shoe upon the deal floor, not only near the bodies but also in a direction toward the door ["The Assassin's Track," *Strange Stories of a Detective; or The Curiosities of Crime*, New York: Dick & Fitzgerald, 1863].

But writers also very occasionally provided settings that seemingly defied the closest observation. These go back to the Rue Morgue and even Minister D—'s apartments. And they place as much emphasis on the detective's intelligence as they do on the setting. These are locked-room mysteries and they literally involve thinking outside the box. More than any other detective stories they call upon the writer to draw a particularly detailed scene, significantly a scene that anticipates readers' questions. Here is such a passage from "Who Killed the Judge? a Mystery of Crime":

> The Court House was on the second street running parallel with the river, and one of the town sewers connected it with the stream. There was a bare possibility that a small man might have obtained ingress into the building by the sewer, but an examination of the mouth dissipated this theory. The Court room was situated on the second floor. The murderer, to reach the Judge's apartment, was compelled to cross the Court room, which, when wrapped in darkness, was no easy task for one unacquainted with the arrangement of the furniture, etc. If the assassin had traversed the room just described, he had failed to displace a single chair, several having been left in the aisles as the Sheriff testified; and the mode and manner of his exit were also left in the dark [*The Junction City Weekly Union*, December 7, 1878].

There were, however, relatively few locked-room plots during the period (see also "The Secret Door," *Marshall Statesman* [April 12, 1876] and "The Left Hand," *The Janesville Gazette* [August 7, 1879]).

Tangentially, railroad cars provide a particularly 19th-century variant for setting in period detective stories. Railroad cars offered a variant on the locked-room plot that Poe introduced in "Murders in the Rue Morgue." Only with cars the observation of the passengers often becomes the point of the story as opposed to Poe's focus on the material things missed by ordinary detectives (and readers). The action of "The Car Acquaintance: or, the Two Bits of Paper" (*Ballou's Dollar Monthly Magazine*, July 1860) offers an early example of a story that takes place entirely on a New York City streetcar and concerns the observations of people and things in that closed environment. The same kind of plot extends to discoveries in railroad carriages, featured in stories such as "What I Learned About Counterfeiting" in *Western Rural and Illinois Stockman* (June 11, 1881, and June 18, 1881) and "An Observing Man: The Capture Made by a Private Detective" in the *St. Joseph Herald* (November 26, 1887). Railroads, of course, were places where people spent a lot of time, and, like the office, the barroom, or the drawing room, provided a fulcrum for storytelling. Here is how "The Telegraph Detective" begins:

> It was in a railroad car that my vis-à-vis, to while away the time—we were obliged to wait, owing to a broken rail—told the following story [*Barnstable Patriot*, June 29, 1880].

In terms of contemporary popular fiction, however, there was no such thing as distinctly urban crime. Gangs, the bane of real cities, are just as likely to do their dirty business in the country as in the cities of period detective stories. And, of course, in terms of popular fiction, readers would not encounter crimes associated with sex, poverty, racism, and random violence for another hundred years.

Police and the City

But one city institution did play a role in determining the character of the mid–19th century detective and detective story: The police department. Most American cities did not have official police departments until the middle of the century: New York City in 1845, New Orleans and Cincinnati in 1852, Boston and Philadelphia in 1854, Chicago and Milwaukee in 1855, Baltimore and Newark in 1857, St. Louis in 1861, and Omaha in 1866. As in Britain, the introduction of plainclothes (or detective) police divisions did not appear until years after the founding of the protective (or patrol) departments. Which came first, however, hardly needs to be asked in the world of popular fiction: detectives existed years before police forces officially added them to their ranks. In terms of fiction, however, being identified as a police detective made a difference then and continues to make a difference to the character of the hero. First, it puts an urban stamp on the narrative which makes a difference to the setting but not the essentials of the story. More importantly, being a member of a police department makes the detective a subordinate in a hierarchical organization. Thus detective narrators sometimes present situations like this one:

> Proceeding at once to headquarters, after a short consultation with the Chief, I received instructions to go immediately with another officer and endeavor to ferret out the perpetrator of this foul deed ["A Detective's Yarn," *The Golden Era*, October 19, 1862].

The complicating factor in the portrayal of city police detectives as heroes is that the early history of police forces in a number of American cities was not a pleasant one. There was the New York "Police Riot" of 1857, and debates over control between city, state, and federal governments sometimes led to violence or threatened violence—as in Denver's City Hall War of 1894. As far back as 1857, as *Harper's* "How Bob Bolter's Prisoner Escaped" documents, fiction makes reference to political differences between city and state regarding policing and police powers. Consequently, while some writers specify that the detective is a part of a police department in order to validate his or her expertise, others while maintaining the label of "city detective" make their characters act like, or very much like, independent individuals—as is the case with Metta Fuller Victor's Mr. Burton in *The Dead Letter* (1866).

While belonging (or not belonging) to a police department affects the detective's character, urban background also contributes to one of the detective's defining characteristics, recognizing criminals—a trait that was increasingly important in the anonymity of 19th-century America. It is this skill (or talent) that brings about the capture in "A Tell-Tale Toothpick":

> Last summer I was on a train coming to New York; between Washington and Baltimore an under sized man, with a long, flowing, gray beard got on. He had between his teeth a visible toothpick, the end of which had been bitten square off. The train got under way, and I rose from my seat, walked leisurely over to the one he occupied, and was about to seat myself on the vacant space beside him, when he looked up, and if terror was ever depicted upon human face—I saw it there—in those wavering, wicked black eyes. It was my man, and he knew me. "For Christ's sake," he whispered, "don't make a scene, and I swear to you, I will not try to escape. I give up!" [*Jackson Citizen*, November 10, 1878].

Indeed, establishing identity in an increasingly anonymous world became the foundation of modern urban policing with Pinkerton's Rogue's Gallery, Chief Byrnes' *Professional Criminals of America*, and Bertillon's biometrics. Below it helps to identify the roué who jilted the country girl in "Her Clay Idol: A New York Detective Story":

My earnestness at last resulted in his reluctantly calling a cab and going to headquarters with me. I showed him No. — well, never mind, in the Rogue's Gallery. The old man staggered back and said: "It can't be him; but what a resemblance." At last when I told him who the man was, and that he had served two terms in State prison, the old merchant broke down, and all he could say was "my poor daughter" [*The Sunny South*, June 10, 1882].

Just as we noted above that New York detectives don't detect exclusively in New York City, having a city detective as the hero does not mean that the stories take place in a city. In fact, many of Ballou's stories featuring the aforesaid New York Detective do not take place in New York. And Sylvanus Cobb, Jr., the star writer for *The New York Ledger*, rarely used any big city as setting for his detective stories, but chose generic small towns, some of which were in the South and some in the West. As in *The Dead Letter* by Metta Fuller Victor, sending for a "city detective" to solve one's problems became a normal part of American detective stories for the rest of the century:

There was no telegraph or railroad to the town in question, therefore, the reports that reached the metropolis were in the first instance vague and contradictory, but they soon assumed a more decided character, and a full endorsement as to their truth was received in the shape of a letter from the local authorities to the police department, begging that a most skilled detective might be sent down, to ferret out the real criminal ["Stabbed in the Back," *Ballou's Dollar Monthly Magazine*, September 1862];

Thus three weeks passed without anything of interest occurring, and at the end of that time I could endure the suspense no longer. Therefore, I wrote to an old friend of mine who was then on the detective force of P—, to come to L—, and together we set about the search ["The Torn Bill," *The Tioga County Agitator*, August 15, 1866];

and

As a last resort, Clara (this was the name of the miser's daughter) went to the city to consult with a skilled detective ["The Murder of the Miser," *The Ohio Democrat*, November 28, 1873].

Mentioning the city, therefore, became a way of validating the hero's expertise rather than having anything to do with where the story takes place. Being a subordinate member of a police department, as well as having a city detective act outside of his or her jurisdiction became important ways of underlining the hero's separation from the crime narrative and became a way of connecting the detective hero with the archetype of the outsider.

In the late fifties and early sixties, then, the Harpers' and Ballou's linkage of setting and hero established a pattern, so that for the rest of the century, whether in New York, Philadelphia, Chicago, or Podunk, the detective is very often a "city detective." None of this, however, means that the city and its detectives suddenly took over U.S. detective fiction. While stories set in New York (and a few other U.S. cities) flourished in the last half of the century, the names of cities also served simply to give readers general geographical sign-posts in stories that establish the detective as the peripatetic hero and put forth the theme (commercially exploited by Pinkerton) that evildoers can run but cannot hide. Thus the rambling title of "Trailing a Thief. A Detective's Long Chase After a Fugitive Cashier. From Minnesota Through Canada, England, France, Spain and Italy to Switzerland—A Clever Ruse to Avoid Extradition Proceedings" (*Pullman Herald* October 19, 1889) represents a class of stories based on American detectives chasing suspects around the city, across the country, and across the world.

Back to England

English detectives were standard fixtures for American readers well before the early1860s. Way back in 1837 there was Burton's "The Secret Cell." It took only two months for Dickens' "The Butcher's Story" to travel from *Household Words* to the October 5, 1850, edition of *Brooklyn Eagle*. Chamber's "Recollections of a Police Officer" came out in 1852 and stories excerpted from it ran in newspapers for years. In the same year *Harper's New Monthly Magazine* printed "A Reminiscence of a Bow-Street Officer" (September 1852). In the late 1850s English detectives made appearances in "The Mysterious Occurrence in Lambeth" (*Harper's New Monthly Magazine*, August 1855), "Retired from the Force" (*The Ladies' Companion*, November 1857), "Finding a Criminal from the notes of an English Detective" (*The New York Ledger*, January 9, 1858), "Coming out of Exile; or the Diamond Bracelet Found" (*The Eclectic Magazine*, October 1858), and "Watched and Watching" (*The Albion: A Journal of News, Politics and Literature,* July 14, 1860). Wilkie Collins' short pieces "A Marriage Tragedy" and "Who Is the Thief?" ran in *Harper's Monthly* and *The Atlantic Monthly* in the late 1850s. While Dickens' shorter pieces on detectives from *Household Words* continued to be pirated and printed in papers across the U.S. for years, in 1861 Robert Bonner paid the celebrated English author the unheard of sum of 1,000 pounds to publish his "Hunted Down" in *The New York Ledger*.

Not surprisingly, most English imports up to the 1860s used London as either setting or as the one of the settings in a hunt-and-chase plot. There is a minor thread of admiration for the glamorous habitat of the aristocratic elite of the capital, as in this piece from Mrs. Henry Wood's "Coming out of Exile; or the Diamond Bracelet Found":

> the stately rooms of one of the finest houses in London were open for the reception of evening guests. Wax-lights, looking innumerable when reflected from the mirrors, shed their rays on the gilded decorations, on the fine paintings, and on the gorgeous dresses of the

ladies; the enlivening strains of the band invited to the dance, and the rare exotics emitted a sweet perfume. It was the west-end residence of a famed and wealthy city merchant of lofty standing; his young wife was an earl's daughter, and the admission to the house of Mr. and Lady Adela Netherleigh was coveted by the gay world [*The Eclectic Magazine*, October, 1858].

But the London mansion—indeed the mansion in general—had not yet become a standard locale in detective fiction. "The Mysterious Occurrence in Lambeth" (*Harper's New Monthly Magazine*, August 1855) takes place in a humdrum, middle-class metropolitan neighborhood, but "Finding a Criminal: from the Notes of an English Detective" (*The New York Ledger*, January 9, 1859) begins in a butcher's stall in Newgate market and "Watched and Watching" begins with a detective's dream about a London similar to that found in Dickens:

It was a bitter cold night in December. The snow was some inches thick in the fields, and in the streets of London all was slop and filth—in a word, everything was miserable. Even the professional thief was afraid to come out of his lair, and the pickpocket could find no one in the streets whose pockets they might pick [*The Albion: A Journal of News, Politics and Literature*, July 14, 1860].

While those two stories begin in London, both involve the detective's travel to another place, a place in the country, to find the criminal. That place in the country in fact became a standard setting for detective stories set in England, a place like Woodcastle:

Woodcastle was a pretty town, and William Starke the richest man in it. Now I have said Woodcastle was a town, but do not imagine a row of cottages fronting the only street, a rickety tumble-down tavern, a blacksmith shop, and forty cur dogs. No; it was a bustling, active place, where a brisk business was pushed, many stores were thriving, and two good-sized factories, three miles back, were running with profit to their owners, and to the satisfaction of their numerous hands ["The Dog Detective," *Puget Sound Herald*, May 3, 1860].

The year 1864 was a big one for English detectives in the U.S. In New York, Dick & Fitzgerald issued pirated versions of two collections of "Notebook" detective stories printed in England: *The Diary of a Detective Police Officer* and *The Autobiography of an English Detective*. *The Diary* contains nine stories, seven of which take place in London. But it is not the London of peers or millionaires. Thus the opening of "The Dramatic Author" from the collection:

During my third year of service in the force I was a frequent visitor in the evenings at the Wrekin Tavern, an establishment well known to most Londoners. My especial business there was to be on the watch for a certain tradesman, whose predilection for convivial, and particularly theatrical society, had led him step by step to distaste for and neglect of his business, and finally to a ruin of a deeper dye than inability to meet pecuniary obligations commonly involves.

Dick & Fitzgerald's *The Autobiography of an English Detective* is something different. First of all, it reprints only eight of the English original's sixteen stories published in two volumes. Three of those, "My First Trip Across the Atlantic," "Detective in the Bud," and "Coiners and Forgers," concern the narrator's personal history as a detective and mention the Bow Street Runners, the Peterloo Massacre, and actual Bow Street Runners John and Daniel Forrester. All of the pieces in the American version of *The Autobiography* depend upon sensation novelesque motifs involving shenanigans among the upper classes. While most of the stories in *The Autobiography* include London as a locale, most of them center on searches which take the hero out of the capital.

By the mid–1860s, detective stories imported from England lost at least part of their luster for American publishers. Their exotic or even foreign allure was diminishing—and now that American cities had (sort of) modernized their own policing, they no longer served as examples for how police and detectives work; although hats were occasionally tipped to real English police figures—as when "A Clever Capture" (*The Indiana Democrat*, January 20, 1881) mentions Sir Richard Mayne, the first commissioner of the Metropolitan Police. Of course stories set in England retained some of the allure of history that crime stories in England always fed on. Thus American publications noticed highwaymen (see "The Mysterious Highwayman," *The Louisiana Democrat*, April 27, 1870) and circumstantial-evidence stories (see "The Left Hand," *The Janesville Gazette*, August 7, 1879). And smash hits in London crossed the Atlantic. Not only did Tom Tyler's 1863 play "The Ticket of Leave Man" tour the United States, its detective gained a short story life of his own in pieces like "Quick Work: From the Diary of Hawkshaw the Detective" (*New York Fireside Companion*, January 31, 1870). And American writers assumed that their readers had read Wilkie Collins' *The Moonstone*:

> "Those who have read the 'Moonstone,'" said Mr. F., "will remember how the experience of Sergeant Cuff was set at naught by the eccentricities of a dreamer [...]" ["A Detective's Experience: The Missing Jewels," *The McKean Miner*, February 3, 1870].

Many of the stories set in England after the 1860, however, dealt with the same kind of world that readers found in many tales set in America. Big cities were rare, as were toffs, swells, and members of the peerage. In the main they took place in small towns with ordinary people and clever detectives. But, then again, since this was before the advent of international copyright, when an English magazine with a detective story in it came into the hands of an editor looking for something popular with readers, it was a gift—no purchase, no translating, no royalties.

France Revisited

If English stories were not exotic enough for American readers, others filled the bill. While by mid-century Vidocq stories were becoming somewhat moth-eaten, France and French detectives did not entirely lose their attraction for American readers. And publishers knew it. Indeed, three of the first detectives to be featured as series heroes in U.S. publications were French. In April 1859 Ballou published the first of these in three detective stories, labeled "From the Journal of a Detective," in his *Monthly Magazine*. They were "A Curious Stratagem" (April 1859), "The Guest Chamber of the Inn at St. Ives" (June 1859), and "The Mysterious Deaths at Castellane" (September 1859). All three of these stories were supposed to have come from the "notebook" of one M. Guillot: "I had been some years connected with the Detective Bureau (so the thief-taker commenced his story), and had naturally arrived at a great degree of proficiency [...]" ("A Curious Stratagem"). In each case the detective does his work outside of Paris:

> My field of operation, as a usual thing, lay within the confines of the department of Lower Alps ["Mysterious Deaths at Castellane"].

Other than the fact that they are not city stories, in terms of the detective plot, their location doesn't make much difference—they could take place almost anywhere.

The year after their publication of *Strange Stories of a Detective; or The Curiosities of Crime*, in 1864 New York publisher Dick & Fitzgerald printed *The Experiences of a French Detective Officer, Adapted from the MSS of Theodore Duhamel By "Waters."* This was a pirated version of the book that was published in London in 1861 and carried the pseudonym also used for or by the author of *Recollections of a Policeman* in the 1852 collection of detective stories pilfered from *Chambers' Edinburgh Journal*. *The Experiences* begins with an essay, "The Difference Between English and French Detectives," and follows with eight first-person short stories, many of which contain what seem to be gaps in the narrative that make the text read like an incompetent translation from a French original. The stories' principal concern lies in describing crime, criminals, and chases about the French countryside rather than in the detective and detection.

Two years after the Dick & Fitzgerald anthology, Ballou began a second series of stories about a French detective, "Eugene Laromie, one of the secret Police of Paris" ("The Tell-Tale Eye"). Published in both *Ballou's Monthly* and *Flag of our Union*, the five stories included "The Tell-Tale Eye" (January 1866), "An Official Blunder" (April 1866), "Seventy Miles an Hour" (June 1866), "A

Lady's Glove" (August 1866), and "A Little Affair" (October 1866). Unlike the previous French detectives who appeared in America, the Laromie stories mostly take place in Paris and their atmosphere reflects the glamour of the Second Empire in France. Thus the author frequently mentions well-known Paris landmarks which are important for atmosphere but not for plot.

Insofar as the all of these stories and heroes possess Frenchishness, each reflects upon both the hero's cleverness and also upon the nature of the French police system. Guillot tells readers that "I have here an alphabetical list, in which I will affirm there are the names of all the notorious rogues in Paris—each and every one of them has his place in this book" ("A Curious Stratagem"). More importantly, the system possesses layers of police and police "spies":

> There is a small hut half-way between here and the farm house—you will see it on the road. It is a kind of depot which I keep for my official use; my spies and detectives often leave their reports and communications there, where I find them whenever I am in this vicinity ["A Curious Stratagem," *Ballou's Dollar Monthly Magazine*, April, 1859].

The Experiences of a French Detective Officer and the Laromie stories (with a new political twist) repeat the point about France and its extensive system of political espionage:

> Shortly after the establishment of the Empire of his gracious majesty Napoleon the Third, it became necessary for the government to be on its guard, to thwart the plots which Socialists were organizing against it in every part of the country. Those arch enemies of order and established government worked their affairs well, however, and gave the officials no little trouble. As fast as one plot was detected and foiled, another was organized, and for awhile the danger seemed to increase daily ["An Official Blunder," *Flag of Our Union*, April 28, 1866].

Part of the reason for the multiple layers of police in 19th-century France was the cyclonic winds of change in the country's government, spinning from Napoleon to the restoration of Bourbons to Louis Phillippe to Louis-Napoleon and finally to the Third Republic. Each turn brought with it renewed attention to France's aristocracy. As a consequence detective stories set in France were far more likely to feature dukes and countesses than contemporary pieces set in England where the focus lay on middle-class characters.

In addition to the influence of politics on stories set in France, there is also a thread of danger associated with France in some stories published in the U.S. This is especially the case in pieces in *The New York Ledger*. Take these passages:

> Yet I would not venture out in such a city unarmed, and I went to my dressing case and took my pistol.
>
> We were soon threading a labyrinth of narrow streets, and I had as much as I could do to keep my guide in sight

> The whole plot was unfolded to me as clearly as could be, I was to be made food for the dissecting-knife of some studious doctor, and was already in the trap! ["An Adventure in Paris," March 6, 1857]

and

> The mansion I had just quitted, stood on the banks of the Seine, about two miles below the old city; and I believe, if I had drank the wine offered me, my rifled body would soon have been cast into the rushing waters. I believe, moreover, the mansion, grand as it appeared, was only a den of robbers and murderers—and that many a poor, unsuspecting soul had taken its flight from there to the eternal world! I did not communicate with the police, for the reason that, in the first place, I could bring no charge of crime against any; and, in the second place I did not wish to become involved with the French courts of law; but, thankful beyond expression for my own escape, I firmly resolved never to risk my life again in another mysterious adventure in Paris! ["A Mystery of Paris," December 10, 1864].

Heirs of the tradition of urban "Mysteries and Miseries" initiated by Eugène Sue's *The Mysteries of Paris* (1843) and carried on by George Lippard's *The Quaker City* (1844), and Ned Buntline's *The Mysteries and Miseries of New York* (1848), stories like these allowed story papers and newspaper fiction to portray the city as a dangerous place—as long as it was a foreign city.

Politics and intrigue, however, are hardly the main concerns of most of the French detective stories of the 1850s and 1860s. Along with the ubiquitous police references, mechanical things play a minor role in them. The Guillot stories, for instance, center on deathtraps, and Laromie's "The Tell-Tale Eye" and "Seventy Miles an Hour" concentrate on technology—photographing images imprinted on corpses' eyes and speedy railroad engines. These plots, however, do not have to be place-specific. With money, a constant in detective fiction, stories set in France are able to link it with a specific place. Thus mentioning the *Palais de la Bourse* in Paris became a common way of indicating the wealth (or lack thereof) of characters in French stories throughout the century. With sex, the other constant, French detective stories offer more plots based in one way or another upon love affairs or marital dysfunction than British or American stories. Thus not only do the Laromie stories "An Official Blunder" and "A Little Affair" center on romantic intrigue, in "A Little Affair" the writer suggests that amorousness may be a national trait:

> She was evidently a lady, and one of the most beautiful the detective had ever seen. As she passed she looked at him with a fixed gaze, and then smiled. Instantly, Laromie lifted his hat and bowed profoundly. When he raised his eyes again, the lady had disappeared. He was annoyed at this, for he was anxious to learn more of the beautiful stranger; and from the smile she had given him, he knew that she was not averse to such a course on his part. Eugene Laromie was a true Frenchman in his love of gallantry; and this was the only thing that ever brought him into any real danger. Several times he had narrowly escaped death at the hands of jealous husbands; and his friends were confident that if he ever died by violence, a woman would be the cause of it [*Ballou's Monthly Magazine*, October 1866].

It may (or may not) have been a coincidence, but when Ballou and Dick & Fitzgerald turned to publishing stories set in France in the early 1860s, detective stories were gaining popularity among writers and publishers in France. This began with Paul Féval's action-packed serials printed in French newspapers and his *Jean Diable* (1862) featuring Chief Superintendent Gregory Temple of Scotland Yard. And his secretary, Émile Gaboriau gained international acclaim with his *L'Affaire Lerouge* (1866). The year after its publication in France, on March 31, 1867, *The New York Times* ran a five-column synopsis of "The Case of the Widow Lerouge." And the novel continued to pop up in American newspapers for several decades—in 1875, for example, *L'Affaire Lerouge* appeared as a serial titled *The Parisian Detective or, A Desperate Deed*, "by Erskine Boyd." Stories, or bits of stories, by Gaboriau continued in American newspapers from "The Bath of Blood" (*Fort Wayne Sentinel*, March 23, 1874) through "An Amateur Detective" in the *Sunday Herald* (March 15, 1885). In terms of setting, although Gaboriau's detectives may come from Paris and his Lecoq belongs to a police department, the scene of the crime in *L'Affaire Lerouge* is decidedly rural; hence the opening lines of the novel set the scene at "a small town near Paris, and situated on the banks of the Seine." After Gaboriau, Imperial France as setting got another boost after the publication of M. Claude's *Mémoires de M. Claude, chef de la police de sûreté sous le second Empire* in 1881, from which Frank Leslie excerpted "The Diamonds of the Duke de B.," "Fiacre No. 2525," and "The Two Chiefs of the Detective Force" in his *Pleasant Hours* in 1885.

Everywhere Else

Because they were there when detective stories began, by 1860 American readers accepted England and France as settings that were as normal as New York or Philadelphia or Mathews Corners. By the 1860s, writers began to occasionally introduce really exotic foreign settings in their detective stories. This meant that stories appeared for the first time using the American West as background for crime and detection. These go from pieces about finding a horse thief in Texas in "The Vigilant's Mistake" (*Chicago Tribune*, August 15, 1875) to an account about finding a murderer in the mines in Yuba County, California, in "Tracing a Murderer" (*Palo Alto Reporter*, October 9, 1880). But writers hardly limited themselves to using the West as a new setting and perspective. New York City policeman George S. McWatters added to accounts of his own experiences stories about detectives in Britain and France as well as Germany, Italy, Spain, Egypt, Russia, and Poland in his *Detectives of Europe and America, or Life in the Secret Service, a Selection of Celebrated Cases* (Hartford: J.B. Burr, 1877). Other writers used Italy ("Medical College Sketches: The Ex-Professor's

Stories: The Skull," *New York Fireside Companion*, June 20, 1869), Egypt ("A Piece of Deception," *Every Saturday*, November 16, 1872), Spain ("The Monk Detective; or The Maniac's Release," *Gleason's Monthly Companion*, January 1879), India ("The Haunted Pool," *Sacramento Daily Union*, June 14, 1884), Mexico ("A Wife's Crime: A Mexican Murder which for a Time Defied Solution," *Fort Worth Dailey Gazette*, January 24, 1883), and South Africa ("Cape Diamonds," *The Delta Herald*, May 16, 1884). Beginning in the 1860s Australia became a popular setting:

> "Australian Detective Story or Murder Will Out" (*New Hampshire Statesman*, February 3, 1865);
> "Story of an Australian Detective" (*Harper's Weekly*, February 4, 1865);
> "In the Cellar" (*Flag of Our Union*, August 1, 1868);
> "In the Bush" (*The New York Ledger*, May 7, 1870); and
> "Murder Will Out: A Gold Digger's Adventure" (*New York Star*, 1877).

Flag of Our Union carried "A Story of Russia" in the sixties (Oct 6, 1866), and in a short time three pieces came out featuring detectives in Russia: "The Twisted Ring: Experience of a French Detective in Russia" (*The Daily Independent*, October 2, 1890); "The Red Chest: An Experience in the Life of a Russian Detective" (*The Freeborn County Standard*, September 17, 1890); and "The Punched Kopeck" (*The Edwardsville Intelligencer*, December 2, 1891).

Useful Anachronism

Forgetting about where they take place, a lot of writers set their detective stories in the past. It was the case before Poe:

> About eight years ago, I was the humble means of unraveling a curious piece of villainy that occurred in one of the suburbs of London; it is well worth recording, in exemplification of that portion of "Life" which is constantly passing in the holes and corners of the Great Metropolis ["The Secret Cell" by William E. Burton, *Burton's Gentleman's Magazine*, September 1837].

And it was the case after Poe:

> It's just about six years ago, now, since information was given at Scotland Yard of there being extensive robberies of lawns and silks going on, at some wholesale houses in this city. Directions were given for the business being looked into; and Straw, and Fendall, and me—we were all in it ["The Butcher's Story—A Detective Police Party" by Charles Dickens, *Brooklyn Eagle*, October 5, 1850].

So, it's not a surprise that the actual narrative in "The Murders in the Rue Morgue" begins with

> Residing in Paris during the spring and part of the summer of 18—, I there contracted an intimacy with a Monsieur C. Auguste Dupin [*Graham's Magazine*, April 4, 1841].

Time has always been an important component not just of the plot but also of the setting of detective and crime fiction. Almost none of it takes place in the present, and in one way or another the uses of history had connections with detective fiction throughout the nineteenth century. One of those connections lies in the fact that presenting events that have supposedly taken place in the past implies both validation and closure. Thus narrating events that occurred a decade or so earlier makes both the narrator and the events seem more credible than would otherwise be the case. And writers of detective tales often do this by adding a small detail noting time and date, as in the following:

> One sultry evening, in 1856, I was pacing the deck of one of our floating palaces on Lake Erie, arm-in-arm with John Smith, who was accounted one of the smartest detectives in his corps ["The Detective's Story," *Flag of Our Union*, April 14, 1866].

Telling stories from the past also carried with it assurance that readers were about to encounter an account of a problem that might have been troubling if it had not been solved:

> In the Summer of 1843 Jackson County was infested by a gang of desperadoes that for a time threatened to overturn the whole arrangement of social and domestic affair ["The Dumb Countersign: A Deputy's Story," *The New York Ledger*, September 1, 1866].

Indeed, history has had a connection with the forms chosen by detective story writers throughout the nineteenth century. For five decades, with a few exceptions, detective stories were (1) cautionary tales about the flaws of Anglo-American law or about the effects of moral decay; (2) embellished reporting of the acts of supposedly real detectives; or (3) pseudo-autobiographies or biographies of fictional official or accidental detectives. All of the stories based on circumstantial evidence fall into the first category. So do the occasional stories that emphasize pathos or that contain jeremiads, like this in "A Mysterious Murder":

> Chicago has always been notorious for its criminals. Other cities can boast of desperate thieves, thugs and murderers, but for ingenious rascality and blood-curdling scoundrelism, the outlaws of the Garden City carry off the palm. No satisfactory explanation of our excessive criminality has ever been given, and it is not my purpose to attempt one. It may be that the lax administration of justice in the city encourages the thief and midnight assassin; it may be that our citizens have learned to look upon pre-eminence in vice and wickedness as an additional feather in the cap of the Northwestern metropolis; it may be that our unchecked gambling dens and our unbridled saloons have had the effect of making our criminals more reckless and daring than the same class in other cities. Whatever the cause, such is the fact.
>
> But it is not alone in the lower and brutal grades of crime that Chicago stands pre-eminent. A certain looseness of morals exists which has no parallel in any other city in the world. The divorce courts are blocked with business, and the deadly canker of domestic

infelicity is daily destroying thousands of homes which should be temples of love and joy and peace [James Maitland, *Suppressed Sensations; or, Leaves from the Note Book of a Chicago Reporter and Detective*, Chicago: Rand McNally, 1879].

The second category, embellished reporting of the accounts of supposedly real detectives, thrived especially in the eighties, during the build-up to the newspaper wars. Here are two examples:

Before I go any further I will take the liberty of introducing myself. I was, at the time I am writing of, the police reporter on a large Washington daily. The young man whom I was addressing was one of the telephone operators at Police Headquarters,—Bob Richards,— and our conversation took place in the telephone room in that building. It was my regular custom to drop in at Police Headquarters every afternoon about four o'clock, get what news I could there, and then, wending my way up to the office, turn in whatever "copy" I might have collected during the afternoon ["A Noble Sacrifice: A Tale of Washington, D.C." by Sinclair, *Ballou's Monthly Magazine*, January 1883]

and

"About the narrowest squeeze I ever had in the course of my profession happened to me while tracing down a gang of counterfeiters in Chicago two or three years ago," commenced a noted eastern detective, who was in the city last week on a visit, in answer to a reporter's request for a "yarn" ["A Detective's Story: Tracing a Gang of Counterfeiters—A Close Call," *St. Louis Globe-Democrat*, May 18, 1886].

Finally, there is the notebook, diary, recollections, casebook, memoirs form that dominated 19th-century detective fiction—and beyond. Implied by Vidocq's so-called autobiography and then put into effect by the 1849 publication of the series of stories *Recollections of a Police-Officer* in *Chambers' Edinburgh Journal*, what came to be known as the notebook form became the most popular narrative vehicle for the detective story in the nineteenth century. The principal virtue of the first-person recollections based on a written text was its pretense of eyewitness, historical authenticity. Which, of course, it wasn't. It was a detective story.

2

LAW AND LAWYERS

> It was a first night on the circuit after vacation, and old Tom Badger's turn for a story.
> Tom's *forte* lay in the "criminal line."
> He had cheated the gallows so often that Bill Quipley used to say he wondered how he could look a hemp-field in the face.
> "Did I ever tell you," said Tom, giving his tumbler of julep an exhaustive suck—"did I ever tell you, boys, about Obed Scott's case?"—"A Lawyer's Story," *The Bloomfield Times* June 16, 1874

Stories about law and lawyers became one of the recurring kinds of popular literature in the United States from shortly after the Revolution through the entire nineteenth century; readers could find them in magazines, in newspapers, and finally, beginning in the 1850s, bound between boards. Given the prevalence of transatlantic literary commerce during the period, some of those stories published in the U.S. focused on law, crime and punishment in England. Indeed, they were pirated copies of stories first run in English magazines. In retrospect, this is hardly a surprise. The legal system in the U.S. may have grown from English common law, but during the late eighteenth and early nineteenth centuries both English law and law enforcement were undergoing seismic changes in theory and in practice. And a lot of people were writing about them. Their concerns were reflected (indeed in some cases anticipated) in the 1790s by the creation of the United States Constitution and especially by the articles of the Bill of Rights—as well as in the reform bills passed by Parliament. According to John Langbein's ground-breaking studies of the history of English jurisprudence, the changes in English courts in the eighteenth century redefined the roles of juries and judges. Beginning in the mid-eighteenth century the English judicial system moved lawyers from the background to newly created prominent roles for them and caused what Langbein calls the "lawyerization" of the court system. The fiction in the 1800s, then, both described the characteristics of what amounted to a new profession and two systems of justice—an old one inherited from the Middle Ages and a new one that changed the way English-speaking society searched for truth in criminal matters, and one that moved lawyers from the fringes into the center of the justice system. Those same dramatic changes in court procedure and lawyering lay at the center of the development of the lawyer story, but they also had a great deal to do with the development of the detective story.

Justice in Transition

One of the reasons Chaucer made the defining feature of his Man of Law that "Nowher so bisy a man as he ther nas, / And yet he semed bisier than he was" lay in the fact that there was not a whole lot for lawyers to do in 1400. Of course from the very beginning, for those learned in the law there was paperwork to attend to—wills, deeds, charters, etc.—but there was practically nothing for lawyers to do when it came to criminal law unless they became magistrates or judges. And that officially remained the case until the end of the eighteenth century.

Crime and Punishment

To be sure, that does not mean that there was no crime in England or that Parliament had been sitting on its hands over the centuries while population and urbanization increased, the British Empire expanded, wealth skyrocketed, and, particularly in the later seventeen century and eighteenth century, crime against persons and property prospered. The Lords and Commons certainly did pass plenty of laws concerning crime. On one hand they tried the stick: by 1800 Parliament had established death as the penalty for 200 crimes, most of them crimes against property. In reality, however, many judges lacked the stomach to hang lots of people, especially for trivial offences against the rich, and consequently the government invented transportation to Georgia and then to New South Wales, housed prisoners in hulks of old warships, and extended the medieval concept of benefit of clergy to anyone who could read a passage from the Psalms as an alternative to the gibbet.

As the stick of punishment was hardly enough to curtail crime, in seventeenth century the government also tried the carrot, and offered cash rewards for those who prosecuted criminals:

> The first permanent act, passed in 1692, offered a reward of £40, plus the offender's horse, arms and money if they were not stolen, for the conviction of highway robbers. This was

followed over the ensuing decades by similar rewards for the conviction of those found guilty of counterfeiting, shoplifting, burglary, house-breaking, horse, sheep and cattle theft, and returning from transportation. Royal proclamations temporarily increased the reward for certain offences during perceived crime waves. In 1720, for instance, an additional £100 was promised to prosecutors for those convicted of highway robbery in and around London. When combined with the permanent reward, this and successor proclamations meant that between 1720 and 1745, and 1750 and 1752, the reward for a conviction of a robber in London was £140 ["Prosecutors and Litigants"].

The carrot of paying people to prosecute failed even worse than the death penalty in preventing crime. In fact, it had a disastrous, multiplying effect, whereby criminals and so-called "thief-takers" regularly accused others (both the guilty and the innocent) for crimes in order to receive the rewards offered by the government. The trials of Jonathan Wild (1725) and Stephen McDaniel (1756) exposed both the failure of the system and the acts of two of these very bad men. Thus, for instance, McDaniel:

Stephen Macdaniel [sic] was one of those detestable villains that no epithet is vile enough to brand their infamy. This fellow, in conjunction with John Berry, James Egan, and James Salmon, followed the profession of swearing away the lives of innocent unsuspecting persons, for the sake of the reward given by government, for the conviction of capital offenders:—the young, friendless, and destitute, were sure to become their prey; and father and motherless lads, of from sixteen to eighteen years of age, were their most favourite game. This profitable merchandise was carried on for a series of years, undiscovered and indeed unsuspected [James Caulfield, *Portraits, Memoirs, and Characters, of Remarkable Persons*, London: Whitley, 1820].

Gagging the Jury

The trials of Wild and McDaniel exposed the defects of the reward system as well as those of the long accepted dependence on direct, sworn, eye-witness testimony. In so doing, they were a shocking public reminder of the innocent people condemned to death by a system that was ill-suited for discovering the truth and protecting the innocent.

By the eighteenth century the English legal system had indeed become increasingly ill-suited to finding the truth or protecting the innocent: it was a cobbled-together product of do-it-yourself procedures put in place over the centuries and out of sync with the social problems of the emerging modern world. The trials of Wild and McDaniel occurred at a time when the jury system was undergoing a radical change. In the eighteenth century the traditional English jury system based on a panel of knowledgeable peers asking questions about evidence changed into one in which jury members became mute evaluators of the probity of the evidence placed before them. As Professor Langbein puts it in *The Columbia Law Review*:

Toward the end of the Middle Ages the trial jury underwent its epochal transformation from active neighborhood investigators to passive triers. The jury came to resemble the panel that we recognize in modern practice, a group of citizens no longer chosen for their knowledge of the events, but rather chosen in the expectation that they would be ignorant of the events. This passive jury required a courtroom instructional proceeding at which outside witnesses could inform them. "By the 1500s," thought Wigmore, "the constant employment of witnesses, as the jury's chief source of information, brings about a radical change. Here enter, very directly, the possibilities of our modern system." Instructional jury trial made the law of evidence possible. Once witnesses routinely testified in open court, the jurors' practical monopoly over knowledge of the facts was broken. Once the trial judge heard the same testimony as the jurors, he was able to comment on the evidence and advise the jury on how to apply the law. And the opportunity arose for the judge to regulate the trial testimony of witnesses.

One immediate and unfortunate effect of the changes of the jury's responsibility was speeding up trials. Thus Alexander Pope's "And Wretches hang that Jury-men may dine" seems hardly hyperbole when viewed in light of an observer at the Old Bailey more than a century after the publication of "The Rape of the Lock":

> The rapid and indecent manner in which the trials are usually conducted at the Old Bailey session-house is a constant theme of censure by those who have ever entered that court. For several sessions I made a calculation of the average time which each trial occupied. I never found it exceed eight and a half minutes, notwithstanding many cases engage the court occasionally a whole day; and in the old court, where most of the capitals are tried, they usually, on the first, second, and third days of the sessions, severally take many hours. The average of eight minutes and a half is made on both the courts, and takes in all the prisoners tried for eight successive sessions. The rapidity with which the trials are despatched throws the prisoners into the utmost confusion. Fifty or sixty of them are kept in readiness in the dock under the court, to be brought up as they may be called for. These men, seeing their fellow-prisoners return tried and found guilty in a minute or two after having been taken up, become so alarmed and nervous, in consequence of losing all prospect of having a patient trial, that in their efforts at the moment to re-arrange their ideas, plan of defence, and put the strongest feature of their cases before the court as speedily as possible, they lose all command over themselves, and are then, to use their own language, taken up to be knocked down like bullocks, unheard [Thomas Wontner, *Old Bailey Experience: Criminal Jurisprudence and the Actual Working of our Penal Code of Laws*, London: Fraser, 1833].

Be Your Own Prosecutor

If by the beginning of the nineteenth century the revised jury system presented a different solution to old problems, policing and detection also morphed into something very different from the ideas embodied in the traditions of common law. Enforcing the law like the formation and function of juries had traditionally been the responsibility of informed members of local communities—thus each parish's elected watch and constables were supposed to keep the peace and arrest malefactors. As late as 1863, years after the founding of the Metropolitan Police (1829) and County Police (1839), James Fitzjames Stevens wrote that

> The Law of England makes no provision either for the detection or for the apprehension of criminals. It permits any one to take upon himself that office, whether or not he is aggrieved by the crime [*The Criminal Law of England*, London: Macmillan, 1863].

Traditionally, there being no police, it was the obligation of citizens not simply to report crimes to magistrates but to identify and capture criminals:

> [...] by the common law every person who hath committed a felony may be arrested and secured by any private man present at the said fact, though he hath no general nor particular authority, *i.e.*, though he be no officer of justice, nor have any writ or warrant for so doing; and such private man may either deliver the felon to the constable, secure him in a gaol, or carry him before a magistrate. And if he refuses to yield, those who arrest may justify beating him; or, in case of absolute necessity, killing him.
> Nor is this arrest merely allowed; it is enjoined by law, and the omission, without some good excuse, is a misdemeanour punishable by amercement or fine and imprisonment [Henry Fielding, *An Enquiry into the Causes of the Increase of Robbers*, London: Miller, 1751].

On top of this enforcement system based upon the concept of citizens' arrest, the individual who reported the crime to a magistrate or apprehended a "criminal" was required, not simply to act as a witness at the trial, but also to act as prosecutor in court: the English government did not supply prosecutors in the trials until almost the end of the nineteenth century:

> Before the *Prosecution of Offences Act 1879* there was no public prosecutor to take criminal cases to court. People had to find their own lawyers or present the prosecution case themselves ["History," *The Crown Prosecution Service*].

You Are on Your Own

While the prosecution was in the hands of individuals, the accused were even more so on their own. The official notion was that if people were really innocent, they did not need any help, so asserts William Hawkins in *A Treatise of the Pleas of the Crown: or a system of the principal matters, relating to that subject, digested under their proper heads*:

> [I]t requires no manner of Skill to make a plain and honest Defence, which [...] is always the best; the Simplicity and Innocence, artless and ingenuous Behaviour of one whose Conscience acquits him, having something in it more moving and convincing than the highest Eloquence of a Person speaking in a cause not their own [Vol. II., Dublin: Lynch, 1721].

The accused needed to look and sound very innocent indeed because they could not call witnesses until 1701 when the courts granted that right:

2. Law and Lawyers

[...] in the sixteenth and early seventeenth centuries in England, a defendant in a criminal trial, while not sworn and allowed neither witnesses nor counsel, was expected to respond to witnesses presented against him and was questioned during trial. Beginning in the middle of the seventeenth century, the accused was gradually allowed to call witnesses. Then, in 1701, the defendant was given, by statute, the right to have witnesses testify under oath on his behalf. The defendant himself, however, was deemed incompetent to give sworn testimony. Nevertheless, he was expected to respond to the evidence against him and his responses were accorded evidentiary weight [Harvey].

But while accused persons gained the right to call witnesses in the eighteenth century, in England they had no right to legal representation. Significantly, before 1836 and the passage of Prisoners' Counsel Act, accused persons did not have the right to have a lawyer defend them in court. As noted below, this exclusion of counsel had notable repercussions in popular literature about crime. But that was England, not the United States. The intent of all of the first ten amendments to the U.S. Constitution was, of course, to affirm and protect the rights of individuals, chief among them the rights denied by the English legal system of the time. In this respect, the Sixth Amendment ("to be informed of the nature and cause of the accusation; to be confronted with the witnesses against him; to have compulsory process for obtaining witnesses in his favor, and to have the assistance of counsel for his defense") was particularly significant. And for almost fifty years America and Britain had very different rules governing the roles of lawyers when someone was accused of a crime. And it didn't take long to discover that that was something to write about.

Evidence 1.0

From the Middle Ages, trials in England depended solely upon direct, spoken, sworn testimony of accusers and their witnesses. But during the eighteenth century what was and what wasn't evidence was mostly a muddle. In 1751 magistrate Henry Fielding wrote that

> There is no branch of the law more bulky, more full of confusion and contradiction, I had almost said of absurdity, than the law of evidence as it now stands [*An Enquiry into the Causes of the Increase of Robbers*].

To be sure, jurists of the period did try to eliminate hearsay from trial testimony and perjury had been a crime since Tudor times—punished in the 1700s by a sojourn in the pillory. A vigorous debate, moreover, developed at the time about the value of indirect, or circumstantial evidence—evidence that required inference as opposed to the direct evidence of witnesses' spoken testimony.

Mistakes Have Been Made

At the turn of the nineteenth century a new attitude about justice began to peep out in popular English publications. When first issued in the eighteenth century, the most popular books about crime in England—the various versions of the Newgate Calendar—had an overtly moral tone. Their titles announced that they brought together tales of the lives of condemned criminals which highlighted

> [...] the regular progress from virtue to vice interspersed with striking reflexions on the conduct of those unhappy wretches who have fallen a sacrifice to the laws of their country. [*The Newgate Calendar or MALEFACTORS' BLOODY REGISTER*, London: Cooke, 1774]

and

> [...] a general Display of the Progress and Consequence of Vice, to impress on the Mind proper Ideas of the Happiness resulting from a Life of strict Honor and Integrity. [*THE MALEFACTOR'S REGISTER; OR, New NEWGATE and TYBURN CALENDAR. CONTAINING THE AUTHENTIC LIVES, TRIALS, ACCOUNTS OF EXECUTIONS, DYING SPEECHES, AND OTHER CURIOUS PARTICULARS*, London: Cooke, 1780].

By 1825, however, Knapp and Baldwin's version of the Newgate Calendar focused on "interest" rather than moral opprobrium; their title was

> *The Newgate Calendar: Comprising Interesting Memoirs of the Most Notorious Characters who Have Been Convicted of Outrages on the Laws of England Since the Commencement of the Eighteenth Century; with Occasional Anecdotes and Observations, Speeches, Confessions, and Last Exclamations of Sufferers.*

Significantly, Knapp and Baldwin also included nineteen cases of people wrongly executed. Indeed, during the nineteenth century, publications that centered on the perversion of justice almost displaced old-fashioned moralistic Newgate literature. Thus in Britain there were titles like

> George Spence's *Considerations on the Criminal Proceedings of this Country, on the Danger of Convictions on Circumstantial Evidence, on the Case of Mr. Donnellan, and on the Alarming Consequences of Prejudice in the Administration of Justice: To which are Annexed Cases of Innocent Persons Condemned and Executed on Circumstantial Evidence, with Remarks Thereon.* [London, 1781];

> John Cecil's *Sixty Curious and Authentic Narratives and Anecdotes Respecting Extraordinary Characters: Illustrative of the cruelty and Fanaticism of Circumstantial Evidence; and Recording Singular Instances of Voluntary Human Suffering and Interesting Occurrences* [London, 1819];

and

> George Bakewell's *Observations on Circumstantial Evidence: Derived from Cases which Have Fallen Under the Immediate Notice of the Author, During the Last Thirty Years; Wherein, Many Innocent Persons Have Been Condemned and Executed...: to which is Added Some Important Remarks on the Impolicy of Capital Punishments and on the Causes of Crime* [London, 1848].

Added to these titles, in the United States such works appeared as *Remarkable Instances of Circumstantial Evidence Given on Trials for Criminal Acts which Has Resulted in the Conviction and Execution of Innocent Persons Together with After Disclosures* (New York, 1833). And, of particular note, Cary and Hart of Philadelphia published *Celebrated Trials of All Countries, Remarkable Cases of Criminal Jurisprudence* (1835) with a section on circumstantial evidence the year after they published Vidocq's *Memoirs*.

The turn of the nineteenth century not only saw these kinds of sensational publications centering on the misuse of evidence, but it also witnessed serious people thinking and writing about the fundamental nature and use of evidence. Jeremy Bentham with his *A Treatise on Evidence* (1825) led the list; but there were others like Thomas Starke's *A Practical Treatise of the Law of Evidence* (1833); Thomas Peake, *A Compendium of the Law of Evidence* (1804); Godfrey Gilbert, *The Law of Evidence* (1805); Joseph Chitty, *A Practical Treatise on Criminal Law Comprising the Practice, Pleadings, and Evidence* (1819); Samuel March Phillipps, *A Treatise on the Law of Evidence* (1838); and Henry Roscoe, *A Digest of the Law of Evidence in Criminal Cases* (1840).

So the way things stood around 1800, criminal law was not in very good shape. In England the accused had almost no rights, prosecution was in the hands of individuals not the state, punishment was supposed to be draconian, the nature of evidence and the roles of different kinds of evidence were in question, and the courts were criticized for fatally mistaken judgments. Efforts were underway, however, to make things better: in the United States with defendants' rights guaranteed by the Constitution's Bill of Rights and in England with the slow passage of legislation to ensure the rights of the accused and organized opposition to capital punishment. Central to our purpose, in both countries lawyers' roles in criminal law increased dramatically—they became the principal figures in what was becoming the drama of the courtroom. All of this happened at the time when popular fiction exploded: at the beginning of the 19th-century new magazines appeared almost overnight and every small town in England and the U.S. had its own newspaper. And each of these new media wanted to introduce their readers to the brave new world that was life and letters in the nineteenth century. And lawyers and law were part of that world.

Law, Lawyers, Literature in America

From August through December 1818, Baltimore's *Robinson's Magazine* ("A Repository of Original Papers & Selections from English Magazines") reprinted seven stories from *Extracts from a Lawyer's Port-Folio* which had appeared earlier in the year in London's *The European Magazine*. The American editor explained that

> [...] they are abstracts of cases tried at different courts in Great Britain, and recorded as memorable instances of "the aptness of human judgement to err in deciding in occurrences involved in mystery."

Admittedly, almost all of the tales begin with observations about laws. For instance this:

> No part of our laws implies a more becoming consciousness of human judgement's fallibility, than the cautious and deliberate procedure in ascertaining mental disease and surrendering a supposed lunatick to the custody of his kindred [Untitled, September 19, 1819].

Or about lawyers:

> It has pleased one of the merriest writers of this age to call the courts of law the chimneys of society, through which all the smoke and black vapors find a vent; thence inferring that the sweepers must have black hands. I am not qualified to decide whether these chimneys of the moral world could be cleansed by besoms, or other machines, as satisfactorily as by human sweepers, alias lawyers ["The Brother's House," December 26, 1818].

After introductory musing like these about laws and lawyers, most of the stories in fact do have to do with crimes, but they have little or nothing to do with evidence or trials. Instead, they emphasize mistakes in matters of laws and courts—the most egregious of which in *Extracts from a Lawyer's Port-Folio* appears in "An Assignment" where a supposed murder victim shows up at the door of his alleged murderer very much alive and trying to settle an estate years after his hypothetical murder. Indeed, all of the stories turn on coincidence and the importance of the lawyer narrators in reality is their humanity which is seen best in their observations about the law, not their technical knowledge, reasoning, or forensic talent.

The Shape of Things to Come

While hardly memorable either as fiction or perhaps even as significant works in the history of lawyer literature, nonetheless the pieces from *Extracts from a Lawyer's Port-Folio* serve as a forecast of some of the things that were going to happen in popular literature about lawyers in the United States.

First of all, the stories and observations in *Extracts* are not American; they come from a British periodical and concern law and lawyers in Britain. While popular stories about lawyers and law that take place in America outnumber British imports throughout the nineteenth century, nevertheless fiction about British law and lawyers did have a significant continuing presence in popular

2. Law and Lawyers

publications in the U.S. Thus lawyer stories reprinted from *Chambers' Edinburgh Magazine, Tait's Edinburgh Magazine, Blackwoods Magazine,* Dickens' *All the Year Round,* and other British publications regularly appeared in newspapers and magazines across America, often within weeks of their original publication. The most significant of the British imports, however, occurred not in a plagiarized magazine piece or two, but in the wholesale piracy of articles collected as two books: in 1852 Cornish and Lamport of New York City published *Experiences of a Barrister,* and *The Confessions of an Attorney; which are added Several Papers on English Law and Lawyers by Charles Dickens.* The Preface of *The Confessions* speaks to the popularity of both of these lawyer books:

> The following "Confessions" are evidently by the author of "The Experiences of a Barrister," a work recently issued by the publishers of this volume, and which has been extraordinarily successful—no less than five editions having been exhausted within a month of the day of publication. It is believed that this work will receive, as it deserves, the same meed of public favor.

Cornish and Lamport filched the contents of both volumes from a series of stories about lawyers and law run mostly in *Chambers' Edinburgh Journal*—the British journal that also ran the series of stories that the same New York publisher pirated and published as *Recollections of a Policeman* in 1852. The lawyer stories (as well as the detective stories in *Recollections*) were quickly pirated by American publishers in other cities as well as by newspapers and magazines. As popular as they were, however, these collections taken from *Chambers',* reflecting on the experiences of men and women faced with the vagaries English law and of their lawyers' successes and failures, were also out of touch with the contemporary state and practice of law in both Britain and America. Thus, for instance, "Circumstantial Evidence" in *Experiences of a Barrister* includes both the point that in England judges were prohibited from questioning defendants and that the point that rights of the accused to counsel were severely limited:

> I hold in my hand a very acute and eloquent address prepared for me by one of the able and zealous gentlemen who appears to-day as my counsel, and which, but for the iniquitous law which prohibits the advocate of a presumed felon, but possibly quite innocent person, from addressing the jury [...]

While England may have corrected this particular injustice by allowing accused persons right to counsel decades earlier, nonetheless the fallibility of English justice by implication became a recurrent theme in American lawyer stories. Throughout the nineteenth-century stories about injustice in the old times in the old country continue to appear in the American popular press. As late as 1882, for instance, *The Stark County Democrat* ran a piece about historical English miscarriages of justice:

> The annals of English Criminal Courts contain numerous cases of the conviction of innocent parties by circumstantial evidence. As late as the year 1827 no fewer than six persons were convicted of capital crimes in the Old Bailey, upon circumstantial evidence, who were afterward proved to be innocent, and were saved from the gallows by the energy of the Sheriff, who was satisfied of their innocence, and succeeded in proving it. Such convictions in cases of capital crimes are not now so likely to occur [August 24, 1882].

Far more prominent than condemnations like these were real and imaginary narratives of sensational historic English crimes and court cases reflecting the new more balanced attitude expressed in places like the 19th-century rewrites of the *Newgate Calendar*, such as *Remarkable instances of Circumstantial Evidence Given on Trials for Criminal Acts which Has Resulted in the Conviction and Execution of Innocent Persons Together with After Disclosures* (1833). Of these historical replays, the bizarre 1736 case in Oxford of Jonathan Bradford (who had planned but did not carry out the murder for which he was condemned) stands out. While the name and crime appear sporadically in fact and fiction earlier in the century, *Jonathan Bradford*, the play, ran at Ford's Theater the year of Lincoln's assassination and its popularity led to "creative nonfiction" pieces about Bradford that appeared in newspapers across the country for the next twenty years.

In addition to its English derivation, Robinson's *Extracts from a Lawyer's Port-Folio* belonged to the same genre used by contemporary magazines and newspapers to attract readers by giving them behind-the-scenes glimpses of the secrets of new or interesting professions. The same year *Robinson's Magazine* printed *Extracts* they also printed "Extracts from a Portfolio of a Man of Letters," "Extracts from an Arctic Navigator's Journal," and "The Librarian's Portfolio." This same motive would lead to Cornish and Lamport's *Recollections of a Policeman* in 1852 and to decades of notebook fiction about detectives. In the case of lawyers, inside-look fiction led to titles like those in this partial list:

> "Pages from the Diary of a Philadelphia Lawyer" (a series in *Burton's Gentleman's Magazine*, 1837–39 consisting of: "The Murderess" [1837], "The Counterfeiter" [1837], "A Chapter on Aristocracy" [1837], and "Unnatural Prosecution" [1838]);
> "Chapters from the Note-Book of a Deceased Lawyer" (*The New Monthly Magazine*, 1834, reprinted in America in the *Southern Literary Messenger*);
> "My Own Peculiar, or Stray Leaves from the Port-Folio of a Georgia Lawyer" (*The Knickerbocker*, November, 1839);
> "Recollections of a Retired Lawyer" (*Southern Literary Messenger*, February 1839);

"Scraps from the Notebook of a Missouri Lawyer" (*The Spirit of Democracy*, October 24, 1846);

"Clock Peddlers in the West: Scraps from the Notebook of a Missouri Lawyer" (*The Spirit of Democracy*, October 3, 1846);

"Leaves from the Portfolio of a Practicing Lawyer: The Bracelet" (*The Middlebury Galaxy*, February 15, 1848);

"The Step Mother: Leaves from a Lawyer's Portfolio" (*The Portage Sentinel*, April 4, 1849);

"A Dark Chapter from Diary of a Law Clerk" (*Harper's New Monthly Magazine*, October, 1852);

"From the Portfolio of a Lawyer: A Diseased Heart Cured" (*Monongalia Mirror*, November 25, 1854);

"From the Note Book of an Eminent Philadelphia Lawyer: Lately Deceased" (*The New Hampshire Statesman*, February 24, 1855);

"The Disguised Robbers; From a Lawyer's Notebook" (*The New York Ledger*, August 8, 1857); and

"A Leaf from a Lawyer's Diary" (*The Anderson Intelligencer*, November 27, 1873).

Using the pseudo-diary form frees lawyer-narrators to both tell their tales and to make asides like this one from "Pages from the Diary of a Philadelphia Lawyer: The Murderess":

> My diary presents to me many appalling evidences of the irresistible truth of my conclusions, and as I have received them from the living impress, so have I recorded them, with nothing extenuated, and surely I may add, "nor aught set down in malice" [*Burton's Gentleman's Magazine*, May 1838].

Or, a year later, from the same series:

> Among the various occupations of man, there are none in which the practitioner is so much exposed to the extremes of human passion and human weakness, as in those which have been entitled *consensu publici*—the learned professions ["Pages from the Diary of a Philadelphia Lawyer: Unnatural Prosecution," *Burton's Gentleman's Magazine*, May 1838].

As in the case of extracts from the papers of other professions, none of the lawyers' portfolios or diaries or notebooks or reminiscences is really a portfolio, diary, notebook or reminiscence; using the term "extract" simply served as a superficial device to justify first-person narration and to promote realism in storytelling, and as such belongs in the same category as dates being printed as 18—, and names being printed as Minister D—.

But narration by lawyers was sometimes more than simply a way to validate the realism of the stories by alleging to describe firsthand what lawyers did in and out of court. It sometimes also reflected the pastime of storytelling and its attendant joys. The institution of travelling, circuit courts in the United States meant not only that the judges rode a circuit around a particular district, but also that lawyers, looking for work, followed them, often in groups. And in evenings they stayed in the same hotels and entertained themselves by telling stories. This is the way "A Lawyer's Story" that prefaces this chapter begins:

> It was a first night on the circuit after vacation, and old Tom Badger's turn for a story.
> Tom's *forte* lay in the "criminal line."
> He had cheated the gallows so often that Bill Quipley used to say he wondered how he could look a hemp-field in the face.
> "Did I ever tell you," said Tom, giving his tumbler of julep an exhaustive suck "did I ever tell you, boys, about Obed Scott's case?" [*The Bloomfield Times*, June 16, 1874]

In addition to the diary format, lawyer stories also reflect the motifs of the initiation story. Thus there are narratives such as "The Young Lawyer's First Case," *Jeffersonian Republican* (March 1, 1849), and "The Jersey Lawyer's First Case in Minnesota" in the *Urbana Union* (November 5, 1862). Toward the end of the century Horatio Alger made the struggle to overcome humble beginnings combined with hard work, honesty and luck the most popular form of initiation. "A Lawyer's Story" (*The Spirit of Jefferson*, February 21, 1888) clearly picks up the pattern, thus:

> Twelve weary months had crept by since I had passed my trying examination and had been admitted to the bar. I hired a cozy little office in a building filled with scores of prominent law firms. After arranging my well stocked library I nailed up a new sign among the rest and waited for my clients to appear. It soon became a sad trial of patience.
> Among the many brilliant lights of the day my own name passed unnoticed. Day after day, and month after month, I attended the courts or passed the time in pursuing celebrated trial cases. Like Macawber, I was waiting for something to turn up. The small capital with which I had started was dwindling away at an alarming pace, and, as yet, I saw no prospective fee.

But this, of course, ends with success, wealth, and a wife.

Both the diary and the initiation story open the way for observations about lawyering and the law. The life offers temptations and battles aplenty, as witnessed in "The Young Lawyer's First Case" by a mother's admonition to her son as he sets out in the world of trial law:

> "But promise me now, that you will never undertake any cause that is unjust, and that you will never aid in screening wrong from coming to light and punishment." The son said something about every man's having a right to have his case presented in the best light he could.
> "I know what you mean," said she: "but I know that if a man has violated the laws of God and man, he has no moral right to be shielded from punishment. If he has confessions and explanations to offer, it is well. But for you to take his side, and for money to shield him from the laws, seems to me no better than if, for money, you concealed them from the officers of justice, under the plea that every man had a right to get clear of the law if he could" [*The Jeffersonian Republican*, March 1, 1849].

2. Law and Lawyers 51

The new fiction not only reproduced old patterns but it also presented readers with a new approach to lawyers and the law that was far different from the stogy pieces which they found in *Extracts from a Lawyer's Port-Folio*. In it communities and courts continued to have the potential to make serious, life-threatening mistakes. In it, however, lawyers were no longer simply sympathetic, intelligent observers but heroes whose talents and gifts could ensure the justice envisioned by the law and enacted by the courts.

The Lawyer as Hero: A Case Study

Nine years after the publication of *Extracts from a Lawyer's Port-Folio*, in March 1827, *The Casket* (a magazine that would one day be subsumed into *Graham's Magazine*) printed "The Blasted Tree." It was a story in which a lawyer, not chance or providence, sets things right. The story begins with a bit of Old World gothic spookiness:

> It was a night in which the fancy of an honest German could not fail to conjure up a thousand phantoms his shrieking ghosts cried from the crevices of every sapless tree; his witches rode on the pale moon-beams, in the distant and scarcely perceptible mist that spread a thin veil over the beautiful stars; and the wandering spirits of departed friends peeped, like premature resurrectionists from behind every thicket.

On this particular dark and stormy night an affable local woodsman volunteers to help a stranger find the river ford he needs in order to make an important engagement. The stranger never shows up at the ford, and dark omens, including a tree that suddenly stops blooming, suggest to the community that dirty work had been done at the crossroads. The locals begin to shun the woodsman, believing, without evidence, that he killed the stranger. Five years later the tree, now dead, is cut down and a skeleton is found among the cordwood. The authorities arrest the woodsman and put him on trial. And then comes the lawyer part:

> The prisoner stood pale and dejected, but silent and resigned, at the bar, and answered with a calm and steady voice, "Not Guilty," to the charge. He was asked if he had counsel, he answered in the negative, and requested that assistance might be assigned him. The judge cast his eyes around the court, as if carelessly in search of some one, on whom to lay what, his manner seemed to indicate, he thought a hopeless task, when an old gentleman, whose presence amid the throng had not been noticed, rose and introduced himself as Mr.—, an eminent lawyer of the city. The court bowed respectfully, and a look of astonishment was visible in every face when he asked the privilege of acting as the defendant's counsel.

The eminent lawyer eviscerates the evidence presented against the woodsman and in so doing identifies the person who planted misleading evidence in the dead tree. In the lawyer part "The Blasted Tree" demonstrates the victory of truth and virtue over superstition and prejudice, reason and observation over guile and appearance, and innocence over circumstance. Most importantly, all of this happens in a courtroom and is accomplished by a lawyer. "The Blasted Tree" not only does all of those things, it also ends with a surprise: it turns out that the eminent lawyer is the stranger who was supposed to be the victim from the beginning of the story.

One of the new roles for lawyers in fiction can be seen by comparing "An Assignment" from *Extracts from a Lawyer's Port-Folio* in 1818 and "The Blasted Tree" in 1827. Both stories center on the dangers of circumstantial evidence, but in "An Assignment" this is manifested only in gossip while in "The Blasted Tree" circumstantial evidence leads to an arrest and trial. Both stories contain general comments on lawyers and the law, but in the first this amounts to including a handful of mild and innocent lawyer jokes while in the second it takes the form of a warning about circumstantial evidence and superstition. Most importantly, in "An Assignment" accident clears up years of suspicion while investigation, facts, and the eminent lawyer's knowledge free the huntsman from the gallows in "The Blasted Tree." This new perspective on what lawyers do provided a number of character types, plots, and themes for 19th-century writers to explore—lawyers as interpreters and/or discovers of evidence; lawyers as advocates for changes in the law; lawyers as actors in the drama of the courtroom; lawyers as counsel in difficult personal or family situations. But by and large these new roles were slow to evolve: until about mid-century many lawyers in popular fiction played roles imposed on them by the popularity of sensation fiction—i.e., the neo-gothic literary fashion for exploring and exploiting suffering, especially women's suffering. In sensation fiction, sentiment takes precedence over reason and evidence, and when shaped around a lawyer, he serves as observer rather than actor. In the first story in "Pages from the Diary of a Philadelphia Lawyer, in *Burton's Gentleman's Magazine*, "The Murderess" (1837), for instance, a lawyer is called upon to defend a woman accused of infanticide. She leaves Philadelphia and is murdered by her second husband, but writes to the lawyer of her fall into a life of crime because of her husband. Readers found the same focus upon sentiment in "The Step Mother: Leaves from a Lawyer's Portfolio" (*Portage Sentinel*, April 4, 1849), in which the lawyer narrator, without mention of laws or court procedure, tells the story of a stepmother who murders her stepson and is punished by seeing her own son killed and becoming a maniac herself. What the writer of "The Blasted Tree" and his or her successors realized was that the process of saving the innocent with facts and reason was just as interesting or even more interesting than demonstrating suffering and pathos—especially in short stories.

2. Law and Lawyers 53

Words, Words, Words

In "Circumstantial Evidence," one of the stories from *Chambers' Edinburgh Magazine* reprinted in *Experiences of a Barrister,* the innocent defendant pleads for the help from a "very acute and eloquent address prepared for me by one of the able and zealous gentlemen who appears to-day as my counsel." He doesn't just ask for facts. He asks for rhetoric.

In some cases, the quality of a lawyer's eloquence measured his success in 19th-century lawyer/law fiction. As much as reason and knowledge of human motives, rhetorical skill was the lawyer hero's stock-in-trade. In some cases writers based lawyer stories on the conflict of good versus bad rhetoric. Thus "John Taylor the Timon of the Backwoods Bar and Pulpit" presents readers with an example of how not to address a jury:

> First of all, three advocates spoke in succession for the prosecution; but neither their names nor their arguments are worth preserving, orators of the blood thunder genius, they about equally partitioned their howling eloquence betwixt the prisoner and her [...] counsel, as if in doubt who of the twain was then on trial [*The McArthur Democrat*, February 12, 1857].

Describing effective oratory, however, was not quite simple. In a retelling of the same plot in the "The Volunteer Counsel" the writer adds allusions to change the significance of the same kind of metaphors used to describe inefficient speeches:

> I have listened to Clay, Webster and Calhoun, Dewey, Tyng and Bascom; but have never heard anything in the form of sublime words even remotely approximating to the eloquence of John Taylor massive as a mountain, and wildly rushing as a cataract of fire. And this is the opinion of all who heard the marvellous man [*Orleans Independent Standard,* January 27, 1865].

Lawyer stories emphasize that effective eloquence is both a talent and a gift: it forms an essential part of the successful lawyer hero's character. It is something the lawyer practices even when out of the courthouse. In "My Own Peculiar, or Stray Leaves from the Port-Folio of a Georgia Lawyer" in *The Knickerbocker* (November 1839), for instance, when at leisure a group of lawyers gathers in a debating society in which members are given absurd topics to argue. And it stays with the lawyer even when he is in his cups: in "Scraps from the Notebook of a Missouri Lawyer" (*The Spirit of Democracy,* October 24, 1846) a drunken lawyer forgets he represents the defense and gives the prosecution's closing argument to the jury but still manages to win the case. But eloquence also comes as a divine gift. This is implicit when in "The Criminal Witness, A Lawyer's Story" (*The Raftsman's Journal,* June 11, 1856) the lawyer-hero says, "[...] if I made them feel that the finger of Omnipotence was in the work, it was because I sincerely believed the young man was innocent, of all crime; and I am sure they thought so too." But in the following the idea of the divine gift is explicit:

> When it came my turn to address the jury it does now seem to me that Divine Providence was on my side. My mind seemed especially clear, my tongue especially available, my voice especially strong. All that I was, of myself, and all I had gathered from the case in my careful preparation of the law and facts. I had especially at command. I am not given to excite people to tears, but when I closed, I must say there was not a dry eye in the house, not even my own. The jury wept. The Prosecutor had fled the court room, fearing that he too might throw off the lawyer and assume the man ["A Lawyer's Story," *The Perrysburg Journal*, August 9, 1889].

Even with the Divine on one's side, however, knowing one's audience continues to the first rule of rhetoric—and the first rule of lawyering:

> I worked hard to get a jury of ignorant men, who had more heart than brain who, if they could not fathom the depths of argument, or follow the labyrinthine mazes of the law could feel for a young fellow in a bad fix, a weeping, pretty wife, nearly broken hearted and quite distracted. Knowing the use of "effect," I told her to dress in mourning, bring her little cherub of a boy only three years old, into court, and sit as near her husband as the officer would let her. I tried that game once in a murder case and a weeping wife and sister made a jury render a verdict against law, evidence and the judge's charge, and saved a fellow that ought to have been hung as high as Haman ["A Lawyer's Adventure," *Bradford Reporter*, July 16, 1857].

But sometimes written words are as important as those that are spoken, regardless of their eloquence. In 19th-century popular fiction lawyers regularly do what lawyers have always done: deal with documents, mostly wills. Stories about wills and the fulfilling the testator's wishes stretch from "The Will," one of the installments of "Pages from the Diary of a Philadelphia Lawyer" in *Burton's Gentleman's Magazine* in 1838, to "A Lawyer's Story" in the Charles Town Virginia's *Spirit of Jefferson* (February 21, 1888). As with other lawyer fiction, the subject of wills gives rise to statements of principle, as in this bit of lawyerly musing in "Romance of Making Wills":

> Wills generally afford a frightful temptation to the worst part of our nature. I really believe that more cunning, more falsehood, more worldly anxiety, and more moral wrong are blended with the subject of "wills," than with the whole mass of law parchments extant. A will should not only be properly made, but properly placed, and more than one should be cognizant of its whereabouts. I have known many cases of gross turpitude in the shape of destroying wills [...] [*Green-Mountain Freeman*, August 31, 1854].

Three kinds of plots underlie almost all stories about wills: (1) the treasure hunt plot in which the lawyer (and others) search for a lost, hidden, or misplaced will; (2) the perjury plot in which the lawyer, often alone, exposes perjured witnesses to the signature on a will; and (3) the forensic plot in which the lawyer (and others) supply the court with physical evidence proving a document to be a forgery. Here is a lawyer's expert witness identifying the date of the paper on which a forged will was written:

> "Your Honor, and gentlemen of the jury," commenced the witness, "this piece of paper which I now hold in my hand was manufactured by myself, and was calendered upon a machine of my own invention. The waterlines, in place of the ordinary blue ruling, was included in my improvement. You will also observe, upon close inspection—though the ink upon the surface has somewhat obscured it—my own stamp in water-marks. Your Honor can examine it for yourself" ["At the Right Time: A Lawyer's Story," *Fayetteville Observer*, October 12, 1876].

In spite of the fact that stories about wills depend upon the sensation novelesque theme of the suffering (woman) innocent, as the century advanced, lawyer/law stories came to depend more and more upon the search for and provenance of evidence in criminal cases.

Evidence 2.0

From the middle of the eighteenth century onward it was becoming clear to a lot of people that finding truth about criminal acts was a difficult thing. The trials of Jonathan Wild and Stephen McDaniel demonstrated the dubious worth of sworn, eyewitness testimony. In the years before (and even after) the advent of modern medical jurisprudence, physical evidence was often suspect as was so-called expert testimony—trials in the U.S. even at mid-century sometimes became battles of conflicting experts' opinions about evidence. It was the nature of evidence in period courts that motivated Blackstone, in his magisterial *Commentaries on the Laws of England* (1765–1769), to write

> All presumptive evidence of felony should be admitted cautiously; for the law holds it better that ten guilty persons escape, than that one innocent party suffer.

As noted above, at the turn of the century a lot of lawyers and would-be lawyers began writing about the nature and rules of evidence. On top of that, Samuel Rommily emphasized the law's mistakes in his campaign against capital punishment which gained traction at the beginning of the 1800s, and Newgate literature began to shift its focus from homilies about living moral lives to emphasizing the sensational mistakes of the courts. Since the fallibility of evidence was very much in the public mind in Britain and the United States at the beginning of the nineteenth century, writing fiction about it was a natural outcome. Just as naturally, with their new roles in criminal justice system, lawyers sometimes (but not always) played principal roles in that fiction about miscarriages of justice.

Circumstantial Evidence

While law/lawyer stories about civil law, especially disputes about wills, occasionally appear in fiction of the period, most of them center on criminal acts—overwhelmingly on murder. Emphasizing the vagaries of the justice system, many of them bear the title "circumstantial evidence." These tales feature sensational, sentimental, newsworthy, or historical examples of justice gone wrong—in spite of or because of the law, the courts, and sometimes even the best efforts of individuals.

Some of the most sensational of the miscarriages of justice made into fiction grew from the limitations of 19th-century culture. In the days before Social Security cards, driver's licenses, photography, dental records, fingerprints, blood typing, DNA analysis, and all the rest, identifying bodies was a pretty chancy thing. In the days when one's community or occupation were integral to one's identity, going missing was too easily coupled with going dead. Thus appeared the missing-body plot. American readers encountered the missing-body plot early in the century in *Robinson's Magazine's* reprint of "An Assignment" (September 5, 1818) from *Extracts from a Lawyer's Port-Folio* where an allegedly dead man shows up surprisingly alive. It appears again in the story "Circumstantial Evidence" reprinted from *The London Keepsake of 1832* in *The Radical* of December 18, 1841. That piece recounts an English tale in which a man is arrested, tried, and incompetently and incompletely hanged and left in chains for the murder of a missing and presumed dead friend whom he meets in the West Indies after his escape from the gallows. In "Circumstantial Evidence, a Strange Instance of its Uncertainty" (*The Cambria Freeman*, November 14, 1867), an accused murderer escapes to Canada to await the reappearance of his supposed victim, who has been shanghaied and returns very much alive after a series of involuntary voyages. Finally, a similar situation turns up in "Circumstantial Evidence" (*The Daily Intelligencer*, June 15, 1879), in which the supposed victim visits her accused and condemned "murderer" in his death row cell.

Just as the uncertainty of missing bodies taints justice in those stories, evidence based upon bloodstains became another way justice could go awry. Until 1901 no tests existed to distinguish one person's blood from another's or even to identify blood as human or animal. But Genesis 4:10 set a very early precedent for blood as defining evidence: "The voice of thy brother's blood crieth unto me from the ground." It came to be that having any sort of red stain on one's clothes or self meant trouble. For example, in "Circumstantial Evidence" (*The Illinois Free Trader*, November 27, 1840), a story reprinted twenty-eight years later as "A Strange Story Wonderful: Chain of Circumstantial

Evidence" (*The Western Democrat*, January 28, 1868), a youth who had been deer hunting is accused of murder because of the blood on his clothes. To add poignancy to the tale, it is his sister who is forced to reveal the apparently damning evidence:

> At the mandate of the court she arose, laid aside her veil, haggard with anxiety and terror, in low, tremulous accents, broken with sobs, she reluctantly deposed, that the clothes worn by her brother on the return from that fatal journey, were torn, soiled with earth, and bloody! An audible murmur ran through the crowd, who were listening in breathless silence the prisoner bowed his head in mute despair the witness was borne away insensible the argument proceeded, and after an eloquent, but vain defence, the jury brought in a verdict of guilty! The sentence of death was passed.

But it was not just old-fashioned misuses of evidence like bloodstains that provided substance for sensational stories about the courts' threats to innocence.

In addition to stories in which the limitations of the court's knowledge potentially condemn innocents, in law/lawyer stories sometimes it is the community that makes justice impossible—or seem impossible. On the American frontier as well as in small communities in the United States and the Old World, impartial administration of justice was often portrayed as being at risk. Some stories made community prejudice the potential impediment to a fair trial. Indeed, the prospect of lynching comes up with fair regularity in the fiction of the period. Thus the lust for vengeance comes out in "Circumstantial Evidence":

> [...] the law seemed too slow and mild for vengeance; and the great crowd, now swelled to hundreds, swayed to and fro shouting angrily for blood [*Cooper's Clarksburg Register*, April 21, 1852].

At the courthouse in "Circumstantial Evidence," citizens view a trial as merely the prelude to an execution:

> "Has she been indicted?"
> "Yes, at the last court; she was indicted and we would have lynched her; yes, sir, we came near stringing her up."
> "We must give her a fair trial before we hang her," I remarked.
> "We don't object to that. Everybody says that she is guilty; and she is guilty, and must be hung, that's all there is to it [...]" [*The News and Herald*, March 1, 1883].

Very occasionally popular stories also will touch euphemistically on community pressure in the form of police coercion of prisoners to gain convictions.

> A stranger was arrested in a town twenty miles away while trying to dispose of a rifle with McWilliams' name engraved on a silver plate in the stock. He was brought to the county seat at once, and when the right pressure was brought to bear on him he made a confession ["Circumstantial Evidence," *Omaha Daily Bee*, July 3, 1886].

In "The Boorn Affair: A Strange Story of Circumstantial Evidence," jailers "work on" an accused but innocent prisoner:

> Although all the testimony when sifted was found to be worthless, yet the two brothers were remanded back to jail, and Jesse was worked upon to make him turn State's evidence. The Jailer tormented him with suggestions, which his wife followed up with womanly adroitness. Neighbors helped. Beset with preaching and prayers, tracts and sermons, religions conversation and pious directions—told that there was no doubt in any one's mind but that Stephen committed the murder—urged to make a clean breast of it and thus save both body and soul, what wonder that the man confessed, or was alleged to have confessed, that Stephen Boorn did murder Russell Colvin? [*The Somerset Press*, June 18, 1875].

Less frequently than community pressure or coercion down in the cells, the process or the law itself sometimes acts as a hurdle to justice in mid- to late-19th-century popular fiction. A few stories about dishonest lawyers pop up during the period—such as "A Case of Conscience—A Lawyer with Conscientious Scruples" (*Spirit of Jefferson*, March 5, 1867), in which a lawyer successfully defends a guilty robber and then objects to being paid out of the proceeds of his robbery. Very occasionally a story about prejudice or corruption of the bench appears. It's the point of "The Culprit Judge: A Tale of Bench and Bar":

> I suspected him of knavery. When prisoners were convicted, and he had the discretion of punishment, his sentences were sadly inconsistent. He fined when he should have imprisoned, and confined when a nominal punishment would have answered the justice of the case. But I never could get any clew, and with the populace he was regarded as a man of rare integrity and firmness of mind [*The Weekly Portage Sentinel*, June 3, 1858].

Readers also encountered a few stories centered on juries. "A Juror's Testimony" speaks to pressure placed upon juries:

> But I doubt if there are many who understand the influence that was brought to bear upon the jury in making up of their verdict [*New York Ledger*, September 8, 1866].

A naively curious countryman on a jury asks all the right questions in "A Verdant Juror" in *The New York Ledger* (September 11, 1869). And the hung jury serves as a plot device in "Fanny Talbot: A Tale of Circumstantial Evidence" (*Edgefield Advertiser*, September 12, 1855).

Along with stories that focus on procedure, sometimes the law itself serves as the subject. Thus, double jeopardy serves as the feature of "A Very Narrow Escape" (*The Butler Citizen*, August 24, 1881) in which two accused men are tried separately, the first is found innocent, and then confesses to the crime at the trial of the second without fear of punishment. In the matter of law, "A Defence [sic] Without Evidence" (*The New York Ledger*, September 15, 1866) goes even further: instead of a providing a surprise way to solve problems, laws become the subject of the story and provide multiple hurdles to the vindication of the innocent. Three different laws keep the lawyer-narrator from ready access to testimony that will free his client:

> 1. "The former was the party accused, and the law, in theory, excluded his testimony, as much out of tenderness to *him*, as because of the great temptation to falsehood offered by his situation";
> 2. "But the rule of excluding the evidence of husband and wife, '*for or against each other*,' at least in some of its applications, struck me as resting on a more questionable foundation"; and
> 3. "An imperative law of the State forbad the introduction of negro testimony in any case in which a white man was the party."

But even with those three strikes, the story demonstrates that virtue is rewarded— along with brains.

Justice Achieved

With only a feeble grasp of science, impatient communities weighted down with prejudice, and rules that could be impediments rather than supports, justice was not easily achieved in the nineteenth century. But in fiction it always was.

In early lawyer fiction, lawyers, judges, and juries have little to do with the discovery of guilt or innocence in law/lawyer stories. That is because a lot of popular literature about the law and lawyers rests on coincidence or Providence. To underline this "Circumstantial Evidence, or The Fatal Resemblance" (*The Spirit of Democracy*, October 16, 1866) even picks up the words from Longfellow's poem "Retribution" to get the point across: "God's mills grind slow, but they grind exceedingly small." With respect to crime, this notion gets summed up in the phrase and the concept of "murder will out." In "A Leaf from a Lawyer's Diary," the narrator literally makes the point:

> And as I passed by his lifeless form swinging from the limb of that tree, I was forcibly reminded of the legal phrase, "Murder will out" [*The Anderson Intelligencer*, November 27, 1873].

To be precise, rather than being a legal phrase or concept, "murder will out" is more literary than it is legal. Indeed, Chaucer used it first in "The Nun's Priest's Tale":

> O blisful god, that art so just and trewe!
> Lo, how that thou biwreyest mordre alway!
> Mordre wol out, that see we day by day.
> Mordre is so wlatsom and abhominable To god,
> That is so just and resonable,
> That he ne wol nat suifre it heled be;
> Though it abyde a yeer, or two, or three,
> Mordre wol out, this my conclusioun.

The precedent of hundreds of years of stories that depend on Providence to work out human dilemmas, joined with the fashion for sensation fiction based on suffering rewarded, produced stories in the nineteenth century with lawyers in them in which neither they nor courts or juries or laws insured justice. But God did.

Not relying entirely on God to do all of the work, however, courts in nineteenth-century law/lawyer fiction often do depend on evidence to bring about justice. In most cases that evidence consists of the real criminal's (not the accused's) confession—the oldest and most basic kind of evidence in church and secular courts. But the majority of the confessions found in law/lawyer stories are more than simple confessions which can be retracted, affected by mental illness, or altered by revelations of other kinds of evidence. They are deathbed confessions which have been equated with direct evidence since the Middle Ages. Thus, for example this tableau from "Fanny Talbot: A Tale of Circumstantial Evidence":

> "Oh, speak not to me! It was I who stabbed Isabel!" exclaimed the young man wildly.
> All were horrified at these words. His mother and sister imputed them to the delirium of the disease; but when he grew more calm, and solemnly repeated the asseveration, they were forced to believe him. Before his death he related the particulars of this unnatural deed [*Edgefield Advertiser*, September 12, 1855].

While with varying degrees of subtlety Providential justice lies under most lawyer/law stories, the assumption that there can be no such thing as unimpeachable evidence also forms the bedrock of law/lawyer fiction in the nineteenth century. In this regard, one popular kind of law/lawyer fiction inevitably follows the pattern of crime, accusation of an innocent, seemingly overwhelming prejudice or evidence against him or her, and then salvation brought in with the introduction of new evidence. Thus plots emerged centered on the surprise exoneration of an innocent based in part on the hero's skepticism about every kind of evidence. They were

(1) The absent-evidence plot—in which the hero (or coincidence) delivers new and exculpatory evidence. See, for example, "The Accusation" and "The Blasted Tree" cited above;

(2) The misinterpreted-evidence plot—in which the hero supplies a different interpretation of the evidence from the accepted one. See the ballistics demonstration in "A Case of Circumstantial Evidence" (*Eaton Democrat*, May 10, 1855);

(3) The false- or manipulated-evidence plot—in which the hero needs to expose the motives of a villain to correctly interpret evidence. Thus, for example, the exposure of perjury through cross-examination in "Miriam: A

Tale of Circumstantial Evidence" (*The Spirit of Democracy*, February 4 and 11, 1852);

(4) The false confessions of guilt plot—in which the hero finds evidence to demonstrate that the accused's confession is (understandably) delusional. Thus the stories "Circumstantial Evidence: An Adventure in Western Virginia" (*The Daily Press*, June 2, 1859) and "A Case of Circumstantial Evidence" (*Eaton Democrat*, May 10, 1855).

As they appear in 19th-century law/lawyer fiction, each of these plots at first substitutes the hero's (usually the lawyer's) intuition for public opinion and superficial interpretation of things and events. In other words, to the heroes, innocent people look innocent—in spite of appearances:

> I was in court when Edward Carson was brought in, and when my eye rested upon him I could not believe him guilty of the crime which had been laid to him. He was not more than five-and-twenty years of age, and was what would be called a handsome man. He was of medium size, with a full, well-developed head; with fine auburn hair; large blue eyes; and with a countenance denoting great frankness and generosity ["A Lawyer's Story," *The New York Ledger*, April 5, 1862].

Innocent people may look innocent, but seeing innocence (or guilt) is a skill especially possessed by lawyers:

> There is no calling in life which affords to the observer so keen an insight into the human heart as that of the law. A man may, with a tolerable degree of ingenuity, succeed for a long time in concealing his true character at least its shadows and minute vanities from the world at large; indeed often from his most intimate friends ["Scraps from the Notebook of a Missouri Lawyer," *The Spirit of Democracy*, October 24, 1846].

While many law/lawyer stories (especially before 1850) center on justice brought about by the lawyer's investigations and discoveries outside of the courtroom, at mid-century things changed. By the late 1850s some writers began to understand the possibilities of courtroom drama. Cross examinations and the lawyer's skill in eliciting the truth from perjured or intractable witnesses became the center of a number of stories run in *The New York Ledger* and miscellaneous newspapers. Thus in "Helen Montressor; Judge Remsen's First Client," conveying his use of the atmosphere in the courtroom is an essential part of the lawyer/narrator's search for truth:

> The excitement had now became overwhelming, and the witness was beginning to fear for his bodily safety—a fact which I determined to use as an additional screw. "I shall ask for but little more information," I replied, "as I do not wish to expose you to the rage of this audience, if you will answer me promptly. Where is the will that old Mr. Gregory executed on the day of his death, in which he made his grandchild, Helen Montressor, his heir, and which your wife stole from the child as she lay sleeping?" [*The New York Ledger*, May 31, 1856].

"The Criminal Witness, A Lawyer's Story" likewise features a surprise revelation that could only happen in the courtroom and in front of a jury:

> "Nancy Luther," said I, turning to the witness, and speaking in a quick, startling tone, at the same time looking her sternly in the eye, "please tell the court, and the jury, and tell me, too, where you got the seventy-five dollars you sent to your sister in Somers?" The witness started, as though a volcano had burst at her feet. She turned pale as death, and every limb shook violently. I waited until the people could see the emotion, and then repeated the question [*The Raftsman's Journal*, June 11, 1856].

The other mid-century phenomena in lawyer/law fiction was the introduction of evidence based on scientific proof. While the period saw the birth of modern forensic science, courts and juries often accepted it only grudgingly—indeed, in England James Marsh, who discovered the standard test for arsenic, failed to win a conviction in his first court appearance in 1832. Nonetheless, basic science does occasionally save the day in period lawyer/law stories, especially when firearms enter as evidence. There is a minor thread of firearms evidence in mystery-related fiction from mid-century onward. Thus Goodfellow's sleight of hand with projectiles is one of the clues in Poe's "Thou Art the Man!" (1844), and Mr. Bucket's (or Mrs. Bucket's) piecing together pistol wadding points the definitive finger in *Bleak House* (1853). In neither case, however, does this involve lawyers or the judicial system—except that lawyer Tulkinghorn is on the receiving end of the bullet in *Bleak House*. There were, however, stories about ballistics that did bring in lawyers. Reprinted for years, "Bullet Marks, a Story of Love and Circumstantial Evidence" (run first perhaps in the *Green-Mountain Freeman* on August 21, 1867) recounts how a condemned man is exonerated when his knowledgeable friend proves by makers' marks that he could not have fired the bullet that wounded his comrade. While "Bullet Marks" makes perfunctory mention of a trial, in "A Case of Circumstantial Evidence" a court-appointed advocate amazes the judges with a new view of hitherto damning evidence:

> The town surgeons attended and declared that as the ball passed through the heart, death must naturally ensue. Lewis wished to know if the ball was still in the body; the surgeon sought for and found it, upon which the advocate sent for the pistol with which the deed had been perpetrated and tried to drop the ball into the barrel—it seemed too large—he accordingly tried it in all possible ways; still it would not go in. That the ball could not be fired by that pistol was evident to every observer, the judges looked at one another and shook their heads—[...] [*Eaton Democrat*, May 10, 1855].

Significantly, here in his discovery and demonstration the lawyer seems to be acting like a scientist, or a detective.

Along with stories about lawyers' victories in court and stories about their successes when acting as detectives, stories depicting lawyers as unsavory characters are not uncommon in the nineteenth century. Dickens' Jaggers and Tulkinghorn represent the English precedent for this view of lawyers. But there are numerous examples of lawyers created in the same mold in American popular media. Thus one of the poems about lawyers to appear after mid-century was "The Devil and the Lawyers," which concludes:

> If all they have said of each other be true,
> The Devil has surely been robbed of his due;
> I'm satisfied now 'tis all very well,
> For the lawyers would ruin the morals of hell.
>
> They have puzzled the court with villainous cavil,
> And I'm free to confess, they have puzzled the Devil;
> My agents are right to let lawyers alone
> If I had them, they'd swindle me out of my throne. [*The Staunton Spectator*, November 5, 1867].

Along with pettifoggery, greed sometimes appears as a hallmark of the profession:

> "What a pity it should end there," was the pensive reflection of more than one "legal mind," accustomed to regard a squabble of some sort over a dead man's money as essential to the repose of his soul, or at least as a mark of decent respect to his memory ["A Legal Slip 'Twixt Cup and Lip," *The New York Ledger*, September 18, 1869].

Lawyers and Detectives

From early in the century writers focused many of their lawyer stories either on (1) the hero exposing bias or deceit through cross-examination, surprise witnesses, or oratory; or (2) the hero hunting for clues and the discovery or explanation of physical evidence. In fact, in that second category lawyers do not act as lawyers but as detectives. And the stories in which they appeared centered on missing or misinterpreted evidence relating to a crime and saving the innocent. They did not necessarily have to end in a courtroom with arguments before a judge and jury—and they rarely do. The whole point was finding evidence. Indeed, after the word "detective" was used in print, not only did detectives begin to appear in fiction, but while writers described curiosity, skepticism, intelligence, the search for evidence, and attention to detail in action as essential traits of lawyers, they also described detectives in the same way. And in fiction they do the same things. Thus the lawyer-narrator in "An Old Lawyer's Story" does not depend upon the knowledge gained from his studies when reading for the bar, but the qualities that made him an efficient detective:

> A great many years ago, while I comparatively a young man, and still unmarried, I resided in a certain city in Pennsylvania, and enjoyed the reputation of being the cleverest lawyer ever

known there. It is not for me to say the praise was merited, but I certainly found myself able to discover loop-holes of escape which surprised even my fellow lawyers. I possessed by nature those qualities which would have made an excellent detective, and I was a thorough student of the law. There was no mystery about it, but among the more ignorant classes I gained a reputation for more than human knowledge. Perhaps it was not polite for them to say that the devil helped, but they did [*The Omaha Daily Bee*, July 30, 1874].

In the story the hero dresses in disguise and reexamines the scene at which three elderly people died, after which he produces physical and theoretical evidence which both doctor and coroner (who were not "deeply scientific men") misinterpreted and thereby avoids the courtroom altogether. Indeed while stories about lawyers acting as detectives do appear throughout the nineteenth century, from mid-century onward when it came to finding facts and saving the innocent, detectives got most of the jobs.

While lawyers continued to act as detectives throughout the century, in fiction detectives began to take over—just as police departments and private detective organization multiplied in cities across America after the Civil War. Occasionally fictional lawyers knew their own limitations: indeed in "The Lost Will: An American Detective Story" (*The Riverine Grazier*, New South Wales, Australia, February 6, 1891), a lawyer, "the shrewdest lawyer in the place, and quite a detective himself," has to consult a detective to save his client's fortune. Some writers, in fact, accepted the notion that lawyers and detectives were essentially different in their approaches to crime problems. The narrator of "A Detective's Story: How He Was Convicted and Sent to State Prison," for instance, emphasizes the difference between detectives and lawyers:

> While the profession [of detective] may make a man hard-hearted and anxious to convict, it is nevertheless a certain fact that a complete chain of circumstantial [i.e., physical] evidence against a criminal will settle his case sooner than half a dozen respectable witnesses. Lawyers can browbeat and confuse, and the veracity of a witness can be slurred or impeached, but when you strike against a circumstance it is not so easy to step over it or explain it away [*The Decatur Daily Republican*, December 2, 1887].

This is the same way Edgar Allan Poe approached things in "The Mystery of Marie Roget," back at the dawn of the formal detective story. Dupin holds that not only bunglers like Vidocq and the Prefect don't know how to solve problems, but lawyers and courts are clueless:

> He has thought it sagacious to echo the small talk of the lawyers, who, for the most part, content themselves with echoing the rectangular precepts of the courts. I would here observe that very much of what is rejected as evidence by a court, is the best of evidence to the intellect. For the court, guided itself by the general principles of evidence—the recognized and booked principles—is averse from swerving at particular instances. And this steadfast adherence to principle, with rigorous disregard of the conflicting exception, is a sure mode of attaining the maximum of attainable truth, in any long sequence of time. The

practice, in mass, is therefore philosophical; but it is not the less certain that it engenders vast individual error [*The Ladies' Companion*, November and December 1842 and February 1843].

And if they are not clueless, lawyers can pervert the course of justice: thus "A Detective's Story" concludes with

> He had rich and influential relatives to back him in this decision, and when the case came to trial he was actually acquitted in spite of proofs enough to convict him ten times over. The defense set up that I, as the detective in the case, could not find the real criminal, and therefore, made my plans to convict young Brush. They even charged me with preparing and hiding the clothes and with buying and fixing the knife. I was denounced as a monster and a dangerous man, and many people shunned me [*Hamilton County Press*, April 27, 1889].

Summation

In 19th-century American fiction, lawyers played many parts. They joined with clergy and physicians as members of the "learned professions," and as such observed and made observations about human nature and the human condition. Like clergy, through rhetoric they sought to open the hearts and minds of judges and juries and make the truth prevail. As respected citizens they became as eminently marriageable as any upper-class male. And just as the term "Philadelphia Lawyer" shifted from describing one learned in the law to one skilled in manipulation, lawyers also became sinister characters and confidence men. Each one of these roles gave rise to a different kind of fiction, from exemplae focused on human behavior to sensation fiction ending in the victory of love and virtue. The most influential of these responses to "lawyerization," however, was to become the "detective story." These narratives about "circumstantial evidence" began as a response to the inequities and mistakes inherent in the law or made by courts in the eighteenth century. They evolved into a kind of fiction loaded with popular appeal, fiction which demonstrated the victory of truth over superstition and prejudice, reason and observation over guile and appearance, and innocence over circumstance. All of this was accomplished by a hero from what was then a newly invigorated profession: a lawyer. Writers soon discovered that the action did not have to literally take place in a court as long as evidence and justice lay at the heart of the matter. At mid-century, moreover, writers discovered another new profession that could find evidence to vindicate the innocent and solve mysteries, that of the detective. As cities created police forces and private detective agencies appeared in major cities, detectives were much in the news. Being a detective, moreover, only required those things that could be found in every reader—reason, close observation, and a commitment to justice. It was a winning combination.

3

Physicians and Forensics

> Once when I attended a lecture by a celebrated man, he had stated that every animal had in its blood globules differing in size from those of any other kind. This knowledge had been arrived at by very slow steps. There was no doubt, however, of its scientific accuracy, or that with the aid of a powerful microscope a professional man of skill and experience could decide, without chance of committing a mistake, from the slightest stain whether the blood, if blood, had flowed in the veins of a human being or other animal. It was the same with minute fibres of fur, hair, &c. This he had said was a most valuable discovery, and he instanced the fact that in France an innocent man might have been convicted of murder owing to a knife having been found in his possession stained with what had every appearance of blood, which stains examined by a skilled gentleman through the microscope was proved to be lime juice.—"Murder Under the Microscope," *Autobiography of an English Detective,* 1863

Lawyers had made a place for themselves in a lot of aspects of 19th-century life; they could, therefore, claim a spot in every variety of the new stories about crime and detection that began to appear in newspapers and magazines—whether about clerks pilfering dry goods, gangs printing bogus banknotes, or black sheep offspring altering wills. Not so with physicians. Theirs was the more mundane task of trying to save lives. And it wasn't easy. Even after Pasteur's demonstrations in the 1860s, knowledge of the role of bacteria in diseases spread slowly to practicing physicians. Continuing medical education was a 20th-century concept. Once a doctor hung out his (and it was always "his") shingle in the 19th century, his obligation to keep apprised of medical advances such as theories of bacteriology, sepsis, and the use of anesthesia by subscribing to medical journals, or travelling to Paris or Vienna, or even talking to his colleagues was mandated by his own curiosity—or not. For most of the century, doctors themselves spread diseases because they did not know how diseases spread. In 1843 Oliver Wendell Holmes argued in an article in *The New England*

Quarterly Journal of Medicine that puerperal fever, a major cause of illness and death of women following childbirth, was contracted from person-to-person contact with their physicians. Holmes' piece was not only highly controversial but "vigorously attacked and ridiculed [...] by two leading Philadelphian obstetricians, Charles Meigs and Hugh Hodge," because they did not understand germ theory or contagion (Dunn).

Until the formation of the American Medical Association in 1847, medical education in the United States was haphazard and decidedly antique. While, as with lawyers, plenty of "note-book" stories about physicians appeared in the popular press, it was only late in the century that they gained much public recognition for the role they could play in solving crimes. This happened because of revolutionary scientific discoveries and in part because of pioneering work and works in medical jurisprudence by physicians in Britain and the United States. But it took time to get these things put into practice. Application of advancements in medicine and science to public policy was glacial. It took until the 19th century in England and America for the state to take over from churches the registration of deaths—and gradually to add cause of death to those certificates. Also, somewhat incredibly, American jurisdictions did not begin to replace elected or appointed coroners—those who determined the official cause of death and culpability—with trained medical examiners until the last quarter of the century. Thus, while random people from off the streets made official pronouncements about deaths, in some of the new detective stories physicians and other savants used science to get at the real truth. The knowledge acquired by science by close observation and reason became an ideal antidote for the ignorance and prejudice that formed the basis of the circumstantial evidence story. But it wasn't always physicians who supplied it.

My Son the Doctor

If the detective story had been a late 20th-century invention, medical doctors and scientists would have automatically been at the head of the line when it came to choosing detective heroes. But that wasn't the case back when the form began. Medicine was a different kind of profession. First of all, in the 19th century admission to medical school was a snap. Abraham Flexner did a survey of medical education in the last century for *The Atlantic Monthly* in June 1910, and this is what he found:

> Between 1810 and 1840, twenty-six new medical schools sprang up; between 1840 and 1876, forty-seven more; and the number actually surviving in 1876 has been since then much more than doubled. First and last, the United States and Canada have in little more

than a century produced four hundred and forty-seven medical schools, many, of course, short-lived, and perhaps fifty still-born. One hundred and fifty-six survive to-day. Of these, Illinois, prolific mother of thirty-nine medical colleges, still harbors in the city of Chicago fourteen; forty-two sprang from the fertile soil of Missouri, ten of them still "going" concerns; the Empire State produced forty-three, with eleven survivors; Indiana, twenty-seven, with two survivors; Pennsylvania, twenty, with eight survivors; Tennessee, eighteen, with eleven survivors. The city of Cincinnati brought forth about twenty, the city of Louisville eleven.

These enterprises—for the most part, they can be called schools or institutions only by courtesy—were frequently set up regardless of opportunity or need, in small towns as readily as in large, and at times, almost in the heart of the wilderness. No field, however limited, was ever effectually preempted. Wherever and whenever the roster of untitled practitioners rose above half a dozen, a medical school was likely at any moment to be precipitated. Nothing was really essential but professors.

There were no laboratory classes: it took until 1871 for Harvard to expand its medical curriculum to a three-year program with a focus on experiential learning though the laboratory sciences of anatomy, physiology, and chemistry and training in bedside practices (Bynum). And nobody had real clinical experience until the end of the century and the creation of Johns Hopkins and other hospital-linked medical schools. This is the sort of education that could lead to physicians like Dr. Puffer:

> [...] an old bachelor—a physician, who belonged to that class of medical practitioners who, having learnt certain rules and laws by rote, and having obtained a diploma, go to work on the principle that all men must be doctored in the same way or in none. And that a patient is a creature formed to swallow nauseous doses which do him no good, without complaint—to foot great bills without a murmur and to die of a dispensation of Providence, making no accusations against the doctor ["Dr. Puffer's Lost Opportunity," *The New York Ledger*, July 13, 1867].

Physicians were trained the same way lawyers were—by being essentially apprentices of experienced practitioners. Thus readers get this bit of background of James Brampton, one of the best-known fictional detectives in the 1860s:

> I was born in New York city. My father was a respectable merchant, and he bestowed upon me the best education that money could produce. He wished me to embrace the medical profession and for that purpose sent me to read with a physician who lived in a village on the Hudson River. This physician was a particular friend of his.
>
> I liked the study of medicine pretty well and remained several years in the physician's office. But a terrible accident happened to my father, in fact, he was burnt to death, and he left his affairs so embarrassed, that my mother could not afford the means for me to complete my medical studies. I therefore determined to seek for some more remunerative employment [*Leaves from the Note-Book of a New York Detective*, New York: Dick & Fitzgerald, 1865].

Whose Body?

Perhaps the most enduring images of traditional medical education from Rembrandt's "Dr. Tulip" to Thomas Eakins' "The Gross Clinic" are those depicting dissections and tiers of students watching an operation being conducted in a place that is still called an operating theater. What this aspect of medical education demanded was a constant supply of corpses, a subject about which polite society was especially punctilious. The supply of executed criminals' bodies often failed to meet the demand of medical schools and individual surgeons who wished to sharpen their skills. Thus, according to W.F. Bynum, the practical study of anatomy was "a source of considerable conflict between doctors and the public":

> Persistent difficulties in supply led to the lucrative business of body snatching and grave robbing, linking anatomy teachers directly to the criminal underworld. [...] The French resolved the legal if not the emotional aspects of bodies for dissection in the 1790s, but in Britain and America problems persisted, fanned by revelations from the 1820s that Burke and Hare in Edinburgh and the Williams gang in London were actually generating their own corpses by murder. There were serious riots against doctors and medical students in New York in 1788 and in New Haven in 1824 [12].

Notably, in 1824 the author of "The Blasted Tree" uses such body snatchers, or "resurrectionists" as part of his or her gothic introduction to the story. The author of "Mademoiselle Jabirouska: The Modern Messalina" (*Holden's Dollar Magazine,* November 6, 1848) is more specific in that while the over-eager body snatchers sell the bodies of their victims to "students of anatomy," the heads they collect are destined for Germany to be used in the study of phrenology. And almost a decade later over-eager resurrectionists play the same role in "An Adventure in Paris":

> Was it not plain enough now? The whole plot was unfolded to me as clearly as could be. I was to be made food for the dissecting knife of some studious doctor, and was already in the trap! And my body would be sold for forty francs! My soul knocked out—my wind stopped—and all for that paltry sum! My soul, what a price for a murder! [*The New York Ledger,* March 6, 1857].

While the idea of grave robbing and dissecting corpses links early detective stories with Gothic fiction, dissection came to play a role in the form of autopsies which provided acceptably definitive answers to questions raised by enigmatic or circumstantial evidence. Although Poe's "The Mystery of Marie Roget" concentrates on *post-mortem* details, the *post-mortem* examination didn't become a standard part of detective stories until mid-century. And by then it was exclusively the province of medical personnel. Indeed, some detective stories centered on careful attention to physical details of dead bodies. In "The

Silver Pin" (*Leaves from the Note Book of a New York Detective*, 1865) former medical student James Brampton discovers the esoteric means used to commit murder, and in "The Pen Knife Blade" (*The New York Ledger*, February 16, 1867) over-zealous medical students and a resurrectionist lead to a surgeon's similar discovery of a hitherto unsuspected means of murder. In these two pieces men with medical training fill the role of detective. The experimental confirmation of their suspicions in the form of a *post-mortem* examination stands as the most important aspect of both character and plot in these few detective stories. Most often, however, autopsies performed by anonymous physicians and surgeons act as supporting documents in detective stories. Sometimes they serve as consultants for detectives:

> The first thing I did was to go to one of the surgeons who did the *post mortem* examination and procure an accurate description of the wound. I learned that the instrument had entered beneath the fifth rib, and thence passing upward, grazed two or three ribs and turned inwards, passing near the heart and producing hemorrhage and death. From this description it was evident that the fork to produce such a wound, must have been nearly or quite perpendicular with the body, and turned in an awkward manner to be used with the hands ["Circumstantial Evidence," *Coldwater Sentinel*, May 11, 1849].

At other times they confirm what the detective suspected:

> This supplied a motive but it was hardly likely in itself to excite grave suspicions against him, if other circumstances had not been developed by the post mortem examination. Two doctors had been appointed to perform the examination, and they were both of the opinion that the man must have been shot by a person who was behind him at the time, though the pistol had been held above him and fired downwards. The reasons they gave in support of their conclusions were so convincing that Boiteler's statement could only be accepted on the supposition that he was so excited at the time as not to be able to remember the exact position of his servant at the instant he fired. It was also shown that the muzzle of the pistol, from which the ball had been fired which killed his wife, must have been held quite close to her, as her dress had been set on fire ["Found Out," *The Mountain Democrat*, February 21, 1863].

In an effort to curtail the effects of too many details that might offend sensitive readers, however, sometimes writers make their autopsies as brief and impersonal as possible, like this one:

> An autopsy of the body, and an analysis of the contents of the stomach, left no doubt as to the cause of death. The presence of arsenic, in a necessary fatal quantity, was indicated by every known chemical test ["Lucky Larceny," *The New York Ledger*, April 16, 1870].

Doctors' Memoirs

In connection with lawyers, we have already noted that one popular kind of 19th-century journalism was the "note-book" story, or pseudo-autobiography.

Newspapers were full of "lawyer's stories" and "detective's stories" but there weren't as many stories titled "doctor's story." But there were some. The earliest "doctor story" in *Chronicling America* dates from 1842: it's "A Doctor's Story," in the *Boon's Lick Times* (February 19, 1842). And the same title crops up occasionally over the next few decades. Unlike the other kinds of pseudo-autobiography, however, no plot pattern emerges to define doctor stories—other than that they are personal accounts of events. Indeed, not all of them actually require an M.D. as the narrator. The story cited above, for example, is a comic narrative about mistaken identity. A few doctor stories appeared that centered on the fear of premature burial (see "The Old Doctor's Story," *Fayetteville Observer*, January 6, 1853; and "The Doctor's Story," *The National Era*, December 3, 1857) and love lost and gained is also a recurrent theme (see "Love and War: A Physician's Story," *Holmes County Farmer*, July 18, 1861; and "How I Won My Wife: A Doctor's Story," *The Tiffin Weekly Tribune*, September 21, 1865). Despite all being labeled "doctor stories," these stories have little in common other than the fact that the narrators identify themselves as physicians. Indeed, one of the few things that they have in common is that they are not very much about physicians or surgeons treating patients—other than watching them die or return from death. Doctor stories aren't about cures or discoveries. In fact, in one of the few stories that describes contemporary medicine ("A Physician's Story," *Wilmington Journal*, January 7, 1848), the practitioner applies treatments (which include bleeding) only to disguise from the family that the patient has passed out in an alcoholic stupor. Instead of evolving a kind of narrative unique to physicians, then, the narrative about a physician's experiences took on the coloring of the gothic tale or the love story. Or the detective story.

The Physician as Hero

Although physicians appear in the majority of period detective stories concerning murder, mostly they appear in cameos to affirm that something medical is right or wrong or enigmatic. While in the late 1860s readers encountered a doctor-hero a year in popular press detective stories, before and after that period they appeared only occasionally. As with lawyer-detectives, doctors made their literary debut in circumstantial evidence stories. In the first of these, "The Rifle" (Mary R. Mitford, *Stories of American Life by American Writers*, London: H. Colburn and R. Bentley, 1830), the writer uses the figure of the physician in a frontier community as an example of the tragic potential of judgment by circumstantial evidence. Doctor Rivington is a paragon—helpful, pious, genial, a practicing physician, and the most respected member of the frontier community. Ballistic evidence makes him look guilty of murder, and he is freed only by a combination of close observation and the ministrations of Providence. There's really nothing about him as a doctor beyond a brief aside about curing a patient. Decades after "The Rifle," a doctor enters to represent the other side of the circumstantial evidence argument—the side that says that evidence really proves what it seems to prove. "The Torn Newspaper" (*The New York Ledger*, October 30, 1858) has virtually no merit as fiction—it's yet another tale of the miseries of love. But the denouement of the story depends on the discoveries of Dr. Thomas, "who was a shrewd man of the world, and who let nothing escape him." Thomas, who has done the autopsy, finds the paper wadding from the murder bullet, and, partly because of his familiarity with the citizens of the small town, traces it to a piece torn from a rarely-read newspaper. He then traces the paper to the murderer, and the rest is history—or as the story puts it, "Providence." The bit about tracing bullet wadding may have come from Mr. and Mrs. Bucket's discovery in *Bleak House* (1853) and the tale certainly gives readers a bit of sensation novel in miniature—so it still dances around being a fully-developed detective story.

Two years earlier "Mysterious Manifestation" appeared in *Flag of our Union* (October 11, 1856), *The New York Ledger*'s principal rival. It's a completely different kind of story with a much lighter tone. It's a presumptive ghost story that is really about problem solving. In it seemingly inexplicable bell ringing frightens a middle-class family. Enter the family physician who figures out that it has all been the work of a larcenous Irish maid who has been making off with the family's silver. While he is never given a name, the doctor establishes his bona fides by rattling off a prescription for the wife's nerves—"I would advise you to take aconite alternate with belladonna; you have that medicine, I presume?"—and by rushing off to see other patients. He also establishes the maid's guilt by conducting an experiment before they search her boxes—which may or may not be science-y, depending on what side of the issue one takes. But his principal character trait has little connection with his medical training. It has to do with being a detective:

> The gentleman proved to be the family physician; a small, brisk man, who carried a little cane, with which he was in the habit of giving vigorous little strokes or thrusts to himself, or anything which came in his way. He had bright, twinkling eyes, which danced from object to object, with the rapidity of thought; he had a quick, nervous way of talking; his hands were never still, his eyes were never quiet; he never sat more than five minutes in a place; he was the spirit of unrest and nervousness. Just the one to delight in a little mystery for the mere sake of ferreting it out.

In 1862 Ballou began publishing an evolving series of stories, this time in his *Dollar Monthly Magazine*, featuring a character identified as a New York Detective. Some of the stories are recollections by a non-detective narrator

3. *Physicians and Forensics* 73

and some of them are narrated by the detective (who acquires the name James Brampton). The thirteen stories were immensely popular, copied by newspaper after newspaper and eventually combined with others and printed in 1865 by the notorious pirates Dick & Fitzgerald as *Leaves from the Note Book of a New York Detective.* Most of the stories have nothing to do with medicos — but two of them do: "The Knotted Handkerchief" (*Ballou's Dollar Monthly Magazine*, July 1862) and "The Defrauded Heir" (*Ballou's Dollar Monthly Magazine*, January 1863). The first is narrated by a medical student:

> About ten years ago I was studying medicine in New York. I had been working very hard, having specially devoted my attention for last six months to pathology. This is a tedious study, demanding the most determined mental attention. I threw myself into it with all the ardor of youth, and consequently at the end of six months I had completely exhausted my mental energies.

On his much needed vacation he meets celebrated detective James Brampton whom he later calls upon to help another medical student who is accused of murder by damning circumstantial evidence — which the detective effortlessly sweeps out of the way. The narrator describes the key to Brampton's talents this way:

> His faculty in this respect was evidently owing to his keen observation, his acute mental analysis and determined perseverance. No difficulty daunted him, in fact his power seemed to increase in proportion as the case was enveloped in mystery. He was a man of great courage, and what was still better for his profession, extraordinary coolness.

Six months after the detective helps out the medical student, "The Defrauded Heir" remakes the celebrated detective's biography and he becomes a former medical student:

> I was brought up to the medical profession, although I never graduated as a physician. It was an incident that occurred during my pupilage which made me adopt the profession of a detective officer, and I cannot do better than illustrate my experience, by relating it to the reader:
> My father was a respectable merchant, living in the city of New York. He bestowed as good an education on me as he could afford, and then placed me in the office of Doctor Lignon, who resided in a huge country village, for the purpose of studying medicine. I was then eighteen years of age, and was to remain with him until I was twenty-one, and then enter a medical college.

Not too much after this background is given, the narrator simply sluffs off how and why he became a detective:

> I need not now enter into the reasons which made me turn detective officer, as they have nothing to do with the matter in question; suffice it to say that in a few years I became quite famous, and had as much business as I could attend to. I married and settled myself in the upper part of New York city.

But the retrospective story does include a number of medical details. They include a grave robbing excursion ("Forgive me, reader, I was an ardent student in my profession, and perhaps might never have an opportunity of investigating this strange malady again. I determined to exhume young Harry's body") as well as a cancer diagnosis:

> [...] he noticed for the first time a small pimple on his tongue. [...] He applied caustic to it, it broke out onto a small ulcer. This showed no disposition to heal, and by-and-by he experienced strong laneinating pains through it. This alarmed him, and he went to New York to consult Doctor M—, and Doctor P—, the famous professors of surgery. The moment they saw it they decided it was cancer, and all that remained for the invalid to do was to go home and prepare for death, an operation being entirely unjustifiable.

The plot turns on kidnapping which is done through a Juliet-like potion to simulate death along with a body substitution. It is possible that Percy Garret (or whoever wrote the New York detective stories) reengineered the narrator of "The Defrauded Heir" because of an idea of how to justify a new kind of surprise ending for this detective story, an ending that depended upon medical explanations.

Before they published the Brampton stories, in 1863 New York's Dick & Fitzgerald cobbled together a collection of stories they titled *Strange Stories of a Detective; or The Curiosities of Crime*, supposedly authored by "A Retired Member of the Detective Police." As filler in both *Strange Stories* and in *Leaves from the Note Book of a New York Detective* the publisher included a doctor story. In the first volume "The Doctor's Story" is a maudlin account of a "fallen woman" and in *Leaves* "A Satanic Compact" is another account of deranged love told by a physician whose

> history can be summed up in two or three words; he is, as he states, a doctor, and has practiced in New York city. But he has studied too much and it turned his brain—in short he is deranged, and has been confined in the State Lunatic Asylum for four years.

In 1866, however, Sylvanus Cobb, Jr., and *The New York Ledger* got back into the doctor business. Cobb, one of the most prolific writers in an age of prolific writers, used lawyers and assorted law enforcement personnel for his detective stories and in 1866 he tried out a physician hero in "The Apothecary's Compound, from a Physician's Notebook" (*The New York Ledger*, July 21, 1866). As in the Brampton stories, Cobb begins his doctor story with medical school:

> At the age of five-and-twenty I graduated from one of the best medical schools in the country; and I do not think I stretch the truth when I say that no man had ever been more untiring in his efforts to obtain a thorough knowledge of all that should be understood by the true physician than I had been. I had entered upon my studies with a love for the profession, and as I progressed I loved it more and more; and when I finally received my diploma,

and our old Professor of Anatomy and Surgery assured me that I was fit to practice anywhere, I was vain enough to believe that he spoke the truth; though now, in the prime of life, I am forced to confess that so far as the theory and practice of medicine is concerned, I have learned wonderful things since the day on which that bit of "sheep-skin" came into my hands.

Settling in Cobb's typical small town, the narrator meets its two resident physicians, whose "systems of medicine are so widely different, and our estimations of pathological conditions so dissimilar, that we could never arrive at the same conclusion touching either diagnostics or methods of treatment." The heart of the story resides in the hero observing the strange symptoms of a patient and his niece and the doctor's (scantily described) lab work that leads to his discovery of arsenic in the patient's wine.

In the late 1860s Cobb and other writers for *The New York Ledger* established the physician as a hero of detective stories. Thus *The Ledger* published Cobb's "The Pen Knife Blade: From a Surgeon's Diary" (February 16, 1867); "The Mad Philosopher: A Startling Adventure from the Diary of a Physician" (September 19, 1868); "A Post-Mortem Discovery: A Scrap from a Physician's Diary" (October 23, 1869); and "Sibyl's Augury: From a Physician's Diary" (July 22, 1871); as well as "Dr. Puffer's Lost Opportunity" (July 13, 1867) and "A Curious Case" (March 26, 1870) by Mary Kyle Dallas and Judge Clark respectively. In each case these stories feature a physician (1) dedicated to his patients' well-being; (2) unwilling to accept defeat; (3) curious enough to methodically seek answers to seemingly intractable situations provided by sickness and death; and (4) possessed of particular knowledge unavailable to lay people. In fact, Cobb often presents his doctor heroes as agents of Providence, accidentally given the means of effecting justice. Thus in both "The Pen Knife Blade" and "A Post-Mortem Discovery," entirely by accident, the narrator hero comes across a disinterred corpse which leads to discovery of a murder passed off as a natural death. The hero of "A Post-Mortem Discovery" in fact, says he's not an avenging spirit:

> "Adam Varney," said I, with slow and stern solemnity, "I am not an avenging spirit. '*Vengeance is mine, saith the Lord!*' For myself, I regard the man who bears upon his soul the memory of a great crime as a sufferer to be pitied; and when I felt assured that he would commit no crime like unto it, I might not deliver him into the hands of the law. Let us suppose a case: Suppose a man—aye, suppose YOU—had committed a murder—Ah—are you ill?"

But he really is an avenging spirit. And in "Pen Knife Blade," "The Mad Philosopher," and "A Post-Mortem Discovery," Cobb has his doctor-heroes talk about death and the divine. He also goes to some pains to present readers with details about surgery such as listing the anatomical terms for the tissues surgeons slice through, and alluding to Valentine Mott, a renowned professor of surgery at Columbia in "The Pen Knife Blade." On science, Cobb and the others are not so hot. They generally fudge things up when it comes to experiments. Thus,

> It is not my purpose here to enter into a detailed account of the manipulations necessary to the result I had in view. Suffice it for me to say that in the end we had a thick ring of metallic antimony in the tube of the apparatus, showing clearly that this poison had been freely administered; and from the quantity obtained it struck me that towards the last the doses had been increased ["A Post-Mortem Discovery"].

Medicine being what it was, it was a lot easier to determine the cause of a mysterious death after it happened than to nip a murderer's plot in the bud. From a writer's point of view, though, each option had its own rhetorical virtues: if detection occurred after the death, then this summoned up the traditional "murder will out" theme; if it prevented the calamity, then this enhanced the role of the hero as well as showing beneficial aspects of a Providential universe. As noted above, autopsies turn up in a lot of period detective fiction. And there was one popular medical resource for the prevented death plot—the stomach pump. Around since the last century, the stomach pump plays a central role in stories like "How He Got a Start" (*The New York Ledger*, March 19, 1870).

By the 1870s doctors in fiction think of themselves as detectives ("I am almost tempted to turn detective, and, if my patients fail me, shall look to you for a position in the force, although I dare say should require in such a profession more patience than ever." ["The Platinum Filling," *The Overland Monthly*, August 1874]). Detectives also began to think of themselves as doctors:

> Being something of a doctor, I naturally examined the wounds, and was satisfied they would not cause instant death. But I did not rely upon my own medical skill in this, but sent for a physician, he came, a sharp fellow named Denning and probed the wounds ["Tried for Murder, A Detective's Story," *The Bloomfield Times*, May 20, 1873].

But, forgetting medical training, knowledge, bedside manner, energy, capacity for analysis, and all of the other qualities that comprise the physician as hero, doctors really don't have to do any doctoring to be heroes in 19th-century detective stories. As Conan Doyle knew, they are ideal narrator-reporters, and as Robert Louis Stevenson knew, they make good companions when searching for treasure and fighting pirates. And so in stories like "Conflict with Burglars, a Physician's Story" (*New York Fireside Companion*, April 4, 1870) and "The Laurieville Mystery" (*The Plain Dealer*, February 14, 1880) physicians are action heroes, tracking down and capturing villains.

Everything Is Chemistry

For most of the nineteenth century, medicine was in the doldrums. Bloodletting was still accounted a cure until mid-century and beyond. Surgeons were doing better with the introduction of chloroform as an anesthetic, but medicine had yet to profit from the immense strides science had been making in the understanding of the physical world. Increasingly, scientists explained unknown phenomena as basic as the physiology of human reproduction and posited and then demonstrated the existence of things that could not be seen by the naked eye—most notably the atomic makeup of all matter. And they did this by asking questions and by conducting experiments. The real hero of a certain class of detective stories after mid-century was the scientist. But as a title "scientist" was too vague; to simplify matters writers used the term "chemist" as the generic name for scientist—which was apt anyway because 19th-century scientists rarely limited themselves to one discrete area of study. There are a lot of chemists around in detective stories. Most conspicuously there is the narrator of "The Chemist's Story; or Science vs. Murder" under the heading "Medical College Sketches," who acts as a shill for chemistry and his own courses:

> I am the Chemist of the Medical College at C—. Man, doubtless would find it difficult to define what the duties of a chemist are, if asked. To such, I may say, a chemist is a collector of facts. It is the business of his life to aid in unmasking, for the world's benefit, the good and evil hovering even in the air we breathe; burrowing in the earth we tread, mingling with the food we eat; swimming in what we drink.
> The miner comes to the chemist with his lumps of gold and silver, to be assured his precious treasures are pure and good. The health officers call to him to examine the atmosphere that surrounds and the earth that makes up the plague ground of cholera. The physicians show him the food and drink of their stricken patients, and beg for aid. Sometimes, but, alas, not as often as he would wish, the chemist has a gift or charm to give that is powerful for good.
> In short the chemist must know the whys and wherefores in everything in the outward phenomena of life, as far as feeble man can know. The composition of the ocean he must be familiar with; he must be able to name the gasses of the air; and capable of resolving the human body itself into invisible vapors! I am the occupant of this responsible position and important Professorship in the Medical College at C—.
> [...]
> My tickets for lectures on chemistry are thirty dollars [full course]. Apply at my office, in the college [*New York Fireside Companion*, April 18, 1868].

As high-minded as this all sounds, the story itself turns on nail-biting suspense and the chemist as hero and not scientific proof. But there was a class of stories in which proof was the role of science. The word "science" lends weight to what might be termed close observation and reasoning, such as:

From an examination of the wound, he inferred positively that the fatal weapon must have been fired by a *left-handed* man. Now, the only left-handed person near the premises, when the crime was committed, was a particular friend of the deceased, and the last man to have been implicated in the matter, but for this *revelation of science*. He was, in consequence, arrested, tried, and convicted, and, before execution, made a full confession of the whole matter ["Gleanings from Dark Annals," *Frank Leslie's Pleasant Hours*, 1867, our italics].

Often, however, writers dial up the aura attached to science and scientists by being more precise and bringing in a chemist:

But proof is the thing. I must get authority for seeking temporary possession of Mr. Allen's jewelry, before those bloody witnesses are removed. How sly it was to wait all these weeks before he let the tell-tale go out of his hands. Then we must hunt up an analytical chemist [...] ["The Murder at Cedar Glen" by Amy Randolph, *The New York Ledger*, November 19, 1864];

My brother was an excellent chemist, and I could rely well upon his analysis ["The Mysterious Murder," *The New York Ledger*, December 11, 1869];

On the following day the carpet bag was taken before the Grand Jury, and the iron case examined by an experienced chemist assisted by an old armorer from the arsenal. It was found to contain a fulminate of mercury, mixed with bits of iron; and it was the opinion of both the chemist and the armorer that the power of the terrific explosive agent, had it been ignited, would not only have been sufficient to blow me to atoms, but that it would also have literally stripped and shivered to fragments all of the house above it! ["The Defendant's Accomplice," *The New York Ledger*, June 10, 1871];

He confided to the detective after his recreant wife was under the sod, that the chemist had analyzed a few drops of the liquid in the goblet [...] it was a subtle poison know to a few as aqua Toffana [...] ["The Disguised Servant," *The Bloomfield Times*, February 1, 1881];

The bottle is now in the hands of an analyst, and he has pronounced the contents to be deadly poison ["Miss Garnett's Tenant," *Ballou's Monthly Magazine*, October 1889];

The bottle of wine and cuspidor I secreted in a paper, and carried them both to a chemist who was a personal friend ["The Fatal Cigar," *Denton Journal*, January 11, 1890].

Bringing in the off-stage voice of a chemist to prove things and thereby solve mysteries smacks of the old *deus ex machina* gambit of the death-bed confession, and it certainly does not reflect actual 19th-century trial practice: high-profile cases like the Parkman-Webster case became exhibitions of dueling experts. Making these chemists anonymous, giving many of them personal connections with the narrators, and bringing their pronouncements in at the end of the stories where rebuttal is unlikely, all serve to enhance their credibility with readers.

On Science

As noted above, the 19th century saw an explosion of scientific investigation and discoveries that are accepted as commonplaces by schoolchildren today—take atoms, for example. Originally none of these things had to do with detectives or the courts. Science's result were just the advancements of knowledge. The use and application of what science learned was up to others. Medicine, in these terms, was an applied science. And when the results of scientific investigation were used in legal arguments or in courts they became forensic (i.e., connected to courts) science. While the 19th century witnessed what amounted to a scientific revolution, in detective stories what readers found contained a great deal of wishful thinking. And a lot of that revolved around the subject of blood as evidence.

Blood Will Have Blood

Blood is the oldest physical evidence used to link individuals to crimes. It's there with Cain and Abel and is one of the drivers of the circumstantial evidence story. Blood from slaughtering a chicken, from a nosebleed, or a splotch of carelessly applied paint—all of them could be, and were, misconstrued by the uninitiated as powerful evidence of murder. Thus in the last quarter of the century any random red stain meant trouble:

> He was dreadfully agitated, hesitated to acknowledge that he had been near the place, and a blood stain was found on the right sleeve of his coat. Before he had been in jail one day even his own father believed him a murderer ["Broken Evidence," *The Lowell Sun*, February 16, 1889].

But even by mid-century writers used this as a narrative straw man to be knocked over by science. Real detectives look at blood carefully. Thus

> I immediately went to my desk, took out Roger Lyon's knife, and handed it to him, asking him to see if there were any pieces of stone in the blood stains which still showed on the knife. He knew my meaning in an instant. And taking a vial he carefully rinsed a portion of the stains with its contents, letting the liquid run upon a glass slide, which he had placed in the sun's rays ["Saved by a Mark," *The Indiana Progress*, December 12, 1872].

Just as often as it eliminates evidence, blood holds out the promise of providing accurate evidence. As early as 1863 at least one writer expressed confidence that analysis of blood (and blood as evidence) was entirely possible. Thus the epigraph to this chapter begins with

> Once when I attended a lecture by a celebrated man, he had stated that every animal had in its blood globules differing in size from those of any other kind. This knowledge had been arrived at by very slow steps [*Autobiography of an English Detective*, New York: Dick & Fitzgerald, 1864].

Almost 20 years later, at least in one place there was certainty (albeit perhaps tongue in cheek) that blood could tell a variety of tales:

"How do you know it was the old man's nose?"

"Because," replied the detective, using a microscope, "the blood globules are those of an elderly person" [James Maitland, "A Mysterious Murder," *Suppressed Sensations*, Chicago: Rand McNally, 1882].

Both assertions, however, were false. In spite of detective stories presenting blood evidence of guilt or innocence as actual and definitive, it was impossible to even distinguish blood types or even human from animal blood before 1901.

Name Your Poison

Poison created a problem when it came to the preference for direct over indirect evidence. Except in cases of suicide, it's administered in secret and, depending upon its type, its effects are not immediate. Besides, in the 19th century, poison of one sort or another was all over the environment, used in households and in the manufacture of household products. Additionally, for most of the century, poisons were relatively unregulated and readily available, as regulatory authority lay with individual states and storekeepers without pharmacists' licenses distributed poisonous substances at will. In England, sale of arsenic was regulated in 1851 and the Pharmacy Act of 1868 regulated strychnine, potassium cyanide, and ergot in all of Great Britain. That same year, the American Pharmaceutical Association called for a similar uniform state law to restrict poisons in the U.S. Opposition to any such regulation delayed the passage of such law; however, by 1890, thirty-three states had adopted some form of the model pharmacy law.

The Poison Book

For detective fiction, arsenic was the poison of choice. It

was readily available and because it is odorless and tasteless, it was undetectable in food or beverages. [...] The most visible symptoms of acute arsenic poisoning—nausea, vomiting, diarrhea, and abdominal pain—could be easily confused with other common diseases at the time [...] [Hughes].

Significantly for detective story writers, a chemical test existed that could detect arsenic: in 1830 Englishman James Marsh developed a test for the poison that was finally accepted as evidence in the trial of Marie LaFarge in France in 1840. After mid-century story papers had a fascination with arsenic poisoning. Thus, it appeared in

"The Two Nephews" (*The New York Ledger*, April 26, 1856);
"Resting Powders" (*The New York Ledger*, September 28, 1861);
"The Apothecary's Compound" (*The New York Ledger*, July 21, 1866);

"Dr. Puffer's Lost Opportunity" (*The New York Ledger*, July 13, 1867);
"The Chemist's Story" (*New York Fireside Companion*, April 18, 1868);
"Our Cook's Revenge" (*The New York Ledger*, November 19, 1870); and
"A Lucky Larceny" (*The New York Ledger*, April 16, 1870).

The newspaper stories we have found that rely on arsenic are

"The Poisoner" (*Columbus Sunday Enquirer*, February 27, 1881);
"The Price of Two Lives" (*Huntingdon Journal*, February 2, 1881);
"Reaped What They Sowed" (*The Marion Daily Star*, August 12, 1886); and
"A Flash of Lightning" (*Warren Ledger*, October 29, 1886).

Given his fascination with physicians at the time, it also comes as no surprise that the *New York Ledger*'s Sylvanus Cobb, Jr., would happen upon arsenic as a means of showing off his hero's knowledge, discernment, and skill. Just as they treated evidence of violent death with conspicuous restraint, when it came to describing the symptoms of arsenic poisoning writers found that the less said the better. Instead of the vomit and diarrhea of arsenic poisoning, the physician-narrator of "Resting Powders" gives his readers this description:

> They had been taken just before noon, with cramps and chills; but they were much easier when I arrived than they were when they sent for me. I saw that their stomachs were out of order; and as I knew that they were both pretty high livers, I was not at all surprised. I gave simple emetics, with some other medications [*The New York Ledger*, September 28, 1861].

Most writers were casual about testing for the presence of arsenic, except the writer of "The Chemist's Story" who gives Marsh credit in this overblown passage:

> I was certain I had discovered arsenic; but to make "assurance doubly sure," I determined to apply Mr. Marsh's test for that poison. Accordingly, I placed in the diluted contents of the poor woman's stomach the usual acids. I then turned on the blow-pipe flame, and presently, upon a white and beautiful porcelain ground, there appeared that brilliant metallic mark—worthy of Cain's brow—which is the sign and signet of the Poison Fiend! [*New York Fireside Companion*, April 18, 1868].

After arsenic, hydrogen cyanide, also called prussic acid, was writers' second-most-popular poison. It occurs in nature in items such as almonds and cherry pits (the latter being a contributing cause of the death of President Zachary Taylor). It's used in

"The Trial for Murder" (*Strange Stories of a Detective; or Curiosities of Crime*, New York: Dick & Fitzgerald, 1863);
"A Noble Sacrifice: A Tale of Washington, D.C." by Sinclair (*Ballou's Monthly Magazine*, January 1883);

"Adroitly Foiled" (*McCook Tribute*, June 3, 1885); and
"Saved by a Telephone" (*Peterson's Magazine*, November 1888).

At mid-century in England, strychnine made the news with the arrest and trial of William Palmer, and it was featured in a poem, "Detective Story" (*Chicago Daily Tribune*, February 15, 1886), and in "Dr. Puffer's Lost Opportunity" (*The New York Ledger*, July 13, 1867). There was a lot of chloroform used in 19th-century detective fiction, but we can find only one occasion in which it was used as a poison: "The Price of Two Lives" (*Huntingdon Journal*, February 2, 1881). Mostly chloroform was used to make victims unconscious, as in "The Abducted Ward" (*The New York Ledger*, February 18, 1865). This, and other detective stories printed in the 1860s served as precursors to a piece by Stephen Rogers, M.D. printed in *The Journal of Psychological Medicine* in 1871 titled "Can Chloroform be used to Facilitate Robberies?" Antimony served as a poison in "A Post-Mortem Discovery" (*The New York Ledger*, October 23, 1869), and Atropia or Atropine (i.e., Belladonna) appears in "The First Case" (*Appleton's Journal of Literature, Science and Art*, October 2, 1869). There were also writers who were undecided and gave readers a menu of poisons from which to choose:

> I examined the mortar, and found some small crystals at the bottom of it, which emitted a strong odor of prussic acid. I also noticed that the bottle containing antimonial wine, and one containing chloroform were displaced ["The Defrauded Heir," *Ballou's Dollar Magazine Monthly*, February 1863].

And, more for the shock than its evidentiary value, some writers had recourse to the unknown poison:

> [The Chemist] alleges the presence of poison, but curiously enough cannot define its nature. How malignant it was we can judge by the effects. ["The Pigot Murder," *Harper's New Monthly Magazine*, May, 1865];

and

> He "swallowed a potent draught of some foreign poison" ["The Murder at Carew Court," *The New York Ledger*, July 11, 1868].

By far the most common use of poison in 19th-century detective fiction is as a means of suicide. Thus we see it in:

"The Mysterious Murder" (*Schenectady Reflector*, April 5, 1850);
"Circumstantial Evidence" by Samuel Warren (*The Experiences of a Barrister, and Confessions of an Attorney*, New York: Cornish, Lamport, 1852);
"My German Tutor" (*The Columbia Spy*, November 19, 1859);
"Hunted Down" by Charles Dickens (*The New York Ledger*, August 20 and 27 and September 3, 1859);

"My First Brief" (*Leaves from the Notebook of a New York Detective*, New York: Dick & Fitzgerald, 1865);
"The Murder at Carew Court" by Amy Randolph (*The New York Ledger*, July 11, 1868);
"The Victory" (*Sioux County Herald*, June 8, 1876);
"Sapphire Eyes" (*Frank Leslie's Popular Monthly*, February 1880);
"Link by Link" (*The Marion Daily Star*, October 6, 1880);
"A Noble Sacrifice: A Tale of Washington, D.C." by Sinclair (*Ballou's Monthly Magazine*, January 1883);
"Who Killed Him? Or, The Twisted Ring" (*Frank Leslie's Pleasant Hours*, 1884);
"Who Is Guilty" by Philip Wolf (*St. Louis Globe-Democrat*, September 5, 1886); and
"Under the Shadow of Death" (*Western Kansas World*, August 3, 1889)

In these cases the poison administered is almost always unnamed. Philip Wolf just states "He died of poison of some kind" ("Who Is Guilty"); above, as mentioned, in "The Murder as Carew Court," "some foreign poison" is employed; in "Sapphire Eyes," the spurned wife uses "the deadliest poison" that our botanist-chemist narrator has distilled from plants; and in "Hunted Down," Dickens merely implies poison in his dramatic description of the death:

> [...] the miscreant suddenly turned away his face, and seemed to strike his mouth with his open hand. At the same instant, the room was filled with a new and powerful odour, and, almost at the same instant, he broke into a crooked run, leap, start,—I have no name for the spasm,—and fell, with a dull weight that shook the heavy old doors and windows in their frames [*The New York Ledger*, September 3, 1859].

Typically in suicide cases, poison is obtained by undisclosed means while the criminals are in custody or is administered just before they are to be apprehended. Often the poison is used to "cheat the hangman" on the eve of an execution or is accompanied by a confession that saves an innocent accused. However it is also used to fake murder and frame another or to save the family name. Rhetorically though, such suicides have clear advantages for authors—they provide closure and retribution without the need of narrating a trial.

It is, however, possible to look at the introduction of poison into the detective story at mid-century as a harbinger of a new approach to writing in the genre. It offered a new approach to the crime problem: knives, hands, and blunt instruments offer opportunities for direct evidence and evidence that doesn't require much in the way of expert analysis. Poisoning requires (or can require) scientific analysis and happens in the absence of witnesses. Without someone to immediately take the blame, it offered writers a variant of the circumstantial-evidence plot and gave the investigator-hero two searches to undertake: (1) finding the means; and (2) finding the culprit. But it didn't quite happen. While the enigma of the mystery itself replaced the accused innocent as the fulcrum for the detective's actions (and had the potential to change the nature of his or her character) the physician/scientist as a character type never matured. Indeed in more than one case, the vocation of detective subsumed that of the physician. Thus readers got Brampton, med student turned detective, in the New York Detective series; the Doctor in "The First Case" (*Appleton's Journal of Literature, Science and Art*, October 2, 1869); and the undercover government detective who uses his "calling as a doctor merely as a blind" in "Catching Counterfeiters" (*Iowa State Reporter*, February 2, 1888).

Ballistics

Americas have been trying to figure out firearms for a long time. For writers of the developing detective story, firearms presented, like poison, the opportunity for murder at a distance—and consequently the chance to exploit and explain the potential uncertainty of who fired the fatal bullet. Indeed, bullets came to be the center of attention in some stories of crime and detection written in the U.S. The bullet, of course, was undeniably at the scene of the crime and if examined correctly became the logical starting place in the search for the person who fired it. Part of the virtue of looking at bullets was that until well after mid-century the projectiles from firearms were lead balls, not the self-contained bullet introduced about the time of the Civil War. Often rifle and pistol balls were somewhat unique objects—made from lead and cast in the users' individual molds. They varied in diameter from .25 to .62 of an inch. And they always were accompanied by wadding, paper or other material inserted into the barrel of the weapon to keep the ball in contact with the powder. There were, then, two things about a firearm death that period detectives could fasten upon: the rifle or pistol ball and its wadding. Size mattered in the earliest stories that centered upon bullets. There was this crucial exchange in court in "The Rifle":

> "The bore of this rifle, Mr. Drill," continued the sagacious lawyer, "is very small. I presume that you are familiar with the size and qualities of all that are owned on the road out to Mr. Buckhorn's. Is there any house at which Doctor Rivington could have stopped, and procured a ball of sufficient smallness?"
>
> "John Guntry's rifle," answered Mr. Drill, "carries eighty-seven or eight to the pound, and one of his bullets, with a thick patch, would suit Buckhorn's pretty well. That is the only one any where near the size" [*Stories of American Life by American Writers*, London: H. Colburn and R. Bentley, 1830].

Poe's narrator in "Thou Art the Man!" makes the most of precise details of a rifle ball that came to be associated with the dead horse:

> and, as if to demonstrate beyond a question the guilt of the accused, Mr Goodfellow, after considerable searching in the cavity of the chest, was enabled to detect and to pull forth a bullet of very extraordinary size, which, upon trial, was found to be exactly adapted to the bore of Mr Pennifeather's rifle, while it was far too large for that of any other person in the borough or its vicinity. To render the matter even surer yet, however, this bullet was discovered to have a flaw or seam at right angles to the usual suture; and upon examination, this seam corresponded precisely with an accidental ridge or elevation in a pair of moulds acknowledged by the accused himself to be his own property [*Godey's Lady's Book*, November 1844].

Following the example of Inspector Bucket in Dickens' *Bleak House*, wadding used to pack down the bullet also can yield incriminating data:

> But there were agencies of Providence at work for the discovery of the murderer. The surgeon who had been called to examine and pronounce upon the nature of the wound, had drawn from the orifice made by the bullet a mass of paper saturated with blood and with river water. He saw that it was newspaper wadding which had been driven into the wound behind the ball. He stated to the coroner, from this circumstance, that the assassin must have stood close to his victim for the wadding to have entered the wound. This assertion threw no light upon the author of the crime, and had little weight with the coroner and his rustic jury. The surgeon, who was a shrewd man of the world, and who let nothing escape him, took the wadding home, and, having removed the stains of blood and dried it, closely examined it. He discovered that it was part of a newspaper called the "Evening Star" ["The Torn Newspaper," *The New York Ledger*, October 30, 1858].

Firearms gave writers of detective stories pieces of circumstantial evidence that given the knowledge of the period could be made specific and convincing. Notably, a lot of the stories featuring ballistic evidence end up in the courtroom and open an opportunity for writers to bring both lawyers and physician/surgeons into the picture as experts. While modern ballistic science did not really begin until the turn of the century with the knowledge of how and why each weapon makes unique marks on the bullet it fires, writers of 19th-century detective stories were on the right track. Significantly, it was a track that emphasized close observation of things as opposed to people. However, it's best to provide a caveat at this point: only a fraction of 19th-century detective stories concern murder and only a fraction of those involve poison, firearms, or "infernal machines." But thieves, burglars, robbers, pickpockets, and other assorted felons as well as murderers have fingers and leave fingerprints.

The Matter of Dermal Papillae

Thousands of years after the Chinese recognized the value of fingerprints as unique identifiers and long before iPhone and 21st-century security experts realized the value of biometrics over passwords to secure personal accounts, detective stories acknowledged the value of fingerprints—and prints made indicating missing digits. Nineteenth-century detective stories were pretty much in sync with forensic science in the matter of the loops and whorls on our fingers. In detective stories the words "fingerprint," "finger-mark," and "thumb-mark" go back to the 1830s. Most mundanely they referred to housekeeping and the smudges left on windows and furniture and how to remove them. The word "fingerprints" also showed up in theological contexts as a metaphor for the indelible intricacy and detail of creation. The concept of fingerprints also appeared in admonitions about omniscience and moral behavior. Thus "Finger Marks," a cautionary anecdote, first appeared in 1854 and was reprinted over and over until at least 1882:

> A mason was employed to thin whiten the walls of a chamber. The fluid was colorless till dried. Being alone in the room, he opened a drawer, examined a pocket-book, and handled the papers, but finding no money, placed all things as they were, forgetting that 12 hours' drying would show the marks of his wet fingers. But the tell-tale finger marks, which he little thought anyone would ever see, exposed his guilt.
> Children, beware of evil thoughts and deeds!—They have all finger marks, which will be revealed at some time. If you disobey your parents or tell a falsehood, or take what is not your own, you'll make sad finger marks on your character [*Centre Democrat*, April 27, 1854].

The earliest published connections of fingerprints with crime scenes occur in newspaper accounts and are used as proof of strangulation or the general brutality of a crime. By the 1870s, however, science and fingerprints began to come together in popular media, first as speculation:

> In a lecture on the uses of the microscope delivered at Washington by Mr. Thomas Taylor, Microscopist of the Department of Agriculture, views of the hand were exhibited, showing the markings on the palm and fingers; and it was suggested that the microscope might be used in the detection of criminals, by comparing the hand or finger-marks often impressed in blood-stains on the murderer's weapons, with the hands of accused or suspected parties [*The Cincinnati Daily Star*, July 14, 1877].

The use of fingerprints in the detection of criminals soon became more than a hypothesis: in 1880, Sir William Herschel published a letter in *Nature* explaining his experiences with fingerprinting. It wasn't long before press in the U.S. picked up on Hershel and the applications of fingerprinting to criminal matters:

> W.I. Herschell [*sic*], an English official in India, about twenty years ago made discovery, or applied an old one with such success that recommends it for adoption as an infallible identifier of criminals or tricky or lost people. It is so simple thing as a finger impression, which may be durably recorded in infancy and preserved till age. The lines and other characteristics of a finger print never change, nor are the finger prints of any two persons exactly alike.

Such a record is worth preserving, for faces and forms change, and may be disguised, but nothing can obliterate the finger print, except the destruction of the finger, Herschell [sic] adopted this detector in India, because of the general resemblance of Hindoo faces, rendering it so difficult for a European to distinguish one Indian from another. It worked well: in fact it never failed. The thumb is generally used for the impression, but any of the fingers will answer the purpose of complete identification in cases of doubt. Every prisoner in jail thus makes his sign manual, and he is always known thereafter by his finger prints. Hershell recommends the adoption of this detector in the British army, for the identification of deserters, and also in the English prisons the more effectually to keep the run of criminals, It is also claimed that finger prints will declare the sex, and the nationality, too, generally with clearness, but not always with accuracy ["An Infallible Test of Identity," *Rock Island Argus*, January 14, 1881].

By the end of the century fingerprints began to be seen as unimpeachable proof of identity and were accepted in British courts as such in the case of Henry Jackson in 1902 and in the United States in the case of Thomas Jennings in 1910.

Going back to mid-century, at least a few writers had had an inkling that the marks fingers left behind could mean something. The earliest of these that we have found is Sylvanus Cobb, Jr., who used finger marks in two early pieces. The first was "The Two-Fingered Assassin," where fingermarks turn the tide in a trial:

> "But there is the mark of a thumb, *very* plainly made," said the doctor; "and here is the mark of the fore finger; and here is the mark of the little, or fourth finger."
> "Yes—it may be," returned the bothered juror; "but what are them marks?"
> "Them" marks alluded to were broad blotches, between the two finger marks, and some three inches below their ends. It was a curious looking mark for the impression of human hands, and no mistake."
> "It must have been the left hand," resumed the doctor, "as you can see by the relative position of the thumb."
> "It 'tis a hand," suggested the juror. "I must say as how't it don't look like a hand to me."
> "Suppose," remarked Parkhill, calmly and distinctly, "I should tell you that the hand which fastened its grip there *had lost its two middle fingers?*"
> "O—oh—yes, yes. Now I see. O, yes. That's it—that's it. Now it's plain. Let's have a look at the prisoner's fingers!" [*The New York Ledger*, June 20, 1857].

Almost a year later Cobb's "The Left-Handed Thief" appeared in *The New York Ledger* (April 10, 1858). In it a falsely accused store clerk applies "red lead" to the knob on the money drawer and uses the prints left by the thief to determine the handedness of the thief:

> "But can you not distinguish thumb-marks from those made by the fingers?"
> "Yes."
> "Then tell me this," I returned:—"Which hand did the thief use most dexterously?"
> Wharton gazed upon the marks and finally gasped—"*The left!*"

Handedness is also a central issue in "The Left-Handed Assassin," in which evidence demonstrates both the handedness of the murderer and that

> The man who had climbed up the spout had but three fingers on the right hand. This was plainly seen by the finger marks on the metal; the spout was marked but in four places by the right hand—the thumb and three fingers, the index finger was gone [*The Coshocton Democrat*, November 2, 1864].

By the early 1880s, however, news about the value of fingerprints in establishing identity had spread widely and quickly. The piece on Herschel cited above, for instance, originated in the *London Globe*, was copied in *The New York Times* (with attribution), then by *The Cincinnati Enquirer*, by the *Argus* in Rock Island, Illinois, and by who knows what other papers. By early 1882 the modern understanding of fingerprints began to appear in detective stories. The earliest we have found is "Story of a Thumb-Mark, Remarkable Detection of a Murder":

> The lines which you see cast upon the screen are the magnified impression of a mark in blood on a sheet of paper which was found on the desk at which your master, two mornings ago, was found sitting dead. It is the thumb-mark of a man—of the man, I believe, who committed the murder; and as it has been shown by scientific men that every individual may be known by the peculiar and special arrangement of the furrows on the skin of the fingers, we have come to ascertain if any one of the thumb marks which you have given us to day agrees with the lines and markings of that now shown on the screen before you.
> [...]
> Mr. Slater and Mr. Carson proceeded with out loss of time to carry out the object of their visit. A smooth tablet had been prepared, with a thin coating of coloring matter on the surface, and it was explained to the men that it was desired to obtain from each of them an impression of the thumb of the left hand. This was done, as Mr. Slater showed, by first coloring the ball of the thumb by pressing it on the tablet, and then transferring the mark to a sheet of paper, by next pressing the thumb thereon. The process was of the simplest kind, and the work was soon begun. Each man after giving the required mark on a separate sheet of paper, duly numbered, was desired to write on the same his name and address, whereupon the paper was handed to a photographer, who was present with his apparatus, and a photograph was taken on glass of each individual mark [*The Wellsboro Agitator*, February 14, 1882].

In 1883, ten years before he used them in the plot of *The Tragedy of Puddn'head Wilson*, fingerprints provided the essence of a detective episode in Mark Twain's *Life on the Mississippi*. In chapter 31 ("A Thumb-print and What Came of It") Twain supplies readers a primer on fingerprints and fingerprinting:

> My apparatus was simple: a little red paint and a bit of white paper. I painted the ball of the client's thumb, took a print of it on the paper, studied it that night, and revealed his fortune to him next day. What was my idea in this nonsense? It was this: When I was a youth, I knew an old Frenchman who had been a prison-keeper for thirty years, and he told me that

there was one thing about a person which never changed, from the cradle to the grave—the lines in the ball of the thumb; and he said that these lines were never exactly alike in the thumbs of any two human beings. In these days, we photograph the new criminal, and hang his picture in the Rogues' Gallery for future reference; but that Frenchman, in his day, used to take a print of the ball of a new prisoner's thumb and put that away for future reference. He always said that pictures were no good—future disguises could make them useless; "The thumb's the only sure thing," said he; "you can't disguise that." And he used to prove his theory, too, on my friends and acquaintances; it always succeeded.

Fingerprints, however, did not become a standard feature in detective stories overnight. Before 1891 they figure into very few stories. In one of the few, "The Missing Picture," the criminal knows not to leave prints behind:

> This was my idea; if Mr. Stanley was the guilty man he had hidden himself in the room of the library, and overheard what I had said; and would, certainly during the night find an opportunity to visit the gallery door, examine it for the fingermarks and obliterate them [*The Columbus Journal*, March 4, 1885].

"The Imprint of a Thumb, Which Caused the Confession of a Thief and Puzzled a Detective" (*The Omaha Bee*, February 11, 1886) used a thumb print to identify a criminal, but avoided talking about the science or the uniqueness of fingerprints.

Although sparsely used by detective writers, by 1890 taking fingerprints was supposed to be part of every "first-class detective's" repertoire:

> I had one clew, a clew so slight that it had been overlooked by the Russian police, but one which no really first-class detective would have passed unnoticed. On the dead man's throat were the black marks of the fingers which had strangled him. The thumb of the right hand had been pressed violently into the skin of the neck, so as to leave a deep abrasion.
> I at once took a careful cast of this thumb-mark with the finest wax, thus reproducing every line exactly.
> I knew that the impressions of no two thumbs in the world are alike. It is the prison-mark in China, remember, and there serves the same purpose as the rogues' gallery in America to identify a criminal.
> One other clew I had to guide me. A plain twisted ring, worn by the murderer, had left its mark distinctly on the flesh. I caused the impression of the hand, ring and all to be photograph ["The Twisted Ring," *The Daily Independent*, October 2, 1890].

Taking a Closer Look

The new focus on minutiae in the examination of blood and fingerprints made both the microscope and the camera normal adjuncts in detective stories after mid-century. Indeed, microscopes were there at the beginning. Although it's difficult to picture how this could have been done, the Paris police resort to a microscope in the examination of Minister D—'s flat:

> We examined the rungs of every chair in the hotel, and, indeed, the jointings of every description of furniture, by the aid of a most powerful microscope. Had there been any

traces of recent disturbance we should not have failed to detect it instantly. A single grain of gimlet-dust, for example, would have been as obvious as an apple. Any disorder in the glue-ing—any unusual gaping in the joints—would have sufficed to insure detection ["The Purloined Letter" by Edgar Allan Poe, *The Gift: A Christmas and New Year's Present for 1844*].

Decades later, either the Paris police had a furniture fixation or readers found an echo of Poe in "His Own Detective":

> His house was probed and ransacked with that particular care and acuteness which Parisian detectives exhibit in a remarkable degree. They searched the walls and floors. They entered cabinets, escritoires, and drawers; they probed beds and chairs; they examined furniture with the microscope; in fact, so complete was their art that nothing could escape their extreme care even a line [*Sacramento Daily Union*, November 19, 1870].

But detectives of the period used microscopes for other purposes. They helped out with things like blood, thus in the epigraph to this chapter we learn:

> There was no doubt, however, of its scientific accuracy, or that with the aid of a powerful microscope a professional man of skill and experience could decide, without chance of committing a mistake, from the slightest stain whether the blood, if blood, had flowed in the veins of a human being or other animal ["Murder under the Microscope," *The Autobiography of an English Detective*, New York: Dick & Fitzgerald, 1864];

and with hair and fibers:

> I once received a letter by post, containing a few hairs, with a request that I should examine them, and adding that they would be called for in a few days. Accordingly, I submitted the hairs to the microscope, when I discovered that they were from the human eyebrow, and had been bruised. I made a note to that effect and folded it with in an envelope, ready for the person who sent them. In a few days a stranger called and inquired whether I had made the examination ["The Microscope as a Detective," *Orleans County Monitor*, July 21, 1873];

as well as written or printed material:

> Some time since the officer of the P— bank in New York gave information to the police that their notes had been extensively counterfeited in a manner so alarmingly perfect, that many of the spurious bills had passed through their own hands without detection; in fact, the first intimation of the crime was the imperceptible inflation of their paper in circulation. Every line and shade of the original bill was reproduced in the counterfeit in such a perfect manner, that without the aid of a microscope, detection was utterly impossible. Once discovered, it was plain that no other counterfeiting process could so completely imitate the genuine but the art of photography, and in that science the manipulators must have been skilled ["The Detective's Story," *Saint Mary's Beacon*, March 27, 1879].

At the same time microscopes came to the detective's aid, they were learning how to use the camera. Early writers had held out some wildly unrealistic hopes for the camera:

> While pondering over the matter—and it was rarely out of my thoughts—one of my friends, who is a photographer, communicated to me some intelligence that he had gained from his reading and studies. He had seen it stated that the last impression made upon the

eye of a dying person would be retained there for a certain time after death. That being the case, he thought it possible to obtain a photographic likeness of that impression, and was very anxious to try the experiment. The matter interested me at once, and I readily promised to give him an opportunity to test it in the next murder case that came within my observation ["The Telltale Eye" by James D. M'Cabe, Jr., *Flag of Our Union*, January 20, 1866. Reprinted as late as *Gleason's Monthly Companion*, January 1881].

Not long after Herschel's descriptions of the reality and utility of fingerprints, detective stories linked smudges from fingers with photography. As noted above, it appears in "Story of a Thumb-Mark, Remarkable Detection of a Murder":

> We must take means to get the finger mark of every man in the establishment of Greig & Co., as also of the deceased man, and of his nephew. This can easily be done; and thereafter, by an idea which had occurred to me, namely by photographing each impression, we will arrive at the fact whether or not any one of these marks agrees with the mark on this sheet of paper [*The Wellsboro Agitator*, February 14, 1882].

In what is one of the best detective stories of the period, Harriet E. Prescott (Spofford) centered her detective's discoveries on both the camera and the magnification:

> Straightway Mr. Furbush made a prize of the operator; and procuring, through channels always open to him, the strongest glasses and most accurate instruments, had the one chosen window in the picture magnified and photographed, remagnified and rephotographed, till under their powerful, careful, prolonged, and patient labor, a speck came into sight that would perhaps well reward them. Mr. Furbush strained his eyes over it; to him it was a spot of greater possibilities than the nebula in Orion. This little white unresolved cloud, again and again they subjected to the same process, and once more, as if a ghost had made apparition, it opened itself into an outline—into a substance—and they saw the fingers of a hand, a white hand, doubled, but pliant, strong, and shapely; a left hand, on its third finger wearing rings, one of which seemed at first a mere blot of light, but, gradually, as the rest, answering the spell of the camera, showed itself a central stone set with five points, each point consisting of smaller stones: the color of course could not be told; the form was that of a star. Held in the tight, fierce fingers of that clenched hand, between the pointed thumb and waxy knuckles, and one edge visible along the tips deep dinted into the thumb's side, was grasped an end of a laced handkerchief. Now the handkerchief of Agatha More, the instrument of her destruction, was always carried folded in the shape of its running knot in Mr. Furbush's great wallet, a large, laced, embroidered handkerchief; that this was its photograph he needed but a glance to rest assured ["Mr. Furbush," *Harper's New Monthly Magazine*, April 1865].

Along with using the rather old technology of the microscope and the new technology of the camera, many detective writers strove to link their heroes with the newest American inventors and entrepreneurs had to offer. Along with all of the railroad settings, the telegraph provided writers new opportunities in pieces such as "'X' and 'H.' A Telegraph Operator's Story" (*The Allen County Democrat*, April 22, 1875) and "The Telegraph Detective" (*Barnstable Patriot*,

June 20, 1880) and even a robber who poses as telegraph repair man in "Thief-Catching in Canada" (*The Plain Dealer*, January 31, 1880). Remarkably quickly after 1876, when Alexander Graham Bell summoned another Watson, telephones started to pop up in detective stories. See

> "Saved by a Telephone" by Ella Higgins (*Peterson's Magazine*, November 1888);
> "Worked by Telephone" (*Stevens Point Journal*, September 5, 1891); and
> "The Terrors of the Telephone: A Detective Story" by Rufus Cyrene MacDonald (*Boston Daily Globe*, October 11, 1891)

Ingenious Devices and Infernal Machines

In addition to killing people the old-fashioned way by bludgeoning them to death or offering them a poisonous brew, some villains in 19th-century detective stories became more inventive, thus allowing them to take their victims unaware and mystify observers. On the simplest level, there were multiple instances of crimes committed with the aid of trick rings. For example, in "A Clever Capture" (*The Marion Daily Star*, February 7, 1881) the thief preys on the wealthy at fancy balls in West End drawing rooms: while his dancing partners are distracted by a small needle projected into their arms by his spring-loaded signet ring, he relieves them of their diamonds. Similarly, but more sinisterly, anarchists plot to assassinate the czar by means of a lethal ring in "The Twisted Ring: Experience of a French Detective in Russia." Thus, the beautiful nihilist baroness tells the undercover detective:

> Take this ring. No, do not place it on your hand yet. Its touch is death, if you are not extremely careful. Keep it in its case, and just before you are admitted to the audience, place it on your finger. The slightest contraction of your fingers will pierce the hand you hold with a small, hollow needle. Retain the Czar's hand in your own, respectfully, for a moment. During that brief interval you can inject into his palm a deadly poison. Its action is sufficiently slow to afford you ample opportunity to make your escape [*The Daily Independent*, October 2, 1890, which cites the *Chicago Journal*].

Such devices add intrigue to the offenses by delaying the discovery of the crime, thus making them howdunits. In this respect, villains also used disguised firearms to dispatch unaware victims and confuse curious detectives: as early as 1858 the highway robbers in "Assassin of Castellane" employ an "infernal machine":

> the outer surface was meerschaum. Within it was a pistol of the finest steel, and of the most exquisite workmanship. The stem was the barrel, and the lock was concealed in the bowl, and covered with tobacco. A thin plate of metal protected the curiously contrived lock, and upon this the tobacco rested. A pressure of the thumb or finger upon the plate discharged

the weapon. In order to cock it, the plate had to be removed. And now comes the *infernal* feature of the contrivance. The powder used in the little barrel was of Cazabon's own manufacture, and very powerful. For a wad a piece of felt was used, and on the top of the wad was placed the missile which did the mischief. [...] The projectile was a tiny arrow, not larger than a cambric needle, with one end sharp and the other beat down to a thin feature. It was fine steel, but coated with a greenish yellow substance, which was the most virulent poison that the chemist's art could concoct. That needle once within the course of the blood, and death was already at the heart [*The New York Ledger*, June 12, 1858].

And in "Number Eight" an innkeeper's son uses a dartgun-type weapon to shoot needles directly into the hearts of their guests when they continue on their journey the next day:

> The weapon, which was of very delicate and ingenious construction, when aimed, as it was designed to be, at a vital part and from a close range would prove as fatal as an ordinary revolver, and it possessed the merit, having regard to its object, of almost defying detection in its results. No blood flowed externally from the wound, death being instantaneous from internal hemorrhage of the heart, the needle sufficing to stop the outward flow as the flesh quickly closed up over the small puncture [*The Waterloo Courier*, December 15, 1886, which cites the *Philadelphia Press*].

Similarly, "how it was possible for anyone to have done the deed at all" was the difficulty facing the detective in the locked-room mystery "The Torn Glove" (*Strange Stories of a Detective; or, Curiosities of Crime*, New York: Dick & Fitzgerald, 1863). Although compressed air rifles had been used for nearly a century, most notably on the Lewis and Clark expedition to the Pacific, the detective officer claims never to have seen them before and the clerk claims "we received them only a week ago from Europe"; he furthermore informs the detective and readers that it is "dangerous [...] in the hands of bad men" because "When they are discharged, they make no report." According to the murderer in Sylvanus Cobb, Jr.'s "the Mad Philosopher" (*The New York Ledger*, September 19, 1868), this is also the benefit of the air gun hidden within his walking staff—his victims experience no pain and "There will be no report— no sound of any kind." These guns act as effectively as a silencer 40 years before Hiram Percy Maxim sold the first commercially successful models of firearm suppressors. Ten years later, the weapon is not an air gun, but an "air syringe." While not quite a gun, the detective in "The Unknown Death" (*The Lake Village Times*, April 25, 1874) is certain that the "verdict of the Coroner's jury would be 'Death from causes unknown'" until he happens to read in the daily paper that "A ghastly scientific discovery is reported from Turin, where Professor Casturini the celebrated oculist has found a way to kill animals by focusing air into their eyes a few seconds, and almost without causing pain." Finding that the son of the murdered man has such a crank-operated killing machine, the detective announces, "Your crime is discovered, sir! [...] You are a parricide and I arrest you for the murder of the man who lies in the next chamber." Rather than asking for a reward, he "carried away the air syringe, and I have it to this day" and makes "repeated experiments" that convince him "the more of its deadly and dangerous character."

Victims are also not safe even in bed. Although found dead on the road, guests in "The Guest Chamber of the Inn at St. Ives" are impaled in a booby-trapped bed before being robbed and dumped in the street (*Flag of Our Union*, September 24, 1859). A more humorous and racist version of the booby-trapped bed is the one under the clock in "A Mysterious Disappearance" (*Palo Alto Reporter*, January 31, 1880): "There was a peculiarity about this clock, for it was surmounted with a wooden nigger's head, whose tongue—a very red one—protruded from his mouth in a hideous grimace." Victims who explore the head on the clock find it is the lever which makes the bed give way and they are plunged "head-over-ears in to black, icy waters"; thus the spinster who had slept in this "haunted" room, fell in water and caught fever and was picked up by a boat on way to Holland, from whence she returned.

Ingenious devices often relied on more than compressed air or just gravity. Thomas Edison had a series of breakthroughs near the end of the century: in 1879 he created an incandescent globe that burned for 40 hours; in 1881 his dynamo was the featured at the Paris Electrical Exposition; in 1882 his first great central station supplied power for 3,000 lamps in London; that fall one became operational in New York City. These 19th-century successes in the field of electricity inspired a series of electrically-charged crimes. On February 7, 1880, "The Finger of Providence" features an "infernal machine"—an exploding box left to seek revenge on the detective Varnoe (*Louisiana Capitolian*). In "The Incendiary," a vengeance-seeking arsonist sets fires by timers he so can secure an alibi:

> With the exception of a few wires and a mainspring, the whole was of wood. A large wooden hammer was drawn back set evidently at the end of a certain fixed time to strike against the butt end of a large phosphorous match which was bound alongside of a file at such an angle that the stroke would be certain to strike fire. Piled up beneath the point of the match were other matches, a sponge soaked in kerosene, and as much as a pound of pitch. The contrivance spoke for itself [*Salt Lake Evening Democrat*, March 4, 1885].

And in "Miss Armstrong's Homicide" by Sam Davis (*Short Stories*, San Francisco: Golden Era, 1886), a scientist is found dead in his own bathtub. Poetic justice occurs in this story in which Croftly the scientist determines to murder his romantic rival "so neatly and scientifically that discovery would be next to impossible," but when he takes a bath prepped for his roommate and enemy, the woman he loves comes home and inadvertently sets off his intricate trap:

At the instant the wires were connected, Croftly was in the centre of the bath. A shock and terrible chill passed through his frame, and he felt a cloud of vapor rising from the surface of the water and sweeping into his face. Myriads of spear-like crystals shot out from the edge of the tank, and converged toward him like so many shafts of death. He realized his situation, and dashed to reach the steps; as he did so, he threw himself against the jagged edge of a sheet of ice half an inch thick. There was a frightful gash in his side, from which blood was streaming. He struggled madly amid the ice, and every throe brought fresh wounds. His limbs moved no longer in water; they were enveloped in slush. The ice closed about him like a vice.

After the evaporation of the chemicals the electricity no longer had any effect, and the heat of the room began to tell upon the ice. The mass melted, and by four o'clock in the morning the corpse of Croftly was floating upon the surface of the bath. He was not missed until nine o'clock next morning, when Dean burst open the door and found him as described.

The rest is known. The jury gave a verdict of suicide and Miss Armstrong and Edward Dean were married on the 22d of the same month.

Hybrid detective and science fiction, like this piece, demonstrates the flexibility and adaptability of the genre and how the contemporary moment is reflected in popular literature. Technically, moreover, using indirect means of extinguishing life changes the nature of the violence, making it more complex, more interesting, and more of a puzzle, leaving readers asking how it was done before they ask who did it. Infernal machines and murder traps also gave writers something about which to write that is much easier to explain than the human motives that lead to cold-blooded murder.

Finally, perhaps the most inventive device in a 19th-century detective story is found in "The Clever Detective" (*Pullman Herald*, March 30, 1889, which cites the *Chicago Tribune*). The detective, Sergeant Fetchem, is none other than a robot made by Edison! A "cunning piece of machinery" created for 10,000 dollars, his "singular skill and adroitness" make him nearly perfect. However, human error spells his end: the chief sends him out on a manhunt that lasts over a week and he winds down and is ruined.

And All of This Means...

During the majority of the 19th century, most readers in the United States encountered detective stories in their newspapers and family story papers. It was, perhaps, this connection with a medium whose avowed purpose was to keep readers abreast of the changes in their world that led to the adaptability of the detective stories they choose to copy, or cause to be created (i.e., those with bylines like "as written for this paper"). It would, therefore, be natural for editors to choose stories that contained references to the latest kinds of technology. Editors also still favor stories about miraculous cures and surprising discoveries. It's what editors do. And, managing commercial enterprises as they do, editors appreciate things that can be both conventional and innovative. That, perhaps, is why early on adaptability became one of the hallmarks of the detective story. They could be urban or rural, serious or comic, simple or semi-profound, anachronistic or futuristic; they could be about men or occasionally women, about police or private detectives, about lawyers or judges, about surgeons or apothecaries, about amateurs or innocents needing to act in their own defense. They could have courtship romance in their background or superstitious taboos. Notably, what detective stories didn't have in the 19th century was politicians or politics—corrupt or honest, dirty or clean. While they included slaves, they did not address slavery or feature the Civil War. What detective stories did was to offer assurance that in spite of however chaotic or confusing things might be civil justice would prevail, order would be restored. And in an era experiencing an explosion of discovery, invention, and technology, detective stories also assured readers that science could cure diseases and expose if not eliminate crime.

The latter, to be sure, was a hard sell. It still is. The connection of science and crime is a vexed one even in science fiction. But there is more to science than discoveries about the workings of the natural world. There is method. From Bacon onward the most important part of science was doing it the right way, taking the proper steps, being impartial, finding evidence, demonstrating the validity of what that evidence seemed to show. In essence, science possessed all of the attributes that 18th- and 19th-century jurists sought when thinking and writing about the need for and uses of evidence in law courts. Impartiality and method stood behind 19th-century science and jurisprudence and it was one of the things that led to lawyer detectives and physician detectives. Toward the end of the century, however, both were supplanted by detective detectives.

4

WOMEN AND DETECTIVES

> Although for a long time detectives of the fair sex—and some of them of good social status—have been employed for the discovery of crime and grave political offenses, and also for making private inquiries where delicacy and tact is requisite, female detectivism has but occasionally been employed in the United Kingdom for public purposes, and even then with merely insignificant results—*Mower County Transcript,* February 20, 1889

And One Woman in Her Time Plays Many Parts…

For most of the 19th century in detective stories women are robbed, murdered, abused, raped, kidnapped, blackmailed, disinherited, or victimized by sadistic husbands and other criminals. They are innocent victims of circumstance and scapegoats for the crimes of others. A conspicuous number of stories have women criminals—sometimes masterminds, but more often they are accomplices or shields for their criminal lovers. But females in detective stories are not all helpless victims or femmes fatales. They are also heroes—most often as amateur detectives taking on a single case but also as ancillary actors (informants and detectives' wives) assisting the police, and in a few instances they act as professional detectives. In some stories females take on both lead parts as hero and villain. But in almost every case their identity as women is integral to the case and to how they are treated.

Women were there at the beginning. In fact, in what is arguably the first story about a detective in English, William Burton's "The Secret Cell" (*Burton's Gentleman's Magazine,* September & October 1837) women play all the central roles, and other than for a bit of heavy lifting, men are not really necessary. "The Secret Cell" is about the abduction of Mary Lobenstein, who had inherited the estate of a wealthy woman by whom she was employed as a companion. The crime is instigated by "the thin and yellow spinster" Elizabeth Bishop, the old lady's "selfish and mercenary" "hypocritical hyena of a niece" who had hoped to inherit the estate. It is Mary's mother, a former washerwoman, who seeks the male narrator's help. The narrator and his detective friend, however, meet with no success at finding the kidnapped woman until the detective's wife takes over:

> My own inquiries in the mother's neighbourhood were not attended with any success; I therefore sent my wife, a shrewd woman, and well adapted for the business. She went without a shawl or bonnet, as if she had but stepped out from an adjacent house, into the baker's, the grocer's, the chandler's, and the beer shop; and while making her trifling purchases, she asked in a careless gossiping way, if any intelligence of Miss Lobenstein had been obtained?

Based on information she has collected, the narrator and detective discover Mary held captive in a monastery where she has been imprisoned as if she were "an insane prostitute [...] who had been annoying some married gentlemen by riotous conduct at their houses." Even when they discover where the villain's thugs had imprisoned her, however, it is a woman who saves the day when the detective's wife recognizes that Mary is indeed alive and not the corpse the men had assumed her to be. This, however, was hardly the role for women in the detective stories set down by Burton's one-time editor, Edgar Allan Poe. In all of Poe's Dupin stories women appear in a very different role. They are all victims. In "The Murders in the Rue Morgue" two women are "murdered" by an orangutan; in "The Mystery of Marie Roget" a woman is killed in what we now know was a botched abortion and tossed into the Seine; and in "The Purloined Letter" a woman is the victim of extortion. All of these crimes occur off stage. The man figures things out.

Victims and Victimized

Seduced and Abandoned

Acknowledging that there are libraries of literature on the subject from every era, in detective fiction, accounts of seducers and "ruined" women go back to Vidocq and the dawn of the genre. Thus "The Seducer," the third "Unpublished Passages in the Life of Vidocq, The French Minister of Police" (*Burton's Gentleman's Magazine*, November 1838), centers on Louise Marcell, who leaves her seducer, declaring "[...] since I am not to be the wife, I will not submit to the dishonor of remaining another day as the mistress of Monsieur de St. Brie. We part, sir, this instant forever." She then sets out alone for home, where she is found by her father lying on the ground and partially covered in snow just outside his door. Her father takes revenge for her mistreatment and death. After Vidocq, the pathos-dominated "ruined woman" theme was common in a certain class of period detective stories. While detective stories universally condemn men who "ruin" women, they also recognize that doing so was not a crime in the eyes of the law. While some writers found ways to combine that theme and a few of the basic elements of the detective story, these stories mostly carry over the motif of the detective as *deus ex machina* of the sensation novel and concentrate on revenge and self-sacrifice as opposed to problem solving. For example, in "A Life's Lesson," it's a "ruined" woman and not the detective who saves another woman from "a fortune-hunter [...] of no reputable character" with a bullet:

> I am by birth and education a gentlewoman, though compelled to get my living as a governess. I bought the pistol, and I shot Edward Conder, and served him right. I would do it again. He ruined me, and left me to shame and misery. He had always promised marriage, but he never meant to keep his promise. I traced him to Hounslow. Then I found that he was making love to another girl. I followed him, buying a pistol first. On that night I saw him cross to the park, I went after him, hoping to speak. I got up to him. I heard him tell a young lady, who was listening to him, that he had never loved before. I called him a liar, and shot him. Heaven forgive us both! [*Gleason's Monthly Companion*, December 1881].

Simply focusing upon the detective's response as a witness to the melodrama and pathos of women who have been seduced and abandoned was a way of combining detectives and the "ruined women" theme. In these stories detectives serve primarily as witnesses to events that emphasize the pitiable end of women deceived by men, as in this passage at the end of "A Detective's Experience":

> The woman told her story truthfully I could not doubt. But, as I supposed, the man was gone. He was never heard of afterward; and this little memory is all that is left of the wrecked and ruined woman [*Sacramento Daily Union*, December 19, 1868].

A particularly gothic instance related to a witness of crime and perverse notions of women's honor occurs in "Crime Detected: An Anecdote of the Paris Police" by Henry Mills Alden (*Harper's New Monthly Magazine*, May 1852). This is the tale of a priest who is blindfolded and brought to the bedside of a woman to perform the sacrament of Extreme Unction. At the woman's bedside the priest is told:

> Minister of God, before you is a woman who has betrayed the blood of her ancestors, and whose doom is irrevocably fixed. She knows on what conditions an interview with you has been granted her; she knows too that all supplication would be useless. You know your duty, M. le Curé; I leave you to fulfill it, and will return to seek you in half an hour.

Although we are not told explicitly what act induced her state, we learn that she is "the victim of a secret family tribunal, whose sentence is irrevocable!" and that she is bleeding profusely, as "her family have condemned their victim to have her veins opened one by one, and thus to perish slowly in expiation of a fault, already more than punished by her mortal agony."

Pathos, revenge, and outrage by themselves, however, run counter to the problem-solution basis of the detective story. But there are stories in which detectives actively intervene and prevent disastrous relationships from being consummated. Such is the case in "How I Won my Wife" (*The Mountain Democrat*, September 17, 1870). In this brief chase story, the detective is charged with preventing a disastrous runaway marriage between a headstrong young heiress and a blackguard, aptly named Jim Dandy. He tracks the couple down at a low boarding house run by Mag Harris (a creature who "knows that to a pure woman her very presence is pollution"). Saving the young woman's virtue by opening her eyes, the detective reveals the would-be lover as a notorious house-breaker and thief, by "pulling off the false hair and whiskers" and leaving the "sinister countenance and coal black hair of the prisoner visible." Replacing false love with true, in this story the detective then decorously woos and then marries the reformed runaway. But here, as in other stories about roués and deceived women, the detective demonstrates his or her perception and knowledge of the criminal world, as well as proving that sexual predation is only one aspect of persons inclined toward other crimes.

At mid-century as detective stories gained popularity, writers also used the seduced-and-abandoned-woman plot to develop details that emphasize the detective's benevolent nature and role in protecting the community. This began in "The Costly Kiss" in *Harper's New Monthly Magazine*. There the detective narrator traces the actions of an embezzler who is also a serial seducer and saves one of his victims from suicide:

> She went on now for some time in such a way that I feared her trouble had crazed her. She paced the room, hardly minding me, now cursing herself, now him—"her *baby*, oh, her *baby*, *his* baby!" And then she fell on her knees at her chair, and uttered one of the wildest, strangest, and yet most beautiful prayers I ever heard. From the tone of the prayer I saw she was thinking of suicide, and I planned how to prevent this. I concluded to take her home with me, and leave her under the care of my mother and sister [April 1859].

Dick & Fitzgerald's *Strange Stories of a Detective; or, Curiosities of Crime* (1863), in fact, has two stories about detectives and seduced and abandoned women. In "The Libertine," a kind-hearted detective intervenes, rescues a woman from her seducer and, after a time at his own home with his wife as nurse, he returns her to her father's home, but in a sadly altered state:

> But every reader can imagine how futile would be any attempt to depict, with any thing like reality, this harrowing scene, and I can only hope that no one who may read this imperfect sketch may ever be placed in a position to realize the awful sufferings of the agonized parent in that trying hour.

His only child, the victim of a villain's arts, was there before him a helpless, hopeless idiot. Hours wore on, and Mr. Moreton still continued his vain attempts to win from Ada one word of reason or one look of recognition. She was lost to him forever; lost to the world; lost, happily, to herself—for a restoration of her reason would only have brought with it the most soul-harrowing, maddening reflections.

There is a somewhat different outcome in the other story from *Strange Stories*, "Moneybags and Son." In that piece there is another embezzling son who has been the ruin of multiple women, "one in a madhouse, the other an outcast." He refuses to marry his current love interest, Henrietta, whom he has impregnated. She, too, talks of suicide, and attempts it after her final impotent and ineffective shaming plea:

> [...] will you be honorable and act like a man? You know my father is rich—not so rich as yours, it is true; but he will give us enough to begin the world with, and what need we fear? Oh! do not cast me away to shame and misery—to shame worse than death! I cannot endure the thought, Edward. *I* am the suitor now, not *you*; and I sue—for what? For the fulfillment of a promise so often made unsolicited. There is no time for dallying. I expected you would have come tonight prepared to act. I told you what I expected; but you seem inclined to do nothing but leave me to my fate.

The detective, however, rushes the laudanum-ridden Henrietta to the hospital, and after the death of his father the roué reforms and marries his former mistress. The detective closes his narrative with "He may prove an exemplary husband. I hope he may for her sake," but with sexual predation viewed as a gateway crime, many period observers may not have gone away convinced.

While many seduced and abandoned stories emphasize pathos and the character of the compassionate detective, by the 1870s writers of clue-oriented stories occasionally used the topic as the hidden motive that the detective discovers after a narrative about finding and understanding details linked to a crime. Thus some basic forensic dentistry leads the detective in "The Platinum Filling" to the seducer and murderer:

> "Since I have been in Paris," I continued, "I have discovered—it will not interest you to know how—that Monsieur Duplessis had an assumed name, this time one of a higher grade; that of the Vicomte Montmarte. I have discovered, too, that under this title he seduced the poor English girl, Ida Gilmore—I can call it nothing else, for the marriage by which he entrapped her was a false one—and then, knowing her to be friendless and alone, and knowing, too, that he would enjoy her little fortune were she dead, and tiring of the affection of the poor little dumb creature, took her to the other end of the world to get her out of the way, and then returned to Paris with the trumped-up lie that the murdered girl had died, and was buried in England" [*Overland Monthly*, August 1874].

While writers did find uses for the stereotypes of the roué and the fallen woman in detective stories, they never comprised a significant percentage of the stories published, and as the genre developed towards the end of the century they became increasingly rare. As narratives became less sentimental and detectives more important, "ruined women" characters became less numerous and even more stereotypical. From the beginning writers based women's susceptibility to smooth-talking lotharios on a few basic elements: (1) women's trivial natures ("Minnie Althorpe was a beautiful girl about nineteen years of age, a light-hearted, merry girl, full of deep feeling, and yet somewhat flighty and capricious in her character" ["A Life's Lesson," *Gleason's Monthly Companion*, December 1881]); (2) women's youth ("In just one week she would be eighteen, but in the meantime she had become acquainted with a young fellow from the City, and fallen in love with him or thought she had, which is just the same with a young girl" ["How I Won My Wife: A Doctor's Story," *The Tiffin Weekly Tribune*, September 21, 1865]); and (3) women's naïve respect for social superiors made so by titles in Europe or wealth in the U.S., as in "The Platinum Filling" (*Overland Monthly*, August 1874) and "The Costly Kiss" (*Harper's New Monthly Magazine*, April 1859).

Rape

While 19th-century detective stories deal with crimes, part of the success of the genre was that only some of those crimes are violent, and in most cases writers found ways of minimizing the effect of even those crimes on their readers. As seen above, stories about seduction often prove an exception, and principally intend to engage readers' sentiments. But that is not quite the case with stories that have to do with rape. First of all, infinitesimally few 19th-century stories have to do with rape, and even those do not use the word "rape." Some certainly imply rape without saying it:

> That a murder had been committed there could be no doubt. The girl lay on her back, her feet drawn up, her clothing badly torn and in disorder, and while one hand clenched a stout stick, the other had a dying clutch on a coat button—just a match for those left on Will Grafton's coat. She had been choked to death and was a horrible sight, her eyes wide open, her tongue out, and a look of agony on her bloated face ["An Innocent Man Hanged," *News and Citizen*, March 24, 1887].

Others employ euphemisms like "outrage." Just as the role of seduction is encapsulated and comes out only near the end of "The Platinum Filling" (*Overland Monthly*, August 1874), rape gets only passing mention when it enters narratives. That's what happens in "Jean Monette" (*Burton's Gentleman's Magazine*, April 1839) when brigands are offered "an adequate share of the booty, *and also the girl herself,* if either of them felt that way inclined, as a reward for their assistance" [our italics]. In "The Second Sight" (*The Detroit Free Press*, December 14, 1863) the story largely concerns the role of detailed premonitions in solving a murder. Only at the very end do readers learn that the motive may have been the victim's probable rape of the murderer's wife:

> I doubt, however, if the deed would have been committed, but for the cruelty practiced by the old man on the wife of this "White Joe," the negress Sue, who was the woman present at the murder.

Brutality and rape, once again of an enslaved woman of color, come up as an ancillary detail in "The Two-Fingered Assassin":

> [...] his poor wife pined away beneath her husband's brutality and neglect; and finally, because she would not give up her couch to a Creole slave-girl, he beat her, and then turned her out of doors! [*The New York Ledger*, June 20, 1857]

The prospect of rape, not rape itself, is central to the "adventure" in "A Night Adventure in New York" (*Ballou's Monthly Magazine*, April 1868). In it a "tall and elegant lady" appeals for help to the boarders of a rooming house, claiming "O gentlemen! do not let us lose time here! My daughter is being carried away, and I want your aid to recover her!" They chase the villains in

> a night for violence, and I shuddered as I thought that possibly we might be unsuccessful in our efforts to deliver the young lady from the hands of scoundrels, who would consign her to a fate far worse than death.

In the nick of time the narrator and his friend find the would-be ravishers and there is a bit of gunplay that leaves one bad guy dead and two wounded. The men return the young woman to her mother and two sentences later the story ends, sealing off discussion and leaving readers with a narrative with melodramatic emphasis on manly obligations rather than consideration of the female victim. Almost ten years later Ballou used the same combination of potential rape, rampant lust, and chivalry in "Unmaked" (*Ballou's Monthly Magazine*, September 1877). This time, however, there is a female narrator and Miss J. Whitney is named as author. While the narrator displays some pluck, saying at one point that "God helps those who help themselves," the contrast between good and bad men nonetheless underlies the entire story. The end of the story, in fact, can serve as an example of Victorian melodrama:

> "A fine race you have led me, but I have you safe!" he cried, with savage exultation. "Cry, writhe and struggle as you will, you are helpless as a babe; you cannot escape, for you are mine, mine forever."
> "Villain, take that!" thundered a voice; and the next moment I was snatched from Elsmere's arms, and the baffled wretch fell to the ground.
> With a low cry of joy, for the first time in my healthy life, I fainted in Erie Faulkner's arms.

The most graphic portrait of rape in period detective fiction appears in "A Mystery Solved"; the story begins with

> In a cornfield, about half a mile from the village, and just off from a small by-road, a young girl, apparently about sixteen or seventeen years of age, had been found dead and decaying, with such marks of violence upon her person as left no doubt that she had been dealt with in a revolting and fiendish manner [*New York Fireside Companion*, February 7, 1870].

The community where this occurred offers a substantial reward for the discovery of the rapist/murderer. Rather than outrage, the detective's motive in taking up the case is the reward plus his technical interest in the case:

> This case, so unusual and mysterious—so out of the usual range of even mysterious murders—particularly interested me; and making myself known to the proper officials, and showing my authority as a secret agent of the government, I offered my services to investigate the matter, which were cordially accepted.

The bulk of the narrative then turns to finding and following up on clues to the murder. As sanitized as it is, "A Mystery Solved" may have played a role in Anthony Comstock's crusade against what he considered obscene as well as against the *New York Fireside Companion* in general.

As in "A Mystery Solved," the detective's interest in clues and the crime of rape come together in "A Pinkerton Detective" in *The Van Wert Republican* (July 5, 1888). Here the detective tells readers about material clues and witness testimony that lead to widespread suspicion of a young man for rape and murder. But the accusation of rape also plays a role in the surprise ending of the detective story when the narrator exonerates the young man and cleverly brings forth the clues that identify the victim's jealous lesbian lover as the killer:

> Briefly told it was as follows: Jeanne LeFavre and Bertha Kelsey had been friends, but Bertha, tiring of the jealous care, almost masculine attention of her companion, and longing for one of the opposite sex, had met Eugene Verder and fallen in love with him, to the disgust and horror of Jeanne Lefevre.

This, one assumes, would have given Anthony Comstock even worse conniptions. History is silent regarding the response of the residents of Van Wert, Ohio.

Physical and Mental Abuse

While mentions of coercive sexual acts are infrequent, mostly oblique, and focused on the detective and not the victim, references to domestic violence are commonplace in 19th-century American detective fiction. While it was often condemned and found shameful, abuse of women was not prosecuted or even prosecutable. Thus we find in 1888 a real detective lamenting "the abuse and abandonment of wives" in an interview titled "A Detective's Opinion of Crime" reprinted from the *Buffalo News*:

You think detectives are hard-hearted. Well, they have to be in a way or they would melt at the sight of sorrow we meet day after day. Poor, hard working women washing and scrubbing to support louts of men, who drink up all they earn. Tender women with little babes at their breasts deserted and struggling from sunrise till late at night to support their little ones and scarcely seeing their children that are big enough to be out of their arms from one day to another. That is the kind of experience that makes a man case harden himself in very self defense, and it is growing. As we become more English in other things, we become like them in our crimes. We become wife beaters and wife deserters like them. I tell you, if the women would promise to establish the whipping post for wife beaters and a chain gang for wife deserters, I would become a suffragist in no time," and he talked so earnestly that his cigar went out, and he flung it from him with an angry vim that showed one thief taker hadn't been hardened farther than the surface [*The Weekly Thibodaux Sentinel and Journal of the 8th Senatorial District*, September 8, 1888].

Again and again, female characters in detective stories are portrayed as abused. Both "The Second Sight" (*The Detroit Free Press*, December 14, 1863) and the "The Two-Fingered Assassin" (*The New York Ledger*, June 20, 1857) mention abuse of women as incidental facts: the first story features a murdered man who was a "hard father" who "practiced cruelty" on a daughter described as ill-used and "half-starved," and in the second story the wife was beaten and evicted. This victimization shown in detective fiction is not related to class: even a countess is abused by her husband in "The Left-Hand Glove":

> Every one of our family are aware that my brother did not behave well to his wife; and that his conduct caused them to separate shortly after their marriage [*Stories for the Home Circle*, New York: G.P. Putnam, 1857].

A Marquis in "The Detective's Story" is also described as an abuser:

> From the beginning of his career of crime he treated his wife with terrible cruelty. He used to beat and pet the woman alternately, like the tigerish brute he is. By threats and blows he may have torn from her—presuming her innocent—sufficient knowledge of her house and its contents to enable him to succeed in midnight robbery—unless he is prevented [*Yorkville Enquirer*, July 12, 1883].

Domestic abuse crosses national and class boundaries and is described in a spectrum from implied to overt. For example, in "Bigamy or Not Bigamy," the heroine's first husband is described as "cursed with a morose and churlish temper and disposition" and having "unhappy cankerous temper," and their marriage is described thus:

> The union was a most unhappy one. [...] and after being united somewhat more than two years, a separation, vehemently insisted on by the wife's father, took place, and the unhappily-wedded daughter returned to her parent's roof [*Leaves from the Diary of a Law-Clerk*, London: Brown, 1857].

In "Malvern Versus Malvern" from the same collection, the reference to the abuse is less oblique:

> Ah! poor soul, nobody will see her long. An unhappy, long-suffering woman; and, decorously as Pendergast treats her before others—though she seldom sees anyone—there is only one thing she dreads more than she does him, and that is death! I have seen her cower beneath that hard, glittering eye of his, like a beaten hound.

Occasionally abuse is central to the crime or mystery:

> One night a young woman came to the station, and complained that she had been brutally ill-treated by a man whose name she appeared anxious to conceal. She did not wish him arrested, but only sought protection for herself from his violence ["A Den of Phantoms," *Santa Fe Weekly Gazette*, October 17, 1868].

This case, as readers should know, is not going to turn out well. In "Eloise" by Caroline Conrad, abuse also lies at the bottom of things. In it a servant explains to the young Eloise that her mother is not dead, as she had believed, but imprisoned and coerced:

> He wants your mamma to make a will and leave him all the money away from you, deary; and now he's made everybody believe she's dead, he can keep her shut up till she does it, he thinks [*The New York Ledger*, November 20, 1869].

And that

> "You musn't brave him, little dear," she whispered the child; "it won't do no good, and he'll make you suffer for it. You won't get out of this room till you promise, if you hold on till you're gray."

In all of these cases the domestic violence in itself is not technically the crime. Writers use it to indicate another aspect of the criminal's nature, to enhance the detective's sensitivity, and to elicit sentiment in the portrait of women victims.

Possession Is Nine Tenths...

Until 1882 any property possessed by a woman belonged to her husband upon marriage. That was England: in 1882 Parliament passed the Married Woman's Property Act, which did away with this legacy of male ownership. Women in most states of the United States, however, had had the right to own property long before that date, but that did not mean that women were unequivocally in charge of their own property or that stories about women's role in the shady transfer of wealth were not compelling reading. It was one of the reasons for the popularity of Wilkie Collins' *Woman in White* (1859). Occasionally a story about forced marriage (based on inheritance) imported from England, like Charles Temple's "Pray, Sir, Are You a Gentleman?" (*The Columbia Spy*, September 21 & 28, 1861), turns up amid American detective stories. Because they were legally supposed to have control of their own property, however, didn't mean that women in American detective stories weren't seen as potential piggy banks. "A Bold Stroke for a Wife" (*The New York Ledger*, August 7, 1869), for example, concerns forgery intending to exert pressure on a woman to marry a man planning to live on her inheritance, and in the "The Pen-Knife Blade" by Sylvanus Cobb, Jr., the dastardly Herman Parkhurst spirits away forty thousand dollars from his new wife by pressing her "so persistently that she was forced to yield" and working up a plan to steal his step-daughter's share of the property (*The New York Ledger*, February 16, 1867). In "The Monk; or The Maniac's Release," women are only means to the end of cash:

> Ishmael and Lendorf with an accomplice arranging a plan, in which the accomplice was to assume a profession, mix freely in society and marry a young woman; after which to murder her guardian, a very rich man, whose property she would inherit, then poison her [*Gleason's Monthly Companion*, January 1879].

In a more convoluted way, marriage as both an easy path and a roadblock to wealth provides the motive for the sentiment and the crime in "The Mystery":

> I first led her astray and then abandoned her. Years after we met, and I married her. She had a marriage certificate. I again left her; and but for the proof of this marriage with her I could have formed a wealthy alliance. It was to get this certificate that I went to see her that night. I could not, however, persuade her to give it to me. She would not tell me where it was. Maddened almost to frenzy, I struck her down at my feet, and prompted by insanity, I believe I killed her [*Fort Wayne Weekly Democrat*, December 22, 1869].

Our Bodies Our Selves?

In 19th-century detective fiction, whether concerned with detectives, criminals, or victims, physical appearance matters, particularly women's appearance. This does not apply to mature women, who are always just "old women," or guilty female servants who lay the blame on their more attractive (and honest) colleagues. It's young women who are described. Thus readers learn that female victims, villains, and heroes are almost universally beauties. While male detectives and even some male villains are described primarily by their actions, such is not the case for many of the roles females play in period detective stories. Consider these descriptions, beginning with Mrs. Malvern, who is a victim:

> One or two questions suggested, rather than directly put, by Mr. S—, kindled Mrs. Malvern's fine, expressive countenance to a flame, and the dark, lustrous eyes sparkled with fire. She was a splendid woman, not more than five- or six-and-twenty years of age, of a Juno-like presence and aspect, and a complexion so fair as to be almost dazzling,—especially heightened and relieved as it was by the glossy blackness of her hair: she was one of the queens of earth, in short, whose sceptres command the homage of the reddest of red republicans ["Malvern Versus Malvern," *Leaves from the Diary of A Law-Clerk*, London, J.C. Brown & Co., 1857].

There is the seductress:

> My Neighbor was, evidently, of Spanish origin, for the rich dark blood of old Castile burned brightly on the clear olive cheeks, whilst the eyes, jetty as the brow above them, blazed forth with a life-like brilliancy which seemed to light up and enliven the whole face.
>
> Her figure, though slight, was graceful and commanding; and though she was sitting, her very attitude was the embodiment of grace.
>
> It was impossible for me to withdraw my gaze, though rude it might seem, and whenever I encountered those lustrous eyes, as I occasionally would, they thrilled through me like an electric shock ["The Detective: A Story of New Orleans," *New York Fireside Companion*, June 29, 1869].

And readers also learn in great detail of the physical beauty of the anonymous corpse in "A Detective's Experience":

> The body was laid out on the pier, and the lovely up-turned face was magnetic in its intense beauty. A wealth of black, wet hair fell back from the broad, low forehead, exposing a face rounded and full in its fresh Spring-time beauty. The long lashes drooped darkly over the pale underlids, and the chiseled lips had not lost their delicate curve and crimson stain. The soft, milky skin showed beneath it the olive tint it had worn in life. The clinging dress but imperfectly concealed each rounded limb and the exquisite outline of body.
>
> I felt a strange attraction in looking at this dead woman. She must have been unsurpassingly lovely when life was instinct in the frame now so chill. The warm sun of her native land could not have been more lustrous than her eyes were then [*Sacramento Daily Union*, December 19, 1868].

Although somewhat more restrained, writers also give readers physical descriptions of their women detectives:

> Lucy Wagner had not shed a tear yet. She was a tall, slim girl, with dark, bright eyes, and a handsome face ["Betrayed by a Button," *The New York Ledger*, February 17, 1877].

There is, however, one significant exception to the beauty-rule when it comes to detectives, Margaret Saunders, a.k.a. "Clubnose," who appears to have been inspired by an actual Scotland Yard operative. The story "Clubnose" (credited to *Chambers' Journal*, and reprinted in a variety of U.S. newspapers) is a biographical sketch that opens with the narrator describing a nurse as "the most hideous and repulsive face I ever saw in man or woman" and announcing "What a dreadful-looking nurse you have there! Why, it must be enough to send a patient into fits to have that face bending over him" (*Burlington Weekly Hawk Eye*, March 25, 1880). The surgeon then reveals that she is an undercover detective, and we soon learn that she began her career after being an innocent accused who vowed she would "never rest" until she cleared her name "by bringing the real offenders to justice." She is described as the most accomplished at disguise of all on the force. While Scotland Yard officially claims not to have employed female detectives in the 19th century, there are a number of death notices of "A Female Detective" published in American periodicals in

1877 and 1878 that correspond with the fictional character of Clubnose. She is described as having "features which might perhaps be compared with those of a bulldog, [... and which] could not fail to inspire a sense of repugnance to those even who were disposed to admire her courage and acknowledge the utility of the services she rendered" (*The Cambria Freeman*, June 8, 1877).

While writers consistently included some mention of the bodies of leading female figures in 19th-century detective stories, they concentrated on their eyes. Those eyes indicated beauty, intelligence, passion, and sometimes had a mesmerizing effect on men. Indeed, a few stories demonstrate how men's susceptibility to women's physical and emotional allure perverts the course of justice. For instance, "First Great Success" (*Galveston Daily News*, April 17, 1889) a first-person story purportedly narrated by New York Police Inspector Thomas Byrnes, tells the tale of a French detective who leaves Paris "without making a report" when he discovers that his girlfriend is the murderer he is pursuing. The detective in "Foiled by a Woman" is similarly thwarted by a female criminal; however, he is not morose but delighted in his failure, as he reflects,

> I was foiled by a woman. Nor could I help rejoicing, now that she had escaped. Innocent or guilty, there was a charm about her none could resist. The spell of her wondrous beauty affected all who approached her. It lingers in memory yet; and I could not have the sin of her blood upon my conscience [*Louisiana Capitolian*, April 24, 1880].

Indeed some women in detective fiction have a positively perverse effect on men. In "The Fatal Woman" a rejected lover murders each successive suitor:

> And even so early as the time of my first acquaintance with her, she was looked upon almost as an object of terror as well as adoration. It was fatal to love her. For, up to that time, every man who had confessed love for her was dead. Yet this horrible fatality, while it repelled, also attracted suitors—among the rest my dearest and most intimate friend, Albert Gowerie; and it was in this manner that I made the acquaintance of Miss Cornelli [*The New York Ledger*, March 22, 1867].

In typical 19th-century fashion, the victim is blamed, both in the title and the final line ("They were married and from that hour Albert has never had any reason to regret that he loved the fair being whose beauty had, in part, proved fatal to so many"). Sexual jealousy is also the theme of "The Ebony Bedroom" (*Bismark Tribune*, July 30, 1880) in which a faithful wife, the Countess of Montfort, is murdered because the Marquis des Medranc who lives next door does not believe that "no means no" but does believe that rejection gives one license to kill. Seemingly a locked-room mystery, in this story the Marquis had entered from a secret passage joining his mansion to the Countess' boudoir, and slain the woman who rejected his advances.

Unlike sexuality, which is a very rare and euphemized subject in 19th-century detective fiction, a number of stories use contemporary notions about women's heightened, delicate sensibilities in their portraits of female characters. Women are much more susceptible than men to emotional turmoil. In this detective stories carried over the suffering, tragic woman character from sensation novels. As early as "The Robbers' Revenge" (1851), writers made an issue of women's physical response to both good news and bad news:

> I caused Madame Duquesne to be as gently undeceived the next morning as possible with respect to her lost child; but the reaction and disappointment proved too much for her wavering intellect. She relapsed into positive insanity, and was placed in Bedlam, where she remained two years. At the end of that period she was pronounced convalescent [*Harper's New Monthly Magazine*, January 1851].

In "The Victim of a Plot" the heart and mind of the innocent-accused give way at what should be the story's happy ending:

> Her reason that had borne such shocks of grief gave way beneath the joy of her acquittal. She rose to her feet, looked with beaming face at her husband, and then before an arm could be outstretched to save her, fell fainting to the floor. From that moment she was hopelessly insane. Months went by, and as her reason clouded her body faded away. Not long the restless spirit fretted in the poor frame, and one night she died—died of a broken heart, a victim of a woman's hate [*Grand Traverse Herald*, January 27, 1870].

Interestingly, even when women in crisis are not clinically insane, their sanity is a constant worry and they are described in terms that suggest their sanity is in danger. Thus descriptions like the following are common: "This was a terrible blow to the young wife and mother, and for a time fears of her becoming insane were entertained, but she braved the billowy sea of grief and soon landed safe on the shores of good health" ("A Singular Story," *The Abilene Reflector*, January 22, 1885). And it is routine for a female character in stressful or tragic circumstance to be portrayed as "nearly insane" or "like an insane woman" ("A Brilliant Confidence Swindle in High Life" by Allan Pinkerton, *Criminal Reminiscences and Detective Sketches*, New York: Dillingham, 1878; "Number Thirty-Nine," *The Hartford Courant*, April 17, 1867).

Higher Love

In addition to using the pathos of female psychic vulnerability, detective story writers also emphasized the tragic nobility of the value women place on love—and the interrelatedness of love and a woman's mental health. Thus, when Alice Stanwright learns that her betrothed has been murdered, she

> was removed to her room and placed in bed, where she remained for two hours in a semi-unconscious state. This was followed by a sort of syncope which the doctor regarded with considerable alarm, being fearful that brain fever might be superinduced. Nor were his fears on this head without good ground, for in the course of two hours more his patient passed to another

change and began to talk incoherently. This brought the case to a settled state, and the doctor knew that he had to deal with brain fever, though, he hoped, in a mild form ["The Invisible Crime or Foot-Print Evidence" by Le Solitaire, *Daily Alta Californian*, October 29, 1871].

And in "The Brown Mystery" when her beloved is arrested,

> Frances was prostrated with brain fever from the effects of the shock which the news gave her, and when she recovered, it was only in the form of a raving maniac. She was taken to an insane asylum and there confined [*Racine Advocate*, March 8, 1883].

Love as tragedy is a repeated theme in the more sentiment-oriented detective stories of the period. Thus in "A Detective's Story," when the detective tries to have a wronged woman help him by exposing her lover's unfaithfulness, she refuses to do so:

> She never did. It was useless to detain her. We let her go, but three weeks afterwards she died of a broken heart. The mystery of the robbery has never been explained [*The Cedar Valley Times*, September 17, 1868].

Likewise, the abandoned wife of a "worthless husband" becomes "his accomplice to save herself from his wrath" and when he is arrested,

> [...] poor thing, she died before her husband was tried, awakening from that swoon, only to be attacked with brain fever, from which she never recovered ["The Robbery of Plate" by Harry Harewood Leech, *Flag of Our Union*, December 17, 1859].

Contemporary readers would not have been surprised that Virginal Howells "died in a mad-house in less than six months" after learning that the thief of her brother's ring was her fiancé on the eve of her wedding ("The Missing Ring," *The Star and Sentinel*, April 7, 1881). And it should appear a normal response when a woman has "a hysterical fit" and is "sick for months" when a detective reveals that her fiancé is a pickpocket ("Her Clay Idol," *The Sunny South*, June 10, 1882).

The conclusions of period stories that feature women reveal a singular attitude about crime and its punishment when the crimes concern women. They sink into insanity, die opportunely, and escape in disguise, and only rarely are they prosecuted. The lack of prosecution is notable because of the stated rationales. Were justice thwarted for these reasons or due to a lack of evidence, readers would see this as unavoidable. But often the detective chooses not to prosecute: for example, in "The Vital Point" by Frank H. Angier, a 20-year-old woman steals her own diamond necklace and murders her mother-in-law and her husband and attempts to murder their lawyer, but when she admits as much to him, he replies:

> I do not intend to seek your punishment, or to pursue you for my own revenge. Your crimes will bring their own retribution. You are free to leave this house as soon as you desire. The sum of money allowed you for your maintenance under your husband's will shall be regu-

larly paid to you or your agent. *I do not forget that you are still the woman whom my poor friend loved* [*Ballou's Monthly Magazine*, May 1881, our italics].

Similarly, in "A Mysterious Murder" by James Maitland, the truth is suppressed when the murderer sends her deathbed confession to the detective Harris, his newspaper-man confidant reflects:

> I must say that the pathos of these dying words of a wretched woman affected me deeply. Harris seemed also very much cut up. We consulted as to the advisability of publishing full particulars of the crime. Harris, however, sank all feelings of personal ambition, and declared against publication on the ground that it could do no possible good. Although such a splendid "scoop" would have added vastly to my reputation, out of feelings of humanity I agreed to suppress the sensation [*Suppressed Sensations, or Leaves from the Note Book of a Chicago Reporter*, Chicago: Rand McNally, 1879].

Equally odd are the endings in which women are the victims; for instance in "A Bold Stroke for a Wife" by Judge Clark (*The New York Ledger*, August 7, 1869) the lawyer detective and her true love promise to keep the secret of the man who forges a will in an attempt to force a woman to marry him as long as he withdraws his marriage request and renounces any claim to the estate—but there is no mandate that he disabuse the would-be fiancée of the belief that her father's dying request was their union. In "Crime Detected: an Anecdote of the Paris Police" by Henry Mills Alden the nobleman who attempts to kill a female relative is merely banished (*Harper's New Monthly Magazine*, May 1852); in "The Major's Wife" the villainous brother who abducts and robs his sister is given money to emigrate (*Daily Alta Californian*, July 20, 1876); and in "A Detective Story" (*The Wisconsin State Register*, March 5, 1887) a father is lured to a murder scene in the pretext of finding his missing fourteen-year-old daughter, and while the murder is cleared up, no mention is made of the daughter again. But the most bizarre ending may be in "A Noble Sacrifice. A Tale of Washington, D.C." by Sinclair, in which a beautiful woman marries and then is murdered by a man who impersonates her fiancé. When the fiancé is about to be arrested for the crime his twin brother committed, he asks to be "spared as much public notoriety as possible" and then commits suicide; the detective and newspaperman duo then "held a consultation, and, comprehending that St. John had sacrificed himself to save the family name, determined on our part to shield the facts from the public gaze" and the coroner declares his death from natural causes (*Ballou's Monthly Magazine*, January 1883). The final line of the story reads "Years have passed since that tragic event happened, but I can never think of it without regarding it as one of the noblest sacrifices I have ever heard of." A 21st-century reader's reaction is less likely to see this as a noble sacrifice than to ask "what about the victim's rights?" and "is there to be no attempt to track down her violator and killer?" The lengthy descriptions of her beauty both alive and as a corpse and her namelessness emphasize her objectification and that the real crime is against the brother, not her. Again and again, the attitude toward crimes against women is revealed to be viewed in terms of how the crimes victimized the men to whom the women are associated.

That antediluvian views of women's nature govern what goes on in a lot of 19th-century detective fiction, in spite of first wave feminism, should not be a surprise. However, here it is particularly significant because it's not just in detective fiction: in most popular period fiction of any sort handsome is as handsome does. Physical appearance reflects guilt and innocence. In terms of the history of popular literature, therefore, it was not only a victory for women but also a sign of the maturing of detective fiction when at the end of the century both male and female appearance came to have no bearing on the identity of the criminal.

One of the most popular roles for females in 19th-century detective fiction in both America and Britain has nothing to do with women as persons or their relationships with others, it has to do with women purely as ornaments. Every detective story about the robbery or theft of a piece of jewelry—and there are a lot of them—speaks if not volumes at least some pithy sentences about the role of women. The purloined jewels in almost every case are unique, highly valuable, ultra-fashionable, and in some cases famous possessions. In general, they are a husband's gift to his wife or family's inherited possession. Since its principal purpose is ostentation, jewelry is customarily only worn on special, public occasions. Thus, at the Paris Opera

> No wonder that bell tinkled unheard, and the curtain went up unnoticed; no wonder that every eye was fixed with a fascinated gaze upon the woman who had just taken her seat, and was calmly with well-bred nonchalance glancing about the house; for upon her arms, blazing like beacons, sparkled the diamond bracelets of which Paris had heard so much, and which royalty had sought in vain to purchase. A hum of admiration, like the murmur of the sea, ran through the house, and then, for the first, the entrancing strains of the chorus were listened to ["The Diamond Bracelet," *Southern Watchman*, November 19, 1873].

Indeed jewelry is viewed by some as the *sine qua non* of belonging to a certain class of society. That view is enforced by a trivial and superficial woman in "The Stolen Diamond" by Frances Henshaw Baden:

> They may do each other good. Annie ought to gain a little appreciation of worldly good, and indeed I wish she did care a little more about dress. Point lace and diamonds afford her no more gratification than plain white linen, or simple jet or gold ornaments.
>
> And poor Lucia would almost sell her heart for diamonds. Indeed, I believe the man who can give her the most of them will win her hand, if her heart should ache for ever after! [*The New York Ledger*, September 17, 1870].

Lucia, like a lot of people in 19th-century detective stories, is mesmerized by jewelry and places a higher value on the material than the human. "The Stolen

Diamond" along with its detective plot contains a homiletic story with a moral about the proper values for women to hold—that women shouldn't value jewelry as enhancements of beauty or as lures for potential husbands. In the world of many of these stories, however, jewelry confers or enhances the worth of the women to whom it is given and who wear it. That men (husbands, detectives, and thieves) are the ones affected by its loss and concerned with its retrieval also carries with it symbolic significance.

Cherchez la Femme?

In 19th-century detective stories there is a gender imbalance when it comes to who is behind circumstance's eight ball. In "Coming out of Exile; or the Diamond Bracelet Found" by Mrs. Henry Wood, the thief and detective have this exchange:

"Then there's no faith in woman."
"There never was yet," returned the officer. "If they are not at the top and bottom of every mischief, Joe, they are sure to be in the middle" [*The Eclectic Magazine*, October 1858].

Echoing the Wronged-Woman theme of contemporary sensation novels, in a number of 19th-century detective stories suspicion falls first on a woman. Thus in "The Wronged Wife" (*The Bismark Tribune*, June 18, 1880), the first wife murders her ex-husband and makes it look like the second wife is guilty; in "A Family Secret" (*The Star and Sentinel*, February 15, 1882) a foster daughter is implicated by the false testimony of the man posing as an heir; and in "Helen Montressor or, Judge Remsen's First Client" by Marl Lee (*The New York Ledger*, May 31, 1856) her employer plants evidence in the beautiful Helen's trunk and then charges her with theft. Most of these stories end with money and marriage when the mystery is cleared up and the innocent woman vindicated. But Wilkie Collins chose to emphasize the pathos of the Wronged-Woman theme in "A Marriage Tragedy" (*Harper's New Monthly Magazine*, February 1858), in which justice does not prevail: the bigamous husband gets away scot-free, and the poor wrongly accused and victimized wife never recovers, indeed "the sad, dull, vacant look in her face never brightened" when she is declared innocent and over the years she "drooped and faded slowly."

In a surprising number of stories, female servants are accused and arrested—often merely because of their social class they are seen as more likely suspects than family members who have the same opportunities for larceny. In "Lost, Stolen or Strayed" (*Columbia Spy*, June 30, 1859) the servants are repeatedly accused and their boxes are searched, although even a novice detective reader would notice that the robberies all occur when Lady Mosshill is visiting.

And of course in Wilkie Collins' *The Moonstone* (1868) Rosanna Spearman is the first suspect brought to readers' attention. This kind of thing occurs in "The Mysterious Occurrence in Lambeth" by G.P.R. James (*Harper's New Monthly Magazine*, August 1855); and "The Thief in the Night" (*Lowell Sun*, August 7, 1880). Perhaps the most intriguing of the maid-didn't-do-it stories may be "A Little Mistake," in which two young, educated, middle-class teachers run away from school and take jobs as chambermaids at a hotel. A robbery occurs and the police on the scene automatically blame the help:

> That night a robbery of valuable jewels was committed in the hotel; and on search, one of the stolen diamonds was found under the mattress of the bed occupied by the two new chambermaids. It was in vain for them to protest their innocence. The fact that they were, by education, and manners, and appearance, *above their station*, told powerfully against them.
>
> Why should *they*—educated and accomplished girls—be in that hotel in disguise, and under assumed names, except for the purposes of robbery.
>
> "It's a put up thing," said the policeman, who was in charge of the matter. "Them girls are in with the thieves, and have been *trained to the business*. Any one can see that!" [*The New York Ledger*, August 1, 1868].

Luckily, a competent detective is soon on the scene and "at once saw that the placing of the diamond under the girls' bed was a mere ruse, to throw pursuit off the scent."

A prominent subset of the female-innocents-accused detective stories in the 19th century are those in which the crime evaporates when the mystery is solved. For example, in "The Left-hand Glove; or, Circumstantial Evidence" (*Stories for the Home Circle*, New York: Putnam, 1857) the death of Edward von Bergfeldt is actually a suicide masquerading as a murder by his ill-treated wife. And a remarkable number of supposed thefts and forgeries are revealed to be the result of somnambulism: the crime in "Mabel's Christmas Gift" by Judge Clark (*The New York Ledger*, January 1, 1870) is the act of a sleepwalking check writer, not a forgery; in "The Thief in the Night" (*Lowell Sun*, August 7, 1880) it is not the niece who opens the complicated safe, but her sleepwalking uncle; and in "Circumstantial Evidence" (*The Franklin Gazette*, September 2, 1881, and reprinted from the *Cincinnati Enquirer*) "pretty Miss Mollie McCann" did not steal $1,045 and a quantity of rare gold coins; rather, the guilty party is Miss Sabine Smith who raised the orphan Mollie as her daughter and hid the treasure in her attic while asleep.

Along with time and place, perverse circumstances also include the company one keeps. Given the strictures of 19th-century society, women were usually associated with a husband, father, uncle, nephew, cousin, brother, or female companion. In the world of detective stories this means the possibility of guilt by association. In "A Work-Woman's Misfortune" (*The New York Ledger*, July

3, 1869), a seamstress who supports her disabled brother is arrested because they rent the attic room above a gang of shoplifters and all in the apartment are arrested as accessories to the robbery. A lawyer, finding out that she does not even know why she is being detained, takes pity on her and seeks a judge in his chambers where the lawyer

> expressed [...] surprise that a woman should have been thus detained in a prison cell, for eight-and-forty hours, upon suspicion, without a hearing. He said it was not uncommon. There was a vast deal of crime transpiring constantly; and the innocent sometimes suffered with, or even *for*, the guilty.

Similarly, in "Tardy Justice" (*The Union Democrat*, Jan 8, 1856), Monsieur and Madame d'Anglade are arrested for living in the same building as the Count and Countess de Montgommeri. When the Count is robbed, they are detained and tortured. The title "Tardy Justice" seems particularly ironic, for although "A collection was made in the court for the benefit of the daughter of M. and Madame d'Anglade, which amounted to above a hundred thousand livres," Monsieur d'Anglade died four months after his arrival on the galleys and Madame d'Anglade while imprisoned "had a dangerous miscarriage" that "brought no amelioration to the rigor of her prison."

The Female of the Species Is Deadlier...

While the villain in "The Secret Cell" by William E. Burton (*Burton's Gentleman's Magazine*, September & October 1837), is a female, she does her dirty work by proxy: she employs men to enact her criminal scheme. Other than that, few female criminals appear in the earliest of detective stories published in America. The first notable female lawbreaker, however, made her mark, and in a big way. In "Mademoiselle Jabirouska" (*Holden's Dollar Magazine*, November 1848), a beautiful temptress and her duenna confederate lure men to her house to be murdered by assassins seeking bodies to sell to students of anatomy and heads to send to students of phrenology. The *Weekly Wisconsin* (December 6, 1848) appears to be the first to reprint the tale, but it certainly wasn't the last: it was widely printed and reprinted over the next forty years and appeared under a variety of titles, including: "A Strange Story from the French" (*The Democratic Press*, June 6, 1860); "The Bath of Blood" (*The Fort Wayne Sentinel*, March 23, 1874), "A Polish Princess' Appetite" (*Logansport Daily Star*, March 18, 1874), and "Twenty-Six Heads" (*Reno Evening Gazette*, June 5, 1888).

But "Mademoiselle Jabirouska" is an exception. Before 1860, those few stories with female characters in them feature them as victims or occasionally as accomplices of male criminals. Furthermore, those who are criminals are usually not violent. For example, a maid named Bridget purloins silver forks and spoons and a few other articles in "A Mysterious Manifestation" by N.T. Munroe (*Flag of our Union*, Oct 11, 1856) and Mrs. Y— trains her pet monkey Jocko to be a thief while she is suffering "under an attack of moral insanity":

> [...] the lady was accustomed to turn her pet loose in the summer evenings when the windows of neighboring houses were open, and after a short absence he invariably returned laden with precious things which were always deposited in the Japanese casket ["The Gramercy Park Mystery," *Weekly Argus and Democrat*, February 17, 1857].

The women "accomplices" are often unwitting accessories, more victims than co-conspirators: Jane Eccles, the sweet, humble, and hardworking "embroideress who adopted her sister's orphan child" is seduced into passing bad bills by a man feigning love and proffering marriage and is convicted and hanged shielding him, as she believes he is also an innocent deceived (*Leaves from the Diary of a Law-Clerk*, London: Brown, 1857). And some of these accessories are coerced into the role of accomplice, for example in "The Robbery of Plate" (*Flag of Our Union*, December 17, 1859) an abandoned wife remarries and is blackmailed into assisting her husband through his threat of exposing her bigamy; and in "Walnuts" the nurse who is caring for the captive father and son does so out of fear for her life from the vengeful Sir Charles Willoughby (*Flag of Our Union*, December 31, 1859). Occasionally, there is no crime involved at all, merely subterfuge, as when a brother and sister pose as runaway lovers to lead astray the detective and allow the true lovers to elope (see "The Double Elopement," *Daily Alta California*, November 27, 1859). The most ingenious of the earliest female accomplices though knew exactly what she was doing: in "The Mysterious Murder" a prostitute goes to visit her lover on the morning of his execution and passes to him though a kiss a vial of poison that allows him to cheat the gallows (*Schenectady Reflector*, April 5, 1850).

In the 1860s the women accomplices take a more active role, but still play mostly adjunct roles. For example, the wife in "'The Car Acquaintance:—Or,— The Two Bits of Paper,"

> afforded invaluable assistance by the ingenuity and adroitness with which she had secreted the stolen goods. The two thousand dollars—the fruits of the street robbery—were, with the exception of one hundred, found concealed in different parts of her clothing [*Ballou's Dollar Magazine*, August 1860].

Another receiver of stolen goods is the wife in "Eleven Thousand Pounds" (*Harper's Weekly*, February 1, 1868), whose pickpocket husband sends her his ill-gotten gains. On being apprehended before even opening the letter, she cries, "It's all up with us!" and the detective remarks to the man who had been robbed:

Ah, poor thing! poor thing! [...] there are generally women mixed up in this sort of thing. Money stolen in this sort of way is almost always sent to women. I suppose they think it is not so likely to be suspected.

Often female accomplices in these early tales are peripheral to the crime being investigated. Their offence is frequently in the form of attempting to aid or protect another or even just acknowledging the criminal behavior of their relatives. For example in the "The Sick Robber: And How Tim Cured Him" by Sylvanus Cobb, Jr. (*The New York Ledger*, August 9, 1858), a murderer's wife scares away visitors to their cabin by warning them her husband has smallpox; in "The English Highwayman" (*The Manitowoc Pilot*, December 23, 1859), the pretty barmaid sabotages the pistols of the victims of the highway robbers; and in "A Detective's Experience: A Female Forger" (*Bangor Daily Whig and Courier*, November 12, 1869), there is no female forger; rather a mother makes a false confession to allow her son time to escape and then dies an hour later, "She had perished by her own hand, from shame and a broken heart!"

Indeed, if you are male and want to escape justice, your best bet is to have a woman on your side. From the daughter pretending to have a cork leg to throw off the detective's pursuit of her father's friend in "The Cork Leg" (William E. Burton, *Burton's Gentleman's Magazine*, March 1838) to the governess who smuggles out the ill-gotten 30,000 pounds to the forger living as a shepherd in Argentina safe from extradition in "A Detective's Great Feat" (*The Fresno Republican*, October 1, 1881), women provide valuable assistance. And they do it in ingenious ways; for example in "Monday" (*Frank Leslie's Pleasant Hours*, February 1875) a forger's fiancée sends his dog to visit him in jail "with a tiny file hidden in his brown, curly coat" and in "The Widow Reed" (*The Star and Sentinel*, May 13, 1880), the widow helps dupe the detectives looking for counterfeiters by disguising them as her neighbor and her stout serving girl. In all of these cases the culprits get clear away. Although occasionally a mother or sister act as accomplices out of family loyalty, most female accomplices are wives or girlfriends. While some may act in the tradition of Eve-Jezebel, luring victims to be robbed or murdered, and others in the tradition of the mother-martyr, illegal or not their acts demonstrate one of two significant themes: (1) the power of women's love and self-sacrifice; and (2) the practicality and ingenuity of women under stress.

There are, however, a number of cases where the woman is the criminal, and her lover is either an accomplice or, more often, too weak-willed to oppose his wife. In fact in "The Black Satin Gown" by John Ross Dix (*Ballou's Dollar Monthly Magazine*, May 1, 1858) and "Hidden Crime Revealed" by Emerson Bennett (*The New York Ledger*, January 14, 1865), writers mention Lady Macbeth to help characterize the nature of their female criminals. Women servants come under the gaze of detectives both as persecuted innocents and as ungrateful fiends. Thus in "The Porcelain Button" (*The Fox Lake Gazette*, May 12, 1859) the servant girl Hannah employs her fiancé to kill her mistress and in "A Sympathetic Link" by A. Ehnenger De Friese (*The New York Ledger*, August 27, 1870) a domestic "whose honesty was not to be questioned" and her lover frame a beggar boy for their "most fiendish and diabolical scheme" to rob and possibly murder her employers.

Revenge killings by females can be found in American detective stories as far back as 1850 when a lady's maid murders her mistress ("The Mysterious Murder," *Schenectady Reflector*, April 5, 1850). But murders like this one are fairly rare. After Reconstruction a lot more women characters become murderers in detective stories, and their motive is overwhelmingly revenge. Indeed, after 1869 there was a serious uptick in this kind of women's crime. Take this list:

"The Mysterious Murder" (*Schenectady* Reflector, April 5, 1850);
"The Diamond Cross or, the Female Assassin" by Oliver Sinclair (*The New York Ledger*, August 2, 1856);
"Guilty or Not Guilty" by Eben E. Rexford (*The Prairie Farmer*, June 12, 1869);
"Murder Most Foul" (*The Sumter Watchman*, March 23, 1870);
"Bob Cheriot, Esq.; or, the Tragedy at Chelmsford" by Warren Walters (*Potter's American Monthly*, January 1877);
"Maria Vassar" (*The Indiana Progress*, August 30, 1877);
"Charming Madame Auvergne" by Frank H. Angier (*Ballou's Monthly Magazine*, January 1880);
"A Detective's Story: The Convict Coachman" (*The Indiana Weekly Messenger*, April 28, 1880);
"The Wronged Wife" (*The Bismark Tribune*, June 18, 1880);
"The Poisoner" by Johnson B. Turner (*Columbus Sunday Enquirer*, February 27, 1881);
"A Life's Lesson" (*Gleason's Monthly Companion*, December 1881);
"A Mysterious Murder" by James Maitland (*Suppressed Sensations, or Leaves from the Note Book of a Chicago Reporter*, Chicago: Rand McNally, 1879);
"A Wife's Crime" (*Fort Worth Daily Gazette*, January 24, 1883); and
"The Fatal Liaison" (*St. Paul Daily Globe*, December 22, 1889).

By the 1880s, jealousy becomes the primary motive for fictional females to murder—whether they murdered their rivals or the men who spurned them. Indeed, in the final tale listed, the wife solves all of her problems by killing her husband and framing his former lover.

A comparison of the crimes by females before and after the Civil War demonstrates a drastic shift in the crimes female characters commit, their motives, and their sole culpability. Prior to 1869 and the first of this new wave of stories, women mostly played the role of victims, but when they were the criminals they were rarely murderers. And when they did murder, jealously was not their prime motive. A survey of women's crimes in the stories before 1869 breaks down thus:

Forgery	2
Inheritance fraud	1
Theft	20
Hires abduction/murder	1
Lures to murder	1
Murder	11
Minor accomplice	7

Furthermore, if we take out the two early instances of murder-for-revenge in the 1850s, the remaining nine murders from that period break down as: seven murders for robbery, one infanticide of a child from a previous marriage, and one murder of an entire family with no motive given. In only three of these cases does the murderess act alone (the mother, the governess, and a seductress thief who drugs her dinner guests and then kills them with a small hammer). The crimes female characters commit after 1869 are distinctly different: after 1869 there are more of them, women commit murders by themselves, and overwhelmingly the motive for the murders has shifted from those associated with theft to romance-related revenge. Furthermore, two stories about women accomplices can be added to this list. "Written in Blood" (*The Herald,* February 5, 1882) concerns a woman who is connected to a murder motivated by lust and greed (her lover frames her husband of the murder of his uncle from whom they will inherit). And in "A Sister's Vengeance" (*The Isola Register,* April 2, 1880) a woman pretends to be her poisoned sister's ghost and haunts her brother-in-law until he composes a written confession she dictates.

This rise in the number and kind of murders committed by women in detective stories might be a response to the rise of the women's suffrage movement after the Civil War. That the rise of vengeful women stories can also be seen as reflecting post-war male anxiety over the rise of female power and the threat it posed. This is suggested by the authorship of the stories. While an increasing number of women wrote detective stories, all of those about women murderers with bylines were written by men. In addition, the role of women in these detective stories may have been inspired by an actual contemporary murder case: that of Adoniram/Andrew J. Burroughs by Mary Harris in 1865. From January through August of that year, the northern newspaper reading public was fascinated with the murder and trial and the letters-to-the-editor which followed. Papers such as the *Washington Intelligencer* and the *New York Times* reported in detail the case of 19-year-old Mary Harris, who came from Iowa to Washington, D.C., to vindicate her honor by shooting the recently-married-to-another 32-year-old Treasury Department clerk at his post. The March 4 issue of *Harper's Weekly* did an illustrated story on Mary Harris. The July 1 article from the *Washington Intelligencer* reporting on the impaneling of the jury included this description of Miss Harris: "The prisoner was tastefully attired in a black silk dress, and a tight-fitting coat or basque of the same material, trimmed with braid and beads; a black bonnet trimmed with straw, and were [sic] a black vail, which almost completely concealed her features. Her hair was worn in ringlets." And the four-page "FULL REPORT OF THE TRIAL" included a complete description of the closing arguments for the defense. The jury returned its verdict of not guilty after deliberating only five minutes, the jury agreeing with the expert witness, that the homicide was not motivated by "hatred or revenge," rather "the act of homicide was the act of an insane impulse." Mary Harris was not the first American to be acquitted using a temporary insanity plea—that honor goes to Senator Daniel Edgar Sickles for shooting his wife's lover in 1859—but it was the second. Furthermore, the *Crime Passionnel* defense of the Napoleonic code traditionally applied only to men—i.e., a husband was permitted to murder his unfaithful wife and her lover, but a wife was supposed to accept her adulterous husband. So in many ways the case was a game-changer, and one that did not end with the verdict—various magazines and newspapers attacked and supported the verdict, articles began with lead-ins like "it was the Mary Harris case over again," and both the murder and acquittal were listed in the "Chronicle of Noteworthy Occurrences for the Year" posted at year's end. Four years later, the *New York Times* reported in its Current Notes section of the paper that "The Washington *Star* reports that Mary Harris, who shot Adoniram J. Burroughs, a clerk in the Treasury Department, has been discharged from the Insane Asylum cured, and is now employed in the Philadelphia Post Office" (November 30, 1869) and in 1883 it reported her marriage to one of the lawyers on her defense team who, now 81, was over twice her age. But the point is that this celebrated case occupied the minds of the reading public—a public that was also reading detective fiction, perhaps in the same issue of the newspaper.

A final intriguing point of comparison of women's revenge stories concerns their conclusions. Only two of these women face the criminal justice system and only one serves her sentence: Maria Vassar was "condemned to death, but the sentence was commuted to imprisonment for life." Of the remaining women:

2 get away with the murder and give deathbed confessions
3 go insane
2 die before their trials (cause of death unknown)
6 commit suicide (one implied, found drowned)

Clearly 19th-century authors and readers want divine justice—they want female murderers to pay for their crimes, but they did not want the State to kill them. Historically, the sentencing to death of women prisoners is rare and the completion of these executions rarer still. While the sentencing statues in the American Colonies mimicked those of England's bloody code, as early as 1778, Thomas Jefferson introduced a bill to abolish the death penalty in Virginia except in cases of murder or treason; and by 1846 treason was the only crime for which one could executed in Michigan. In fiction, the gentler sex seemed to require a gentler death than public hanging, and like Mary Harris, depending upon how wronged they had been, should perhaps go free.

Professional Criminals

The few professional female criminals in detective fiction of the period fall into two categories: pre- and post–Civil War. Before the war there were relatively few women professional criminals. Of those few, most are apprehended. Of the relevant four antebellum stories that clearly feature women in other than ancillary criminal roles, one is a comedic piece about a family of criminals, narrated by the patriarch ("The Pet of the Law," *Harper's Weekly*, February 27, 1858); two are about Jezebel-esque women leading men to their deaths: "Mademoiselle Jabirouska" (*Holden's Dollar Magazine*, November 6, 1848) and "The Female Assassin" (*Prairie du Chien Patriot*, August 14, 1850); and the most original and interesting of these stories, "The Young Widow" (*Wisconsin Patriot*, December 3, 1859). This Vidocq-in-reverse tale tells the story of Madame Delauney, a widow of the Assistant Intendant of the French Police. Prior to his death, she had lived honestly, but poverty had since driven her to become a pickpocket—and one who capitalizes on the expertise of her husband, for "she had first learned the art of theft from her husband, who was accustomed to show her each new scheme of villainy that was revealed to him in his connection with the Paris police." "Beautiful and amiable," an American by birth, she has returned to New York City, and attends all the soirees to which "the elite of the city are invited"—and she attends them ingeniously dressed in widow's weeds with many secret pockets and a ring that had "had a spring diamond knife for a setting." Unfortunately for her, she is caught when she acquires an undercover detective's watch by cutting through his watch chain.

During the Civil War, even the fictional women appear to have been too busy to turn to crime (although a few turn to detecting) but after the war, there is a marked increase in the presence of women who are professional pickpockets, shoplifters, thieves, and practitioners of confidence tricks. They are forgers and members of gangs of robbers. Notably, they rely on the traditional 19th-century occupations for women to succeed at their non-traditional profession—they pose as maids, governesses, and seamstresses to inveigle their way into their victims' households. Unlike in antebellum fiction, after the war half of the women criminals in detective stories escape through their wit, beauty, or being underestimated. They often escape disguised as boys or as old women. As before the war, they continue to play the temptress, as in "The Detective" by Binnacle (*New York Fireside Companion*, June 29, 1869) when the beautiful, foreign lady-in-distress lures the detective into her carriage, only to turn him over to a "notorious gang." However, they also seem to find new distinctly feminine criminal activities, such as in "A Detective's Story" (*Valley Herald*, February 3, 1870). While this story focuses on a widow who cases a New York City department store for her confederates, when the police attempt to reclaim the stolen goods, they find that

> Mrs. Wilson had been the manageress of a baby institution, and derived large profit therefrom. How she obtained the children is and ever will be a mystery. Certain it is, that the police when they searched the house discovered several infants, and all the necessary appliances for many more. The nurse in charge (for the babies were well tended) implied that a great number had been sent away at various times, and the only probable solution of the strange matter was, that there existed in New York a class of people who were able and willing to pay heavy premiums to any person charitable enough to relieve them from the trouble of rearing their offspring.

The legality or illegality of managing a "baby institution" in New York in 1870 is questionable, as the first adoption law aimed at protecting children was the Adoption of Children Act passed in Massachusetts in 1851 and the orphan trains began in New York in 1854. The New York State Charities Aid Association was organized in 1872; however, it was not until 1898 that the state established a specialized child-placement program. Regardless, from a 21st-century standpoint, such a manageress, whether working within the letter of the law or not, is unsavory. She would have been a godsend, however, to the murderess in "The Detective Officer" who kills her baby from a previous marriage when the woman she was paying to care for it attempted to return it to her before emigrating to Australia, as the murderess has concealed her first marriage and motherhood from her new husband (*The New Monthly Magazine*, August 1857).

In the 1880s, the list of crimes with which women in detective stories are associated continues to grow and includes bootlegging, mesmerism, and arson. While this increase probably reflects the cultural interests and occurrences of the day, after 1885, by far the greatest number of female villains continues to be thieves. An overview of crimes committed by female characters in these stories breaks down thus:

Arson	1
Political conspiracy	1
Framing another for a crime	2
Murder	8 (2 as accomplices of their lovers—one of whom later kills her)
Miscellaneous	7
Theft	23

While the number of murders in the stories of the period is on the rise, and will become the major focus of mysteries in the 20th century, in the era just before the Sherlock Holmes stories arrive in America, women are interested in theft. Those murders that women do commit are still motived by jealousy and lust, or they play the accomplice to a greedy lover. Most interesting is that these robbers span the socio-economic spectrum, as well as the proficiency continuum. They are kleptomaniacs and shoplifters in the new emporiums; one runs up to men in train stations embracing them—and then shrieks at mistaking them for a loved one (while picking their pockets); another is an expert thief, accepted as the wealthiest, handsomest, and most respected woman in town; one is a captain of a gang of stagecoach robbers in Mexico; another is a wife of a lawyer and runs a ring of teenage boys who both rob and sell the goods for the woman they love; and yet another is a Russian countess who is the "head of a band of criminals which had long terrorized the region in the vicinity of Odessa" ("The Red Chest," *Freeborn County Standard*, September 17, 1890).

Female Detectives

A Historical Digression

The bulk of archival work concerning female detectives and the historic role of females in policing in general remains to be done. While women began serving as police matrons in the United States in 1854, mostly to search and care for female prisoners, the official story of women in law enforcement begins in the 20th century: when Lola Greene Baldwin joined the Portland Oregon Police Force in 1908 and when Alice Stebbin Wells joined the Los Angeles Police Department in 1910. However, in the private sector, the story begins earlier. The most famous early female detective is undoubtedly the Pinkerton operative, Kate Warne, who joined the agency in 1856 and is best known for being part of the team that helped foil the 1861 plot to assassinate president-elect Lincoln. The public's ambivalent attitude toward female detectives may be best expressed in this excerpt of a front-page untitled opinion piece that doubles as a death notice for Kate Warne:

> [...] it excites a very disagreeable feeling to think that a society of women exists in this country for the discovery of crimes, conspiracies and such things. The chief of this band was Mrs. Kate Warn, a native of N.Y. State, who lately died at Chicago. She was engaged in this business fifteen years ago, by Mr. Pinkerton, of the National Police Agency. She did good service for many years in watching, waylaying, exploring and detecting, especially on the critical occasion of President Lincoln's journey to Washington in 1861. In 1865 she was sent to New Orleans, as head of the Female Police Department there. The idea of a woman going about and groping among the rogueries of men in that way is terribly repulsive, and the life of such a woman must be very trying and exhaustive. Mrs. Warn died at the early age of 38. All things considered, this female spy system or detective system seems strangely at variance with the moral pretensions and genius of the American people [*The Wheeling Daily Intelligencer*, March 18, 1868].

As the article notes, Kate Warne is just "the chief of this band," but other notable 19th-century female private investigators include Pinkerton operatives Kitty Parker and Jennie Hughes, as well as Mrs. Ellen Peck. But even a cursory search of newspapers of the period reveals a host of lesser-known female detectives who are credited with recovering money and putting robbers and murderers behind bars: Mrs. Mahon, Mrs. McCann, Mrs. Mary J. Tompkins (who claimed to be "the only woman in the United States who keeps a detective agency"), Sadie Sevier, Miss Kale Mason, Nellie McPhearson, Mrs. Clara Therman, Luvena Mabry (whom the headline claims is the only female detective in the South and "A Very Charming Young Person"), Mrs. Johnson, Cora Munn, Mrs. Kirby, and Mrs. Mina Dykman and Emma Bottchers, sisters who are "the only female, detectives known in Minneapolis." A number of other articles cite unnamed detectives identified by the city in which they worked, such as a testimony given by "a female detective from Detroit." Similarly, there are a number of one- and two-line announcements, such as "They have female detectives on the Constantinople police force" (*Evening Star*, March 4, 1870); "There is a female detective on the Chicago police force" (*The True Northerner*, July 20, 1877), "The New York police force employs female detectives. They are great on a trail" (*The Wheeling Daily Intelligencer*, September 12, 1884), and "The Pittsburg law and order society employs female detectives" (*Pullman Herald*, March 30, 1889).

An often reprinted article cites a New York City superintendent of detectives claiming that

We don't employ women [...] because it is our firm conviction that women cannot be relied on. We have tried them and found them wonderfully quick at divining the source of a mysterious crime, patient in testing a plan for capturing a suspected person, and—yes, and uncommunicative. There is just one reason, and only one reason, why they are not to be trusted—no one can tell who has the most influence over them. Anyhow, we can't afford to take time risk of employing and being betrayed by them [*The Sun*, January 13, 1884].

Clearly, however, they did employ women. The private detectives mentioned above are often described in relation to their connection to police forces:

Mrs. Johnson, A FEMALE DETECTIVE of New York, at one time connected with the Chicago force [...] [*Omaha Daily Bee*, April 7, 1884];

"The first detective work I ever did," said Mrs. Tompkins, "was thirteen years ago [1875], when I worked up cases for Capt. John Irving, who was then inspector at police headquarters. I worked for him two years and then I started in business for myself" [*St. Paul Daily Globe*, October 28, 1888];

One smart female, whose services have been at certain times availed of by the New York police, is Mrs. Ellen Peck [*The World: Saturday Evening*, August 24, 1889];

and

Mrs. Mohan, formerly a Miss Keelan is THE CRACK WOMAN DETECTIVE of the Hub. [...] She had a sort of mania for detective work and was unhappy until she became associated with the Boston police [*The Gazette*, 1890].

By 1889, these women are described as "semi-detached," doing "occasional jobs for the police" in the often reprinted feature story, "Vidocq in Petticoats," which argues that "Inspector Byrnes owes some portion of his phenomenal success as rogue-catcher to the fact that he has not hesitated to employ women whenever he could do so to advantage, although all the traditions of the Central Office were opposed to them. Hardly a day passes without one or two of these female Hawkshaws calling on the big-mustached chief of the detective squad in the white marble building in Mulberry street" (*Sacramento Sunday Union*, September 1, 1889). While they performed services that required little detecting (such as searching female prisoners and serving subpoenas) they also went undercover as domestics to acquire evidence.

It should also be noted that a large number of women were employed in "female detective corps" in drygoods stores and emporiums to apprehend shoplifters. They went undercover for the state board of pharmacy to ensnare those selling drugs without a registered clerk. They worked as early as 1865 as female revenue searchers, and by 1874 when bustles became the fashion these customs officials found the garments a "convenient storehouse" to smuggle goods into the country (*National Republican*, May 2, 1874). And they worked as spotters on the streetcars and "special agents" on railway cars; "they watched the porters and they kept a lookout for the passengers as well," reporting, among other things, any use of "strong language" or attempt to defraud the company by Pullman car porters (*The River Press*, July 6, 1887).

So why was there a recognized need for this small but very real female presence in nascent age of modern law enforcement? The same reason that is given for fictional detectives: they can do things and go places that male detectives cannot. And they have honed skills (although usually termed "intuition") that our culture defines as feminine. In one article, Captain John S. Young, "for years the head of the detective police force of New York" is quoted as saying, "I would give five years of my life if I could tell all about a thief as quickly and as truthfully as a woman can tell about another woman" (*The New Bloomfield, Pa. Times*, September 3, 1878). The reporter goes on to claim that

> There was a great deal of force about Young's remark. Women have an instinct about womanly things, which is finer, more subtile [sic], and generally more sure than man's mere reason. They know each other; there is no glower about their relations; they discount each other; they can probe all the shams and subterfuges to which they resort; and were all criminals female, and did all crime concern only sentimental matters, would make by far the best detectives in the world; in fact, they would be the only detectives, worth calling so.

A dozen years later, in an interview with Inspector Byrnes, New York's "Hunter of Men," he expresses contempt for female detectives, but he also admits,

> Women will identify better than men. They are far more observing. If a man has any conversation with a woman she will remember everything about him, from the color of his eyes to the cut of his clothes. Under similar circumstances a man will say of a woman that she was nice or pretty, but he can't for the life of him describe her eyes hair and clothes. Yes, women will identify both men and women far better than men can. If a man attempts to defraud a woman in any way she will always remember him. Men won't [*The Evening World*, February 25, 1890].

Another article quotes "an old chief in the detective service" as saying that

> the Pinkertons have found, in their long experience in this business, that there are many cases in which the patient search, untiring energy, and almost fruitless sagacity of the most experienced detectives avail nothing while an experienced woman operative, with the use of a little tact and finesse, can readily ascertain the clew and proof desired [*Millheim Journal*, July 21, 1887].

And he supports this assertion with an example of a female detective who went undercover in society and then left town, never revealing her true identity; the example ends by his describing that the female detective "got the $8000 reward, in addition to her $4 per diem and expenses for the job, and I don't believe there is a man, or less clever woman, who could have worked up the case at all. She is in New Mexico now, and I understand she is successfully following her occupation." These real-life descriptions of the effectiveness and sagacity of female detectives are mirrored in the fiction of the day. For example, *The Female Detective* by Andrew Forrester (1864) relates the exploits of the first fictional professional female detective; its introduction outlines the need for female detectives, the most salient reasons being 1. female criminals, and 2. the fact that "in a very great many cases women detectives are those who can only be used to arrive at certain discoveries [...] the woman detective has far greater opportunities than a man of intimate watching, and of keeping her eyes upon matters near which a man could not conveniently play the eavesdropper" (London: Ward, Lock, and Tyler, 1864).

I Will Make Him a Helpmeet

Almost from the very first detective story published in America, female characters assist professional detectives in their search for truth and justice. As mentioned at the start of this chapter, in 1838 the detective in "The Secret Cell" sends his wife undercover to obtain information he could not otherwise gather. And then in "Mary Kingsford" from *Chambers'* "Recollections of a Police Officer" stories, Inspector Waters relies on his wife to recognize that the expensive brooch that had been recovered is not in fact a splendid emerald surrounded by brilliant diamonds but a paste replica (first published in America in *The International Monthly Magazine*, April 1851). Similarly, in "The Victory" (*Sioux County Herald*, June 8, 1876), Detective Lambert asks his wife to call on a suspect "on pretense of employing her to do some light washing, but in reality to look around and note anything that was unusual in her abode"; what his wife notices leads to a chain of discoveries that bring the murderer to justice and frees three falsely-accused men. It is telling that all three of these stories take place in England, where, according to the Metropolitan Women's Police Association, as late as 1922, a member of the House of Commons suggested that "Policemen's wives could do Women Police Work" when women officers were eliminated in a cost-saving measure.

But the informants are not just spouses. Waters from the *Recollections* series relies on a female informant, Sara Purdy, in "Flint Jackson" (*Tioga Eagle*, January 8, 1852) who is promised "the Queen's mercy would be extended" to her for her assistance and to whom he grants all the credit for the successful resolution of the case; and Detective Berton relies on Mag Dufries to lead him to the villain's hideout, and once he is captured Mag helps him escape despite being threatened with a pistol should she attempt any deceit or trickery in "Mag Dufries: or, The Lost Child" by Fred. Hunter (*Flag of Our Union*, March 31, 1855). The good guys also get assistance from women who are neither relatives nor women of suspicious character. "The Art Detective" (*Memphis Daily*

Appeal, May 9, 1869) describes a French woman who for several years sent the Paris police notes "in a carefully disguised female hand, pointing out certain malefactors, or indicating crimes which were contemplated or had been committed." Other women who aid in solving crimes are approached by the detectives. For instance in Wilkie Collins' "The Stolen Letter: A Lawyer's Story" (*Harper's New Monthly Magazine*, February 1855), the lawyer-hero acting as detective employs the aid of the head chambermaid where the blackmailer is staying, allowing him access to retrieve the incriminating letter. And in "Doctor D'Arsac," the second of the many "Unpublished Passages in the life of Vidocq, The French Minister of Police," Vidocq asks a fellow wedding guest to act as his spy after she recognizes a brooch on the bride as that belonging to a murdered woman (*Burton's Gentleman's Magazine*, October 1838).

Amateur Detectives

On December 10, 1856, one of the earliest tracings of detective work, the story "Treasure of Rampsinitus" derived from the writings of the ancient Greek historian Herodotus, was printed in Steubenville, Ohio's *True American*. In this tale, Egyptian King Rampsinitus "employed his daughter as the detective" and she figures out the mystery of the theft from the king's coffers. Men also depend on women in "Convicted but Innocent" (*Denton Journal*, September 20, 1873), where the lawyer's wife plays armchair detective, informing him that he has condemned an innocent man and presenting him with a much more plausible solution. However, being set on the trail of criminals by one's father or simply thinking through the solution is unusual; in the majority of the cases in which a woman takes on the role of amateur detective her motive is (1) revenge for a past wrong; (2) self-defense for a wrongful accusation; or (3) defense of a falsely accused loved one. For instance, in the revenge department there is Lucy Wagner's proclamation "He killed grandma for fear she should wake and call someone and he shall hang for it, if I can find him; and I'll never stop trying till I do" ("Betrayed by a Button," *The New York Ledger*, February 17, 1877). Similar vows are made by domestics attempting to clear their own names. Thus in "The Strange Discovery," perhaps the earliest example of a female detective, "Though absolved from all participation in the murder by the laws of her country, Julie was a girl of too much spirit to suffer the least shadow of guilt to hang around her, if by her unceasing endeavors she could bring the truth to light" (*Burton's Gentleman's Magazine*, January 1839); and in "Lost, Stolen or Strayed," the first-person narrator announces:

> I was no more individually suspected than any of my fellow servants; but I had a sturdy honesty of soul, and it galled me terribly to think my honesty should be suspected. I

frequently declared that I should never rest till the real thief was discovered; and, to say the truth, my restless and suspicious vigilance rendered me as good a detective as if I had been trained to the business [*The Columbia Spy*, June 30, 1859].

Some women become detectives to clear an accused family member, usually their lover/fiancé. For example, stories such as "Coming out of Exile; or the Diamond Bracelet Found" by Mrs. Henry Wood (*The Eclectic Magazine*, October 1858), "The Murder at Cedar Glen" by Amy Randolph (*The New York Ledger*, November 19, 1864), "Guilty or Not Guilty" by Eben E. Rexford (*The Prairie Farmer*, June 12, 1869), "The Girl Detective" (*The Allen County Democrat*, July 26, 1877), and "The Maimed Hand" (*The Allen County Democrat*, February 27, 1879) all involve women following up clues, searching crime scenes, or even going undercover to find evidence to save their beloveds. Unlike sensation novels or courtship narratives, these stories feature real detective work involving attention to detail and reasoning. In "The Maimed Hand," the thought process of the detective is revealed as the hero considers the button and bootmark upon which the old constable based his investigation:

> In a moment Ruth Hartly thought, as she examined the waistcoat, "If the button was torn off when the thief was climbing in at the window, how did it happen that it came from almost under the collar of the waistcoat?"
> She examined the thread that had fastened the button to the cloth, and she found that it had not loosened, but that the different stitches had all been broken through, so that great force must have been used. It had not dropped off; it had been torn away, and yet the waistcoat showed no sign of having been injured. Then she went out and compared the foot prints in the front and back garden.
> She saw that the distance between the footsteps in the front garden was greater than that between the marks in the ground in the back of the house, while the prints farthest apart were deepest.
> So she reached the conclusion: "There is no doubt that the same boots made the mark in both the front and back garden, but they must have been worn by different persons. He who made the marks in the background (those effected by the burglar) being the lighter man, so the less depression of the ground; and the shorter man, hence the shorter distance between the footsteps in the back ground.

The most daring and ingenious of detectives whose motive is exonerating a lover is Alice Warren in "A Story of Circumstantial Evidence" by L.H. Wells (*Sioux County Herald*, September 9, 1880): she tells him, "Harry, I believe you are innocent of this terrible crime, and it shall be the work of my life to see that your innocence is proven; it may be a long time before this can be done, but I know God will aid me in this holy work" before handing him a file and convincing him to escape; she then tracks down a gun made-to-order by the murderer to replicate the one owned by the man he framed. Again the plucky girlfriend, with ultimate faith in the innocence of her betrothed despite evidence and public opinion, vindicates her beloved so that they can wed, she can give up her life as a crime fighter, and they can live happily ever after.

Working Women

These traditional romantic and emotional motives may have been more acceptable to the reading public than a woman's need to support herself in a world in which few professions were open to her. However, making a living was the motive for most actual female detectives: 19th-century female professional detectives were in it for the money—and the money was considerable. Newspaper accounts of the day refer to rewards of $10,000 or more and one article cites female detective pay as "$8 a day and expenses, with a $2,000 bonus if she won" (*Pittsburg Dispatch*, February 27, 1890); in this same era, women factory workers earned on average a dollar a day. Additionally in Forrester's fictional *The Female Detective*, Mrs. Gladden repeatedly refers to detectives as inspired by the standard government reward of £100, as does Mrs. Paschal, the detective featured in *Revelations of a Lady Detective* by William Stephens Hayward (London: George Vickers, 1864), who also admits to following up cases for their posted rewards, even if the cases are not assigned to her.

Despite the publication of Forrester's and Hayward's collections of stories about female detectives published in England in the 1860s, the fame of Pinkerton operative Kate Warne, and the appearance of real female detectives in newspaper articles, female professional detectives did not appear in American fiction until late 1870s. In this, America was behind both English popular fiction and the American stage. From Richmond to Sacramento and from St. Paul to New Orleans audiences from 1860 onward watched plays featuring women detectives, including:

> *The Lady Detective*;
> *Plot And Passion; Or, The Female Detective*;
> *Minister of Police and the Female Detective*;
> *The Female Detective, or The Boathouse on the Lake*;
> *Baron Ludwig, or the Female Detective*; and
> *The Female Detective, or Women Against the World*.

Some of these are probably the same play as advertisements for them are often accompanied by such descriptors as "Lotta in six characters," "the thrilling drama made famous by Lotta," and "Miss Herring in 6 roles."

The first fictional female professional detectives began to appear in U.S.

periodicals in the late 1870s. In 1877 Leopold Davis introduced two female detectives in a short story in his *Strange Occurrences* (Boston: Published for the author, 1877). The narrator-detective introduces the woman he is about to install as an undercover agent:

> In the year in which this robbery took place, very little was yet known of female detectives; still there were only two women in the service,—one an elderly American lady; the other an intelligent young German girl of fine appearance and good address. The name of the last was Lisette Bremer. She was shrewd and reliable, and would be the very person to aid us in this matter.

Lisette is not the hero of the tale, but she provides valuable assistance, insinuating herself into the household in a manner the lead detective could not; and she is presented as a working person and her relationship to the case is purely professional. While Christine Erickson seeks vengeance for her father's murder in "Brought to Justice" by J. T. Hunter (*Sterling Standard*, June 3, 1886) she is also a deputized police officer. When Christine and her mother are left penniless after her detective father is murdered by a robber, she is enticed into the role of female detective by the "Chief." Although she found the title "female detective" "dreadful," she is persuaded to take up the offer, because "the compensation was liberal," and "for the sake of the support it afforded us," she "overruled my mother's objections and conquered [her] repugnance for the work"; for she recognizes that if she could "secure the reward offered, the money would buy us a tiny home [...], and with a roof of our own over our heads, I would defy want or care." Similarly in "The Missing Jewels" (*The Columbus Post*, September 6, 1882), Anne Bardulph, possibly the first fictional female private investigator, is tempted by the reward offered for the recovery of Mrs. Dorman's diamonds and goes undercover as her housekeeper. By the end of the tale, she has solved the mystery and has two men interested in her, but she turns down the proposal of the first saying "I have a profession now, and I must not wed one who knows nothing of the instincts and requirements of my calling" and instead begins a relationship with the detective who had accused her of being the accomplice of the robber. In "The Lost Lady" by Clarence M. Boutelle (*Frank Leslie's Popular Monthly*, August 1886), Lillie Grimshaw turns to detecting in the place of her brother, a former operative for the private detectives Craft & Quick, who is laid up with a broken leg. As they are both "L.E. Grimshaw," she can show up in his place and earn the desperately needed salary of $100 a month plus expenses.

In the most finely-crafted story about a female detective, "Personal to Mr. Gimblett" (*The Fort Wayne Gazette*, February 1, 1885, which credits the *London Truth*), a woman controls the entire investigation and at the end becomes a private detective. It begins as many innocent-accused stories, with Martha

Chale, a maid whose father had been on the force, employing the now-private detective Gimblett to clear her name. But here the similarity to the hackneyed tales end. In an era when it was still usual to have stories such as "Murdered Himself" (*Freeborn County Standard,* June 15, 1887), in which the author gives away the mystery in the title, "Personal To Mr. Gimblett" gets it right. The tone is playful, characters develop, and the plot twists. In the course of the story, Martha Chale plays both the client and the detective. Seemingly in the manner of the love romance the story ends with Mr. Gimblett's proposal, "Martha, if you will only consent [...] I'm older than you, but we're suited for one another in every way. We should run well in double harness, my dear, both in business and domestic life." But here, too, the story does not end with the typical pronouncement that they-lived-happily-ever-after with Martha's response to his kissing her hand: "For a moment Martha Chade's dark eyes flashed furiously, and she looked inclined to box his ears. But she finally didn't."

Female detectives of this era are often referred to as "spies" or in "secret service." Even in "Brought to Justice" by J.T. Hunter, the Chief of Police wishes to entrust to Christine "a delicate secret service." Similarly in "A Woman of Mystery," an odd journalistic piece that begins as if a news item but then metamorphoses into a first-person detective story, the woman of mystery is described thus:

> She is, in short, a detective; a female spy in the employ of the Police Commission of this city; hired to discover culprits whom the Central Office detectives are unable to detect; and many a man whom she has bewitched has poured unwittingly into her ear secrets connected with his business operations, or a story of some irregular proceedings, which have led to the detection and arrest of some of the most accomplished and shrewdest swindlers who have operated in the metropolis. She is and has been for several years the most successful and efficient detective in America [*St. Louis Globe-Democrat,* January 26, 1879].

In a precursor to the paranoia about and suspicion of Mormons that Arthur Conan Doyle will later capitalize on in "A Study in Scarlet," "A Mormon Way" by Belinda Belnheim (*Barnstable Patriot,* October 2, 1883) does not even reveal the object of the detective's investigation: the first-person narrator relates how their cook "whom we loved and whom we trusted so implicitly, was, during all the years she was in our house, the paid spy of a secret society." The family is not told why they were the object of surveillance but are assured that "there were hundreds of spies in every large city at the bidding of the society."

American readers also came across a number of stories in which females serve the French police in a variety of situations from capturing common criminals to high political intrigue. The most well-drawn spy is La Cocotte, who in 1862, is "the best female agent in the service," years after the story ends, the narrator tells us:

She is still an extremely handsome woman and the best female detective in the service. She no longer operates, in the zone of the fortifications, in low cabarets; but her undeniable ability is exercised in detecting political offenders. She has an ample income from the government. She moves in the best society; and among those with whom she mingles, none suspects that she is the one, who directs, under the minister, a large and important branch of the secret service, and in whose presence all should be extremely careful of what they say if they are not above suspicion ["The Bohemian's Story of 'La Silhouette'" by Edward Dusseault, *Ballou's Monthly Magazine*, June 1880].

"An Embarrassed Detective: A Story of the French Prefecture" (*St. Louis Globe-Democrat*, September 25, 1880) is a satire of the French system of policing at the end of which the chief of the service complains to the detective that he has been policing "in a whimsical fashion, each one on his own account, without instructions and without discipline" and he calls in the female detective upon whom he has been reporting and who has been reporting on him and announces: "Now take a good look at each other, and have the kindness whenever you meet in the future, to remember that both of you are in the police service."

On the opposite end of the seriousness spectrum, "Anastasie Jouvin" (*Frank Leslie's Pleasant Hours*, February 1884) deals with attempted regicide rather than humor. In the beginning of this tale, a teenage girl warns the tutor of Napoleon III's son to "get out at once" of the military cafe where they are breakfasting for it is not safe for the Prince Imperial; but the story does not follow through on this political plot: the majority of the tale focuses on the attempt to discover the identity of the girl, who is revealed at the end of the story to be "Mademoiselle Anastasie Jouvin, the chief of the female detective staff of Her Majesty the Empress." These stories and the women in them reflect long-standing Anglo-American attitudes toward the French police system, which reflected both repugnance and admiration, both fear of the intrusion of the secret police system put in place after the Revolution and envy of the fashions and style of the Second Empire.

In Britain and the United States, however, detective stories avoided politics and the roles of seductresses, schemers, plotters, and counter-plotters imposed on women in political intrigue fiction. In American (and British) detective fiction while males retain and even enhance their identity when they become detectives, women are forced to become something other than themselves in order to fulfill roles not related to being detectives but imposed on them by their superiors and by society. Thus like Lizette in Leopold Davis' story, they take on the roles of servants—maids and housekeepers usually. Just as much as beauty attracts notice and approval in 19th-century fiction, disguised as young boys and old women female detectives escape notice in the power dynamic of the period. In an era of elaborately gendered clothing and strict gender norms, female heroines especially rely on disguises. The female detective narrator in "Brought to Justice" by J.T. Hunter boards the train with two disguises: "one of which had often metamorphosed me into a bent old woman, and the other which I prayed heaven I might never be obliged to don—a suit which would fit a boy of just my size" (*Sterling Standard*, June 3, 1886). Realizing that she cannot thwart the desperate villain on her own and knowing that she must obtain aid without arousing the murderer's suspicion, the female detective dresses to evade notice: "When the train stopped and the other passengers left the coach, an (apparently) old lady, with snowy hair, spectacled, bent and leaning on a cane descended upon the opposite side."

Such disguises also allowed female criminals to go undetected, at least for a while. A number of female accomplices dress as young boys so they can protect their villainous husbands, one of whom when captured and commits suicide is viewed as "the bravest and prettiest criminal he had ever known" ("The Coiners of Kansas," *The Weekly Register*, November 10, 1880). More daring is the murderer who dresses as a man to obtain medical aid when her victim bites off her finger ("The Withered Hand" by Marah Crosse, *The Charleston Daily Supplement*, December 24, 1870). But again, an intriguing part of female disguises is when they interfere with justice—providing another avenue for women to escape their detective pursuers. And they do so in a wide variety of disguises, and often use multiple disguises, as various as a limping old lady who leaned on a gentleman's arm ("Major Truslow's Mistake" by Amy Randolph, *The New York Ledger*, March 18, 1871); a boy with a clubfoot and crutch ("The Diamond Cross" by Frank H. Angier, *Ballou's Monthly Magazine*, January 1876); and a double disguise—first as a mulatto messenger boy and then as an old man ("Foiled by a Woman," *Louisiana Capitolian*, April 24, 1880).

Disguise, in fact, is one of the few unique characteristics of women in detective fiction before the 1890s and the appearance of new female heroes like Loveday Brooke, Lady Molly, and Constance Dunlap. While writers developed and sometimes dwelled upon special attributes possessed by male heroes in detective stories—knowledge, acute perception, patience, close reasoning, physical courage, stamina, objectivity—most women in their stories have a limited repertoire of personal talents and gifts. Their tradecraft almost always resides in looking and listening. It's not that they do it better than men, it's because the principal virtues of female detectives lie in the facts that they can go where men cannot and that no one notices them. They also differ from male detectives in motivation. While men do become amateur detectives by accident and necessity, they become professional detectives because of vocation: they have or acquire a calling to be detectives for the sake of being detectives.

Females, however, become detectives because of necessity. And while it may sometimes be economic necessity, even that is linked to providing for a family or family member. Women in period stories do not become detectives out of a personal need or for individual satisfaction. They become detectives to serve the needs of others.

5

CRIME AND CRIMINALS

> At least two scholarly journals explained that this unhappy childhood was the reason he killed women in his basement for their skins. The words crazy and evil do not appear in either article—Thomas Harris, *The Silence of the Lambs*

Looking back, there was a lot written about crime and criminals in the 19th century. Some of the century's classics are about the subjects: *Les Misérables, Crime and Punishment,* and *Bleak House* all appeared between 1853 and 1866. But that is not all, not by a long shot. One cannot leave out Poe's fascination with crime in all of his prose, and there is a lot more. Whole schools of contemporary writers made their mark depicting crime and criminals. There were the "misery and mystery" works of Eugène Sue, copied in England by George W.M. Reynolds and in the U.S. by Ned Buntline and Poe's friend George Lippard. The Gothic fiction of writers like Monk Lewis can hardly exist without the larger-than-life criminal; the Newgate novels of Ainsworth and Bulwer-Lytton depend on legendary criminals like Spring-heeled Jack and Dick Turpin; and the sensation novels of Wilkie Collins, Ellen Wood, and Mary Elizabeth Braddon depend upon the anguish, misery, and suspense that attend criminal actions. And there is still more. The first stage melodrama, Thomas Holcroft's play *A Tale of Mystery* (1802), revolved around murder, and from then on crime became a fixture for most of the melodramas on the Victorian stage. Indeed, "crime plays" (dramatizations of actual crimes) became a subset of melodramas in the 1800s, beginning with *The Red Barn* (1828) which was based on the murder of Maria Marten that took place the year before the play's premiere. In Philadelphia, John Wilkes Booth played the role of Sergeant Sam in one of those crime plays, *Jonathan Bradford, or Murder on the Roadside* (1833), a drama that was part of the repertoire at Ford's Theater in Washington, D.C.

But 19th-century literature was hardly the first time literature touched on crime. Murder has always been an important subject. Eating the forbidden fruit was, after all, the First Crime. There is a good bit of carnage in Greek and Roman drama and without murder there would be no *Hamlet, Macbeth,* or *Othello*. The same holds true for mainstream Victorian writers who gave the world murderers like Eugene Aram, Old Rudge, and Jonas Chuzzlewit. Significantly, it didn't used to take a detective or even a judicial system to reveal and punish crimes. This is the case because traditional literature about crime wasn't much about society—it was about what crime does to one individual. Indeed, the psychology of the criminal was also one of the principal concerns of William Godwin's *Caleb Williams* (1794), a novel that is sometimes cited as one of the forerunners of the detective story.

At the same time that traditional literature, books and plays, increasingly turned to crime and criminals as subjects in the 19th century, the explosion of newspapers in Britain and the U.S. greatly expanded the number of people who read about crime and criminals. Fascination with crime has a long history in tract literature and in pamphlets released on the occasion of the most sensational crimes—and their punishments. In the 19th-century newspapers, especially in the U.S., secularized crime and criminals. Crime and criminals were not just pure sensation; they were news. What turned up in newspapers wasn't simply moral opprobrium or hearsay or legend, it was the coroner's report, police findings, or the daily testimony of lawyers and experts at the trial. To be sure this usually only happened in the case of crime in big cities—in the U.S. that meant New York, Philadelphia, and maybe Boston—but news of particularly horrific crimes or celebrity trials spread across the country to local papers anxious for anything to attract readers and fill space. Thus, for instance, there was the Parkman-Webster case at Harvard in 1849 that turned on dental evidence, and the case of John Rulloff in 1871 whose brain came to be preserved and exhibited at Cornell's medical school. These cases stayed in the public consciousness for years. Indeed, the Parkman-Webster case continued to be mentioned in American papers through 1890. Exposure in the new media offered readers a new view of crime and criminals; it was a view that focused on evidence and process rather than censure and admonition—except censure and admonition directed at the police. Additionally, in the U.S. geography gave newspaper readers a unique perspective about crime and criminals, in that, unlike Britain and France, the crimes and criminals they read about took place hundreds, even thousands of miles away, in an environment very much unlike their small towns in Minnesota or South Carolina or Arizona.

For a lot of readers, many of whom were only marginally literate by 21st-century standards, witnessing detailed and prolonged personal self-destruction featured in serious literature may have been too difficult, too depressing, too serious, and perhaps even too much about the human condition. And there was an alternative developing. The traditional way of dealing with crime and criminals wasn't entertainment—and it was also not in step with the new age of technology when efficiently figuring how something worked became as important as understanding why it worked. And it didn't fit with the gradual appearance of leisure. The new detective story developed new ways of dealing with crime and criminals designed as diversion rather than as admonition or censure or intellectual and spiritual contemplation. And most of those ways depended upon reducing attention devoted to the moral and psychological effects and emphasizing the routines of the detective.

A Digression on the Victims of Circumstance

Part of the difficulty with the study of detective stories, especially early ones, comes when one turns to character and characterization. There isn't much of the latter. It is one of the effects of the short-story form: a writer can't do a lot to draw a complex character in 2,000 to 5,000 words. But with detective stories, it's not just that. With detective characters what the hero does is more important than who he or she is; and with criminals it is not only that, but also that their principal function is to stay in the background until the end of the story. Simply put, plot trumps character. That was certainly the case in the earliest kind of detective story, the circumstantial evidence story. But the circumstantial evidence story added a third necessary character to the mix—the victim, but not the victim of the crime but the innocent victim of wrongly applied circumstantial evidence. And that was the first way writers turned readers' attention away from crime and criminals. They were not as important as the innocent victims of justice gone wrong, who became more important than the victim of the crime.

As seen in an earlier chapter, the first real stirrings of the detective story occurred in the circumstantial evidence story as it evolved at the beginning of the 19th century. While their numbers drop off in the 1870s, stories that rely upon the theme of threats resolved by providential justice (often with the giveaway titles "circumstantial evidence" or "murder will out") continue throughout the period. While period detective stories in general were not always about murder, circumstantial evidence stories usually were. They do not, however, focus on the victim of the crime (or the criminal) but concentrate on a person who is falsely accused and sometimes wrongly convicted and executed and the evidence that leads to the injustice. Circumstantial evidence stories, therefore, presented striking examples of the cruelty of laws, the frailty of human judgments, and absence of reason and compassion on the part of those who enforced the laws. But explicitly or implicitly, they also justified the ways of God to readers by providing the solution to the crime (from offstage in the beginning), by including the characterization of those who suffer false accusation and by focusing on those who save them.

About suffering, the Job story comes first. Suffering tests and demonstrates faith. It became the mainstay of most forms of popular Victorian fiction. As Dickens knew, in 19th-century society, after women and children few could less deserve to be behind fortune's eight-ball than virtuous working people. It's something detective story writers also knew quite well, too. Take Eugene Aubrey in "Not a Ghost Story," for example:

> [...] the person accused of the atrocious deed, was a young artisan of hitherto unblemished character, and the only child and sole support of his widowed mother [*The New York Ledger*, July 17, 1869].

But it is not usually men, it's honest but defenseless women who are in the wrong place at the wrong time:

> The girl's name is Sybil Clarke, some nineteen years of age, and said to be very beautiful. I have not seen her yet. She is an artificial flower maker and being all alone here, occupied a furnished room on Crosby Street—a not unusual style of living among girls of her class ["The Silver Arrow," *The Lebanon Advertiser*, July 6, 1864].

The suffering of innocents, moreover, does not only apply to working-class folks. Gents get arrested and accused, too. In "The Detective's Story" (*The Richwood Gazette*, October 1, 1874), the pig-headed authorities accuse "This young man, Ellis by name, [who] was really a very fine fellow, with an unspotted reputation." And often, accusing a member of the "respectable" class shows pretty clearly to everyone but the authorities that something is seriously amiss. It's bowdlerized tragedy: if gentlemen get thrown in the cells for things they didn't do, it can happen to you, too.

Bringing with it the black-and-white aesthetic of contrast, another way to pull on readers' emotions was to demonstrate that suffering can also interrupt prosperity and celebration. A lot of 19th-century detective writers knew this, and jailing lovers on the eve of their weddings became a favorite pattern in the creation of accused innocents. After his arrest, Tom May's fiancée says:

> Oh, surely this be some terrible dream, for which we shall all wake, ere long—a dark mystery, but God's hand holds the clew! ["The Murder at Cedar Glen" by Amy Randolph, *The New York Ledger*, November 19, 1864].

And then there is calamity as the result of behavior. Sometimes momentarily letting things slip can bring an otherwise worthy and upright person to court on a murder charge. In "Second Sight," wrath begets the circumstantial evidence:

[Tom] Sanders, after one of these quarrels, had been heard to threaten that he would be revenged, that it was better the old brute should go to his own place, than live to torture the girl—words which might have been uttered in the heat of passion, but to which the subsequent event gave terrible significance [*The Detroit Free Press*, December 14, 1863].

With Edward Carson, in "The Lawyer's Story" (*The New York Ledger*, April 5, 1862), dice and drink put him in a fix: "I could see that he had been dissipated, and that his generous and social qualities had led him into excess."

Readers accept the innocence of these characters in part because they suffer—thereby expressing humanity unavailable in evil characters. Readers also accept their innocence because they look innocent in a world where looks counted and because narrators all but tell readers that guilt lies elsewhere. Thus the cases of Charles Ashcroft and Harvey Johnson:

Charles Ashcroft, a young man of five and twenty—intelligent and handsome—and about the last man in the world one would have selected as a murderer ["Convicted but Innocent," *Denton Journal*, September 20, 1873];

and

Harvey Johnston is arrested on suspicion of having committed the deed; but I know him to be innocent! ["My First Brief," *Leaves from the Notebook of a New York Detective*, New York: Dick & Fitzgerald, 1865].

When these kinds of stories appeared, they focused on the responses of the person falsely accused of the crime. Thus in a piece titled "Circumstantial Evidence," with his dying fiancée in his arms, the accused hero paints himself as a Byronic hero:

The world—the uncharitable world—they who believe me a murderer, and have tortured the most innocent actions into proofs of deliberate villainy, will not hesitate to brand you a victim of a cold-blooded felon. And why should I fly? To live a wretched wanderer, with the brand of Cain on my forehead, and a character stamped with infamy? [*The Illinois Free Trader*, November 27, 1840].

Even after American short detective fiction leaned more toward evidence-centered stories, suffering innocents continued to appear in pieces set on the Continent. Thus "A Case of Circumstantial Evidence," set in France ends with a depiction of a priest ruined by false accusation and conviction:

When this unfortunate man was declared innocent and set at liberty, his bishop offered to restore him his clerical faculties, and even to give him charge of a parish. But, although grateful for the kindness, he could not be prevailed upon again to take upon himself the duties of his calling. He said that the twenty-five years' residence at the *bains* had been such a pollution to his very soul, and that his body was so weakened and his whole nervous system so overset, that he was not fit to resume his functions. At the representation of the bishop, an allowance of £20 a year was made to him by the Government and he retired to the small town where I met him, and where, after living for many years a most holy life, he died in peace six or seven years ago. The French people have a sort of instinctive horror of any and every person—whether innocent or guilty—that has ever been connected with the *bains*, and this was the reason why they would not answer me about Pere Francois until they knew me better. I question whether any one ever suffered more from false circumstantial evidence than did this poor priest [*Daily Gazette*, July 17, 1869].

As if readers actually needed to be told how to respond to suffering innocents in circumstantial evidence stories, the writer tells them what to do at the end of "A Case of Circumstantial Evidence":

Let the sympathetic reader now endeavor to form some conception of the transport of Lewis on having saved his friend. Let him figure to himself the joy of George, when the painful consciousness of an atrocious crime was thus removed from his bosom! He was unanimously declared innocent of the murder; his passion cost him two months imprisonment, and it was long before the tears ceased to flow for his departed friend [*Eaton Democrat*, May 10, 1855].

Even in the first half of the 19th century, however, some writers recognized that detective stories could or should do more than depend upon the suffering of innocents for their impetus. Poe definitively knew this and miniaturized the circumstantial evidence elements in his stories: it's easy to overlook LeBon in "The Murders in the Rue Morgue" because he appears in name only, and the jack-in-the box in "Thou Art the Man!" tends to erase readers' memories of Pennifeather's persecution. In a sample of 133 murder stories from 1859 to 1879, only 35 percent of them use the suffering innocent character of the circumstantial evidence story as the motive for the detective's actions. From the mid–1850s writers began to fashion circumstantial-evidence plots that substituted a seemingly intractable problem for the falsely accused innocent, or found other kinds of plots centered on crime and detection. Thus stories based on evidence, on chases, on cyphers, on disguises, on capers, on escapes from danger, and even on heroes' mistakes appeared in newspaper and magazine fiction from then on. But they all needed crimes and criminals to showcase the character and abilities of their detective heroes.

Reading the Crimes: The Oldest Sins, the Newest Kind of Ways

In England and the United States the huge increase in wealth brought about by the Industrial Revolution and global trade lay at the core of a lot of what went on in the 19th century. While some have always had more wealth than others, now the haves not only had a lot more, there were also a lot more things to be had, an array of things that Dickens classed as "portable property."

Silver and gold plate, Kimberly diamonds, gold from Australia and then Sutter's Mill, paintings, silks: the wealthy bought and displayed all that they bought. And there was money, paper money floating around, issued by private banks until 1844 in England and until 1863 in the U.S. when their governments established central banks with uniform paper currency. As ever, there were also people anxious and able to relieve other people and institutions of their money and possessions. There were more people gathered in one place as American cities expanded during the century—more pockets, more purses, and more shops selling more things. And the 19th century presented new opportunities for criminals. Counterfeiting and banks and safe cracking quite obviously couldn't exist before paper money and safes—both were 19th-century novelties. It was also easier to get away with murder: the test for arsenic poisoning wasn't successfully used in court until the LeFarge case in 1840. We should note here, however, that some crimes never appear in period detective fiction. Graft, political corruption, corporate fraud—most of the subjects taken up by the Muckrakers—were taboo. The assassination of two presidents during the period had no effect on detective fiction. There was only desultory mention of slavery and the Civil War. Race crime and lynching associated with race scarcely came up—although lynching does occur in stories in which race was not a factor. Rape, even in euphemistic references, was very rare and other sex crimes were entirely ignored. While criminals often "look like" criminals in detective stories, the notion of there being a criminal class was a non-starter as were crimes against minorities and immigrants. Detective stories were mostly about a kinder, gentler world than the real one.

And it was not all about murder. For 21st-century readers, "mystery" and "murder" are nearly synonymous. But this was not the case in 19th-century detective fiction. Throughout the century, stories about other crimes consistently number twice as many as those about murder. Even when one generously includes in the "murder" stories those which are about attempted murder, suicides-faked as murder, and theft-gone-wrong murders, and those in which the detective reveals no murder actually occurred, these stories are doubly outnumbered by stories about theft, robbery, embezzlement, fraud, shoplifting, pickpockets, arson, kidnapping, extortion, smuggling, counterfeiting, escaped criminals, burglary, blackmail, forgery, gambling, moonshining, spies, confidence games, and inheritance cheats.

Stand and Deliver

Highwaymen were among the first hero-villains to be featured in English and French crime literature. They had their share of space in the various editions of the Newgate Calendars, and in Ainsworth and in Bulwer-Lytton. In name at least their heirs and assigns appeared in imported detective stories printed in the U.S., stories like "The Mysterious Highwayman" (*The Louisiana Democrat*, April 27, 1870) and "The Scourge of the Highway" (*The New York Ledger*, December 23, 1876). In the opening paragraph of "The Fashionable Highwayman," in fact, the writer tips his or her hat to Dick Turpin *et al.*:

> Perhaps no other country in the world had so much romance connected with its highway robberies, as England during the last century; and notwithstanding that the penalty for this daring crime was death by the hangman, there were never wanting bold knights of the road, ever ready to demand a purse and take the chances of ending their lives by the rope [*The New York Ledger*, December 24, 1864].

In America, however, especially in the West, "old knights of the road" lost all of their panache. They became thugs:

> At this time Mountain Kentucky was in a state of anarchy. Law and order were but little regarded, and the woods were filled with armed men engaged in those terrible family feuds which have made the dark and bloody ground famous. It was the famous rendezvous, too, for a much worse class of criminals. Thieves and counterfeiters made their headquarters among the wild gorges and deep forests from which they emerged, at frequent intervals, to prey on the fatness of the rich-grass country but a few miles distant. Robberies were of frequent occurrence, and stolen horses and cattle were stampeded out of the low country by the hundred head. They would be secreted here until the hue and cry was over, and then conveyed across the Ohio river and sold. It was known to the authorities that the desperadoes were well organized, and all efforts to break up the gang were fruitless ["The Romance of Cracker's Neck," *The Bee*, June 10, 1882].

In 19th-century detective fiction, highwayman becomes "highwaymen," plural; they are assemblages of bad men who do bad things without bothering about stealth or deception. Everyone knows who they are, and the character of their leader defines the gang:

> The occurrence created a great excitement in San Francisco. Robberies and murders were, at that time, by no means unfrequent, and it was known that an organized gang, composed in great part of escaped Australian convicts, was burrowed among the sand-hills of the neighborhood, and most of the nightly burglaries and outrages were attributed to its members. This gang was under the leadership of one James Stuart, a desperate scoundrel, whose name was a terror throughout the entire State; and many crimes had been fixed upon him, and, among others, the murder of the sheriff of Yuba County. By his great skill and finesse, however, Stuart had always succeeded in eluding the search of both the regularly-constituted police, and the sharper, more lynx-eyed detectives of the Vigilance Committee ["A Case of Mistaken Identity," *The Galaxy*, February 1868].

Rampaging Australians compose the gang back in their own country, too, in "In the Bush" (*The New York Ledger*, May 7, 1870). But America had its own home-grown thugs who popped up across the country. Thus this sample:

"A Detective's Adventure" (*Daily Evening Bulletin*, July 30, 1881) takes place in Texas;
"The Murders at Sunset Canyon" (*Harper's Weekly*, August 18, 1866) takes place in California;
"Robbers' Roost" (*White Cloud Kansas Chief*, January 25, 1872) takes place in Mississippi; and
"The Romance of Cracker's Neck" (*The Bee*, June 10, 1882) takes place in Kentucky.

In the most sensation-oriented and youth-oriented publications gangs also terrorize Eastern cities, as in "'Earless Bill' the Detective" (*New York Fireside Companion*, February 14, 1870). Unlike other period detective stories, however, in stories about gangs, citizens and communities do not need a "lynx-eyed" hero, they need a detective with bravery, cunning, and endurance. But gangs of robbers did not pose the greatest problem to contemporary detective heroes. Gangs of counterfeiters did.

Shoving the Queer

Before there was paper money to copy, there was coining, which goes back to antiquity. Tracing those who made fake coins had its brush with greatness when Isaac Newton was Warden of the Royal Mint and personally led the investigation and prosecution of William Chaloner who struck as many as 30,000 counterfeit guineas. Once there was paper money it was easier to make a lot of dishonest dollars than it was striking bogus coins out of base metal. In the U.S. before 1863 one estimate reckons that one third of the paper currency in circulation was counterfeit. It should also be noted that that currency was issued by private banks, a major percentage of which were as unsound as the currency. After a national currency was established in 1863, the federal government moved to pursue counterfeiters and it authorized U.S. Marshals to hire "special" detectives to do the work. It comes as no surprise, then, that counterfeiting became a popular crime in the detective stories of the 1860s. Hence this sample from the 1860s:

"A Detective Taken In" (*The New York Ledger*, May 25, 1861);
"The Coiners" (*Ballou's Dollar Monthly Magazine*, September 1862);
"The Counterfeit Detective" (*The Puget Sound Herald*, February 20, 1862);
"A Detective's Story" (*Continental Monthly*, October 1863);
"The Trap" (*Strange Stories of a Detective; or, Curiosities of Crime*, New York: Dick & Fitzgerald, 1863);

"Breaking up a Gang: A Detective's Story" (*The New York Ledger*, February 4, 1865);
"The Last Crime" (*Eau Claire Free Press*, October 12, 1865);
"The Tell-Tale Eye" (*Flag of Our Union*, January 20, 1866);
"A Possible Case of Circumstantial Evidence" (*Frank Leslie's Illustrated Newspaper*, April 6, 1867);
"The Counterfeit Bill" (*The New York Ledger*, August 10, 1867); and
"A Den of Phantoms" (*Santa Fe Weekly Gazette*, October 17, 1868)

In a number of ways, counterfeiting differs from the other crimes that fictional detectives solve. First, it involves two distinct stages, making and then passing the fakes. They are made in one place and distributed in another: "The first important matter, according to my view, was to trace some of these notes to the first circulators, and then lay some plan to get into their confidence, and gradually work my way back to the principals" ("Breaking Up a Gang," *The New York Ledger*, February 4, 1865). Frequently this meant travel. In "A Detective Taken In" (*The New York Ledger*, May 25, 1861), for example, the hero crosses the border and detects in Canada.

Counterfeiting also requires equipment and technical skill. Writers don't bother much about this beyond brief mentions of presses and plates. Ned Buntline's "The Last Crime" gives readers more details than most:

> They had presses at work, and were printing off, signing, numbering, and cutting from the sheets vast numbers of counterfeit United States notes of various denominations, from fifty cent currency stamps up to Treasury notes of large amounts.
> Silently, steadily they worked on, those four dark and desperate looking men, each at a different process, but all working together, for hours.
> At last one who had been scrutinizing each bill carefully, putting the signatures on all which passed his critical eye, and destroying those which he deemed imperfect, gave a signal, and the other three at once ceased their work, and came to the table where he was seated [*Eau Claire Free Press*, October 12, 1865].

In this connection, however, it is worth noting that "The Detective's Story" (*The Daily Kennebec Journal*, November 8, 1872) does bring the innovation of photography into the story. Unlike other detective story crimes, counterfeiting is a crime against institutions not individuals—in England, in fact, counterfeiters were charged with treason. Indeed, writers often begin their stories by citing their heroes' corporate employers:

> In that other time of which I have spoken the business community of New England was startled by the appearance of new and dangerous counterfeit bank notes. They came, no one could tell whence; but they came in great quantities; and ere long nearly every trader in the country had suffered in the possession of one or more of these promises-to-pay. The flood of counterfeits increased as the weeks passed on, and so nicely executed were they

that people began to lose their confidence in all kinds of bank paper ["A Detective Taken In," *The New York Ledger*, May 25, 1861];

and

> Some years ago, it matters not how many, several of the leading banks of the country, located in Boston, New York, and Philadelphia, made a startling discovery at the same time, not only that an immense number of counterfeit issues of their respective institutions had been suddenly put in circulation, but that they were so perfectly executed as to have deceived, in many instances, the officers themselves. This alarming state of affairs led to the conclusion that there must be a large organization of the most adroit scoundrels at work in concert, which would require all the detective skill in the country to ferret out and suppress; and every man of any note in this line of business was forthwith called upon to act, my humble self among that number ["Breaking Up a Gang," *The New York Ledger*, February 4, 1865].

Counterfeiting in period detective fiction is not typically an urban crime. Counterfeiters have inaccessible hideouts and funny money comes from out-of-the-way places:

> About ten years ago I was especially detailed from headquarters at Washington to proceed to a small town on the New England coast, where it was suspected a gang of coiners were at work. It was an out-of-the-way place, little more than a fishing village, and though now taken in by a branch railway, at the time of which I write the only means of reaching it was by a stage from the nearest town of any importance, which was fifteen miles distant ["The Buried Bullet: A Detective's Story," *Newark Union*, November 1, 1879].

The remote locale contributes to the nature of the plot as well as to the actions of the detective, who needs to depend on travel, disguise, and impersonation more than searching for clues and studying suspects. Unlike many other crimes, counterfeiting involves more than one person. In the argot of the detective story, counterfeiting involves gangs. Before cattle rustlers and before organized city crime, writers focused on gangs of counterfeiters. While creating passable false coins or bills and developing a network for distributing them would seem a practice calling for expertise and finesse, such is not the case in period detective fiction. It's done by gangs composed of professional criminals, dangerous professional criminals among whose number inevitably resides a villain who has had contact with the detective. The threat of exposure always brings with it a physical threat. Because they involve discovering and exposing groups of criminals, counterfeiting stories typically also involve corporate law enforcement—usually a posse or a police force—to corral all of the criminals at the end of the adventure.

A Nation of Shopkeepers

For those inclined to be felons in the 19th century, cities and towns provided easier pickings than skulking about on highways and byways. Robberies of city shops and warehouses formed part of the conversation of the first cadre of real detectives when they sat around with Charles Dickens telling him about the job. Thus

> It's just about six years ago, now, since information was given at Scotland Yard of there being extensive robberies of lawns and silks going on, at some wholesale houses in the City. Directions were given for the business being looked into; and Straw, and Fendall, and me—we were all in it.

This excerpt from Dickens' "Detective Police Party" appeared in *Household Words* on July 7, 1850. Three months later, on October 5, 1850, it appeared in the *Brooklyn Eagle*. But it wasn't just professional burglars who plagued retail establishments; employees could illicitly dip into the till. Employers had to keep an eye on them, and they became the first suspects:

> "Now, lads," said I, "as soon as you have got through with R—'s affair, I have another job for you, which will amuse you on evenings. Bartons, of Broadway, suspect some of their clerks of robbing them, so you must watch them at night when they quit the warehouse, and see how they amuse themselves" ["The Confidential Clerk," *Strange Stories of a Detective; or the Curiosities of Crime*, New York: Dick & Fitzgerald, 1863].

And sometimes employees were more than suspects, like the boss' son in "The Costly Kiss: A New York Detective's Experience" (*Harper's New Monthly Magazine*, April 1859). In addition to being targets of embezzlers (those in a position of trust who misappropriate funds), stores, shops, and warehouses were susceptible to night-time burglaries:

> Mr. Amos Smithers was a jeweler; his shop had been broken open the night before and now was holding a consultation with Detective Drake, who was examining into the matter with an eye to every detail of the robbery ["The Matched Button," *Gleason's Monthly Companion*, September, 1879].

As in England, shops big and small became targets for a variety of robbers, thieves, and burglars in the U.S. Indeed the large new emporiums where customers were allowed to touch the merchandise gave rise to new types of crime that became featured in detective stories after the late 1860s:

> New York at this time was infested by a gang of rogues who had introduced a new system of shop-lifting, and had successfully victimized many of the larger storekeepers in the city. As their course of action was entirely fresh, a new name had to be invented for them, and they were christened "sneak" thieves by the police, from the cunning way in which they effected their depredations and the difficulty experienced in detecting them. ["A Detective Story," *Sacramento Daily Union*, April 9, 1870].

Professional shoplifters became occasional culprits in period detective stories. There is "Crazy Sal," "shoplifter and confidence woman" who "has had a place in the 'Rogues Gallery' for several years" in "Why I Became a Detective"

(*Daily Alta Californian*, January 6, 1873), and the suspect in "A Detective's Story":

> [...] I escorted her to the police head-quarters, where she was searched, and all the missing property found upon her, and she at last confessed she was a noted French shoplifter" [*Gleason's Monthly Companion*, January 1879].

As with burglars, shoplifters were often professional thieves, known to the police whose task it was to catch them in the act or to find them and the evidence needed to convict them. Stories about them, as well as those about larcenous clerks, often do not turn on the theft of money, but on the theft of goods, goods that reflect the values of the second half of the 19th century. Thus stories like "The Stolen Silks: A Detective's Story" (*Daily Bulletin*, August 24, 1867) and "Stolen Laces" (*The Ledger*, December 7, 1888), as well as those about jewels and plate discussed below, reflect the kind of conspicuous consumption that moved Twain and Warner to call the end of the 19th century the "Gilded Age."

That's Where the Money Is

Nineteenth-century banks were not quite the places that criminal legend Willie Sutton robbed in the 1930s. Banks were relatively new parts of daily life in the 19th century, and they went through a lot of growing pains between 1800 and 1900. Up to mid-century banks were privately owned and depended solely on the judgment and responsibility of the owners. They were also subject to the vagaries of international finance and the periodic financial panics that occurred almost every twenty years during the period. Bank failures were not unusual occurrences, nor were depositors' and investors' runs on banks. These realities drove the plot in a few detective stories:

> Her husband at one had time lost a considerable amount by the breaking of a bank, and since then no one could persuade her to have anything to do with any bank ["The Porcelain Button," *Fox Lake Gazette*, May 12, 1859];

and

> The fears of the depositors had been excited by certain conduct of the missing man, which seemed at the time to point directly toward bankruptcy; and their promptness in seeking legal remedies proceeded from their convictions that the apparently prosperous banking-house was coming down with a crash on the heads of its depositors ["The Great Seymour Square Mystery," *Flag of our Union*, Oct 17, 1868].

The image of the masked robbers terrorizing bank patrons and tellers, made familiar by 20th-century films, had no relevance to detective-story writers in the 19th century—neither did that of the cracksman or safe-cracker lighting a fuse, given that TNT and dynamite were not invented until the mid–1860s. In most of the 19th century, the means of safeguarding valuables were rudimentary: modern locks with keys did not come about until the inventions of Chubb and Yale, and combination locks and time locks did not appear until after mid-century. Thus, in "Told by a Detective," the veteran detective narrator observes that

> In those days the banks were poorly equipped compared to the inventions now in use. Not one of the four had a time lock, and, instead of chiseled-steel vaults, they had big safes set in recesses or brick vaults, bank burglars could get into any safe in three or four hours [*Boston Weekly Globe*, June 9, 1889].

Even after mid-century, many banks depended on strongboxes or key-operated safes, and many of those safes were on wheels:

> That night, about twelve o'clock, I was coming up my beat, when I saw four men pushing a small safe along the streets. It was an extraordinary sight, and I suppose they expected that the very boldness of the act would be their greatest protection. It was a clear, starlight night, and every one of their movements was perfectly plain to me, I recognized the safe, at a glance, as the property of Messrs. Cuttworth & Co., and I was confident that these men were engaged in a daring robbery ["The Fatal Safe," *Flag of Our Union*, Aug 25, 1866].

While early detective fiction frequently has something to do with banks, stories that revolve around banks as physical entities are less numerous than stories about bank practices, bank staff, or bank customers. An early exception to this is "The Bank Vault" (*The New York Ledger*, August 22, 1857), in which the robber tunnels into the bank. Another example is "On a Field of Azure a Silver Star" which begins with a detailed description of how a bank vault was burgled by a professional:

> The bank had been entered between the hours of six p.m. and six a.m., evidently by a regular cracksman. The outer door leading into the hall had an ordinary triple bolt-lock, the catch operating on three steel bolts running at different sections of the door into closely fitting grooves. The lock had been tampered with but had not yielded. The sawing in two of the bolts was assayed, and the marks indicated, but had been abandoned as a bad job. Then the iron casing into which they ran had been drilled near the bolts and a saw inserted in the holes. The bolts had thus been reached, wrenched back, and an entrance effected.
> I traced the robber from this door to the inner vault-room door, a thick oak door, studded with beads, and heavily locked. This had been forced by a chisel applied so as to loosen the hinges, and the robber—for it was apparent there was but one—found himself in the same room where I now sat with the president.
> Here a door having a Yale lock led into the vaults. This had been tampered with; but singular to relate, the audacious robber had picked away the plastering and laths for two feet above the door of the vault, and had lifted himself over the heavy plate-iron roof of the vault. Here he had drilled holes at irregular points through the sheet iron, and then with a chisel had cut a hole through, and dropped into the vault, with only the door of the burglar proof safe between him and his expected booty [*Warren Ledger*, August 30, 1878].

Rather than focus on banks as places with safes and cash drawers to be stealthily opened by professionals, however, a majority of bank-related detective fiction concentrates either on what banks do or on the people who work in them. Lost, stolen, or strayed mortgage payments offer writers opportunities to rend hearts, as in "Seven Up," in which detectives track down sharpers who cheated a youth out of his family's payments:

> I know it, mother. All these years we have toiled to pay off that mortgage left on the farm at my father's death, and now it has all come to nothing. Sit down in your chair, mother, and I will tell you the truth, as I trust I have ever done. I do not fear your blame, as I have always loved your praise. This one egregious error has taught me great lessons already. They say women can bear troubles better than men [*Hartford Courant*, April 25, 1863].

In addition to safeguarding valuables and lending money, as noted above, banks played a major role in many period counterfeiting stories. Since they were the ones to take the financial hit from the passing of bad bills, banks were major employers of detectives in fiction and in life—indeed, Allan Pinkerton's first case was arresting counterfeiters. After counterfeiting, which was a crime perpetrated by gangs, forgery and forgers were a crime and a type of criminal character that occur with regularity in stories of crime, especially English stories of crime. The criminal in "Jules Ingram, or a Race Down the St. Lawrence,"

> was an accomplished penman, scholar, and bookkeeper, thoroughly conversant with business details, and had so mastered the secret of the postal system, that he could operate by proxy, and ubiquitously. He was believed now to be dwelling on the frontier; and the bankers of all the Atlantic cities had subscribed funds for his apprehension and conviction at whatever cost [*Rockland County Journal*, December 24, 1864].

And it was in part professional criminals like this who caused bankers to hire detectives to chase them down, arrest them, and bring them back. There are, of course, other ways that signing a name can be a criminal act: writing checks without funds to cover them. Check "kiting" may be as old as checks. Thus

> He might have given those checks in confidence of selling those bonds, and placing the bonds to his account. In due course, these checks, which were crossed, would have been brought to the clearing house, and have been presented on the morrow. But it seemed his creditor had some mistrust of him, and caused the check to be demanded out of due course ["An Uninvited Guest," *Defiance Democrat*, December 18, 1873].

Those with the most opportunity to dip into banks' tills, however, were bank employees. Bankers were well aware of this and, like other 19th-century businesses, took measures to ensure the honesty of their employees—they spied on them:

> There is a very amusing story told of a bank president who used to have his clerks watched by a detective after office hours, so that he could keep himself properly posted as to any fact which might render any one of them liable to appropriate funds belonging to the bank. He

had hauled up several clerks about their improper and extravagant expenditures, and was, as the story goes, sitting in his private office waiting the appearance of the new assistant teller, Ferdinand Algernon Vere de Vere, who had been duly shadowed and reported on by Operative P.Q., of Judas & Gehazi's secret service ["The Banker's Clerk," *The Long Island Traveler*, September 30, 1881].

Bank presidents, cashiers, clerks, and tellers were among the popular characters in early detective fiction. While a president is discovered with his hand in the till in "The Bank Vault" (*The New York Ledger*, August 22, 1857), writers usually treat chief executives—and bosses in general—as responsible, even compassionate community leaders. Not so with watchmen, cashiers, clerks, and tellers: they are the usual suspects when the books don't tally or a bum check gets cashed. Echoing the circumstantial evidence story pattern, these occupations theoretically give characters the opportunity to commit crimes because they handle money, and when it's discovered that they have assets above their station, things look bad for them. Part of the detective's discovery in these stories is to uncover the source of these assets—which is often explained by extra hard work and penury in order to support a widowed mother or to build a marriage nest-egg to impress a fiancée's father. In these sentiment-tinged stories the detective's job is both to save the innocent and to uncover the real villain, the one driven by the motives of greed or revenge as opposed to those of sacrifice and love. In "How Linton Bank Was Robbed," a bankteller is made a scapegoat because the villain desires

> the daughter of President Goodnow, and knowing that John Earnest was the young lady's favorite he planned and carried out a scheme to steal the money in such a way that suspicion would rest upon the young teller, and through the disgrace thus produced the attachment between the couple would be broken off [*Semi-Weekly Bourbon News*, October 1883].

Portable Property

There were more things to covet and to steal, rob, or burgle than banks' assets—and a lot of them were easier to acquire illegally. Gold was always in fashion, and so was silver; sheets of both were hammered into plates, platters, tureens, and other dining and serving pieces which came generically to be known as "plate." A well-to-do family could accumulate a considerable weight of dining and serving pieces. And they had to be both displayed and kept safe. The bother of having and safeguarding the family's plate comes out in "My Wife's Maid":

> Both my wife and myself had inherited a large amount of bulky family plate, and besides this useless metal, which never came out of the safe, I had several costly services presented on the occasion of our marriage, three large salvers, etc., testimonials from societies which I had been an active member, to say nothing of a complete and varied assortment of small articles in silver and gold [*The Stevens Point Journal*, March 28, 1874].

It was the kind of thing crooks went after in stories such as "The Robbery of Plate" by Harry Harewood Leech (*Flag of Our Union*, December 17, 1859), and "Who Stole the Plate?" by Andrew Forrester, Jr. (*The Revelations of a Private Detective*, London: Ward and Lock, 1863).

Jewels were also tempting targets for thieves and burglars. Unlike plate which had some utility, the only purpose of jewelry was ostentation. Jewels got top billing in stories such as "The Missing Jewels" (*The Columbus Post*, September 6, 1882) and "A Detective's Experience: The Missing Jewels" (*McKean Miner*, February 3, 1870). But it wasn't just any kind of jewels—it was diamonds. After mid-century they became a writer's best friend. Here, for example, is a sampling of diamond detective story titles from the 1880s:

"The Diamond Necklace" 1881;
"The O'Shaughnessy Diamonds" 1882;
"The Romance of a Diamond" 1883;
"The Diamonds of the Duke de B." 1884;
"Cape Diamonds" 1884;
"Dolly's Diamonds" 1886;
"The Great Diamond Robbery" 1888; and
"The Bride's Diamond" 1889.

In practical terms, diamonds became *de rigueur* after Queen Victoria received the Koh-i-Noor diamond in 1849 and then after the discovery of South African diamond fields in 1869. But in literary terms diamonds got their big boost from Wilkie Collins in 1868:

> "Those who have read the 'Moonstone,'" said Mr. F., "will remember how the experience of Sergeant Cuff was set at naught by the eccentricities of a dreamer. My own life furnishes an episode somewhat similar to it, but with this difference: The party most interested here was guilty of meditated wrong, while there the effect of the imagination and great anxiety united to confound the experience of the great London detective" ["A Detective's Experience: The Missing Jewels," *McKean County Miner*, February 3, 1870].

The other objects that got a lot of play in 19th-century detective stories were wills, documents with signatures of the testator and witnesses. They are stolen, hidden, lost, and forged. At first it was lawyers who discovered that a member of the family did the stealing, hiding, losing, or forging. And then detectives took over.

Murder

Beginning in the 1920s, if the subject were detective stories, then murder was the natural place to start the discussion. The notion that detective stories had to be about murder was in fact codified in 1928 in S.S. Van Dine's "rules" for writing detective stories. Demonstrably, however, such was not the case when detective stories began. As noted above, stories about other crimes outnumbered stories about murder in detective stories published in the U.S. throughout the 19th century at a rate of approximately 2 to 1. It wasn't that 19th-century America lacked examples of horrific crimes that could have served as models for make-believe detectives to solve. Lizzie Borden was a novice when compared to other 19th-century criminals: Lydia Sherman poisoned three of her husbands and seven of her children; Sarah Jane Robinson poisoned almost all of her relatives; the "Bloody Benders" killed at least ten people in Kansas; and the Harper Brothers murdered as many as 40 people in Tennessee and Kentucky. These crimes and criminals stayed in the public consciousness for years. Amateur historians continue to track down details of old crimes and criminals like these, details of which seem attractive beginnings for detective stories, especially to those conditioned by modern detective novels. It's what Poe thought, and after the success of "The Murders in the Rue Morgue" he turned to real crime. But his attempt to convert the death of Mary Rogers into fiction ran into problems as facts came to light and "The Mystery of Marie Roget" did not turn out well. Indeed, in "The Mystery of Marie Roget" Poe failed to find the middle ground between objective reporting and lurid sensationalism that was essential to the development of the detective story.

Finding that middle ground when the subject was murder was not simple. It was a lot easier to create detective stories around counterfeiting and burglary than around murder. Readers, after all, react differently to the loss of a jewel in a debutant's tiara in a distant city than to the murder of someone in his or her own bedroom. Property crimes need a lot less sanitizing than murder to make them agreeable and popular fiction. And that goes double for crimes against institutions like banks and the government. When the subject was murder, the 19th-century detective story writer's principal task lay in finding how to lessen the effect of an atrocious action without minimizing the significance of the crime.

One of the ways of reducing the effect of violent death on their readers lay in downplaying the importance of the victims in stories. As noted above, one principal way writers did this was to concentrate on the wrongly accused innocent. In this respect, the speed of the short story helped too: in the typical detective story murder comes up very early, gets only brief mention in the narrative, and then the readers' attention is directed to the detective's actions. Besides that, readers do not get a chance to know the characters who are victims—victims usually get a sentence or two of identifying description, rarely more. It is a very atypical period detective story that encourages readers to consider the meaning or the effect of the victim's death on those in the world of the story. Sentiment belonged to other kinds of fiction, not detective fiction. It's one of the reasons that in some stories victims don't even have names: they have generic labels indicating gender (which is usually male) and profession (jewelers seem to have a high mortality rate). Numbers, if used strategically, ironically can also dilute the effect of death. Stories about detectives sometimes deal with the murder of anonymous victims. Thus at the beginning of the second Guillot story, "The Guest Chamber of the Inn at St. Ives," the sub-agent gives the detective this background:

> Certainly not; have I not facts to deal with? Supposing, M. Guillot, that half-a-dozen dead bodies were to be found in a certain neighborhood in rapid succession, and under very suspicious circumstances—would it not be a fair conclusion that there had been foul play somewhere? [*Ballou's Dollar Monthly Magazine,* December 1859].

The only things that make these six people important lie in the fact that they are dead and that that fact magnifies the problem and consequently enhances the success of the detective. To lessen the effect of death, writers also sometimes linked the deceased with antisocial behavior. Misers especially do not fare well in detective fiction. The title character in "The Murder of the Miser" (*The Ohio Democrat,* November 28, 1873) doesn't even have a last name. And those standing in the way of true love (usually fathers) don't invite much sympathy from readers either. Misers, their hoards, and bad dads, are, of course, extreme cases. Bad dads lack love and represent social prejudice based on income and class, and misers stand for an extreme of the possession of wealth. Writers often used those extremes to minimize the effect of their death on readers. There is also flagrant ageism in 19th-century detective stories. It's not surprising to find victims like these in detective fiction of the period: Old Jake Adams, Old John Ryder, Old Pigot, Old Jeffrey, Old Lispenard, and Old Logan. Most don't even get two names. Sometimes writers let readers know how advanced the ages of victims are—some are even as old as sixty: Moses Parker, the dead man in "The Apothecary's Compound" (*The New York Ledger,* July 21, 1866) is "a man past three score"; "A Detective's Sketch" (*New York Fireside Companion,* August 3, 1869) has Mr. Thomas Seymour "a man of about sixty years of age"; and in "A Post Mortem Discovery" (*The New York Ledger,* October 23, 1869) a "man of about sixty, named Ebenezer Varney" dies a suspicious death. Departed characters full of years have less of an effect on readers than those who die in or before their prime—and not many of that kind of character die in detective stories of the period. But writers found additional ways of obscuring the reality of violent death.

Lethal Weapons

One of the hallmarks of the modern detective story is the demonstration that there are countless ways to take human life: indeed inventing and detailing a new and ingenious way to kill people has been a requisite in a certain type of 20th-century detective story. That was not the case in the 19th century. Writers had far more limited options: at first it was death by edged weapons, hatchets and axes, firearms, blunt instruments, or strangulation, and later in the century it was by poison and infernal machines. Interest in forensics notwithstanding, it is not unusual to find period stories centered on murder that make no mention of how the victim met his or her untimely end. Late in the period the appearance of poison, infernal machines, and medical novelties marked an accelerated interest in crime scenes and forensics, but that, too, was yet another way to remove attention from the victim as a human being and emphasize the victim as an anatomy lesson.

As detective stories developed, the way an individual met his or her end became far more important than the life or identity of the victim. Analysis of 133 stories about murder published between 1859 and 1879 yields the following ways murderers used to kill their victims:

Edged weapons: 50
Blunt instruments: 26
Firearms: 14
Poison: 12
Axes/hatchets: 8
Suffocation: 7
Other or unspecified: 16

There were a lot of sharp things readily available back then: kitchen cutlery, cooking and butchering knives, straight razors, pocket knives, daggers, Bowie knives, paper knives, scalpels, oyster knives, bayonets. Knives were popular. Many trades had specialized knives, and during the Civil War most photos of enlisted soldiers show them with a gruesome blade in their belts. In taverns and in streets, knife fights became the low-rent 19th-century version of the gentleman's duel. The present danger to life and limb moved some state legislatures to pass laws restricting the ownership of large knives, especially after the War. Writers who chose edged weapons as murder weapons had a lot of choices available. And from a story-teller's point of view, knives provided objects that all listeners understood—they didn't ask for the kind of elaboration necessary with poison, or even firearms. Providing even a perfunctory description of the knives used in fictional murders is very rare in period detective stories. Most simply state that the murder was committed with a knife. The same thing can be said for other forms of inflicting untimely death. Wanting the kind of examination of minutiae spotlighted in the Sherlock Holmes stories, clubs are just clubs, axes are just axes, and strangulation is just strangulation. The same holds true of firearms. While gun makers Colt and Smith and Wesson were well-known during the period and a lot of people owned different kinds of guns, in detective stories firearms usually get the same generic treatment given to knives. In "The Invisible Crime," for example, the only mention of the lethal weapon is the following:

> That the deceased, Edward Stanton, came to his death by a wound inflicted by a pistol ball, willfully fired by some person unknown, and that said person is guilty of murder in the first degree [*Daily Alta Californian*, October 29, 1871].

While there were a lot of them around, until 1857 firearms were relatively inconvenient. Before Smith and Wesson introduced the self-contained metallic cartridge in 1857, to fire a pistol or long gun one needed to load the bullet, loose powder and wadding and then position a percussion cap. A knife, club, or rock was a lot more convenient for a murderer and for a writer.

Just as modern crime fiction often emphasizes the shocking reality of violent death with detailed descriptions of crime scenes and autopsies, 19th-century detective and crime fiction sought to avoid them. While the knives were the most popular means of murder, scarcely a drop is shed of the ten pints of blood bodies contain—except on the murderer's clothes as the way Providence exposes homicides. Even the occasional macabre story about so-called "resurrectionists" which includes body snatching in the detective's investigations scarcely even mentions the disinterred body (see "The Pen Knife Blade," *The New York Ledger*, February 16, 1867). Most detective stories during the 19th century get the details of violent death out of the way as quickly as possible. Here is a sample of typical crime scenes:

> Mrs. Weldon must have been asleep when the deed was done. She was described discovered hanging half out of bed with her throat cut in a frightful manner ["The Porcelain Button," *Fox Lake Gazette*, May 12, 1859];

> The young man was lying before the fireplace quite dead. His throat was cut in a fearful manner. Some of his hair which had evidently been pulled out by the roots, lay scattered about the room ["The Knotted Handkerchief" by Percy Garrett, *Ballou's Dollar Monthly Magazine*, July, 1862];

> His partner and companion had been murdered and robbed, and he himself had been slightly cut across the face and gashed on the left arm, and he was all excitement, lamenting his dearest friend, and vowing vengeance against the assassin ["The Murderer's Ordeal" by Emerson Bennett, *The New York Ledger*, August 10, 1861];

> The body had been found just on the inside of the front door, and directly at the foot of the stairs. A single glance was sufficient to see that the bloody deed had been accomplished by the aid of the "Bowie" or some other similar sharp-cutting instrument ["A Detective's Yarn," *The Golden Era*, October 19, 1862];

and

> The body of the man had been found under such circumstances as to leave no doubt that he met his death by lawless violence ["A Defence [sic] without Evidence," *The New York Ledger*, September 15, 1866].

This was the kind of thing anyone in a Victorian household could read or turn a blind eye toward without too much indignation—even grandmother, mother, maiden aunt, and children. Whether it came from (1) the conventions of the time; or (2) the drive to be accepted and widely read by a hyper-sensitive reading public; or (3) the desire to concentrate on the character and actions of the detective; or (4) all three, minimizing and neutralizing the character of the victim and the means of his or her destruction was the making of the detective story.

Who's Got the Mark of Cain?

When it comes to criminals in traditional literature, a few writers made them rebels or romantic heroes, but most either wanted to terrify their readers by creating soulless monsters or wanted to frighten and enlighten them by showing a character's tragic self-destruction—thus villains were either motiveless monsters like Iago or conscience-wracked average people like Macbeth. In the 19th century maybe Dostoevsky wanted to probe the consciousness of the criminal, but most detective-story writers really didn't want to. What they wanted to do was to showcase the detective's discovery and capture of a hitherto unidentified individual. They wanted to focus on answering the question of who rather than dwelling on the answer to the problem of why people do wicked things.

Discovering who did (or didn't) do it formed the foundations of the newer kind of detective story that evolved during the 19th century. The other kind of story depended not on identifying an unknown but finding a villain whose identity was known. But the detective's job was a lot more complicated when the second kind of story emerged in the early 19th century. Wanting voice prints, retinal scans, DNA, fingerprints, or even photographs, the detective's job was not easy. Before Inspector Byrnes' *Professional Criminals of America* (1886) and the systematic photographing of criminals, the only way for law enforcement agencies of fiction and fact to identify them was with verbal descriptions, a routine that appears so frequently that it is simply taken for granted in many early detective stories: heroes depended on verbal descriptions of their quarry from Vidocq onward. As dubious as it seems today, narrator-detectives had faith in those descriptions. Criminals did, too. And since detective and criminal knew one another, disguise was a common motif in early detective stories. Indeed sometimes in the pseudo-biographical notebook stories, readers find that the criminal wears a disguise to avoid capture and the detective also wears a disguise to mask his identity as a thief-taker. In these kinds of stories the central object for the detective (and the reader) is to locate and unmask the villain rather than discovering his or her motive. In fact, in some period detective stories disguise takes on a life of its own, particularly when it comes to cross-dressing. By the middle of the century men dressing as women and women dressing as men became a popular detective story gambit. Using the villain's cross-dressing as the detective's discovery and as the story's surprise became a feature in a certain type of story, as in "Resting Powders" (*The New York Ledger*, September 28, 1861), in which a long-lost heir poses as a female nurse and administers poison in order to gain an inheritance. More commonly, however, cross-dressing added elements of comedy or farce that had the potential to change the tone of the detective's story. This can be seen in stories such as

"Hunt on the Highway" (*The Kenosha Telegraph*, September 6, 1860);
"The Golden Haired Wig" (*Strange Stories of a Detective; or, Curiosities of Crime*, New York: Dick & Fitzgerald, 1863);
"The Jewel Thief" (*The New York Ledger*, August 13, 1864);
"Romance of a Railway Carriage" (*Engineer's Monthly Journal*, January 1870); and
"Our New Pupil" by Hester Bittersweet (*Ballou's Monthly Magazine*, November 1870).

Comic disguise and cross-dressing, in fact, became such a cliché that a piece made the rounds of newspapers in the U.S. and abroad in which a woman and a man are traveling together in a railway carriage and each asks the other to avert his/her eyes and so that they can change clothes. The man transforms into a woman and the woman transforms into "Detective J— of Scotland Yard" ("A Detective's Story," *Fort Wayne Sentinel*, December 8, 1880).

The disguised-detective plot often centered on finding known, professional criminals. But finding an unknown criminal—sorting out the innocent from the guilty—was often a different kind of story. It depended on finding and judging evidence as well as finding and judging people. In the 19th century a few briefly prominent people (Gall, Lavater, and Lombroso) tried to simplify judging people's character by trying to make it into a science. Looking at the bumps on heads was phrenology's answer to the enigma of human behavior—

based on the belief that development of certain parts of the brain (representing different aspects of personality and deportment) produced discernable changes in the shape of one's skull. Describing, and therefore defining, a character by means of phrenology does occur in period detective fiction, but not very frequently. In the following pieces the pseudo-science only gets passing mention:

> His head was large—very large—the frontal region being of uncommon fullness, and the upper portion, where phrenologists locate Firmness and Reverence, was remarkably high. The top of his head was entirely bald, and the skin had a thin, smooth, transparent look, as though the skull beneath had swelled almost to bursting it ["The Mad Philosopher," *The New York Ledger*, September 19, 1868];

and

> The lady's attendant was a dark, compact, muscular-looking man, with a hard square face and massive features. His forehead was specially noticeable. It was high enough, and very wide, but retreating; being particularly prominent just over the eyes, where phrenologists place the perceptives. The countenance of the man was an intellectual, but, on the whole, not an altogether agreeable one somehow. As John used to say, "It had one expression too many" ["Saved by a Detective," *The Star and Sentinel*, August 5, 1878].

There is, however, one story in which phrenology plays a headline role. In "Mademoiselle Jabirouska: The Modern Messalina," which was also published as "Twenty-Six Heads":

> The woman whom he had encountered in his travels served as a lure for the young men who were abducted. These unfortunates, after having been enticed to their ruin by this modern Messalina, who appears to have been a sort of monomaniac in the indulgence of her passions, were delivered over to the assassins, who, having put them to death, separated the head from the body. The latter was sold to the students of anatomy while the head, having been prepared and embalmed, was valuable at that time in Germany, in the pursuit of a science which has since become somewhat fashionable—we allude to the science of which Gall and Spurzheim were the principal propagators [*Holden's Dollar Magazine*, November 6, 1848].

Unlike phrenology, the pseudo-science of physiognomy held that character could be predicted not by bumps but by facial characteristics. It is all over 19th-century detective fiction. Innocent people look innocent and evildoers look like evildoers. One way writers used phrenology was to have characters couple it with their skills as detectives. Thus

> I was always fond of the science of physiognomy. From my youth up, I was noted for my proclivity for reading the character of a man from his face; and I finally became such an adept in the art, that I could occasionally guess the very thoughts of the individual whose countenance I was studying ["The Murderer's Ordeal" by Emerson Bennett, *The New York Ledger*, August 10, 1861];

> Well, gentlemen, I shall begin at once; I should like to go through your warehouse, and take a look at your assistants. I am something of a physiognomist, and can tell a thief almost as soon as I look at him. ["The Confidential Clerk" *Strange Stories of a Detective; or, Curiosities of Crime*, New York: Dick & Fitzgerald, 1863];

5. Crime and Criminals

and

> I certainly had no occasion at that time to suspect him of having been concerned in the robbery; but my long acquaintance with villains of every grade, and my natural aptness in reading physiognomies, led me to think to myself that I had never met a man who had more natural qualifications for a rascal than he had ["The Resurrectionist" by Sylvanus Cobb, Jr., *The New York Ledger*, June 30, 1866].

Even when the detectives don't fashion themselves as experts, physiognomy comes in to a lot of stories. Some of them supply readers with lengthy passages of applied physiognomy ("The Apothecary's Compound" [*The New York Ledger*, July 21, 1866] devotes over 400 words to a complete physiognomical analysis of Luther McVauglin). Most commonly, however, writers get by with a lot less. It is not uncommon, whether literally or implicitly connected with physiognomy, to find brief descriptions of faces that telegraph characters' innocence or guilt:

> The expression of anxiety detracted somewhat from her beauty, and as I looked upon her now, seeing her face in a different light, I was struck with a sort of snake-like cast which was perceptible in the whole character of her features ["Hunt on the Highway," *The Kenosha Telegraph*, September 6, 1860];

> His eye changed expression, and brightened, and emitted a strange and peculiar gleam; and my attention being thus directed to his eye, I now bethought me that I had never seen one exactly like it—one capable of being to apparently open down to the soul while concealing so much. It was off its guard now—the door was really open down to the soul of the man—and I looked in at that door, that opening, *and saw that the soul of that man was a dark one* ["The Murderer's Ordeal" by Emerson Bennett, *The New York Ledger*, August 10, 1861];

and

> His features were regular, but there was an expression about his mouth which I did not admire. His moustache hid the entire upper lip, but what I could see of the under lip made me shudder. There was such a blending of scorn and contempt about his mouth, though it appeared to me that he tried to wear a continual smile, which I almost invariably found polished villains to assume as a mask to hide the workings of their scheming brains and bad hearts. His eyes were deep set, and of that cold steel-blue shade that men of cool, calculating temperaments generally have ["Our Cabin Passenger" by Mary C. Young, *The New York Ledger*, September 8, 1866].

Even if some characters are so steeped in evil as to be able to hide their villainy until the end of the narrative, it comes out at the accusation or the trial:

> At first the young man's face flushed scarlet red, but only for an instant, for the color disappeared as suddenly as the flash of midnight lightening, and then a ghastly pallor overspread his features, which seemed to shrink, and collapse, as I remembered to have seen those of the miserable victims of Asiatic cholera, whom I had encountered in the hospitals of New Orleans.

> A tremor as of ague seized upon him—his lips moved, but no articulation proceeded from them ["The White Perfumery Bottle" by Dr. S. Compton Smith, *The New York Ledger*, October 13, 1860];
>
> Had a thunderbolt struck the guilty wretch, he could not have fallen more suddenly to the ground. He was not hardened in crime; and this abrupt accusation of murder overcame him ["The Horse Detective" by Dr. S. Compton Smith, *The New York Ledger*, March 30, 1861];

and

> I never saw, before nor since, a face express so much terrified amazement as his did at that moment. All color forsook it, every lineament quivered, and, clutching his throat convulsively, he rather gulped out than articulated ["Murder Will Out" by Emerson Bennett, *The New York Ledger*, December 4, 1864].

In a not-too-subtle manner, writers' use of phrenology in 19th-century detective fiction ultimately connects with the belief in a providential universe and the faith that murder will out—in secular terms, it is a conviction that justice will prevail because of (or even in spite of) a system of laws and with the help of a gifted hero. In a sense, recognizing a villain by his or her appearance comes from the same system of belief as falling in love at first sight. In the world of detective fiction all of this means that one kind of stories is not really about discovering who committed the crime because that was written on the villain's face and deportment; instead they are about finding sufficient evidence to prove that that person did it. And that was important.

But literary antecedents existed that showed a very different approach to crime—works that concentrated on the difference between appearance and reality and that a person, as in *Hamlet*, could actually "smile and smile and be a villain" a "remorseless, treacherous, lecherous, kindless villain." So in the middle of the century detective stories appeared which reflected skepticism about judging a character according to his or her looks. Such skepticism, for example, comes up in "The Porcelain Button":

> I found a good looking girl about twenty-two years of age. The countenance was an open one, but there was an expression of deceit about her lips which I did not like. I haven't much faith in physiognomy, so I put it down for as much as it was worth [*Fox Lake Gazette*, May 12, 1859].

By the late 1860s in some stories like "The Devitt Will Case," the superficial categories of physiognomy have become dated obstacles to solving crime:

> "God forbid," I said, gravely, "that we should ever begin to portion out punishment by the lines of the countenance. It's too slippery an index, sir" [*Peterson's Magazine*, April 1867].

Accompanying these stories, others occasionally put forward descriptions of characters that demonstrate that looks can be and are deceiving:

> I had expected to see a person of sinister countenance, but was woefully mistaken. He was a man of about twenty-eight years of age, with a cleanly shaven face, and was neatly dressed.

His eyes were large and expressive, and the noble looking forehead told me he was intelligent. Though his looks spoke well of him, I thought he needed watching, and determined to do it ["The Pious Robber," *The McKean County Miner*, June 10, 1869].

These put the puzzle above the person.

Why?

All of this begs the question of what really makes someone commit a crime. Readers didn't get (maybe didn't want) much insight into that question in 19th-century detective fiction. In spite of a few phrenology hits, biological determinism rarely appears. The notion of the born criminal was a virtual nonstarter, as was the idea of a criminal class, perhaps because one was too potentially gothic and the other because of the detective story's inclination to stay away from the conditions of real cities. But this hardly meant that writers portrayed criminal acts as motiveless and random. In most cases, crimes in 19th-century detective fiction have something to do with characters' relationship with power. Many stories turn on banker-cashier, merchant-clerk, wife-housemaid, farmer-hired hand, lawyer-clerk, foster parent-foster child, relationships. In one variety of story someone is accused who turns out to be innocent—the accused innocent is invariably of lower social status but a paragon: the most efficient clerk or the hardest-working housemaid or the most loving ward. This fact, in turn, echoes in multiple contrasts between accused innocents and actual criminals—courage versus cowardice, forthrightness versus lying, openness versus obfuscation, discipline versus passion, friendship versus jealousy. Lack of discipline resulting in dissipation (usually drinking or gambling) sometimes gives the Goofus-and-Gallant contrast in pieces like "A Detective's Sketch," in which there are two nephews, both seemingly alike in dignity, but one of them is a rotter:

> Yes; on several occasions, recently, my uncle has severely reproved Ralph for his extravagance and dissipated habits; and, but a few days since, he threatened that unless he immediately reformed, he would disinherit him [*New York Fireside Companion*, August 3, 1869].

Criminals in this order of detective fiction mostly occur in homiletic works about amateur criminals that can be traced back to the circumstantial evidence stories and "murder will out" pieces in which Providence sorts thing out and patient suffering is a virtue. But moral admonitions also play a role in more modern stories that banish the accused innocent and replace him or her with clues and legwork. Thus the detective in "The Costly Kiss" discovers that the boss' son has been pocketing company funds in order to live the life of a roué who would flirt with sewing-girls while engaged at the same time to be married to a rich and fashionable young lady, educated, refined, and all that; and more than this, who would steal his own money, so to speak, to the tune of sixteen thousand dollars, was bad enough for anything [*Harper's New Monthly Magazine*, April, 1869].

But 19th-century detective fiction also includes some criminals who are professionals. In terms of criminals, however, the term "professional" means two very opposite kinds of people. There are professional thugs, gangs of evildoers who habitually commit illegal acts that succeed because of the defects in law enforcement. Most of stories about detectives and this type of villain take place in the South or the West. No one ever explains why these characters rob, murder, and pillage—they just do. And it's the detective's job to stop them. At the other end of the spectrum there are professional criminals who possess skills, commit complicated illegal acts, and hope to escape detection. Thus, for instance, Slippery Bill in "On a Field Azure a Silver Star,"

I knew it was Slippery Bill. A dress from Worth is known from its superior style and finish; a painting from Landseer embodies the noblest attributes and poses of the animal delineated. The work of a cracksman is characterized by the same proficiency and marked individuality of execution. The work on the doors, the method of entering the vault, the nerve and audacity of the burglar, tended to one conclusion: Slippery Bill had cracked the vault [*Warren Ledger*, August 30, 1878].

These characters at least fall back on the motivation of monetary gain. Insofar as motive goes, writers used gain far more often than revenge or mental illness. It stands behind stories about robbery, theft, embezzling, counterfeiting, and many cases of murder. Stories involving gangs of robbers or gangs of counterfeiters portray gain as a corporate motivation. It's also there as motive in stories about wills, inheritance, and succession.

A quick look at older literature centered on murders, however, reveals that most are motivated by ambition or sex—they drive characters to monstrous acts in almost every literature in every age and clime. Ambition doesn't really enter much as a motive in 19th-century detective stories, but it should come as no surprise that when the detective story arrived on the literary scene its heroes would sometimes find clues to reveal love, jealousy, and sex at the end of their searches. There are interrupted marriages, spurned lovers, intransigent parents, abusive partners—whatever can go wrong with love goes wrong in these detective stories. Here it may be sufficient to say that all the ways love can go wrong have the potential to be troubling, messy, nasty, and even sometimes repugnant. Not light reading. In the 19th century, however, misery was really the province of the courtship romance or the sensation novel. So how did detective stories incorporate troubling motives associated with love and sex gone wrong? How did they deal with any sort of motives? First, as with the presentation of the crime scene, detective stories do not dwell on overexplaining why bad things were done. Writers handle love/sex the same way they treat *post-mortem* lividity, gaping exit wounds, and other realities of violent death, they get it out of the way as quickly as possible—isolated and encapsulated in a sentence or two. Also detective stories made revealing motives part of detectives' closing presentations. These center on process just as much as they do on the conclusions. And motives served as only part of those presentations—they also included explanations of evidence and exculpation of suspected innocents. Only a very small minority of detective stories—like those published in the *New Orleans Picayune*—end with emphasis on the pathetic and sentimental, i.e., the motives and their consequences. Readers, after all, were not reading a criminal's story but a detective's story, so the focus of the conclusion was necessarily on the detective's cleverness as much or more than it was on the criminal's motives.

One of the stories which turns on love/sex as a motive for crime, however, does add a 19th-century dimension to the age-old motive of love gone wrong. At the end of "A Detective's Experience: A Life of Crime" the murderer tells the detectives that

> "I am guilty," she said—the same low tone of sorrow—"yes, guilty in the eyes of the world, but not in the eyes of heaven. I was insane when I did the deed. Insanity has its cunning—delirium its passionate sense of revenge. They broke my heart, destroyed in their bloom all the flowers of my life. I am a maniac even now, for I feel no terror in my crime" [*The Times-Picayune*, November 15, 1868].

Here the writer describes a woman's murder of an entire family not as a crime of passion but as temporary insanity. Insanity as an acknowledged motive for criminal acts, particularly murder, certainly existed from before the 19th century. In Britain, in fact, Parliament passed the Criminal Lunatics Act in 1800. In terms of American detective fiction, writers seeking a bit of sensation would have readers believe that every town had a neighboring lunatic asylum with very lax security. For writers who either kept to the old ways of story-telling or were not over-punctilious about readers' responses to solving problems, wrongful imprisonment could crank up suffering, the escaped lunatic could serve as an updated *deus ex machina*, and packing an evildoer off to an asylum did avoid the gallows. While writers use the terms "mad" and "insane" casually to describe fleeting moments of emotional duress, debilitating mental illness plays a prominent role in a only few stories during the period. Those few would include:

"Ten Millions—An Extraordinary Story" (*Frank Leslie's Pleasant Hours*, 1867);

"Guilty or Not Guilty" by Eben E. Rexford (*Prairie Farmer*, June 12 & 19, 1869);
"The Mad Philosopher" (*The New York Ledger*, September 19, 1868);
"The Monk Detective; or The Maniac's Release" (*Gleason's Monthly Companion*, January 1879); and
"Man or Demon" (*The Cheyenne Daily Leader*, December 2, 1888)

These stories show both the criminals' acts and make a stab at rudimentary explanations of monstrous acts, most relying upon parallels with demonic possession, but substituting stress or obsession for the influence of Satan and his minions. While these stories center on the actions of a detective figure, they also sit on the gothic edge of the genre because they deal with particularly shocking acts motivated by irrational human behavior. There arose a class of motive, however, which relied on a kinder, gentler form of aberrant behavior— but this time a diagnosable one, somnambulism. From mid-century onward writers semi-regularly used somnambulism as their detectives' solutions to enigmatic circumstances. In "The Mysterious Burglar: A Detective's Story" (*New York Fireside Companion*, November 29, 1869), for example, the narrator-detective discovers that the up-town New York businessman has been opening his own burglar-proof safe and burgling his own money. At the end they both have a good laugh over the embarrassing circumstances. Sleepwalking in stories like this represents one more way in which writers of detective stories used to minimize the effect of the crime and to shift readers' focus to the actions of the detective.

Consequences

Theoretically, ending a detective story is not a problem: explain facts of the crime, identify the criminal, and, if necessary, exonerate the innocent. That's all. The finality of converting suspicion into a formal charge gets the unpleasantness over quickly—especially in short stories. There is sometimes an explanation but never a rebuttal. Crisis has been averted. The reader can go away happy because the problem has been solved and the world has been returned to normal. Showing the problem finally and neatly solved is also the most satisfying part of the process for the writer. After all, did Poe tell the readers that the orangutan was euthanized or Minister D— sent to Devil's Island? Occasionally, 19th-century detective stories take this route: the writer simply ends the narrative. So "Lou Lispenard's Escape" by Caroline Conrad ends with "They convicted him easily enough. There were a hundred damning evidences of his guilt brought to light, when once public attention was called to him" (*The New*

York Ledger, September 22, 1866). The same thing is done, albeit more artfully, in Harriet E. Prescott Spofford's "In the Magurriwock," which concludes with

> the hoops had been knocked off the barrel, the staves had fallen apart from side to side with the fury of the outpouring liquor—and there lay the ghastly skull, the arms, the half-bleached skeleton of the murdered man they sought.
> They stood around the dreadful and disgusting sight in a horrified silence. The two men saw that there was no escape. "Well," said the elder, in the wolfish audacity of his confession, "I suppose you know what that sound up stairs means now?" And listening they could hear the words of the woman on the dismal hearth above, as she rocked herself feebly to and fro, and made her moan: "Three men went down cellar, and only two came up!"
> [*Harper's New Monthly Magazine*, August 1868].

For many writers, though, the issue of what to do at the end of the story becomes crucial, especially in stories about murder, a capital crime. To include descriptions of arrest, trial, and punishment of course can take away from the main surprise of the detective story, but in an era censorious about even minor moral lapses, how can a popular writer avoid mentioning punishment in some way?

When it comes to murders in 19th-century detective fiction, there are several answers to that question. The most popular way to deal with murderers after identifying them was to get things over as economically as possible by simply saying that the culprit was executed—without elaboration. The ending of "The Walker Street Tragedy" is typical:

> Two months after Seroque was hanged—and one year after I witnessed the wedding of Doctor Seyton and Miss Clara Alford [*Leaves from the Notebook of a New York Detective*, New York: Dick & Fitzgerald, 1865].

Perhaps out of a sense of delicacy some writers avoided using the word "hanged," and chose to try to get the point across through equivocation:

> for he recovered, and underwent his sentence in a manner prescribed by the Judge. ["Found Out," *The Mountain Democrat*, February 21, 1863];

and

> And in a few weeks I was able to appear against them, when all had sentences passed upon them as their crimes merited ["'Earless Bill' the Detective," *New York Fireside Companion*, February 14, 1870].

Others chose to be euphemistic:

> and two months thereafter terminated his wicked and eventful career by suffering an ignominious death at the hands of an offended justice ["A Detective's Yarn," *The Golden Era*, October 19, 1862];

> Was this the end? No—for murder will out, and the murderers now languish in the darkness of their dungeon cells awaiting the fate which slow justice meets out to the guilty ["The Last Crime," *Eau Claire Free Press*, October 12, 1865];

and

> A subsequent confession removed all doubt of the prisoner's guilt, and in due time the law's dread penalty was exacted without misgivings as to its justice [A Defence [sic] Without Evidence, *The New York Ledger*, September 15, 1866].

And still others ascend the pulpit:

> The tooth of the platinum filling had found a mighty tongue to cry aloud for vengeance; and the slow, terrible sword of Justice is at last laid bare—let us hope, never to find its scabbard till judgment to the last awful jot and tittle be executed on the murderer of Ida Gilmore ["The Platinum Filling," *Overland Monthly*, August 1874].

But, for period detective stories, discovery, trial, and execution were not the only proofs of God's justice. There was suicide:

> "My God!" he cried, "my crime has found me out!" and then, before either of us could divine his intention, he drew from his breast, a small pocket-pistol, placed the muzzle against his temple, there was a flash, a sharp report, and Ralph Darwin lay dead at our feet ["A Detective Sketch," *New York Fireside Companion*, August 3, 1869].

And other visitations of God

> But the murderer answered no more questions, for when they entered his cell in the morning he was quite dead. "It was not suicide," said the surgeons who examined him, "but a visitation of God." He had died from heart disease ["ZiZi the Little Detective," *The Galaxy*, July 1877].

Even if the murderer escapes trial and punishment a moral still needs to be drawn. It's what happens in "A Detective's Experience" (*Sacramento Daily Union*, December 19, 1868) where the writer invokes pathos: "But, as I supposed, the man was gone. He was never heard of afterward; and this little memory is all that is left of the wrecked and ruined woman." On the other hand, "The Apothecary's Compound" by Sylvanus Cobb, Jr., ends with atonement and forgiveness:

> He wrote to me that he had seen Luther McVaughn—that McVaughn had been assistant surgeon in one of the western regiments, and on the afternoon of the last day of the battle of Nashville, he was shot through the head and instantly killed.
>
> I read the letter to Uncle Moses, and when he heard it he bowed his head upon his hands, and I fancied that I heard him pronounce his sister's name. In a little while he looked up and said to me:
>
> "Surely we may thank Heaven that the poor man has this made some atonement for his sin, and for myself, I am willing to take that atonement as full and ample. May a merciful God forgive him as I do!" [*The New York Ledger*, July 21, 1866]

Just as 19th-century detective story writers sought to minimize the effect of the violent crime in their stories by minimizing details about the crime at the beginning of their narratives, they tried to do the same thing at the end. But they could not wholly escape including abbreviated statements about justice, thereby coupling the acts of the detective and the state with the workings of providence. In doing so they joined the underlying messages of the circumstantial-evidence story and the murder-will-out story: the writer nods to the power of providence to expose and punish sin while illustrating repairs being made to a fallible system of justice.

The discovery and punishment of the criminal clears the slate. It brings justice and makes society whole again. Innocence is rewarded and faith restored. That is the way 19th-century detective stories work. In most cases the detective does his or her job and then disappears without much fuss—much like a visiting physician, a contract employee, or a temp. To be sure some stories feature amateurs who solve crimes in order to save a loved one, but increasingly during the century detectives take over detective stories—or at least the middle of detective stories. If they were present at the beginning there would be no story and at the end they have no more to do in the world of the fiction. Except in a very, very few cases. The first of these is in "Mr. Furbush" by Harriet E. Prescott Spofford (*Harper's New Monthly Magazine*, April 1865), in which the burden of understanding and revealing crimes makes the hero quit the police force after uncovering the murderer: "You will not find Mr. Furbush's name on the list of detectives now. He has sickened of the business." The second is "Brought to Justice" by J.T. Hunter in which a woman finds her father's murderer and testifies at his trial. After his sentencing

> Although I knew that the doom that was dealt was richly deserved by the confessed murderer, I almost repented my part in the transaction, and could think of nothing for days but the terrible words of his sentence, "You shall be hanged by the neck until you are dead, and may God have mercy upon your soul" [*Sterling Standard*, June 3, 1886].

Both of these stories demonstrate the understanding that the detective is more than a means to solve crimes and make communities whole and that detectives do not simply disappear and move on to the next case. It is a particularly modern insight. Both stories were written by women.

6

DETECTIVES AND
THEIR STORIES

> There is a good deal of excitement and no little romance in the profession of the detective. He must be very shrewd, understand human nature, be prolific of resources and inventions, cool, self-reliant, courageous, and resolute. He goes everywhere; adopts all disguises; plays many parts; combines, analyzes, manipulates, manages, and does work often that is a credit to his brain and a discredit to his principle—Junius Henri Browne, *The Great Metropolis,* 1869

A Digression on Words

In the beginning the word was not "detective." Nevertheless, a century before Scotland Yard became Scotland Yard there were people in England whose job was to track criminals down and bring them to justice. They had a generic name: thief-taker. While the abominations of thief-takers Jonathan Wild and Stephen McDaniel, and unflattering portraits by Godwin and a number of other Victorian novelists made it an unsavory profession to follow, in his 1755 dictionary Dr. Johnson simply defined a thief-taker as "One whose business is to detect thieves, and bring them to justice." That the term "thief-taker" was current in the U.S. at the beginning of the 19th century is witnessed by this piece from the *Burlington Free Press,* February 10, 1837:

> In the course of the trial, the most clever and celebrated thief-takers have been examined, and scenes of ingenious villainy have been disclosed which have inspired us with wonder, approaching to admiration.

In addition to its connection with some very corrupt and bad men, the term "thief-taker" lacked finesse, polish, and accuracy—they captured more than thieves. The French, however, provided an alternative in the life and works of Eugène François Vidocq. Two years after Cary and Hart published their translation of Vidocq's *Memoirs,* the French police agent's name became a generic term used in America to describe a person who would later be described as a detective. Thus, concluding a piece on an unsolved crime on January 22, 1836, *Vermont Phœnix* suggested that "If the people of Hudson choose, they may have a Vidocq from our Police Office." Even after the term "detective" came into common usage, writers employed the French detective's name for effect—as in "Who would wish to play Vidocq to the nine muses?" (*New York Daily Tribune,* July 31, 1857).

After "thief-taker" and "Vidocq" came the word "detective." "Detective police" was occasionally used in American newspapers, and can be found as early the November 23, 1844, edition of the Bowling Green, Missouri, paper *The Radical's* reference to fugitives captured by English detectives in Ireland. In the year Poe died, *Chambers' Edinburg Journal* followed its series of stories about lawyers with a series based on the adventures of a plainclothes police officer titled "Recollections of a Police-Officer." The first story in the series had no subtitle in the original publication (July 28, 1849) but was later titled "One Night in a Gaming House." In it the narrator, a former uniformed policeman, begins the action of the story by saying, "I was to be at once employed on a mission which the most sagacious and experienced detective officers would have felt honored to undertake."

The next year Dickens got on the bandwagon of the New Police and his magazine, *Household Words,* ran "The Modern Science of Thief-Taking" (July 13, 1850) which uses the word "detective," and two weeks later he recounted hanging out, smoking cigars, and listening to stories from some of the original cadre of official detectives in "A Detective Police Party" (July 27, 1850). Both Chambers' "Recollections of a Police-Officer" stories and Dickens' other articles about detectives appeared in American newspapers almost as fast as a ship could cross the Atlantic. In 1852 in New York publishers Cornish and Lamport scooped up Chambers' "Police-Officer" stories and published them in a pirated volume titled *Recollections of a Policeman.* Their only addition to this collection of stolen stories was a description of the detective in the Preface:

> The Detective Policeman is in some respects peculiar to England—one of the developments of the last twenty-five years. He differs as much from the informer and spy of the Continent of Europe, as the modern Protective Policeman does from the old-fashioned Watchman. In point of fact, he is a preventive as much as a detective. His occupation is as honest as it is dangerous. Its difficulties and danger give it an odor of the romantic. The record of "hair-breadth 'scapes," which follow, is another verification of the old saying, "Truth is stranger than fiction" [Preface, *Recollections of a Policeman,* New York: Cornish and Lamport, 1852].

By mid-century it was all clear enough: the term "detective" took over. It grew from the actual appearance of plainclothes investigative police officers who became the official detective branch of the Metropolitan Police in the 1840s. Thus, a "detective story" was one about the experiences of a plainclothes public official who investigated crimes and caught criminals. This led to all of the pseudo-biographical "notebook" and "diary" detective stories which would continue to be published almost until the end of the century.

But perspectives changed in the 1880s. Scotsman John Henry Ingram began a Poe revival when he published *The Works of Edgar Allan Poe*, issued in monthly volumes in Edinburgh in 1874–75 and reissued in 1880. Even a cursory reading of "The Murders in the Rue Morgue" is enough to convince anyone who asks that it has little to do with the kind of story about detectives that was going to develop in England and America. And there is not a whole lot of Vidocq in it either. It was a different kind of story about a different kind of investigator which arose from some very different traditions. And eventually, every time he was asked, Arthur Conan Doyle freely admitted that Poe inspired his Sherlock Holmes stories. At Columbia University in New York in the 1890s, Professor Brander Matthews became a Poe enthusiast—and a detective story enthusiast, too. Among his discussions about Poe's short story accomplishments, Matthews, and others, made the assumption that since Poe's Dupin had only a playfully adversarial relationship with the police, a person didn't need to be a "detective" to be a detective. Added to that, perhaps because of "The Gold Bug," they believed that a detective story need not be about crime as long as it was about reasoning and problem solving. All of this occurred during the surge of popularity of detective stories caused by the advent of Sherlock Holmes, a phenomenon that moved academics like Matthews to think about the history of the genre. For them, detectives didn't have to be deputized public officials or solve real crimes; they figured that anybody could be a detective, and they went looking for detectives and detective stories in every countries' literature, ancient or modern. And they found detectives in Herodotus, Voltaire, and in the Bible.

The upshot of all this was that for many, beginning early in the 20th century, two kinds of detective stories existed. One centered on the straightforward narration of the acts and monuments of an official or specialist (i.e., lawyer, physician, etc.) detective, or one acting in his or her stead. The other was a more "literary" narrative centered on problem solving by both the detective in the story but also sometimes the reader as well, in which intellect and cleverness made more difference than the profession of the hero.

Another Digression: On Police

It's hardly necessary to say much about what happened in England with Robert Peele, the New Police, Scotland Yard, and all the rest. It did not hurt, of course, that Charles Dickens was one of the most enthusiastic supporters of the detective corps—if not ordinary beat coppers. In England and America the police largely avoided areas where crime, vice, and poverty resided—as long as their inhabitants didn't impinge on the property and lives of "respectable people." Even though many Americans thought they were imitating the English system when it came to creating police departments, things in the U.S. were very, very different. Instead of a metropolis, there were small towns and seemingly limitless space; instead of an entrenched class system, everybody was supposed to be equal (except the enslaved and free African Americans, Asians, Native Americans, and women); instead of a stodgy legal and judicial system that changed glacially, there were new laws to be made and individuals' rights to be nurtured and protected—at least hypothetically. Additionally, because early in the century the French had instituted a widespread and intrusive system of policing, as in England many in America feared that the police could become snoopers and spies who meddled with their rights and freedom. It was a fear around which Peele and early English police executives skillfully navigated. It was much harder to convince Americans that they needed more than the watch and constables system inherited from the Middle Ages.

On paper (or on the official Web sites of police departments), it's not difficult to trace a steady march of police departments being established in major American cities in the middle of the 19th century: Boston 1835, New York 1845, San Francisco 1849, Baltimore 1853, Philadelphia 1854, Chicago 1855, Saint Louis 1861, Cleveland 1866. But it's a misleading timeline. In most cases the dates cited are for when a relatively stable organization began, after years, even decades when failure and mismanagement marred attempts to provide adequately for public safety. The whole period was marked by power struggles between city and state government and also between individuals over control of police departments. There was the police Civil War between local New York City police and a force established by Albany. In 1861 the Illinois legislature revoked Chicago Mayor John Wentworth's police authority and he, in turn, fired the entire police force. These were not atypical phenomena. There was even more of a muddle with the beginning of detective divisions. Although the New York department had plainclothes officers for a long time, its detective division wasn't properly organized until Thomas Byrnes became its head in 1882. Politics and the spoils system played an influential role in the conduct of police business with jobs handed out in exchange for votes, political favors, or cash. Bribery and extortion were common practices among patrol officers and detectives. If a cop on the beat received a monthly "gratuity" to ignore taverns and brothels, detectives made a lot more:

> The chief detectives have a salary of $2,500 a year, but they make five or ten times that sum often, and frequently acquire a large property [Junius Henri Browne, *The Great Metropolis*, Hartford: American, 1869].

The unreliability and incompetence of official police departments during their formative years created periodic public outcries. Thus this piece credited to the *New York Sun* ran in the *The Evening Telegraph*, December 14, 1870:

> The method upon which the municipal detective service is conducted in the principal cities of this country requires a thorough overhauling and an immediate reform; for at present it is utterly demoralizing in its tendency, and in many instances affords protection and encouragement to the most hardened thieves and transgressors. From the first introduction of the infamous "stool pigeon" system the service has been going on from bad to worse, until now its practical operation has become simply intolerable. We do not say that there are not honest and well meaning men engaged in the vocation of detectives, although it is a wonder that any such are to be found under the system now generally in vogue.

Meaningful reform of America's police departments didn't take place until the 20th century. In the 19th century, therefore, there was a felt need for an alternative. And private detective agencies—sometimes called detective police agencies—were that alternative. They sprang up in every major city in the U.S. Frequently begun by former police detectives, there were entities such as Matsell's independent police agency in New York; Bradley's detective police agency, Tuttle's detective agency, and Allan Pinkerton's National Detective Agency in Chicago; and Smith, Pierson & West in Baltimore. They had big clients, like railroads and banks, and had the advantage denied to police of having no jurisdictional prohibitions. It was not uncommon for private detectives to consult or act with official police in pursuits or investigations, and U.S. Marshals subcontracted with private detectives to track down counterfeiters since the department had neither the personnel nor the funds to take on the task. Advertisements for private detectives frequently appeared in period newspapers, and Allan Pinkerton advertised the prowess of his works in print beginning with the narrative of his agency's success in *The Expressman and the Detective* (1874).

Origins

Forgetting, for the moment, the investigations of assorted lawyers, physicians, scientists, children, friends and lovers of accused innocents, and paying scant attention to grouchy geniuses—important as they are—the detective story owes its real beginning and continued existence to the appearance of professional detectives in American magazines and newspapers. The first of those to gain popularity in the United States was Eugène François Vidocq.

Vidocq was exceptionally good at self-promotion: he talked himself from being a police stool pigeon to being head of the *Sûreté Nationale*, and when politics turned against him he established the first private detective agency. For Americans there was lots to read about Vidocq. In 1830 the *Philadelphia Album and Ladies Literary Gazette* published "Vidocq and the Sexton"; Cary and Hart printed *Memoirs of Vidocq, principal agent of the French police until 1827* in 1834; and in 1838-39 William Evans Burton included nine stories in the series "Unpublished passages in the Life of Vidocq French Minister of Police" in *Burton's Gentleman's Magazine*. Papers published stories with Vidocq as their hero through April 21, 1872, when "A Night Adventure" appeared in the *New York Times*. The short fiction about him portrays several Vidocqs. One is Vidocq the con man—in disguise, romancing suspects, plying them with drink, and bargaining about rewards as in "Vidocq and the Sexton." Thirty years later the gun-toting, sure-shot Vidocq shows up in "Vidocq; or, The Charcoal Burners of France" (*M'Kean Miner*, November 24, 1860). In between, Burton's "Unpublished Passages" stories, written (or translated) in the first-person, largely choose to emphasize the pathos of crime, betrayal, and miscarriages of justice rather than the capture of criminals. On top of all of this Poe has Dupin in "The Murders in the Rue Morgue" fault Vidocq for his mundane methods and superficial analyses.

William Evans Burton (1804–1860) is more than the bridge between tales by or about Vidocq and Poe, whom he hired to help edit *Burton's Gentleman's Magazine* in 1839. He also wrote two detective stories, "The Secret Cell" (September & October 1837) and "The Cork Leg" (March 1838), which he published in his magazine. They both feature the work of plainclothes police officers. In the first story the narrator gives readers a police officer who acts as a detective before the Metropolitan Police had detectives:

> I had a friend in the police department—a man who suffered not his intimacy with the villainy of the world to dull the humanities of nature. At the period of my tale, he was but little known, and the claims of a large family pressed hard upon him; yet his enemies have been unable to affix a stain upon his busy life. He has since attained a height of reputation that must ensure a sufficient income; he is established as the head of the private police of London—a body of men possessing rare and wonderful attainments.

Although he does not quite rescue the kidnapped maiden, Burton makes his proto-detective a paragon possessed of intelligence, drive, and persistence. DeTurgot, the Paris detective in "The Cork Leg," on the other hand, he made into a meddling twerp, albeit a clever one, whose case disappears along with his hopes of promotion and fame at the end of "The Cork Leg." Rather than being an investigation of the intellect, rigors, benefits, or anything else about detectives, Burton's two stories are fundamentally literary. And they come from Burton's instincts as a comic actor, a profession that brought in most of his income. Thus, "The Secret Cell" begins with a tongue-in-cheek juxtaposition of clichés of Gothic literature and examples of real life: the narrator claims that in his tale

> a conspiracy, an abduction, a nunnery, and a lunatic asylum, are mixed up with constables, hackney-coaches, and an old washerwoman. I regret also that my heroine is not only without a lover, but is absolutely free from the influence of the passion, and is not persecuted on account of her transcendent beauty [September 1837].

"The Cork Leg," in the manner of a three-act farce, centers on a whole household in a French chateau pretending to have artificial limbs in order to confuse the detective who comes in search of the man who, it turns out, committed no crime at all.

In 1841, then, while hardly more than an occasional oddity, American readers had encountered plainclothes officers who solved crimes—but those crimes were in England and France. Poe certainly knew about Vidocq and, having worked for him, knew about Burton's two stories. That's part of why he chose France for the setting of what became his new take on the short story. Whatever inspired him to write "The Murders in the Rue Morgue," it seems pretty clear that he had a good time doing it—carefully stringing readers along and setting them up for the punch-line surprise of the orangutan. In his tales of ratiocination, Poe contributed a great deal to the modern detective story: the unique personality of the hero, the red herring, the exultation of reason, the obtuse narrator, the surprise ending, and the concentration on minutiae. He changed the geography of the narrative from tracking across country to focusing on one particular place and time. All of these things were and are fascinating and imitable. The detective story should have been an immediate inspiration to writers in Philadelphia and New York and Boston. But it wasn't. The French may have liked Poe's detective tales, as did Collins and Dickens, but they did not take off in America. Before the end of the century, the tales of ratiocination remained obscure in the U.S. Not only that, "The Murders in the Rue Morgue" suffered the indignity of being rewritten as a third-person narrative starring M. Allard, a pupil of Vidocq, who solves the double murder of Madame l'Esparaye and her daughter. Sometime before the ending (where he is made chief of the Paris police) the narrator spoils Poe's surprise this way:

> And day after day, Allard patiently read over the Paris papers in search of an advertisement of the lost orang-outang. But he saw none. "Very well," said he to himself, "we must now advertise an orang-outang found. My belief that an ape only committed that murder is not

to be overthrown. If the owner of the orang-outang, which I am sure must in any event have made its escape, is innocent he will undoubtedly be on the look-out for his precious animal" ["'Who Was the Murderer!' from the German," *The Plymouth Weekly Democrat*, May 13, 1869].

On July 28, 1849, *Chambers' Edinburgh Journal* published the first of ten stories that formed the series titled "Recollections of a Police-Officer." It was modeled on the journal's earlier "Experiences of a Barrister" stories, some of which ran at the same time that the "Police-Officer" stories appeared. The "Police-Officer" pieces are also the first stories about crime fighting published after the creation of an official detective division of the Metropolitan Police. They began to be published one year before Dickens turned his attention to police and detectives with "The Modern Science of Thief-Taking" in *Household Words*. A detective named Waters narrates the *Recollections* stories and the writer adds bits of personal information to bolster the notion of biography. Readers learn that the narrator was once a gentleman brought low by gambling and bad company, that he was reduced to becoming a policeman, that he was promoted to being a detective, and that he has a wife concerned for his safety. Although some of the stories are loosely connected to one another, most are separate cases of bringing malefactors to justice. Thematically they also echo certain elements in *Chambers'* lawyer stories in "Experiences of a Barrister"— "Guilty or not Guilty," for example is an overt circumstantial evidence story and "The Twins" contains a long passage on courts and the absence of public prosecutors in English law. Most of the "Recollections" stories make passing reference to police procedures, mentioning records, hierarchy, and the like. And to make things seem more authentic, one story even records a failure: in "The Pursuit" the embezzler outwits the hero several times and manages to escape to America. The repeated use of "energy," "duty," and "watchfulness" serve to establish the essence of the hero's character and secrets of his success. In the main, however, the *Recollections* stories center on the practical skills of the tracking and surveillance of known criminals which culminate in their arrest—unlike the Poe stories, which implicitly present readers with crime-scene problems to ponder. For good or for ill, the "Recollections" stories were the first detective stories to spread across the United States in newspapers anxious for copy and excitement.

The Paper Trail

The "Recollections of a Police-Officer" stories appeared in American newspapers throughout the 1850s. But perhaps the most important company that led the *Chambers' Edinburgh Journal* bandwagon (and, in time, that of the American detective story) was Harper and Brothers publisher. In June 1850 the New York publisher launched its new magazine, *Harper's New Monthly Magazine*. In November, as its monthly press run was about to reach 50,000, *Harper's* started with the *Chambers'* police pieces; they retitled "Recollections of a Police-Officer: Legal Metamorphoses" and printed it as "Villainy Outwitted." Two months later, the January 1851 edition of the magazine contained "Robber's Revenge" a piece taken from *Chambers'* "Recollections of a Police-Officer: The Revenge" printed in Britain on November 9, 1850. *Harper's* next early foray into the world of British police was "A Reminiscence of a Bow-Street Officer" in September 1852.

But by 1852 the Harpers had picked up a passing fascination with British lawyers—or a copy of *Leaves from The Diary of a Law Clerk*, a volume of dubious parentage, published by the well-known New York pirate publisher Cornish and Lamport, who added *"By the Author of 'Recollections of a Police-Officer' etc. etc."* to the *Law Clerk* title. *Diary of a Law Clerk* yielded the stories "Edward Drysdale," "The Incendiary," "A Dark Chapter," and "The Temptress" in *Harper's*. Because, or in spite of, this move to lawyer heroes of crime stories, *Harper's* published two significant stories about lawyers in 1855: "The Stolen Letter: A Lawyer's Story" (February 1855) and "A Mysterious Occurrence in Lambeth" (August 1855). The former *Harper's* attributed to Charles Dickens but it was actually "The Fourth Poor Traveller" from *The Seven Poor Travellers* by Wilkie Collins, which was published in the Extra Christmas Number of *Household Words* for December 1854. Likened to Poe by some historians, "The Stolen Letter" follows a lawyer as he makes sense out of cryptic notes in order to thwart a blackmailer. While "The Mysterious Occurrence in Lambeth" by G.P.R. James is a traditional circumstantial evidence story, nonetheless, the urbane lawyer-narrator makes comments about observing and reasoning, and the story ends with a substantial surprise. Lawyers, however, were not the future of the detective story.

In 1857 Harpers, the publisher that had, along with others, brought the detective story to America in the shape of "Reminiscences" stories from *Chambers'*, became the publisher that made the detective story American. In the first issue of their new magazine, *Harper's Weekly*, they printed "A Police-Officer's Seven Thousand Mile Chase" by J.B. Armstrong (January 3, 1857). While this may have been the first extended story featuring an American detective in America, the title telegraphs the essence of this humdrum chase narrative. The important thoroughly American detective story came in *Harper's Weekly* of July 25, 1857, with "How Bob Bolter's Prisoner Escaped." "Bob Bolter" takes place in New York and features a New York police detective, New York criminals, and refers to the police "Civil War" of 1857. More important than all of these is the tone of the story—the relaxed, casual conversation over cigars that leads the ex-police officer to tell his friend about one of his own experiences that illustrates the ingenuity of criminals and the intelligence of detectives. The next of *Harper's Weekly's* new detective stories, "The Button: An Experience of a New York Detective, Related by Himself" (October 16, 1858) features the same conversational, colloquial narration:

> I expect you've no idea how scientifically burglars do their work sometimes. It's a regular trade; I don't know but you might call it one of the arts and sciences. Folks generally think a burglar is a rough-looking villain, with a horrid face and bushy eyebrows, who breaks into any house or store where he thinks there's anything worth taking, and kills everybody that makes any resistance. Just let me show you a burglar (turning to the Rogues' Gallery), one of the best of them. There, that fellow, number 203; you wouldn't think *he* was a rascal; he looks more like an Episcopal minister, doesn't he? Now that fellow had as nice a kit of tools as you'd care to see. His "skeletons," with movable wards, were made with a polish on 'em. Give him a chance and he'd open any lock in town. He never "weeded" a place till he knew just where he was to go and what he was to do.

Both "The Button" and "The Costly Kiss: A New York Detective Experience" in *Harper's New Monthly Magazine* (April 1859) share the same purpose: as the detective narrator of "The Button" puts it, "I was going to tell you of some smart work there was done some years ago by three men, down in Maiden Lane and thereabouts." Both of these *Harper's* stories focus on telling reader/listeners about police procedures: tracing material things, knowing criminals' habits, disguises, and thoroughly knowing their environment. They apply what Dickens did for detectives in London to detectives in New York. "T4FG2G: A Detective Experience" in *Harper's Weekly* (December 4, 1858), however, was something different. The detective narrator in the story, if anything, is even more relaxed and conversational than in the other *Harper's* stories of the time. The difference lies in the fact that the story is not about finding clues but interpreting them. This begins with a joke about the French for the number 48 (*quarante huit*): "Well, one of 'em, just as they started, sung out to the other, 'Current wheat!' or something that sounded like that. Did you hear it?" The plot then moves to finding a paper written in gobbledygook that forms the center of the cipher narrative—and marks out a new kind of detective hero:

> It *is* all Greek to you, I presume; but it is easy enough to make it out if you go to work in the right way. Now such puzzles always please me. If I had thought that the letter contained nothing worth knowing I should have tried to understand it, just for the fun of it. As it was, for both reasons I went to work, and could read it all in about two hours.
>
> It isn't anything to boast of, though; for the cipher is perfectly simple. It didn't take an extra smart head to plan *that* out. I've *seen* puzzlers, though—some that took all my spare time for weeks.

This is right out of Poe's pieces about cryptography—which he never applied directly to his detective stories—and posits a new kind of writer and a new kind of reader of the detective story, both of which add intellectual challenges and even playfulness to hunting and chasing that were parts of the detective stories inherited from England and France.

About the same time *Harper's* ran these New York detective stories, the *Atlantic Monthly* printed Wilkie Collins' tongue-in-cheek piece "Who Is the Thief? (Extracted from the Correspondence of the London Police)" (April 1858). And in the spring of 1865 the Harpers published three significant detective stories: *Harper's New Monthly Magazine* saw Harriet E. Prescott Spofford's "Mr. Furbush" in April and C. Davis' "The Pigot Murder" in May; the anonymous "After those Seven-Thirties, a Simple Job" followed in *Harper's Weekly* in July. After this brief burst of popularity in magazines, detectives and detective stories largely became the province of story papers and newspapers.

Well before dime novels, at mid-century story papers—tabloid-sized publications containing short stories, poetry, and serials—were outlandishly popular. *Flag of Our Union*, for example, had normal weekly press runs of 100,000 in the 1850s, and *The New York Ledger* by the 1870s was printing 1,000,000 copies of sample issues. Plainly put, story papers invented popular fiction in America. And the two most popular of them, *Flag* and *The New York Ledger*, had a real affection for detective stories and detectives. Maturin Murray Ballou, publisher of *Flag* included the first reference, albeit a passing one, to an American detective that we have found, in "Mr. Snicker's Misadventure" in his *Ballou's Dollar Monthly* in January 1856. In the late 1850s, Robert Bonner's *Ledger* ran a number of crime stories set in a America written by Sylvanus Cobb, Jr., but at that time Cobb's hero was usually a lawyer, as in "The Bank Vault: From a Lawyer's Notebook" (*The New York Ledger*, August 22, 1857). While stories about heroes called detectives set in the United States became regular occurrences in both *The Ledger* and *Flag*, perhaps one of the contributions of story papers was the reintroduction of the series character. The first of these series characters began in *The New York Ledger* with "Assassin of Castellane, From the Records of a French Policeman" (June 12, 1858); it may (or may not) have been cribbed from French originals, and was perhaps connected with Vidocq's death in 1857. In the spring of the next year, Ballou followed this up with "A Curious Stratagem" (*Ballou's Dollar Monthly Magazine*, April 1859) and "The Guest-Chamber of the Inn at St. Ives, From the Journal of a Detective" (*Flag of Our Union*, September 24, 1859), both credited to James F. Franklin. All three feature Guillot, a hero who "had been some years connected with the Detective Bureau [...] and had naturally arrived at a great degree of proficiency" ("A Curious Stratagem," *Ballou's Dollar Monthly Magazine*, April 1859).

They also favor murder by means of unexpected devices. Within the first year of their publication, the Guillot stories appeared in papers from coast to coast: from *The Oconto Pioneer* in Wisconsin to Placerville, California's *The Mountain Democrat*. Their popularity, however, was dwarfed by Ballou's New York Detective series about detective James Brampton, which began in germ with "Masked Robbers: A Leaf from a Detective's Notebook" (*Ballou's Dollar Monthly Magazine*, April 1862) and ended with "Mr. Sterling's Confession" (*Ballou's Dollar Monthly Magazine*, January 1863). The Brampton pieces highlight the accomplishments of "a man of extraordinary sagacity, [... who] had succeeded in discovering the perpetrators of crime, when to ordinary men all clues appeared to be lost" ("The Knotted Handkerchief" by Percy Garrett, *Ballou's Dollar Monthly Magazine*, July 1862). Stories about this model detective which celebrate close observation appeared frequently in newspapers across the country as well as in a pirated volume *Leaves from the Note-Book of a New York Detective: The Private Record of J.B.* (New York: Dick & Fitzgerald, 1865). The Brampton stories did so well for Ballou that he came out with a second series hero; this time featuring the French detective Eugene Laromie. Laromie appeared in five stories in 1866 all attributed to James D. M'Cabe, Jr.: three were published in *Flag of Our Union*, beginning with "The Tell-Tale Eye" (January), followed by two published in *Ballou's Monthly Magazine*, ending with "A Little Affair" (October). Reflecting the same soupçon of danger found in other period stories set in France, Laromie

> had passed through some wonderful adventures and been nearer death than most men cared to be. His success in ferreting out and bringing to light crimes of all kinds had won for him the bitter enmity of all offenders, both political and criminal, in the city. They had repeatedly vowed vengeance against him, for they declared that there was no chance for them while he remained in Paris. Laromie only laughed at their threats, and kept his wits about him. He declared his eagerness to meet them whenever they [chose] provided they gave him fair play ["The Little Affair"].

In addition to series detective stories, story papers ran stand-alone stories about detectives. Indeed, one-shot heroes were the rule rather than the exception. Sylvanus Cobb, Jr., one of the most prolific contributors to *The New York Ledger*, for example, wrote detective stories in the early 1860s about the triumphs of a variety of lawyers, sheriffs, and physicians—with an occasional detective thrown in.

By the 1870s things in publishing began to change. Beadle and Munro's dime novel detective titles became significant forces in the market, and may have been one of the reasons for the decline and disappearance of detective stories from many established magazines. Story papers continued to attract huge audiences, and by the 1880s began to include detective serials with short stories about crimes and their solutions. For main-line detective stories, one of the most significant developments in the last quarter of the century was the emergence and growth of syndication of materials for newspapers—in both England and the United States. We know that by the 1870s Ansel Nash Kellogg and Irving Batcheller's syndicates supplied material, including fiction, to any newspaper belonging to their syndicate. It was the same way that S.S. McClure introduced Sherlock Holmes to American readers in 1891.

Newspaper editors had a fondness for detectives and detective stories going back to the 1850s. Back then few of the stories were original: editors found them in magazines and happily pirated them whenever they had empty space. By the 1870s, on top of syndicated stories, newspaper detective stories outnumbered those that appeared in magazines, and many of them were written specifically for newspapers and carried a writer's name and the announcement that the story was "written for" newspaper X. By the end of the 1860s the first series hero begun in a newspaper appeared in the *New Orleans Picayune* which ran five stories narrated by an anonymous detective whose assistant is Mr. I—. Reprinted by papers across the nation, these trenchantly sentimental stories began with "A Detective Experience: A Female Forger" and included "A Detective's Story: Tragic End of a Brilliant Songstress," two stories titled only "A Detective's Experience," and "A Detective's Experience: The Missing Jewels." That these were published and republished in newspapers signals a shift in the center of detective stories in the United States. A decade later another series hero, apparently originating in a Louisiana paper, appeared in at least five stories. Narrated by Detective Varnoe, these stories reflect the increased sophistication and focus on problem solving that occurred in newspaper detective fiction in the 1870s. They include "A Bit of Mystery," "Story of Crime," "The Finger of Providence," "The Poisoner," and "A Double Crime." Two of them carry the author's name as Johnson B. Turner.

Parentage

Although short fiction had been around for a long time and had appeared under a number of guises, the short story was distinctly a mid–19th-century creation. And detective stories were there at the start. From the beginning, detective stories were up front about their subject; readers knew what they were going to find before they began reading, because detective stories typically announced what they were about—detectives. Preponderantly first-person narratives, in the beginning their titles often included the authenticating phrases "Leaves from the Diary (or the notebook) of a Detective," or "The Experiences of a Detective." But after mid-century the most popular titles for detective stories became simply "A Detective Story," "A Detective's Story," "A Detective's Experience," or "A Detective's Adventure." It was pretty clear to anyone that a detective story was a story about a detective. But what kind of story was it? The fact is that there was not one kind of detective story; several kinds evolved in the 19th century. But they did have some common literary ancestors and these left their marks.

Melodramas and Sensation Novels

At this juncture, it's important to point out the literary roads not taken by detective stories in the mid-nineteenth century—in spite of significant temptation. They were not ghost stories, Gothic stories, melodramas, or miniaturized sensation novels. All of those forms touched on or depended upon crime and criminals. But their writers placed emphasis on affecting readers' emotions by evoking (with apologies to Aristotle) pity and fear. Melodramas and sensation novels may have centered on crime but they magnified the role of the victim and made criminals and not detectives the principal characters. Detective stories had detective heroes who relied upon observation, logic, and evidence, elements that were not the focus of the other forms of popular literature. Granted, a small number of stories, principally those published in the *New York Fireside Companion*, dwelt upon the detective hero facing fiendishly dangerous criminals and sought to stimulate the cheap thrills provided by stereotypes in capture-and-escape plots. The narrator of "A Detective's Story" (*New York Fireside Companion*, November 22, 1869), for instance, describes helplessly watching maniacal counterfeiters crush fellow detective Jack Findall between two huge stone rollers. But this kind of detective story gave rise to the youth-oriented dime novel and the dime-novel detective—quite different from mainstream detective fiction of the day. Also out of the mainstream of 19th-century detective fiction, the *New Orleans Picayune* published a series narrated by an anonymous detective and dominated by attention to women victims of crime and male perfidy. If the *Fireside Companion* stories aimed at readers' adrenalin, the series from the *Picayune* laid claim to readers' compassion.

This does not mean, however, that the simplified emotions and emotional appeals of melodramas, sensation stories, and homiletic, tract literature had no place in 19th-century detective fiction. But they were encapsulated. It is not unusual, therefore, to find sentimental material in the background of the action in detective stories; accounts of separated lovers, prejudiced fathers, wealthy uncles, and other stereotypes often figure in the detectives' solutions. But they are subordinate to the detective's method of discovering the truth. There are also stories that explain criminal behavior by bringing in drink, gambling, and dissolute companions, but these are very different from simplistically moral Victorian tract literature. In detective stories, readers do not find out the identity of the real criminals until near the end of the narrative, at which point the courts—and/or sickness, suicide, exile, etc.—conclude things very quickly. Detective stories depended upon solving problems to which the answer was not apparent to those in the world of the narrative—versus the exaggerated nature of the villains and heroes of melodramas and sensation novels. Other than nodding to a grief-stricken widow or widower, or briefly mentioning the angst of a wrongly accused innocent, minor characters in detective stories act principally as observers who are sometimes superficially curious, or befuddled and perplexed, or bigoted. The surprising thing about most 19th-century short detective fiction may be that it is not more melodramatic than it is. But the combination of the brevity of the short story form and the increasing stress placed on method and material clues in detective fiction makes this departure from and avoidance of melodrama almost inevitable.

Notebook Stories

If it weren't for notebook fiction, there is a good chance that we would be examining lawyer and not detective stories. The early 19th century's fascination with detectives was stoked by the fashion for the "notebook" form of prose fiction, a genre which sought to attract readers by promising them an inside look into the life of a practitioner of a newly prominent profession such as law or medicine or detection. And, as seen above, detection was newer than most. In the spirit and the manner of *Chambers'* "Recollections of a Police-Officer" series, American (and English) writers from mid-century onward used the term "notebook" in their titles and included bits of information about police procedure, organization, and history in their narratives. Here's an "inside" view of police history from "The Scarlet Ribbon: A Detective's Story" by Rett Winwood:

> In the first place, I was only a watchman. When the police system was started, I went into that corps. I can honestly say that I always tried to do my duty, in either situation. My superiors seemed to think so, too, for by-and-by my name was up before them for the new detective force that was to be organized. I was counted "knowing," and had done some pretty sharp things by way of hauling up offenders, during my life, and when the subject was once agitated, I was of course sure of my place, and on the whole, ready enough to accept it.
> [...]
> After I came to be detective, there seemed a little better chance for running about, but I kept steadily at work, early and late. I found enough to keep me busy, hands and brain. There was always some sink of iniquity to be cleaned out, or some case of mystery and crime to be cleared up. All this was bringing me in a little money, and some fame, for I met with wonderful success in my efforts. Perhaps it was owing to this close work, mental and physical, that I put upon every case that came under my notice. However, I believe constant

6. Detectives and Their Stories

toil and steady perseverance had as much as anything to do with it [*Ballou's Monthly Magazine*, December 1866].

The notebook tradition also gave rise to inserted asides about crimes and criminal behavior which served both to inform the reader and to further the authority of the speaker as a detective. Thus this quasi-public service announcement:

> Before the telegraph came into use, the counterfeiters—or "horse-dealers," as they call themselves—drove a much better trade than they do now. When they had started a good bill it would run two or three days—or a week even before the public generally would find it out. But now-a-days, since we have had the telegraph all over town, they find themselves brought up with a short turn. Deputy Carpenter has arranged a plan which spoils their fun completely. Just as soon as information is received at any station that a counterfeit has been offered, that station communicates directly with headquarters, giving a description of the bill; from head-quarters the news is telegraphed immediately to every station in the city; the patrolmen are called in, the captain or sergeant reads the description to them, and they go back at once to their beats and warn all the shopkeepers—in fact every body likely to receive money in business—that such a bill is out. So, in an hour after the counterfeiter starts a new bill, the whole island is on the look-out against it. I'll tell you a good story how one country "horse-dealer" got "took in.'" It was while was with Chief Matsell—say about ten years ago ["The Trap," *Strange Stories of a Detective; or Curiosities of Crime*, New York: Dick & Fitzgerald, 1863].

From the beginning, bits of police history and inside information about criminals like these established part of the atmosphere of the detective story, the part that, to some extent, authenticated the promise of the "detective" portion of the title.

Diary Stories

Even going back to *Chambers'* lawyer and detective stories, however, the term "notebook" was misleading. Notebooks contain notes, not finished narratives. "Robbery at Osborne's Hotel" by "Inspector F." makes this clear:

> I do not know that I should have yielded to the suggestion, had I not a few months since made acquaintance with a gentleman who writes for the best of the London periodicals. He warmly urged me to pitch together the incidents retained in my memory with the memoranda thickly scribbled in my note-book, promising on his part to see the product carefully through the press [*The Brooklyn Eagle*, January 29, 1864].

The so-called "detective notebooks" actually were quite different from the abbreviated form the term "notebook" suggests. One contemporary alternative to using the "notebook" tag was to use the term "diary" to describe what the readers were going to encounter. Applied more often to stories about lawyers or physicians, writers sometimes used the term "diary" in their narratives when the detective hero refers to a text for confirmation of a fact or writes down something of possible importance. "Diary" also occasionally turns up in titles. Publishers used it for one of the flood of story collections from England supposedly written by Waters—thus *Diary of a Detective Police Officer* (Dick & Fitzgerald, 1864). And it turns up in titles such as "A Leaf from the Diary of a Detective" (*The New York Ledger*, January 15, 1870) and "Quick Work, from the Diary of Hardshaw [sic] the Detective" (*New York Fireside Companion*, January 31, 1870). The term "diary," of course, suggests more intimacy than the term "notebook." And there is a class of 19th-century detective stories that uses superficial intimacy as part of their draw. This is the case in each story (and there are a lot of them) in which the rescue of a beloved is at stake. It's also the case, as the titles announce, in "How I Won My Wife" (*The Mountain Democrat*, September 17, 1870) and in "His First Case, How a Detective Found the Lost Money and a Wife" (*The Chillicothe Constitution*, March 20, 1891). The glance into a character's life is also one of the features of stories about how a character became a detective (see "Why I Became a Detective," *Daily Alta California*, January 6, 1873) and those giving details of detectives' first cases. Indeed, by the 1880s "how I became a detective" had almost become a genre cliché; thus this comment: "Some of our fellows who have been relating histories in your paper have informed you how they became detectives. All true, I believe; but there was no romance in my case" ("Caught by a Thread," *The Delta Herald*, August 3, 1883).

Memoir Stories

Going back to Vidocq, another form that affects 19th-century detective fiction is the memoir—an individual's record of significant moments or events that took place during his or her life. Like histories, memoirs aim to describe events and cite facts—even if the dates leave out a digit or two. Names, dates, places, and times, after all, underpin most detective stories. And even as the form was developing, one of its requisites was a compact description of the events and facts associated with the crime near the beginning of the narrative. And the fundamental structure of most detective stories is the description of a process: first I did this, then this, then this. Thus the ubiquity of "How" titles, as in "How the Burglars Were Taken," "How the Burglars Were Trapped," "How I Captured the Burglars," "How I Got Promoted," "How Linton Bank Was Robbed," "How to Prove an Alibi," "How We Caught Him," etc. This tendency ramifies in several directions. It connects with the aim of notebook literature to give readers an inside look at the way a profession, in this case the detective, operates. But it is also related to the urge of writers to particularize the talents and skills of their individual detective heroes, which frequently resides in their demonstration that their heroes are more logical—which often just means more methodical—than the rest of the inhabitants of the world of the story.

Connected to the memoir tradition is the fact that detective stories center upon remarkable events. One of the earliest detective stories, William Evans Burton's "The Secret Cell," starts readers off with the word *curious*:

> About eight years ago, I was the humble means of unravelling a curious piece of villainy that occurred in one of the suburbs of London; it is well worth recording, in exemplification of that portion of "Life" which is constantly passing in the holes and corners of the Great Metropolis [*Burton's Gentleman's Magazine*, September 1837].

Several years later Poe used the term "outré" for events in "Murders in the Rue Morgue." More prosaically, but still a notch above "remarkable," the term "singular" became the catchphrase for detective story writers in describing what readers were about to encounter:

> "I have a singular case before me this morning," he began. "And I am about to try your ingenuity to unravel it" ["The Young Widow: A Leaf from a Detective's Portfolio," *Wisconsin Patriot*, December 3, 1859];

> But it appeared to be one of those singular cases that defy human detection, and which are generally abandoned by those appointed to discover the culprit, and left to divine vengeance ["The Left Handed Assassin: A Detective's Story," *The Coshocton Democrat*, November 2, 1864];

and

> I had not been in the detective service long when a singular case came under my notice. I was sitting in my cozy little office looking over the county newspaper, when the door opened and a tall man walked in ["My First Case," *New York Fireside Companion*, June 27, 1868].

Teasers like these also had the advantage of drawing from readers' interest in sensationalized coverage of real crimes. Memoirs and detective stories focus on a participant in important events—indeed the principal actor in those events. It's either a happy accident or appropriate, then, that the term "memoirs" appears in the title of the second collection of Sherlock Holmes stories.

Detective Story Plots

As noted above, a number of different kinds of detective stories evolved during the 19th century. They fall into two general categories.

Circumstantial Evidence Stories

One kind of detective story plot that appeared during the 19th century evolved from 18th-century stories based on the misuse of circumstantial evidence. Originally the circumstantial evidence story was an account of injustice based on a faulty interpretation of material clues and circumstances attached to a crime and crime scene. Begun in Newgate literature as tragedies, accounts in which Providence supplied the truth after an innocent had been executed, by the first quarter of the 19th century, circumstantial-evidence stories began to show individuals instead of Providence taking over, finding real evidence, and, often at the last minute, exonerating wrongly-accused innocents. Thus began the narrative pattern of

    1. The problem: a crime, often a murder;

    2. The wrong solution based on misinterpretation of facts or bias, sometimes with dire consequences; and

    3. The right solution based on objectivity and facts

In the beginning it was lawyers who found the new evidence needed to bring about the real solution to the crimes. In "Circumstantial Evidence" (*Coldwater Sentinel*, May 11, 1849), for example, the lawyer-narrator takes the case of a man widely assumed to be guilty (blood on his clothes and flight from the scene of a murder), revisits the evidence, including conducting an interview with the physician who did the *post-mortem*, and uses scientific evidence to exonerate the man widely assumed to be guilty. Significantly, a few years earlier, Poe discussed the abuses of evidence in "The Mystery of Marie Roget," and even earlier included the topic in the plot line about the police mistakenly arresting LeBon for the grisly murders in "The Murders in the Rue Morgue." In "Thou Art the Man!" he also portrays an accused innocent—this time condemned to death by a gullible jury of rubes—who is saved by the narrator's jack-in-the-box conclusion. By the late 1850s detectives took on the role of saviors of innocents alongside lawyers. After a decade they had almost entirely taken over the role (which came to be identified as that of the detective) in stories which presented details of a crime, followed by a wrong solution, and capped off with the true solution.

One of the attractions of the plot based on the wrong solution to a problem being replaced by the right solution was its adaptability. Its basic form provided a variety of satisfactions for the writer and reader—including setting up and knocking down a straw man, overturning stubborn authority, and liberating the innocent. Indeed, it was possible, even desirable, to leave out the wrongly-accused innocent part and focus on examining an intractable problem and then unfolding the solution. By providing so much detail about the crime scene, Poe almost did this in "The Murders in the Rue Morgue," but somehow felt that he needed to include the wrongly accused LeBon. After mid-century some writers chose to keep the accused innocents in their plots and others eliminated them and expanded the focus of the problem. This brought about four basic plots of this kind of detective story:

1. Plots that depend upon crime scene investigation and demonstrate that the detective sees better than others (e.g. seeing the broken nail in the window frame);
2. plots that depend upon missing evidence and demonstrate that the detective is more adept at finding things and people than others (e.g. the missing witness);
3. plots that depend upon enigmatic or misleading circumstances and demonstrate that the detective reasons better than others (e.g. ciphers, riddles, rigged evidence); and
4. plots that depend upon intransigent evidence and demonstrate that the detective can find a new way of understanding things and events (i.e., new forensic methods and, ironically, dreams).

Each of these plots could be, and was, combined with one or more of the others to produce a more complicated narrative. And more than one solution could be produced to the problem—as when rival detectives produce contesting solutions. Additionally, stories could end with the problem unsolved, or with the discovery that there was no problem in the first place—see, for instance, "Identified by His Corns" (*The New York Ledger*, November 10, 1866), and "Detective Pierson's Queer Dream" (*The Indiana Progress*, October 17, 1872).

Hunt-and-Chase

While the 19th century witnessed the creation of a variety of plots centered upon discovery and interpretation of evidence, writers also made detectives heroes of plots anchored on hunting and chasing. These narratives begin with a very different premise than circumstantial evidence plots: the crimes are solved and perpetrators known when the story begins. They are "How Catch 'Ems" instead of "Who Done Its." And examples go back to the beginning of the detective story in the United States. One of the first "Recollections of a Police-Officer" stories to be purloined by American papers and published in this country was "The Pursuit" (see *Wisconsin Argus*, October 22, 1850). And Harper Brothers' first foray into detective fiction, as noted above, was "A Police-Officer's Seven Thousand Miles' Chase" (*Harper's Weekly*, January 3, 1857). Titles of this kind of plot frequently include the words *hunt* ("Hunt on the Highway; from the Record of a Sheriff," *The New York Ledger*, March 26, 1859); *find* ("Finding a Criminal; from the Notes of an English Detective," *The New York Ledger*, January 9, 1858); *catch* ("Catching Counterfeiters," *Iowa State*

Reporter, February 2, 1888; and *adventure* ("A Detective's Adventure," *M'Kean Miner*, May 22, 1873). Unlike evidence stories where the evildoer remains hidden until the end of the narrative, this type of story begins with the identity of the criminal—often with someone (banker, police chief, agency head) assigning the hero to arrest him or her.

If, in these stories, the criminal is known, so is the detective. And this becomes a problem, since his or her success depends upon anonymity. Consequently, disguise provided a favorite motif in this kind of plot, and the searching detective is disguised instead of the criminal. This provided readers suspense as well as a bit of actual detective tradecraft: Allan Pinkerton, in fact, would show off his closet of disguises to visitors. Disguises became so common in detective stories that comic detective stories appeared based on crossdressing detectives and criminals. Thus, in "A Detective's Experience: The Romance" (*The Corrector*, October 3, 1868) the detective becomes infatuated with the escaping forger who is disguised as a woman. It was not unusual for the object of the hunt to be the leader of a notorious and violent gang, which intensifies the danger of the task. The hunt-and-chase plots also tend to elevate the power and intelligence of the criminal who can commit crimes, avoid capture and punishment, and serve as an opponent worthy of the hero. To the same end of magnifying the hero's achievements, finding and catching villains also often involved travel to out-of-the-way uncivilized places. Occasionally writers emphasize this aspect of the story:

> as all know who are conversant with the history of the "Lone Star," the whole country was filled with outlaws and desperadoes of every description, from the common gambler and thief, down to the highway robber and cold-blooded assassin. In every settlement of note they could be found by scores, and sometimes by hundreds; and in many places they formed by far the largest portion of the population. Where this was the case they ruled in blood, might made right, and woe to him who dared to breathe of law and order. Texas at that time was to some extent composed of the refuse of creation, the scum of the earth, the dregs of society—scoundrels and villains of various nations and climes ["Arresting a Murderer" by Emerson Bennett, *The New York Ledger*, June 17, 1865].

With all of this in mind, it's not too difficult to plug in all of the things that have been said about the archetypical quest story—physical and moral trials of the journey, figurative salvation of society, etc.

Detectives

On the most elemental level, plot defines the detective. Thus by showing a tracker or a problem solver's successful action, the writer has accomplished the basic requirements of the generic detective story: the detective detecting.

It's a job that requires little in the way of characterization, and, if one factors in the traditional notion of the detective's role as furthering Providential justice, it's one that doesn't even require a human actor. Even at the middle of the century stories appeared that clearly made that point. There were dog detectives (see "The Dog Detective" by Dr. S. Compton Smith, *Puget Sound Herald*, May 3, 1860), horse detectives (see "The Horse Detective," *The New York Ledger*, March 30, 1861), and even monkey detectives (see "Zizi, the Little Detective," *The Galaxy*, July 1877). And, to be entirely frank, in some stories the characterization of the human detective does not rise much above that given to detective dogs. But that is hardly the case with the majority of detectives in 19th-century short detective fiction.

Who's the Boss?

Superficially, it is not difficult to classify detectives in 19th-century fiction: some are professionals, some are amateurs, and some are situational detectives. Thus, the wife who sets out to prove her husband's innocence is a situational detective, and the hobbyist is an amateur, but with the professional things become muddy. Just what is it that makes someone a detective? Originally being a plainclothes police officer made one a detective; that's the definition in Dickens as well as in the stories run in *Harper's* magazines at mid-century. But because of the chaos caused by political as well as garden variety corruption in American police departments, private police and detective companies sprang up in cities across the country. Also, nothing prevented individuals from running advertisements in papers and calling themselves detectives—there were no licensing laws until late in the century. On top of this, police and agency detectives often acted like independent agents—at least in the fiction—with no reports, no offices, and no schedules. While in stories imported from England and France the detectives are almost always identified as government agents, with stories about American detectives sometimes it's hard to tell if a character is a copper or a private eye, especially after 1860. Granted, some stories make the detective's employer clear. "A Detective's Story: Hasheesh" by James McMillen, for example, contains one of the few mentions of the Pinkerton Agency in newspaper fiction:

> In the fall of 1870 I was recalled from the southern part of the State, where I had been "working up" a horse case, and ordered to start immediately, upon the arrival of my relief, for Chicago, and report myself to our chief at headquarters. (I may here premise that I had been, for a number of years, a detective belonging to Pinkerton's force, and had always been considered an efficient officer by my superiors) [*Massachusetts Ploughman and New England Journal of Agriculture*, April 15, 1876].

But, considering that superiors in both police departments and private agencies carried the title "chief," often it is not simple to tell one from another. Even a reference to a particular city attached to the detective's title (for instance "Philadelphia Detective") doesn't always mean much, in that the city reference can either refer to the police force of that city or be used as a hero's credential to authenticate experience and expertise—as in the oft-reprinted New York Detective stories of the early 1860s. Sometimes, however, the reader can make a determination by inference. Thus there are stories that probably refer to a police force:

> Sitting in the front office one morning, engaged in perusing the New York papers, I heard the chief's bell tinkle rather excitedly. The sergeant answered it ["The Young Widow: A Leaf from a Detective's Portfolio," *Wisconsin Patriot*, December 3, 1859].

Some others probably refer to a private agency:

> One morning I was sent for by the chief to take up a new case, and when I entered his office I found a lady present ["A Detective's Story," *The Dunkirk Observer-Journal*, July 14, 1887].

And, finally, there are some that defy easy categorization:

> Thirty years have I been authoritatively engaged in detecting crime, and at least two thirds of my efforts have been directed against forgers, counterfeiters, coiners, and passers of spurious money. Of course I have seen brought about some curious developments in my time, and more than once I had reason to thank God that some adventure of my own did not terminate with my life ["Breaking up a Gang," *The New York Ledger*, February 4, 1865].

This vagueness stems, in part, from the tension between the belief (and reality) of the unreliability and corruption of actual police departments and the desire to demonstrate the hero's expertise. Insofar as character and theme go, however, it doesn't make a lot of difference whether the detective belongs to a government police force or a private one: as noted above, the detective is not a part of the world of the crime and is at least nominally subordinate to someone else. Most stories, however, make it clear that while the detective may belong to some sort of organization, people, usually rich and powerful people, ignore hierarchy and go right to the detective:

> I well remember when Lansing, Lyon's lawyer, called upon me and begged me to try my best to clear up the mystery. At this time I had been in the detective force nearly four years, and, of course, knew the ropes pretty well. But for a month I confess that at times I was nearly baffled ["Saved by a Mark: A Detective Story," *The Indiana Progress*, December 12, 1872].

Even when the text suggests that the detective is, as it were, a private contractor, he or she ultimately works for someone else. While this has a negligible effect on most stories, and detectives sometimes insist that the search for truth alone will govern their inquiry, a consequential number of stories do end in crimes, even murder, being hushed up, because it's the family or individual that pays the piper.

Why Be a Detective Anyway?

It's an implicit question in a number of period stories. The answer, in fact, was a natural place for a writer to start. And it was where writers separated amateurs from professionals, and was also where divergent views on police and detectives appeared. Social class had much to do with those views. Back at the beginning, class mattered to the writer of "Recollections of a Police-Officer" stories. The detective in those stories is explicitly a gentleman come upon hard times and forced to become a police officer to feed his family. Dickens, on the other hand, chose to emphasize the common touch and accessibility of his detectives at "A Detective Police Party." In spite of the fact that Vidocq was an ex-con, writers, especially American writers, portrayed their fictional French detectives as aristocrats. The stereotype carried over to Poe and endured throughout the period. Readers were not surprised when they found this Dupinesque introduction to a French detective in "The Tell-Tale Eye":

> "I think I must have been born for my profession," said Laromie, brushing the ashes from his cigar; "for in my childhood I was always finding out other persons' secrets. My companions could hide nothing from me, and it seemed to me that events had only to happen for me to know them. Many that I did not seek to learn forced themselves under my very eyes, and frequently in my great annoyance. As I grew up, this talent, for so I consider it, increased. When I came of age, I found myself in possession of an ample fortune which was left by my late father. There was no necessity for me to adopt any profession, or enter any branch of business, for my support was already guaranteed; but in order to give my talents room for legitimate use, I determined to enter the secret service of the government. The chief of the secret police was a friend, and I sought him, and asked admission into his force. At first, he advised me strongly against the course I wished to pursue, giving me many reasons which it is useless to mention here. Some of them were good, others of no consequence; but none of them sufficient to alter my determination. I pressed my application with so much earnestness that the chief at last consented to take me on trial for six months" [*Flag of Our Union*, January 20, 1866].

When it comes to writers describing the background of American detectives, the same social dichotomy existed. But the distinctions between groups were not quite the same.

Among the native detectives found in American fiction, two types of background emerge soon after detective stories begin—but the social position of detectives in the U.S. had more to do with status than class. In the introduction to the collected stories about detective James Brampton, readers learned the continuing hero's background:

> I was born in New York city. My father was a respectable merchant, and he bestowed upon me the best education that money could produce. He wished me to embrace the medical profession and for that purpose sent me to read with a physician who lived in a village on the Hudson River. This physician was a particular friend of his.
>
> I liked the study of medicine pretty well and remained several years in the physician's office. But a terrible accident happened to my father, in fact, he was burnt to death, and he left his affairs so embarrassed, that my mother could not afford the means for me to complete my medical studies. I therefore determined to seek for some more remunerative employment [*Leaves from the Note-book of a New York Detective*, New York: Dick & Fitzgerald, 1865].

Detective Brampton's personal history echoes that of Poe's Dupin and of Waters, the narrator of "Recollections of a Police-Officer," except that in Brampton's case education sets him apart. And it became a pattern. While they are efficient, helpful, and dedicated to their callings, physician detectives definitely belong to the uptown set:

> I could not help admiring the "Doctor." He was one of the handsomest men I ever saw—tall, compact, clear-cut, with an amiable face, and a perfect dresser; always looking as though he had—to use a very original phrase—just stepped out of a bandbox. He sat with his legs under my mahogany, or black oak, and sipped Amontillado, and ate broiled woodcock, precisely as though they were his daily fare. The doctor would not, perhaps, have been considered exactly the associate for a man in my position, the head of a first-class commercial house—barring all egotism—but I would have defied anyone by his looks, to have named his profession ["The First Case," *Appleton's Journal of Literature, Science and Art*, October 2, 1869].

In addition to physicians, there are lawyers, chemists, and assorted rich guys who became heroes in detective stories published in American newspapers and magazines. In fact they occupied what might be called a separate compartment of the genre. But there were other sorts of heroes who possessed entirely different backgrounds:

> George Gregory had originally begun life on the Erie Canal, and, from driving team, had, by dint of perseverance and industry, risen at last to the position of Captain of a boat. An accident at length threw him out of employment, and sent him adrift on the land. How he came to be a detective was never rightly understood, for Gregory could be reticent on that score as well as others, else be would never have achieved a reputation as a secret officer of the law, silence being naturally a golden rule in the profession ["The Detective's Story," *New York Times*, April 30, 1871].

Detective Gregory's background may be a bit of an anomaly, but it emphasizes the point that in many cases all that readers know about American detective heroes is that they work. The toffs who become detectives do so from a variety of intellectual and personal motives, but in many cases being a detective begins with needing a job:

> In the spring of 1850 I entered the detective force. I will not here give the whys and wherefores for so doing, but leave the reader to conjecture. It is said that when a man becomes a detective—a man hunter—he is desperate. The saying was applicable to my step. But why did you do it, Captain? Asks an inquisitive reader. Perhaps, my dear friend, I had been jilted; perhaps a great commercial crash had left me penniless, or doubtless I found the years of bachelorhood gathering about me, and I, with "no visible means of support." The last conjecture is most probable, don't you think so? ["Signed with my Own Blood," *The Indiana Democrat*, June 2, 1870].

And in the force, one does not start at the top. There are incentives besides finding the truth:

> "Well, good luck to you, Banks," said the superintendent, at parting; "and if you wanted, which I don't believe, any further inducement to do your best in forwarding this important capture, I am in a condition to supply it. The commissioner especially selected you for this duty; adding, that in the event of success, you might expect your immediate promotion to inspector. Now, good-by, and don't fail to bring Jennings back with you" ["The Detective as Forger," *The Berkshire County Eagle*, November 7, 1861];

and

> Of course I was too proud-spirited, despite my poverty, to receive anything, but I have always thought that he may have had something to do with my promotion, as I am sure he had influence with my superiors. Nevertheless, I like to attribute my rise entirely to my own deserts, and I may be right, after all ["The Scarlet Ribbon: A Detective's Story," *Ballou's Monthly Magazine*, December 1866].

The Policeman's Lot

Police officers' pay in the 19th century was regular but hardly generous. Beat patrolmen's wages equaled those of farm workers and police detectives' pay didn't match that of those in private practice. Because of their brevity and focus on the problem and not the person, period detective stories do not usually reflect much upon the lives of police officers in the real world. But sometimes they do. Fiction of the period contains a few comments on the economic status of the profession; comments like these:

> Jack had been a member of the police force for two or three years when I left home, and I was hardly prepared to find in the spruce, smartly dressed, gentlemanly appearing individual, my quondam friend; for it is a maxim among the blue-coated and brass-buttoned gentry that "once a policeman always a policeman."
> It was evident at a glance that Jack's "lines had fallen in pleasant places"; and the first greetings over he made me acquainted with the causes which had led to his altered condition. He was still occupied in the favorite pursuit for which he had always evinced a remarkable aptitude—the pursuit of criminals; but he was now, to use his own words, "his own man," having established an independent detective agency, whereof he still retained the head and management ["State's Evidence, A Detective Story," *Holmes County Republican*, December 15, 1870];

and

> At that time our detective system was in its infancy; and as I had recently achieved quite a reputation by the skill I displayed in ferreting out a dangerous band of burglars. I was entreated by the Chief to undertake the detection of the perpetrator or perpetrators of this foul crime. As might be expected, I set out at once to investigate the affair, and I may as well here state that I had just retired for a time from the police force, to fill a more lucrative position in a heavy importing house in Beaver Street, and that in my former occupation, I was considered one of the most expert of the detectives, and had been promoted in consequence thereof ["The Assassin's Track," *Strange Stories of a Detective; or The Curiosities of Crime*, New York: Dick & Fitzgerald, 1863].

But there were ways for police detectives to supplement their income. In *The Great Metropolis* (1867) Junius Henri Browne discusses this aspect of the compensation package of the actual New York City police force:

> Their regular pay varies from three to eight dollars a day for "piping," "shadowing," "working-up," etc.; but they have such latitude in "contingent expenses," "special arrangements," and "individual enterprises" that no limit can be fixed to their profits. The chief detectives have a salary of $2,500 a year, but they make five or ten times that sum often, and frequently acquire a large property. Bank officers and persons having responsible positions in stores are watched, the moment the least suspicion is excited by their conduct; and, if they are using money not their own, they are always found out and reported, unless they happen to pay the detective better than his employer does.

In 1898 the Lexow Committee's report revealed that the New York Police Department was built on a structure of bribery, extortion, and graft. Patrolmen had set fees they charged various kinds of businesses on their beats, and hiring and promotion both depended on bribery. It was a pattern followed by police departments across the U.S. Additionally, one of the accepted parts of detectives' lives was the reward system, a practice whereby victims of robbery offered monetary rewards for the return of the stolen article, not the arrest of the criminal. Writers occasionally mention this, usually in passing. Thus, in "The Costly Kiss" the detective narrator says

> And then another thing, the *recovery of the money* was really my main business. Justice is all very well, of course, but I knew that the hardware firm down town cared considerably more for their sixteen thousand dollars than for the appropriator thereof, especially, mind you, if said appropriator should prove to be *one of themselves*, as I may say [*Harper's New Monthly Magazine*, April 1859].

"The Detective's Story," which the *Times* advertisement ballyhooed as "Being an original tale of particular interest, embodying incidents which have their counterparts in actual occurrences," mentions rewards, too, but adds the most corrupt part of the system: collusion between criminals and the police:

> That was pretty good for those days, though I presume the "fly cops," nowadays, wouldn't think much of it. No reward was offered for the stuff carried off, as the common practice

now, so there was no inducement to look for the goods except for evidence. Merchants in these days know their own business best, I suppose, else they would not send the Police after stolen property to gain big rewards. I could give you many a queer case where burglars got good hauls in ready money by surrendering their swag to detectives, who, in return, pretended they couldn't find the criminals, and yet shared the rewards with them [*New York Times*, April 30, 1871].

This aspect of the reward system also formed the target of a short satirical piece ascribed to Mark Twain titled "Making a Fortune" (*The Indiana Democrat*, November 2, 1871) in which a bank custodian extorts a reward for the return of stolen money. The majority of period fiction, however, did not examine the whole system of rewards too closely. Instead rewards largely served as suitable recognition and compensation for work well done. Fictional detectives display a variety of attitudes toward rewards. These include the purely materialistic:

> For a month or more, while among my friends in Vermont, I thought little of the occurrence. It is true the thousand dollar reward would occasionally come into my mind; but as I was not employed in the case, the prospect of getting it was exceedingly small ["The Detective's Story," *Janesville Weekly Gazette*, March 4, 1864].

But most commonly, rewards serve to complement the success of the detective solving the crime problem—typically the detective enables others' happiness by exonerating an innocent and receives a reward to enable his or her own happiness. Not surprisingly, this often takes the form of acquiring the cash necessary to marry the partner of his or her dreams. But the detective's life included other incentives.

Along with cash rewards, promotion played a role in the life of the fictional detective of the period. The most overt example is "How I Got Promoted: A Detective's Story" (*The Decatur Daily Review*, December 20, 1880), which originally ran in *Chambers'*, but it wasn't only British detectives who mentioned promotion as part of their professional lives. Plenty of American stories mention it, too; here are two printed in Iowa in the 1880s:

> He then returned to the car and sat closely watching his prey. They did not indulge in any more conversation of a criminal nature, but Hiram did not relax his espionage on that account. He felt that he now had his future in the hollow of his hand, and visions of special promotion in the detective force flitted before his eyes ["A Private Detective," *Sumner Gazette*, October 19, 1882]

and

> My firm—a detective agency—had been instructed by the authorities at Mineral Point to depute some one to attend the inquest and to sift the affair to the bottom. An intimation was given me that speedy promotion would follow on my unraveling the mystery, and as I got unlimited discretion concerning my line of action, whether as regards the time I should occupy about the business, the expenses I might incur or the assistance, if any, I should

avail myself of, I felt that my professional reputation was at stake and that if another such murder were to be committed ere I had unearthed the guilty parties, the sooner I changed my vocation for some other the better for myself and my employers ["Number Eight," *The Waterloo Courier*, December 15, 1886].

While rewards and promotions were a faint reflection of facts connected with the real profession of detection, they also helped establish fictional detectives as people who worked. Implications of the relationship between detective and client regarding class and power were no doubt irrelevant to most writers and readers because they and their publishers had a different perspective. They were part of portraying the hero as a secure middle-class person. Indeed, they represented an American and British effort to portray policing and detection as part of the community as opposed to control and surveillance imposed by the government—i.e., the French way of policing. Thus the detective resembled an intelligent, approachable, hardworking, helpful neighbor. The stories with emcee narrators begin with the suggestion that the detective is someone who is recognized, respected, and that others will want to hear his or her story. And, for better or worse, another way of creating a middle-class hero was through wives. This began with the earliest stories, with the detective's wife in "Recollections of a Police-Officer" in the 1850s: Waters becomes a cop to support his wife and family. Wives and families continue in stories throughout the period. In almost all of the Brampton stories of the late 1850s and 1860s the detective's wife enters briefly to play a supporting role ("On one cold January night I was seated lazily by my fireside enjoying a cup of tea which my wife knows so well how to make, when a violent ring at the front door bell disturbed the reverie in which I was indulging" ["The Club Foot," *Ballou's Dollar Monthly Magazine*, August 1862]). "The Pigot Murder" by C. Davis, in fact, begins with a description of the comfortable middle-class life, in which the wife fulfills the 19th-century man's dreams of a comfortable life:

> I had been eight years on the special detective force in Philadelphia when that trouble about Joe Myers turned up. Joe was an old chum of mine: the only red-headed fellow I ever did trust, by-the-way, but it was a matter of propinquity; my father's tavern and old Pete Myers' shop were close beside each other, on the L— turnpike; he and I were in the same classes in the district school; and after that, worked together on Squire Hall's farm, year in and year out, until I got the chance of an opening up in town. The fact is, whatever success I met with there is due to a succession of lucky chances—hits, as I may say, at discoveries in my line of business, rather than any astuteness of mine. That troubled me but little; it was enough that I did succeed; at the end of the eight years had a snug marble-slabbed brick house out on Green Hill, which my wife had as prettily fixed up as any of the old blooded nobs in town. She had a fanciful way of hanging plant baskets about, and matching colors in carpets and the other trumpery, that set off a room somehow; she got up prime little game suppers for our friends, in winter, too; we had the boys at good schools; and altogether, bid fair to settle down early into a comfortable, easy middle age. Next to Pike (the chief) I had

the best salary on the staff; and no man on the force was so often called on for fancy jobs; and they always pay well [*Harper's New Monthly Magazine*, December 1864].

Enter the Amateur

While one of the intents of 19th-century detective stories was to convince readers that professional detectives were useful, admirable, necessary, hard-working, and even wholesome individuals, nevertheless a lot of stories centered on amateur detectives. Because amateurs played different roles from professional detectives in their respective fictional worlds, readers developed different relationships with them than they did with professionals. Those relationships, however, were various because amateur detectives came to play a variety of roles in 19th-century detective fiction. Sorted out, those roles fall under six headings.

Lovers: In some detective stories the pursuit of truth coincides with the pursuit of a life partner, and the solution to the problem enables the union of the lovers. The circumstantial evidence plot was made for lovers, as seen in "A Bit of Detective Business" (*Frank Leslie's Pleasant Hours*, February 1868) in which the amateur narrator saves the beautiful governess Miss Armingdon from false accusation and winds up marrying her. Without the suspense of freeing an innocent, love provides sufficient inducement for an amateur hero to track down the villain as in "A Wild Goose Chase" (*Sullivan Republican*, August 23, 1889) in which the amateur detective finds (and later marries) the missing legatee, or in "Justice vs. Mercy" (*St. Tammany Farmer*, April 27, 1889) in which the amateur hero finds the embezzler and gets the boss' daughter. As well as serving as motive and reward, love persists beyond the grave; it prompts the bereft lover in "The Brand of Cain" (*Turner County Herald*, September 8, 1887) to find the murderer of his beloved. To be sure this kind of amateur detective story crosses over into the category of courtship romance—and *vice versa*.

Women: As seen above, the biases of the time denied women access to most professions, including that of detective. Even though unheralded, women actually acted as detectives during the period, but when they appeared as heroes in detective fiction it was inevitably as amateurs. Their roles often mirrored those of the amateur lover heroes but hedged with the constrained roles imposed on women. Frequently those constraints necessitated playing unaccustomed roles or acting in disguise.

Nuisances: Enthusiasm and faulty judgment are not good companions. They lead to demonstrably wrong answers. Nuisance detectives either catch Betteredge's "detective fever" or share a Walter Mitty–esque dream of being sleuths:

> Hiram Hazlett had for months been much interested in newspaper accounts of cases in which private personages attained fame by acting as amateur detectives in cases where professionals had failed. He was constantly revolving in his mind the possibility of sometime acquiring fame in such line himself, and was fond of picturing his course of conduct under circumstances which he would imagine himself in. With this proemial clause, we will proceed to follow Mr. Hazlett on his way to catch the early morning train for the city, where he was engaged in the hardware business ["A Private Detective," *Sumner Gazette*, October 19, 1882].

Typically they get in trouble by suspecting the wrong person, which leads to discovery and then deflation. Thus this rebuke at the end of "A Fourfold Alibi":

> The superintendent sent for Mr. Pryor the next day and told him that Mr. James Anderson had conclusively proven his innocence. "Let me advise you," he continued, "to leave your present boarding house at once. You are liable to arrest for breaking into other people's rooms; and if you ever breathe another suspicion against anybody in connection with Mr. Anderson's death, I will have you arrested at once for burglary. If you have any business of your own, attend to it and leave eavesdropping and spying to men who are paid to do such dirty work [*Wellsboro Agitator* February 6, 1877].

These stories run to farce, comedy, and satire, as in "Mr. Buston's Eye: Amazing Detective Work Performed by That Organ" (*Abilene Weekly Reflector*, September 26, 1889). Their relative popularity provides a perspective on the maturity of the detective story as a genre.

Boys: Part of the growth and development of the detective story involved the emergence of boys' literature in the form of boys' story papers and dime novel "libraries":

> The adventures in the adult papers were not beyond the capacity of the boys; but one, and then another, conceived the idea of conciliating their especial interest by making a paper for them, till this branch, with its Boys' Journal, Boys of New York, Boys of America, Boys of the World, Young Men of New York, Young Men of America, has become rather the larger of the two. The heroes are boys, and there are few departments of unusual existence in which they are not seen figuring to brilliant advantage. They are shown amply competent as the Boy Detective, the Boy Spy, the Boy Trapper, the Boy Buccaneer, the Boy Guide, the Boy Captain, the Boy Robinson Crusoe, the Boy Claude Duval, and the Boy Phoenix, or Jim Bledsoe Jr., whose characteristic is to be impervious to harm in burning steamboats and hotels, exploding mines, and the like ["Story Paper Literature," *The Atlantic Monthly*, September 1879].

In some quarters this led to a debate about the harmful effects of boys reading detective stories and being drawn in to a world of fantasy criminals and detectives. It's what happens in "An Amateur Detective" by James M'Cabe:

> This young gentleman's ideas had not been derived from his native town; for among his other accomplishments was a decided familiarity with a certain species of literature commonly known as "yellow covers," and devoted to the exploits and achievements of such

heroes as Tom King, Claude Duval, and Dick Turpin, and others of more modern fame. Being well acquainted with the thieving community through these mediums, young Harper recognized at once the robberies the work of some most accomplished burglar. As he kept his familiarity with the works I have mentioned a secret from his parents, he was unable to give any reason for his assertion that there was nothing superhuman in the affair, and was commanded by his father to hold his tongue in the future. Anxious to distinguish himself, and burning to excel the famous thief-takers of whom he had read, young Harper quietly formed the daring resolution of attempting to discover the thief who was committing so many depredations in B—, and to bring him to justice [*Flag of Our Union*, October 12, 1867].

In this case, however, the boy detective reasons better than the adults in his community and identifies the thieves. But this is an anomaly in the world of adult story paper and newspaper detective fiction, which assiduously stayed away from boy heroes throughout the period.

Heroes: C. August Dupin, of course, is the star turn of early detective fiction. He is emphatically not a professional detective; if anything Dupin is a gentleman intellectual. Not a lot of writers followed Poe's lead. In France, Émile Gaboriau did—sort of: his M. Lecoq began as an amateur polymath detective and appeared as such in the U.S. in a variety of translations, including "An Amateur Detective" (*The Sunday Herald*, March 15, 1885). Late in the century with accelerating advances in forensic sciences, the occasional superstar detective does appear in print. Thus the hero of "The Print of a Finger" by David Ker:

Born of an English mother and American father, he had inherited the beauty of the one with the keen intellect of the other, and had made his nickname of "The Amateur Detective" famous in every part of the world.
Why he had taken up this singular pursuit, devoting himself to hunting down criminals, as other men take to botany or geology, no one could tell; but his name had long since become a proverb for reckless daring and super-human ingenuity, and it was a common saying with the police of London and New York, that "for anything with a knot in it, there wasn't nobody like the 'Amateur'["] [*Frank Leslie's Popular Monthly*, January 1882].

For most of the century, however, most amateur detective stories were not about leisure-class geniuses. A significant portion of them related the experiences that convinced individuals to become professional detectives. In effect they are stories about interns or apprentices. The narrator of "The Detective's Story" puts it this way:

Perhaps, however, I should call it an amateur rather than a professional experience, for I was not then a member of the force, and took hold of the case merely because it interested me deeply. It was my success in this case and the reputation it gave me that afterwards decided me in the choice of our really glorious profession [*The Richwood Gazette*, October 1, 1874].

Other amateur detectives become heroes because they have to—to free themselves from suspicion or accusation. Finally, one early amateur detective stands out. He appears in Harriet E. Prescott Spofford's "In a Cellar." The author uniquely drew a character who actually thinks seriously about his actions:

> As I sat actively discussing the topic, feeling no more interest in it than in the end of that cigar I just cut off, and noting exactly every look and motion of the unfortunate youth, I recollect the curious sentiment that filled me regarding him. What injury had he done me, that I should pursue him with punishment? Me? I am, and every individual is, integral with the commonwealth. It was the commonwealth he had injured. Yet, even then, why was I the one to administer justice? Why not continue with my coffee in the morning, my kings and cabinets and national chess at noon, my opera at night, and let the poor devil go? Why, but that justice is brought home to every member of society,—that naked duty requires no shirking of such responsibility,—that, had I failed here, the crime might, with reason, lie at my door and multiply, the criminal increase himself? [*The Atlantic Monthly*, February 1859].

But this is a very rare glance into the conscience of any kind of detective—not seen again until Prescott Spofford's "Mr. Furbush" (*Harper's New Monthly Magazine*, April 1865).

Dogs, and Assorted Other Animals: It is, of course, not quite accurate to include animals as amateur detectives. But in the old fashioned murder-will-out detective story they serve as detectives, identifying evildoers aiding in their capture and punishment. They feature (in order of frequency) dogs, horses, cats, and monkeys.

Speakers and Listeners

A lot of mid-century detective stories assume the form of an imagined conversation between a detective and a listener or listeners, conversations like:

> The first step I took was to get my cards printed. Here's one of them that I keep as a memento of the case. You see, I describe the bills, noting particularly the private mark—the "Co"—and offer a reward to any one giving information at police head-quarters of the person offering such bills [...] ["The Costly Kiss, a New York Detective Experience," *Harper's New Monthly Magazine*, April 1859]

and

> Yes, sir, as you say, a detective's life is full of danger, and often accompanied with something not unlike romance. Perhaps you would like to hear a short narration of one of my experiences in the work? ["A Detective's Story," *Flag of Our Union*, June 1, 1867].

These conversations quickly turn into narratives about something the detective's profession led him or her to encounter and surmount—an adventure, a problem, or both. The narratives fall into two categories. One is the straightforward, presumptive autobiography in which the reader is the listener. These can begin as professional anecdotes like "The Mysterious Advertisement" from the New York Detective series that begins without preface with "The nature of my profession brings me in contact with every description of person. I have formed through its agency many pleasant acquaintanceships, to which my memory often reverts with pleasure" (*Ballou's Dollar Monthly Magazine*, July 1862). The detective speakers also sometimes embed a professional anecdote in a frame story about a personal experience, as in "A Detective's Story":

> I was a poor man, he said, and the profession of a detective a precarious one. His daughter loved me, he could not deny that—but she was his only child, and her wealth and position demanded a match with some social equal. He would not break her heart by absolutely refusing to sanction our engagement, but if, within a year, I could secure a fortune of $25,000 lucrative business, and Edna was still of the same mind—well, he would consider the matter [*Defiance Democrat*, October 17, 1878].

The second pattern of these first-person narratives in effect employs an emcee who introduces the detective and acts as audience. Thus "The Detective's Story" begins this way:

> I was pacing the deck of one of our floating palaces on Lake Erie, arm-in-arm with John Smith, who was accounted one of the smartest detectives in his corps. Business relations, to which I may take occasion to refer at some future time, had brought us in contact, and a casual acquaintance had ripened into intimacy [*Flag of Our Union*, April 14, 1866].

Unlike the "Watson" character introduced by Poe, the emcee steps away and the detective takes over and finishes out the narrative by recounting his or her own experiences. Stories like these then have two narrators and two listeners, the emcee and the reader.

In many 19th-century detective stories, there is, in fact, a noticeable movement away from the tone associated with the diary and notebook forms, the first intimate and personal and the second terse and official. In detective stories of the period, readers commonly find themselves included with the audience inside the narrative. Some early stories, like "The Costly Kiss," present a deferential speaker who explains the curiosities of detective work to visiting gentry. Others, however, introduce what was going to be the dominant tone of detective narrators: a casual, friendly, even welcoming atmosphere. It's an atmosphere conveyed and enhanced by the use of the term "yarn," a term denoting an informal narrative shared with companions sometimes perhaps even stretching the bounds of credulity. It's used in titles, like "A Detective's Yarn" (*The Golden Era*, October 19, 1862) and "Beat the Brace Game: A Detective's Yarn of the Early Days of the Mississippi" (*St. Paul Daily Globe*, March 15, 1888). And it comes up in narrators' dialogue:

> I think I can make out a story that you won't get tired listening to. Some of my friends tell me a good parson was lost to the world when I turned policeman. Well, anyhow, here's a

straight yarn this time, if I know how to spin it, and I'll do my best, I promise you ["A Detective's Experience," *Harper's Weekly*, December 4, 1858];

Now that I have spun my yarn, and finished my cigar at the same time, let us adjourn to the saloon, and renew our game of draughts ["The Detective's Story," *Flag of Our Union*, April 14, 1866];

and

On a dismal, gloomy evening in the fall of 18—, some half dozen of us sat in the back parlor of the café Bordeaux, quaffing our coffee, speculating on our future prospects, and now and then spinning a yarn ["The Detective," *New York Fireside Companion*, June 29, 1869].

The last example joins telling stories with a comfortable, convivial atmosphere—the same kind of atmosphere found in "How Bob Bolter's Prisoner Escaped" in which the detective "loves to take a quiet 'drop' into my easy chair in the little study, and with a Romano cigar in one corner of his mouth, play narrator from the other side" (*Harper's Weekly*, July 25, 1857). Indeed, smoking serves as the fulcrum for a lot of detective storytelling. Like the comfort (and companionship) of cigars, it is not unusual to find stories begin with the narrator next to a fire or stove on a raw and blustery day:

I was sitting in the office of our chief about nine o'clock in the morning—let me see, it was much such a day as this—raw, and damp, and blustering. I was tucked up near the stove ["Robbery of Plate" by Harry Harewood Leech, *Flag of Our Union*, December 17, 1859];

I sat by my fire late in the evening gazing intently on the blazing coals, and hoping some "job" would turn up in a day or two, for rent was high, and coals and brandy-and-water were absolutely necessary to keep out the cold ["Watched and Watching: A Detective Story," *The Albion: A Journal of News, Politics and Literature*, July 14, 1860];

and

While sitting alone in my London office once one dull, dark, drizzly October afternoon, indulging in the luxury of a quiet smoke, the door opened in a timid, hesitating manner, and an old, wrinkled, gray-headed, gray-bearded man... ["Mysterious Robberies: A Detective's Story," *The New York Ledger*, March 1, 1862].

This repeated unpretentious, homey atmosphere at the beginning helps to establish fellow feeling between the narrator and the reader/listener. It also sets up the contrasts between inside and outside, action and repose, safety and danger, peace and chaos, creative thought and conventions, comfort and adventure.

A number of detective narrators connect their stories with a stage in their professional lives. Typically these begin at the beginning and recount first successes. Thus

I had not been in the detective service long when a singular case came under my notice. I was sitting in my cozy little office looking over the county newspaper, when the door opened and a tall man walked in ["My First Case," *New York Fireside Companion*, June 27, 1868]

and

Nancy Harrigan was convicted of grand larceny at the next term of Court, and the Chief was so well pleased with me that I was placed off the regular force; and thus it was that I became a detective ["Why I Became a Detective," *Daily Alta Californian*, January 6, 1873].

And detective narrators are not coy about characterizing their yarns before they tell them. Readers are frequently promised thrills, not just in the stories' titles but also in openings like these:

Few men in the Secret Service have attained a higher reputation or encountered more perils that Ambrose Beckham. I knew him for years before I could ever prevail on him to recount any of his adventures; but meeting him in Boston about a year ago, I succeeded in getting several interesting stories from him, among them the following, which he related in his modest way ["A Mountain Adventure," *Defiance Democrat*, February 25, 1875]

and

What life is more thrilling than that of a police detective, what more full of startling adventure—An incident in the experience of two men well known in the city of New Orleans, as the most skillful and accomplished detectives in the Southern country, has been related to the reporter ["A Detective's Story," *The Cedar Valley Times*, September 17, 1868].

As noted above, most 19th-century short detective fiction has first-person narrators, whether they are detectives, lawyers, physicians, amateurs, friends, or family. There are, however, some third-person narratives about detectives. Third-person narratives engage readers in a different way than do first-person stories. And, other than the subject being a detective solving a crime, little about most of the third-person short detective fiction makes it stand out from other kinds of third-person storytelling. But there are a few exceptions. Two of them are "The Victory; a Strange Crime and Its Solution" (*Sioux County Herald*, June 8, 1876) and "The Left Hand" (*The Janesville Gazette*, August 7, 1879). Both relate stories about detectives solving murders, but both pause in order to provide readers with lists highlighting significant facts about the crime and crime scene. Coincidentally both lists consist of six items. In "The Victory" point six makes it clear to even the most obtuse that Mrs. Duncomb had a great deal to do with her husband's murder:

6. The blood from the wound in Mr. Duncomb's throat had spurted over the bed, and the sheets and pillows on Mrs. Duncomb's side were spotted with it, but there was no stain of blood on Mrs. Duncomb's night clothes. Moreover, the stains were on the bottom sheet on Mrs. Duncomb's side, and on the inside of the top sheet, but none on the coverlet—a proof that she could not have been in the bed when the wound was inflicted, but that the clothes on her side were turned down.

In "The Left Hand" the last of the "numerous and pregnant" points prefigures the famous dog-in-the-night query:

> 6. Were the dog and the murderer old friends? If they were the savage beast's quietness was accounted for.

Both of these stories, then, seek to make the reader into an active participant in the problem solving that lies at the center of the detective's role. But this did not become a requisite part of the detective story for another half-century.

It's Not Just a Job

For one thing, detective stories make the point that detectives are necessary. Imported stories made the point:

> I am a detective. I am not ashamed to own it; indeed, I am proud of my profession, as every good detective ought to be. I know some people look down on a policeman. I should like to know what they should do for aid against the rogues and swindlers who always abound in wealthy cities if it were not for us. The very people who make the most fun of us are the first to seek our aid if they are robbed and swindled ["Caught by a Thread: An English Detective's Story," *The Delta Herald*, August 3, 1883].

And, in very different context, American stories, too, demonstrated the necessity of detectives. Small towns sometimes needed detectives and sent for them, and they played a role in taming the frontier:

> The Vigilance Committee was then a thing of the past; there were rude court-houses, sheriffs, half-civilized policemen, and other formulas, and frequently honest attempts at the administration of justice, to be met with even at the foot of the Sierra Nevada; and consequently my profession found employment as the emergencies of the times arose ["The Murders at Sunset Canyon," *Harper's Weekly*, August 18, 1866].

Consistently, detective heroes talk about themselves as belonging to a profession. Brampton, in the New York Detective stories, repeatedly brings up the term:

> The nature of my profession brings me in contact with every description of person. I have formed through its agency many pleasant acquaintanceships, to which my memory often reverts with pleasure ["The Mysterious Advertisement," *Ballou's Dollar Monthly Magazine*, July 1862].

Belonging to a profession carries with it a certain éclat not attached to a mundane endeavor like a job or a trade. It's a source of pride—which the narrator of "The Buried Bullet" expresses at the beginning of that story:

> I had first become a detective from choice. I felt pride in my profession and took especial pleasure in the working up of intricate and mysterious cases, and the one thus accidentally brought under my notice interested me at once.

And one acquires a reputation for professional expertise, a reputation that needs to be maintained:

> He had only an unintelligible paper to work upon, and the government expected him to discover the whole matter. Laromie was a shrewd man, and now that he felt that his reputation was at stake, he resolved to exert himself to the utmost to succeed ["An Official Blunder" by James D. M'Cabe, Jr., *Flag of Our Union*, April 28, 1866]

and

> If we had been superstitious, we must have come to the conclusion that witchcraft was at work. As it was, we only felt chagrined and angry, and firmly resolved that, as our very reputation was at stake, we would leave no stone unturned to ferret out the mystery ["A Sewer Rat: A Leaf from a Detective's Life," *Frank Leslie's Pleasant Hours*, November 1873].

There is more to belonging to a profession, however, than social utility and personal satisfaction. By definition, professions require members to possess particular education and training, and to demonstrate specific skills, unknown among lay people. So, what is it besides a badge that makes a detective a detective? Especially since badges are rarely mentioned in period fiction anyway.

Professional Requirements

Most detectives have had some kind of experience with a police force where lessons can be learned:

> When I first entered the force I was told that I must cultivate my bump of patience, and I have had occasion to learn the value of the advice. It was annoying to have day after day go by with no advance made in my work, but there was no help for it. It was nearly a week before I got even a nibble ["The Costly Kiss," *Harper's New Monthly Magazine*, April 1859].

Size and strength, among the few qualities required in real police forces, are assumed and receive scant mention in period fiction. Indeed writers spend little or no time in the physical description of their detective heroes other than giving them Anglo-Saxon names. Background and gender are only mentioned in the rare cases of women detectives or the occasional detective of exotic origin—typically Germanic. Patience, along with diligence, watchfulness, and alertness were the qualities long associated with the watch and the beat patrol officer. And they were the principal qualities necessary for most heroes of hunt-and-chase stories. Indeed, "track" and "tracking" appear in, and form the basis of, lots of detective stories throughout the period. It was something that titles advertised: e.g., "The Assassin's Track" (*Strange Stories of a Detective; or Curiosities of Crime*, New York: Dick & Fitzgerald, 1863); "On his Track, a Detective's Story" (*Massachusetts Ploughman and New England Journal of Agriculture*, October 10, 1885); and "A Detective Story: Tracking a Burglar" (*Grant County News*,

July 24, 1890.) At mid-century *clew* (or *clue*), the word for a thread from a spool or a string from a ball of yarn to follow and wind up, became a ubiquitous term and an essential concept in detective stories. Further, by the end of the century not just chasing or following but also "shadowing" (i.e., following unnoticed) became a normal part of the detective's repertoire. It gets triple billing in Lawrence Lynch's novel *Shadowed by Three* (1879) and by 1890 the skill also became associated with the most tawdry part of the private detective business in "Tale of a Shadow, Many a Merry Chase After an Eccentric Young New Yorker. The Divorce Detective's Puzzle" (*Pittsburg Dispatch*, October 26, 1890).

From the beginning of stories about detectives, disguise served as a necessary adjunct to tracking. A set of false whiskers formed part of many detectives' kits. Here's one of the many references to them:

> It was my first evening in town, and as I was sitting within the friendly walls of the St. Nicholas, wrapped in a cloud of tobacco smoke and a fine specimen of the latest style of false whiskers and moustache, I saw enter a very dear friend, from whom, two years before, I had parted in California.
>
> As he passed, he glanced at me, but did not recognize me. I was glad of it, for it assured me that my false whiskers would be a valuable aid to me as a disguise in the search which on the next day I intended to commence ["How I Wasn't Taken Down, from the Journal of a Detective," *Vermont Watchman and State Journal*, March 29, 1861].

While he disdains disguises in the first two stories and emphasizes more esoteric skills, even Dupin resorts to a disguise when he visits Minister D— in "The Purloined Letter." From the writers' point of view, the disguised hero supplied opportunities for suspense and danger due to the possibility that the detective's identity might be revealed and his life endangered—as in stories like "A Detective Story" (*New York Fireside Companion*, November 22, 1869), in which the narrator watches his colleague murdered by a gang. The disguised hero also served to magnify the intelligence and threatening character of the villain—as in "The Purloined Letter," in which Dupin dons green specs to visit the villain's apartment. Disguise also carries with it the possibility of understanding the mind of the criminal through role-playing, but this is a strictly 20th-century idea.

The one universal attribute possessed among detective heroes is that they see better than anyone in their worlds. They notice things others do not and therefore both avoid errors and come to better conclusions than those who do not look as carefully or as well or as objectively. Noticing and understanding the tuft of hair, the sailor's ribbon, and the broken window lock allow Dupin to solve the mystery in "The Murders in the Rue Morgue." This focus on the scene of the crime—CSI if you will—slowly gained traction among writers beginning in the 1860s, when it became a standard part of detective fiction.

6. Detectives and Their Stories 209

Thus, in the eight stories we have found published in 1862, one depends on a trained horse, one on surveillance, one on courtroom cross-examination, two on knowledge of criminals' history, and three on crime scene analysis. Significantly, all three appeared in *Ballou's Dollar Monthly Magazine*:

> "If this is all the proof they have got against your friend, it does not amount to much," said he. "With respect to the handkerchief, you see it is only bloody in spots; had it been used in murder it would have been saturated equally through the whole fabric; the blood on the knife is at least two weeks old, and the challenge evidently written two or three months ago—you see the paper looks quite yellow, and has already faded" ["The Knotted Handkerchief" by Percy Garrett, July 1862];

> "Here are the stockings," I replied, going to a comer of the apartment, and taking from it a pair of woolen stockings—"which you wore over your boots, and here are some small pieces of paper still adhering to them with which the floor of the study was strew when you entered. I have also discovered a letter which your wife was writing at the time you stole behind her" ["Stabbed in the Back," September 1862];

and

> Examine the back of your coat. Do you see those two leaves from the almond tree sticking to it? They are fastened there by the blood of your victim. The high wind blew them after you, as you had in all probability turned to leave the spot, and there they are, a damning proof of your guilt ["The Accusing Leaves," November 1862].

Indeed, some writers wove the ability to see and remember facts into their hero's thought patterns:

> With the rapidity of lightening I recalled each peculiarity which I had noticed in the manner and bearing of the sub-agent since his arrival at the farm-house; and the rapid deduction which I was instantly able to draw from them was such as to almost to [*sic*] disbelief ["A Curious Stratagem" by James F. Franklin, *Ballou's Dollar Monthly Magazine*, April 1859].

Late in the century the notion appeared that close observation was a trait acquired from Native Americans. Thus a variously titled story, about white settlers' encounter with crime and a Native American, circulated in American, Australian, and New Zealand papers in the mid–1880s:

> The story about an Indian who found a white man lying dead in the woods with a bullet hole in his forehead is one of the best illustrations of the habit of observation which a detective must cultivate. The Indian came into the white settlement and told the settlers his story: "Found white man dead in woods. Had hole in his head. Short white man shot him with long gun. Ramrod of gun three inches beyond muzzle of gun. Wore grey woolen coat. Had little dog with short tail. Had waited long while for dead man to come along."
> "How do you know all this? Did you see it?" was naturally demanded of the Indian.
> "Oh, yes I me saw; now show you."
> The settlers visited the scene of the murder, and the Indian showed them the spot where the murderer had waited for his victim. He had set his gun against the tree. It was a long one, because the bark was grazed high up, and about three inches above the mark left by the

muzzle there was a slight mark made by the ramrod, showing that it projected three inches. The man wore a gray woolen coat, because where he had leaned against the tree little particles of grey threads had been caught by the bark. There was the place where the little dog sat on his haunches—his stump tail left a mark in the yielding soil. The murderer was short, became when he reloaded his gun he set the butt a good way from his feet. The trail he left coming and going showed he was white, because he turned his toes out. Indians never did. The trail also showed that the one coming to the tree was older than the one going away from it—hence the murderer had waited ["The Detective Quality," *Weekly Valley Herald*, February 7, 1884, which credits as its source the *New York Times*].

Whatever its origin, being an acute observer became one of the professional qualifications of the detective story detective. In the last quarter of the century, however, detectives and their stories invented or acquired new ways to see and new means to interpret what they saw. Enter then stories that turn on photographs (see, especially, "Mr. Furbush," *Harper's New Monthly Magazine*, April 1865) and microscopes (see "Saved by a Mark: A Detective Story," *The Indiana Progress*, December 12, 1872). Enter roles for chemists (see "The Mysterious Murder, Leaves from the Diary of a Detective," *The New York Ledger*, December 11, 1869) and too many autopsy surgeons to cite. As for new ways to interpret crime scenes, as seen above, there is an increasing interest in fingermarks in stories throughout the period, tests for poisons (especially arsenic) appear, and in American stories in particular, detectives in stories discover that bullets reveal their history by themselves.

Seeing details, no matter how minute they are, however, ultimately returns the readers and writers to the fundamental definition of evidence: things are things, not direct evidence; they require inference and explanation and therefore are circumstantial. Things might be sufficient evidence for convictions someday in the imagined future, but they surely weren't in the 19th century. Writers could not simply displace suspicion and bad evidence with good evidence and a packaged conclusion. Or rather they could do so by introducing an offstage deathbed confession, or the providential return of a victim, or the accidental discovery of the jewelry the housemaid was accused of stealing. But as the conventions of the detective story developed, doing any of those things was either out of bounds or served as the basis of comedy or other kinds of literary light fare. Providence may have been good enough in old stories about justice, but in detective stories if unseen hands were there at all they had to work through detectives. And detectives had not only to see things, they had to explain how they noticed what they noticed and what it all meant.

Gifts and Talents

Providence, of course, could work its way back into a detective story the same way it had done so for millennia, through dreams. The solutions in a few period stories depend upon dreams; stories such as "Saved by a Dream" (*Grand Traverse Herald*, July 24, 1873); "My Uncle's Story: How a Murderer Was Discovered by Dreams" (*Chicago Tribune*, January 24, 1875), and "A Clew in a Dream: A Detective Who Firmly Believes in the Truth of Visions" (*St. Louis Globe-Democrat*, June 10, 1886). But on the subject of dreams, there is also "Detective Pierson's Queer Dream," which finishes with

> "Well," said Detective Pierson, "that was the queerest of all. I didn't. He wasn't the man, being the son of a rich merchant in the West. He had lost his finger in the war, never had any whiskers, and his teeth were his own. To crown all, the man I wanted was subsequently arrested in Texas. Since then I never believed in dreams" [*The Indiana Progress*, October 17, 1872].

It may not be a dream, but intuition can sometimes work and be just as non-rational as dreams. Some detective heroes use it, but see intuition as inexplicable:

> During the transaction I had more than once glanced at the man, that I might fix his features upon my mind, as I had actually become possessed of the idea that the notes might be counterfeit. Why I cannot tell. Was it intuition? or was it that vague warning which nature sometimes gives to one's inner consciousness when danger is near, and yet none is apparent to the senses? ["Shoving the Queer," *Ballou's Monthly Magazine*, July 1884].

Some try to account for it, but do so feebly:

> In cases of many conjectures, I have often been correctly guided by a remarkable power of intuition, answering to the instinct of the animal, but which I cannot explain or account for on any known hypothesis; and bringing this particular faculty to bear upon the subject that occupied my attention, I summed up in this wise: that the murderer was about five feet eight inches in [height], of medium proportions, good figure, fashionably dressed, of pleasing manners, with a dark complexion, a keen, scrutinizing countenance, and a dark, restless eye. Of course this was all, or nearly all, conjecture; but such was the figure my fancy drew—such the figure that presented itself before my mind's eye ["Detecting a Murderer" by Emerson Bennett, *The New York Ledger*, November, 7, 1863].

But still others accept the guidance of intuition and revel in its inexplicability:

> The great secret of Mr. Gimblet's tablet's success in his peculiar line of business was a singular knack of forming a correct conclusion without the process of reasoning. He was by no means wanting in logical perception, but he was frequently aided in his investigations by a sort of intuition which put him on the right track when others were vainly groping in the dark ["An Amicable Agreement," *Gouvernor Free Press*, July 2, 1884].

While outliers existed, the evidence-centered detective story could not get by with dreams, intuitions, fugue states, Ouija boards, and the like. Mainstream detectives not only had to come up with evidence, they also had to explain how they put the whole business together to prove their new point. Since reason trumps superstition, bias, and ignorance, the simplest solution in this respect was to talk about the detective using reason. Often writers use the term "reason" to explain the process of putting two and two together. Here are two examples:

> On the soil outside the window there were impressions of his knees, two toes, and the left hand only. The person forcing the lock of the desk had leaned against the right wall, and evidently worked with his left hand. The person who wielded the fatal knife had used the left hand, for the wound slanted upward from the edge, and was made from the left side. If made from the left side with the right hand it would either have been straight down or inclined from the entrance of the knife downward. A moment's thought will show the justness of this reasoning ["The Left Hand," *The Janesville Gazette*, August 7, 1879];

and

> The more he thought of it, the more he felt convinced he was right. No conspirator would have made use of so simple a cipher, and the perfumed note paper, and the delicate hand in which the sentence was written, made it plain that a woman was concerned in the matter. Reasoning thus in his mind, he entered the Rue Rivoli, and soon came opposite the mysterious number forty-eight ["An Official Blunder" by James D. M'Cabe, Jr., *Flag of Our Union*, April 28, 1866].

There were, moreover, more detailed and fully precise ways to describe the transition between specifics and generalizations than simply using the term "reason." Some writers knew this and used other terms to describe what went on in the detectives' minds. One of them was the term "hypothesis"—a tentative answer based on evidence, but evidence that might not be complete. Further, there can be serial hypotheses where one supplants another or hypotheses that compete with one another. Both cases need sorting out and provide additional opportunities to review the evidence. Here is the process at work:

> From this point, impenetrable mystery hung over the whole matter. Had Thompson decamped with the money, or had he been the victim of some foul play? The first hypothesis was scouted by Thompson's friends and fellow-workmen. He had shown himself for more than twenty years a man of probity; he was a sober and prudent man, whose only delight was in his home and his children. He was always preaching habits of saving and economy to the men under him, and when he disappeared, it was found that he had a considerable sum in the savings bank, which he had never touched. It was incredible, therefore, that he could have embezzled his employer's money. The second hypothesis seemed the more reasonable one. But if he had been murdered, how had his body been disposed of? ["Story of a London Bank Cashier," *St. Joseph Herald*, January 12, 1878].

But "hypothesis" was only one of the terms writers used when explaining the hero's thought processes in solving a problem. Detectives in stories talk about "theories" as ways of dealing with facts as often as "hypotheses" and "reason." Here Detective Brampton tells readers how he got from evidence to theory as part of solving the crime:

It follows, then, whoever committed the deed must have done it instantaneously to prevent the victim from crying out. He must, at the same time, have placed one hand over the old gentleman's mouth, while with the other he gave the fatal blow. Had he not done this, however deep the wound might have been, it must have elicited a cry. But then in this case we meet a great difficulty; from the position of the wound, no one man could possibly have done this. And yet it is evident that a hand was placed over the mouth, for the marks of the fingers were still to be traced on the face of the deceased when I saw it. My theory is, that two persons were concerned in this murder ["The Bowie Knife Sheath," *Leaves from the Note-Book of a New York Detective*, New York: Dick & Fitzgerald, 1865].

But a theory is just a theory.

The significant point here was that theories like hypotheses may sound scientific, but they can't stand by themselves. They have to be proved. And proving theories also provides an additional means of expanding the plot. The detective can be faced with sorting through multiple theories:

I knew she was innocent, for she had nursed her master when he was a baby and loved him tenderly. I was satisfied the servants were guiltless. I must start a new theory. Did I murder him myself? No, I certainly did not. I had read of somnambulists who had committed strange freaks and frightful deeds. Could it be that I, in a somnambulistic state, had gone to Sir The's room, cut off his head and concealed his body? No, no, the thought was too horrible. It could not be; there would be some evidence of it ["My Uncle's Story: How a Murderer Was Discovered by Dreams," *Chicago Tribune*, January 24, 1875].

But they, too, need to be sifted:

One thing seemed alone certain amid the maze of perplexity; the house-breakers must be sought from amongst neighbors, servants, friends or relations. Now the neighbor theory, upon investigation, seemed utterly futile, and one glance at old Frederick was enough to make one dismiss all thoughts connected with the second term in the list ["A German Detective Story," *Denton Journal*, April 4, 1879].

All of this can be seen as elaboration of the circumstantial-evidence plot which goes from an erroneous theory accepted as fact (X is guilty) to an alternate theory (Y is guilty) grounded in facts. It also makes detectives more than trackers and followers of clues. It makes them thinkers.

All of this brain work, however, created a kind of tension. Was the detective some kind of egghead or a regular guy? A very few stories took the egghead route. The hero in "Bob Cheriot; or the Tragedy at Chelmsford" certainly seems to fill the bill:

Mathematics were my delight; in them I imagined I found the centre and basis of everything. Music, painting, sculpture, and everyday life found in my theory their ground work in that exact science. Form, fancy and fact, were all but different shapes for figures—they were the *motif* of all things, and by them all things were solved. In them I found study and recreation, oftimes amusing myself by forecasting from accident and life-tables the births, deaths and mishaps in my neighborhood. With this study in my thoughts it came across me one day that with the aid of figures I might find a solution to the dire tragedy at Chelmsford.

> Given a secret, the answer strongly desired, would my favorite study give me an insight into its closed chamber? I was staggered at the thought, but rather than relinquish my pet hobby, I began to make a statement in algebraical symbols, somewhat in this form:
>   Let x represent the murderer [*Potter's American Monthly*, January 1877].

And several years later a hero articulates the 19th century's dream of a utopian future in which science will take over the detective business:

> However, as the years move on, greater wisdom and wider tolerance are shown by the law; and it is to be hoped that in our day—at all events, in those of the generation who will immediately succeed us—that circumstantial evidence will be reduced to rules as certain as those of mathematics ["The Maimed Hand: A Tale of Circumstantial Evidence," *The Allen County Democrat*, February 27, 1879].

Most writers, however, did not endow their heroes with preternatural intellectual powers—that was something left to Poe and saved for writers at the turn of the century. A telling demonstration of this is that in a search of over a thousand period detective stories the word *genius* never appears attached to a detective hero. The only place that it does occur is in the description of characters with an "evil genius." Rather than the word *genius*, writers frequently use the words *clever* and *shrewd* to describe their detectives; in their excess, however, satirists also use them but use them to spoof both amateur and professional detectives who are "too clever" or "too clever by half."

Along with the implication that while detective heroes are smart they are not geniuses, there are other things that 19th-century detective heroes are not. While they are flanked by Dupin and Sherlock Holmes, they are not eccentric. While they were created during a period of epidemic political corruption, they have nothing to do with politicians or political issues. While emancipation and immigration created theoretical diversity, they are overwhelmingly white, Anglo-Saxon men. While on the frontier and in cities violence was common, they rarely confront situations in which violence occurs. While they identify and capture criminals, they do not examine the causes or the effects of crime, and they do not affect them—except in a few very, very rare cases. What they were was just the kind of hero a lot of people in 19th-century America wanted to read about, again and again.

AFTERWORD

Along with mentioning a handful of books and miscellaneous magazines, we have inundated readers with parenthetical notes that cite decades' worth of detective stories printed in family story papers and newspapers in cities, towns, villages, and hamlets across America and even in the so-called Indian Territories. They make it clear, we hope, that we take it as a given that detective stories were very much alive in the United States before Conan Doyle was born, and even before "The Murders in the Rue Morgue" appeared in *Graham's Magazine* in 1841. Indeed, the case can be made that detective stories were one of the first (and most important) indigenous popular literary forms in America—beginning long before and vastly outpolling the Western. This is the case because of a number of factors. One of them is luck. Just as part of Conan Doyle's success came from the coincidental popularity of illustrated magazines and the energy of the editor and illustrator of *The Strand Magazine*, combined with the publication of Poe's works in Edinburgh, the beginning of detective stories in America coincided with the rippling explosion of newspapers and magazines across the United States in the 19th century and what amounted to seismic changes in law and jurisprudence in the Anglo-American world. Newspapers, as it turns out, were immensely important to the history of popular literature in the United States, as indeed they were to the popular literatures of other countries. Appropriately, the National Library of Australia named its online database of historical newspapers "Trove" (http://trove.nla.gov.au). Lacking news from outside their own local community, the front pages of most U.S. papers through the 1860s typically contained a short story, a poem, perhaps a tidbit of news, and a column or two of advertisements. Courtship romances, ghost stories, and detective stories regularly appeared as the short stories in those papers. There were a lot of them—in our case, there were a lot of detective stories published in newspapers before our cut-off date of 1891 (the publication date of "Scandal in Bohemia"). That's one fact. Another important fact about newspaper fiction is that it was viral—which is a current way of saying it was widely stolen, plagiarized, or copied. Stories like Dickens' "A Detective Police Party," for instance, could come from England, be printed in New York, Philadelphia, or Boston, and then spread to newspapers in places like Indiana, Pennsylvania; Denton, Maryland; Nashville, Tennessee; St. Cloud, Minnesota; Red Cloud, Indian Territories; and finally San Francisco. So could stories about American detectives.

Newspapers in the 19th century were very cheap, sometimes even free, and their distributions was subsidized by the federal government. They were—and still are—driven by advertisements; at mid-19th century many papers carried more advertisements than copy. Until after the Civil War many areas of the country did not have access to telegraphs or railroads. Additionally, halftone engraving was not widely used until 1890s, so illustrations in early newspapers were rare. With meager news to print and few if any illustrations not connected to advertisers, many newspapers had to rely heavily on fiction (and poetry) to draw in readers. That's "readers" plural, because unlike books, newspapers were read by more than one person. Indeed, they were read by every literate person in a household—which meant that women and adolescent children formed a significant portion of newspaper readership. Inclusive readership and the mores of the time had more than a bit to do with shaping newspaper detective stories.

Nineteenth-century America had its share of sensational crimes, crimes which modern-day enthusiasts have taken pains to meticulously chronicle. Those sensational crimes certainly made a splash in newspapers of the day. Unless they were very unusual crimes, hotly contested in court, and involving specialist witnesses (often "professors"), however, the crimes and the trials that they recorded were big-city crimes—typically taking place in New York. A look at 1879 serves as an example. There were three big arsenic poisoning trials in that year: Hayden, Riddle, and Cobb. Two were in New York City and one in Norwich, Connecticut. The Hayden trial, in fact, featured dueling experts on the arsenic question—the kind of material a writer might clip and put in a folder and eventually use as the basis of a story. But, at least according to our sample, it didn't happen. Arsenic poisoning, for example, occurs in a sprinkling of detective stories before 1879 (in 1856 "The Two Nephews"; 1861 "The Resting Powders"; 1866 "The Apothecary's Compound"; 1868 "The Chemist's Story"; 1867 "Dr. Puffer's Lost Opportunity"; 1870 "Our Cook's Revenge"; 1870 "A Lucky Larceny"; and 1874 "The Mysterious Mark"). However, in the twelve years between 1879 and 1891, only two stories even mention arsenic. Therefore, it looks very much like a very sensational trial and a notorious kind of poisoning had negligible effect on contemporary detective stories—at least in the U.S. While patterns can be found in 19th-century detective fiction (the rise of stories tied to chloroform or somnambulism or kleptomania, for example) responding to or reflecting current events was not their purpose. Distasteful, shocking, and morally troubling situations and people were hardly acceptable family reading. Never mind turning a blind eye to its horrific carnage, it's worth noting that the Civil War is hardly mentioned in period detective stories. While sensation novels, courtship stories, and even perhaps glimmerings of the first wave of feminism affected the role of women in some detective stories, in general the new genre accepted the mores of the time. The whole idea of the detective story was putting things back to normal. If after the Civil War news from the outside world began to seep into even small-town papers, directly and indirectly the ideal of family reading colored the nature of newspaper fiction. There was, in fact, a significant 19th-century movement to protect women and children from "unsuitable" facts and ideas in what was available for them to read. In 1807 Thomas Bowdler's *Family Shakespeare* expurgated things Dr. Bowdler thought too vulgar or shocking for his wife and children. Later in the century Anthony Comstock took over the job in the U.S.; he went at it with a vengeance and he zeroed in on newspapers. Thus this tirade in his *Traps for the Young*:

> These details familiarize their readers with crime; they even tend to glorify it. A simple statement that a foul deed has been committed is sufficient to acquaint the public with that fact. The youth who reads the loathsome details as above described might almost as well pass his time in the society of criminals. He could scarcely learn more of vice if he associated with thieves, murderers, libertines, and harlots. The presence of the criminal would inspire a fear, and their coarse loud talk ungarnished by an editor's pen would disgust and in part counteract the force of an evil example. The story in the paper puts them in precisely the same companionship, without the power by its presence to create the checks of fear and disgust.
>
> Is it too much to ask of the mighty press of the land that accounts of crimes shall not be wildly sensational nor specific, and especially that those against purity shall not be set forth with prurient minuteness? [New York: Funk and Wagnalls, 1881].

So, perhaps in their own defense, in detective stories violent death was euphemized, the character of the criminal was minimized, and punishment shunted off stage. Newspaper writers made the story be one about the detective's success and not the horror of the crime, the suffering of the victim, or the angst of the criminal. While detective fiction certainly had its gothic branch, mainstream detective writers took all of the big, troubling, scary, confusing questions related to crime, criminals, victims, and detectives as people off the table. Depending upon the notions of justice and a Providential universe, writers of period detective fiction steered clear of mentioning religion or asking, "Why?" about a lot of things. They could do this in part because they were using the new form of the short story and because all of the distasteful stuff, after all, was the province of gothic tales, sensation novels, and even the pulpit. In short, newspaper writers made the detective story acceptable reading for anyone in a 19th-century household.

Stories about detectives had particular attraction for newspaper readers because they contained both an introduction to something new (detectives) and a supposed inside look at what they did. The idea of the "notebook" story was an attractive one for 19th-century readers, and British and American magazines used it to introduce readers to the "inside" world of physicians, lawyers, explorers, and even librarians. Led by *Chambers' Journal*, British publishers zeroed in on detectives—because the detective branch of the Metropolitan Police was new. Reading about how the British solved the problems of policing in general and of detective policing was particularly attractive to Americans who were trying to solve some of the same problems about crime and public safety that led Parliament to establish the New Police. Detective notebook stories, furthermore, were hardly humdrum accounts of the rigors, routines, and minutiae of the job; they were tales of chases, captures, escapes, hiding, and seeking—with a bit of personal detail about the detective narrator thrown in.

Because 19th-century detective stories—even Poe's—were commercial entities, writers wished to appeal to the largest possible audience. As it happened, detective stories evolved in a manner that enabled them to attract readers with diverse tastes in fiction, and they did so by, in effect, combining with other literary fashions and forms—a faculty that would eventually bring readers priest detectives, cowboy detectives, space detectives, boy detectives, and perhaps even hominid detectives. The first detective stories imported to the United States, however, carried with them the appeal of the exotic: just as papers and magazines across the country published an occasional tidbit about London or Paris, the first detective stories to appear in America took place in France or in England. In a few years, however, detective stories began to exploit the variety of American land and cityscapes. New York, Chicago, New Orleans, and San Francisco all had stories; action took place from Maine to California, and from Minnesota to Texas; mansions and rooming houses served as settings; so did farms and forests. Detective stories could be peripatetic and follow a hero around the country or around a city. All of the action could take place between a few people in one room in a house or in front of a crowd in a courtroom. In addition to the advantages of versatility for plot, character, and theme of different settings, detective story writers discovered that they could focus their stories on people or things, or both. Thus they could concentrate on motives or means, on who really gained from the murder or what the bits of bullet wadding meant or how to find an absconded embezzler.

Detective stories also merged with the two other prominent types of fiction featured in 19th-century newspapers: courtship romances and gothic tales (i.e., ghost stories). Sensation novels, to be sure, had combined the basics of both of those types of fiction with a detective thrown in to boot; they could do this because they were triple-decker novels. But it wasn't possible to combine sentiment, suspense, and a detective in a short story, especially a 2,000-word newspaper story. Thus the sentimental detective story emerged as a variety of romance in which the hero/narrator witnesses the pain and tragedy of betrayal, and likewise the gothic story appeared in which the hero enters a world full of peril and physical threats. So detective stories both found means of packaging in miniature some of the emotional gratifications of the sensation novel and its offshoots and, more importantly, restructured one of its principal sales advantages—the hanging problem and surprise solution that was essential to 19th-century serial novels. In detective stories readers didn't have to wait until the next week or month to discover the solution to the mystery: it popped up the end of a couple thousand words. Finally, by the time of the Civil War the idea of the detective and the detective story had matured enough to inspire writers to develop comic stories and satires featuring detectives. These kinds of detective stories commonly focus on a hero who meticulously examines evidence only to be proved wrong at the end of the narrative and as such follow the pattern of the joke in establishing and then upsetting false assumptions—the same thing Poe did in "The Murders in the Rue Morgue." Finally, and for some most importantly, and once again in the tradition of Poe, the story of a crime and an investigator joined with whist, checkers (draughts), odds and evens, conundrums, ciphers, and other games to become the puzzle story.

In addition to the intrinsic adaptability and flexibility of detective stories, from the beginning they possessed the capacity of reflecting (and thereby enforcing) social norms, often without overt didacticism. This is perhaps most apparent in the roles and motivations of female characters in period detective stories. Willingly or unwillingly, most female characters are victims whose actions are determined either by dedication to love or nurturing or by societal prejudice. Also, just as one of the functions of comedy is to restore order (usually by means of marriage) to a disordered world, the fundamental purpose of detectives and detective stories was to demonstrate the inevitable justice of the universe. This was one of the basic themes of literature for centuries. Plays, poems, and narratives demonstrated that, while very bad things happen, justice will prevail because of providential circumstance or because of the workings of consciences—both ultimately attributable to acts of God. A lot of this goes on in Shakespeare's plays. But in the 19th century things changed and Providential justice only worked alone in simplistic moral tales. Even the device of pulling a *deus ex machina* out of a hat became relegated to unsophisticated stage melodrama. In detective stories, providential justice and order worked because people acted to defend the innocent and to unmask the guilty.

As it turns out, newspapers served as a refuge for the detective story during the last quarter of the 19th century. During its early years, detective fiction appeared both in newspapers and in middle-class magazines like *Harper's* and *The Atlantic Monthly*. In the 1860s first story papers and then dime novels came on the scene and, especially the latter, aimed for a significantly different audience—principally adolescent males. Middle-class journals stopped printing detective stories from the 1860s and didn't resume running them until the Sherlock Holmes craze late in the century. But newspapers never stopped. Indeed while dime novels detective stories came to depend more on action and less on problem solving, newspapers continued to print more sophisticated detective stories because they wished to appeal to all readers but especially to middle-class readers. While detective stories in short-story form certainly remained a popular feature in newspapers in the 1870s and 1880s, increased competition among papers and the beginning of the "newspaper wars" of the 1890s made serial detective novels attractive to American newspaper publishers anxious to gain and hang on to readers. It was perhaps the advent of the serial that stunted the development of recurring detective heroes in short detective fiction in the U.S., and gave an opportunity for Arthur Conan Doyle. And it was the advent of new illustrated, middle-class magazines, combined with the sorry state of law enforcement that made the strange bedfellows of Sherlock Holmes, S.S. McClure, and the Muckrakers. That combination, along with the Poe revival of the 1880s, gave the detective story back to middle-class readers.

In respect to ensuring justice in detective stories, the checkered history of official police and detectives in the United States had a significant effect. While one of the aims of 19th-century fiction lay in depicting the detective as dedicated, intelligent, high-minded, knowledgeable, helpful, and friendly, the institutionalized corruption of American police and detective departments was an open secret. This goes largely without direct comment in popular fiction. Depicting corrupt cops was taboo, and torture, the "third degree," was scarcely mentioned. The lack of trust in police can be seen, however, in the vagueness about whether detectives are public or private employees as well as in many stories in which detectives are directly contacted by aggrieved people, thereby perpetuating the notion of making individuals and not the state responsible for justice and public safety. This, as it turns out, enacted both the traditional basis of English criminal law which made each citizen responsible for the arrest and prosecution of evildoers and the principles of self-reliance being preached by Emerson and Thoreau at the same time detective stories were being developed in popular media. Coincidentally, as they developed, different varieties of detective stories reflected the dichotomy of the individual's responsibility versus the state's responsibility that remains a vexed issue in American society. Thus in the mid–19th century one kind of story follows a detective as he or she alone solves a problem, and in the other kind he or she acts as a government agent seeking a person identified by the authorities as a criminal.

The 19th century was the first period of Western history in which it began to be possible to determine with some degree of accuracy how people died. During the century new approaches to where to look and how to look for causes of death appeared. Scientists developed tests for various poisons, and late in the century Koch, Pasteur, and Lister demonstrated that microorganisms caused diseases. Discoveries related to blood, however, did not occur until the turn of the 20th century and the practice of medicine also did not change substantially until the end of the century—except in the area of surgery in which anesthetics were introduced in 1846. Imaging, seeing things, however, changed—first in refined microscopes and then exponentially with the invention of the camera at mid-century.

Much of what we have found suggests pretty emphatically that detective stories began as stories about the tragic mistakes caused by misleading circumstantial evidence and the impotence of accused persons before the law in 18th- and early 19th-century England. In older literature this elicited themes including the virtue of patient suffering and Murder Will Out—in part because society had yet to come to terms with the manifest defects of a mediaeval system of justice or understand the nature of physical evidence. Thus, in England accused persons were not allowed to have lawyers (or anyone) speak for them in court until the passage of the Prisoners' Council Act of 1836. But that was in England. Protection of people accused of crimes—the right to counsel, prohibition of unreasonable search and seizure, self-incrimination, etc.—was perhaps the principal concern of the creation and passage of the Bill of Rights in the United States. For almost 50 years, then, criminal jurisprudence was very different in the two nations. Narratives centered on convictions and executions of innocent people based on the misinterpretation of evidence cropped up in popular books about criminals and crime and in literature protesting the death penalty in both countries. Connected with this, a new type of fiction appeared to highlight the defects of the old system and the benefits of the new way of dealing with accusations and trials—the circumstantial-evidence story. It had a simple yet adaptable plot: (1) based on faulty evidence, X is arrested for committing a crime; (2) a detective figure reinterprets or finds new evidence; and (3) the court exonerates the accused and convicts and punishes the real criminal. We have found this kind of story as early as March 1827 in "The Blasted

Tree" published in *The Casket*, and Poe included the concept of circumstantial evidence and the circumstantial evidence story in his tales of ratiocination in the 1840s.

All of this happened before detective police were introduced. During the first half of the 19th century, it seemed a good bet that lawyers would be the heroes of circumstantial-evidence stories. They did, after all, have to do with evidence and the courts. Physicians also seemed like they might have a chance when murder was committed by esoteric means. While lawyers still had a monopoly on stories that turned on points of law or when things got so bad that there had to be a trial, by mid-century the focus of stories shifted from saving an accused innocent to finding evidence. That's when detectives took over as heroes.

As we noted in the introduction, we have based all of the preceding descriptions, discussions, and conclusions on material that has not been available until the last decade. We have collected and published online a hefty package of those stories published in America and will continue our searching, editing, and publishing enterprise after this book is published. But it wasn't just the American popular press that was responsible for the creation of the detective story—the reciprocal relationship between newspapers and magazines in the United States, Britain and, to a lesser extent, France played a major role in its creation and development. Consider that in 1883 George Newnes ran "The Reminiscences of an American Detective" in his *Tit-Bits from All the Most Interesting Books, Periodicals and Newspapers in the World*. That was eight years before he ran the first Sherlock Holmes story in *The Strand*. This suggests that there is a lot more story to tell.

APPENDIX:
WOMEN WRITERS

Please note we have found another 109 stories that may have been written by women but whose attributions are gender indeterminate. Additionally, more than half of the stories we have uncovered are anonymous or "by a detective" and many of the stories that appear to be authored by men may have been published pseudonymously.

Ashmore, Anna
Belnheim Belinda
Bigelow, Elizabeth
Bittersweet, Hester
Burton, Jennie Davis
Campbell, Elizabeth
Campbell, Lizzie
Champney, Elizabeth
Clarke, Anne Taylor
Clarke, Ethel Gorman
Conrad, Caroline
Crosse, Marah
Denison, Mrs. M.A.
Dallas, Mary Kyle
Edson, Mrs. R.B.
Eytinge, Rose
Field, Anna C.
Graham, Amy
Green, Anna Katharine
Hale, Mrs. Amanda M.
Halpine, Mary Grace
Hatch, Mary R.P.
Heey, Mrs. Cashel
Higginson, Ella
Howard, Mrs. F.M.
Hunter, J.T. (pseudonym of Carmen Overland)
Kyle, Hattie
Lingard, Alice Dunning
MacDowell, Blanche L.
Meridan, Kate
M'Keever, Abbie C.
Orme, Mary
Orne, Mrs. Caroline
Phillips, Louise
Preston, Masie
Randolph, Amy
Richardson, Frances T.
Rosavo, Narissa
Schoolcraft, Frances Mary
Soule, Mrs. C.A.
Spofford, Harriet E. Prescott
Thorne, Barbara
Thornton, Mrs. Emily
Vaughan, Mary C.
Victor, Metta
Willian, Miss Camilla
Whitney, Miss B.J.
Woodruff, Allie
Young, Mary C.

Bibliography

*All fiction cited in this book can be found
at the Westminster Detective Library: www.wdl.mcdaniel.edu*

Newspapers Cited

Abilene Reflector, Abilene Kansas
Abilene Weekly Reflector, Abilene Kansas
The Allen County Democrat, Lima, Ohio
The Alma Signal, Alma, Kansas
Alpena Argus, Alpena, Michigan
The Anderson Intelligencer, Anderson Court House, South Carolina
The Arizona Kicker, Tombstone, Arizona
The Athens Messenger, Athens, Ohio
Bangor Daily Whig and Courier, Bangor, Maine
Barnstable Patriot, Barnstable, Massachusetts
The Bee, Washington, D.C.
The Berkshire County Eagle, Pittsfield, Massachusetts
The Bismarck Tribune, Bismarck, North Dakota
The Bismarck Weekly Tribune, Bismarck, North Dakota
The Bloomfield Times, Bloomfield, Pennsylvania
The Boon's Lick Times, Fayette, Missouri
The Boston Daily Atlas, Boston, Massachusetts
Boston Daily Globe, Boston, Massachusetts
The Boston Weekly Globe, Boston, Massachusetts
Bradford Reporter, Tawanda, Pennsylvania
The Branding Iron, Atoka, Oklahoma
Brooklyn Eagle, Brooklyn, New York
The Buffalo News, Buffalo, New York
Burlington Free Press, Burlington, Vermont
Burlington Weekly Hawkeye, Burlington, Iowa
The Butler Citizen, Butler, Pennsylvania
The Cambria Freeman, Ebansburg, Pennsylvania
Catoctin Clarion, Thurmont, Maryland
The Cedar Valley Times, Vinton, Iowa
The Centre Democrat, Bellefonte, Pennsylvania
The Charleston Daily Supplement, Charleston, South Carolina
The Cheyenne Daily Leader, Cheyenne, Wyoming

The Chicago Daily Tribune, Chicago, Illinois
Chicago Journal, Chicago, Illinois
Chicago Tribune, Chicago, Illinois
The Chillicothe Constitution, Chillicothe, Ohio
Cincinnati Daily Star, Cincinnati, Ohio
The Cincinnati Enquirer, Cincinnati, Ohio
Coldwater Sentinel, Coldwater, Michigan
The Columbia Spy, Columbia, Pennsylvania
The Columbus Journal, Columbus, Nebraska
The Columbus Post, Columbus, Nebraska
The Columbus Sunday Enquirer, Columbus, Georgia
The Cooper's Clarksburg Register, Clarksburg, Virginia
The Corrector, Sag Harbor, New York
The Coshocton Democrat, Coshocton, Ohio
Daily Alta Californian, San Francisco, California
Daily Bulletin, San Francisco, California
The Daily Evening Bulletin, San Francisco, California
Daily Gazette, Billings, Montana
The Daily Independent, Monroe, Wisconsin
The Daily Intelligencer, Seattle, Washington Territory
The Daily Kennebec Journal, Augusta, Maine
The Daily Press, Cincinnati, Ohio
The Darling Downs Gazette, Toowomba, Queensland, Australia
The Decatur Daily Republican, Decatur, Illinois
The Decatur Daily Review, Decatur, Illinois
Defiance Democrat, Defiance, Ohio
The Delta Herald, Delta, Pennsylvania
The Democratic Press, Fond Du Lac, Wisconsin
Denton Journal, Denton, Maryland
The Detroit Free Press, Detroit, Michigan
The Dunkirk Observer-Journal, Dunkirk, New York
The Eaton Democrat, Eaton, Ohio
Eau Claire Free Press, Eau Claire, Wisconsin
The Edgefield Advertiser, Edgefield, South Carolina
The Edwardsville Intelligencer, Edwardsville, Illinois
The Ellensburg Dawn, Ellensburg, Washington
Evening Star, Washington, D.C.
The Evening Telegraph, Philadelphia, Pennsylvania
The Evening World, New York, New York
The Fayette County Herald, Washington Court House, Ohio
The Fayetteville Observer, Fayetteville, Tennessee
The Fort Wayne Gazette, Fort Wayne, Indiana
Fort Wayne Sentinel, Fort Wayne, Indiana
Fort Wayne Weekly Democrat, Fort Wayne, Indiana
Fort Worth Daily Gazette, Fort Worth, Texas
The Fox Lake Gazette, Fox Lake, Wisconsin
The Franklin Gazette, Fort Covington, New York
Freeborn County Standard, Albert Lea, Minnesota
The Freeport Daily Bulletin, Cairo, Illinois
The Fresno Republican, Fresno, California
The Galveston Daily News, Galveston, Texas
The Gazette, Fort Worth Texas,

Bibliography

The Golden Era, Lincoln, New Mexico
Gouvernor Free Press, Gouvernor, New York
Grand Traverse Herald, Traverse City, Michigan
Grant County News, Canyon City, Oregon
The Green-Mountain Freeman, Montpelier, Vermont
The Hamilton County Press, Hope, New York
Hartford Courant, Hartford, Connecticut
The Herald, Syracuse, New York
Holmes County Farmer, Millersburg, Ohio
The Holmes County Republican, Millersburg, Ohio
Huntingdon Journal, Huntingdon, Pennsylvania
The Illinois Free Trader, Ottawa, Illinois
The Indiana Democrat, Indiana, Pennsylvania
The Indiana Progress, Indiana, Pennsylvania
The Indiana Weekly Messenger, Indiana, Pennsylvania
Iowa State Reporter, Des Moines, Iowa
The Isola Register, Isola, Kansas
The Jackson Citizen, Jackson, Michigan
The Janesville Gazette, Janesville, Wisconsin
The Janesville Weekly Gazette, Janesville, Wisconsin
The Jeffersonian Republican, Stroudsburg, Pennsylvania
The Junction City Weekly Union, Junction City Kansas
The Kenosha Telegraph, Kenosha, Wisconsin
The Lake Village Times, Laconia, New Hampshire
The Lebanon Advertiser, Lebanon, Pennsylvania
The Ledger, Warren, Pennsylvania
The Lincoln County Herald, Troy, Missouri
Logansport Daily Star, Logansport, Iowa
The Long Island Traveler, Cutchogue, New York
The Louisiana Capitolian, Baton Rouge, Louisiana
The Louisiana Democrat, Alexandria, Louisiana
The Lowell Sun, Lowell, Massachusetts
The Manitowoc Pilot, Manitowoc, Wisconsin
The Marion Daily Star, Marion, Ohio
The Marshall Statesman, Marshall, Michigan
The McArthur Democrat, McArthur, Ohio
The McCook Tribute, McCook, Nebraska
The McKean Miner, Smethport, Pennsylvania
Memphis Daily Appeal, Memphis, Tennessee
The Middlebury Galaxy, Middlebury, Vermont
Millheim Journal, Millheim, Pennsylvania
The Monongalia Mirror, Morgantown, West Virginia
Mountain Democrat, Placerville, California
Mower County Transcript, Lansing, Michigan
The National Era, Washington, D.C.
National Republican, Washington, D.C.
The New Bloomfield, Pa. Times, New Bloomfield, Pennsylvania
New Hampshire Sentinel, Keene, New Hampshire
The New Hampshire Statesman, Concord, New Hampshire
The New Orleans Picayune, New Orleans, Louisiana
New York Daily Tribune, New York, New York
The New York Star, New York, New York

The New York Times, New York, New York
Newark Union, Newark, New York
News and Citizen, Morrisville, Vermont
The News and Herald, Winnsboro, South Carolina
Oconto Pioneer, Oconto, Wisconsin
The Ohio Democrat, Canal Dover, Ohio
Omaha Daily Bee, Omaha, Nebraska
The Omaha World Herald, Omaha, Nebraska
The Orleans County Monitor, Barton, Vermont
Orleans Independent Standard, Irasburg, Vermont
The Oshkosh True Democrat, Oshkosh, Wisconsin
The Palo Alto Reporter, Emmetsburg, Iowa
The Perrysburg Journal, Perrysburg, Ohio
Pittsburg Dispatch, Pittsburgh, Pennsylvania
The Plain Dealer, Cleveland, Ohio
The Plymouth Weekly Democrat, Plymouth, Indiana
The Portage Sentinel, Ravenna, Ohio
Prairie du Chien Patriot, Prairie du Chien, Wisconsin
Prairie Farmer, Chicago, Illinois
The Preble County Democrat, Eaton, Ohio
The Puget Sound Herald, Steilacoom, Washington Territory
Pullman Herald, Pullman, Washington Territory
Racine Advocate, Racine, Wisconsin
The Radical, Bowling Green, Missouri
The Raftsman's Journal, Clearfield, Pennsylvania
Reno Evening Gazette, Reno, Nevada
The Richwood Gazette, Richwood, Ohio
The River Press, Fort Benton, Montana
The Riverine Grazier, Hay, New South Wales, Australia
Rock Island Argus, Rock Island, Illinois
Rockland County Journal, Nyack, New York
The Rocky Mountain News, Denver, Colorado
Sacramento Daily Union, Sacramento, California
Sacramento Sunday Union, Sacramento, California
St. Joseph Herald, St. Joseph, Michigan
St. Louis Democrat, St. Louis, Missouri
St. Louis Globe Democrat, St. Louis, Missouri
The St. Mary's Beacon, Leonard Town, Maryland
St. Paul Daily Globe, St. Paul, Minnesota
St. Tammany Farmer, Covington, Louisiana
Salt Lake Evening Democrat, Salt Lake City, Utah
The Sandusky Daily Register, Sandusky, Ohio
Santa Fe Weekly Gazette, Santa Fe, New Mexico
Schenectady Reflector, Schenectady, New York
The Sedalia Weekly Bazoo, Sedalia, Missouri
Semi-Weekly Bourbon News, Paris, Kentucky
Sioux County Herald, Orange City, Iowa
The Somerset Press, Somerset, Ohio
Southern Watchman, Athens, Georgia
The Spirit of Democracy, Woodsfield, Ohio
The Spirit of Jefferson, Charles Town, Virginia
The Star and Sentinel, Gettysburg, Pennsylvania

The Stark County Democrat, Canton, Ohio
The Staunton Spectator, Staunton, Virginia
Sterling Standard, Sterling, Illinois
Stevens Point Journal, Stevens Point, Wisconsin
Sullivan Republican, Laporte, Pennsylvania
Sumner Gazette, Sumner, Kansas
The Sumter Watchman, Sumpterville, South Carolina
The Sun, New York, New York
The Sunday Herald, Syracuse, New York
The Sunny South, Aberdeen, Mississippi
The Tiffin Weekly Tribune, Tiffin, Ohio
The Times-Picayune, New Orleans, Louisiana
The Tioga County Agitator, Wellsboro, Pennsylvania
Tioga Eagle, Wellsboro Pennsylvania
True American, Steubenville, Ohio
The True Northerner, Paw Paw, Michigan
The Tuapeka Times, Lawrence, New Zealand
Turner County Herald, Hurley, South Dakota
The Union Democrat, Sonora, California
The Urbana Union, Urbana, Ohio
The Van Wert Republican, Van Wert, Ohio
Vermont Phœnix, Brattleboro, Vermont
The Vermont Watchman and State Journal, Montpelier, Vermont
Warren Ledger, Warren, Pennsylvania
The Waterloo Courier, Waterloo, Iowa
Weekly Argus and Democrat, Madison, Wisconsin
The Weekly Portage Sentinel, Ravenna, Ohio
The Weekly Register, Point Pleasant, Mason County, West Virginia
The Weekly Thibodaux Sentinel and Journal of the 8th Senatorial District, Thibodaux, Louisiana
The Weekly Valley Herald, Chaska, Minnesota
Weekly Wisconsin, Milwaukee, Wisconsin
Wellsboro Agitator, Wellsboro, Pennsylvania
The Western Democrat, Charlotte, North Carolina
The Western Kansas World, WaKeeney, Kansas
The Western Rural and Illinois Stockman, Chicago, Illinois
The Wheeling Daily Intelligencer, Wheeling, West Virginia
White Cloud Kansas Chief, White Cloud, Kansas
Wilmington Journal, Wilmington, North Carolina
Wisconsin Argus, Madison, Wisconsin
Wisconsin Patriot, Madison, Wisconsin
The Wisconsin State Register, Madison, Wisconsin
The World: Saturday Evening, New York, New York
Yorkville Enquirer, Yorkville, South Carolina

Story Papers Cited

Flag of Our Union, published weekly in Boston from 1846 until 1870. Founded by Frank Gleason, it was purchased in 1854 by Maturin Murray Ballou. Its contributors included Edgar Allan Poe and Louisa May Alcott.

The New York Fireside Companion, founded by George Munro in 1869 as "A journal of instructive and entertaining literature." In 1872 in his story paper Munro introduced the character of "Old Sleuth," one of the first of what would become dime novel detective heroes.

The New York Ledger, established in 1855 by Robert E. Bonner. Its contributors included Henry Ward Beecher, John Greenleaf Whittier, Henry Wadsworth Longfellow, Edward Everett, Louisa May Alcott, Harriet Beecher Stowe, William Cullen Bryant, and Alfred Tennyson. And Charles Dickens.

Magazines Cited

The Albion: A Journal of News, Politics and Literature. est. 1857. New York, New York, weekly.
All the Year Round. est. 1859. London, England, weekly.
Appleton's Journal of Literature, Science and Art. est. 1869. New York, weekly, then monthly.
The Atlantic Monthly. est. 1857. Boston, Massachusetts, monthly.
Ballou's Dollar Monthly Magazine. est. 1855. Boston, Massachusetts, monthly.
Ballou's Monthly Magazine. est. 1865. Boston, Massachusetts, monthly.
Beadle's Monthly. est. 1866. New York, New York, monthly.
Burton's Gentleman's Magazine. est. 1837. Philadelphia, Pennsylvania, monthly.
The Casket, or, Flowers of literature, wit & sentiment. est. 1826. Philadelphia, Pennsylvania, monthly.
Chambers' Edinburgh Journal. est. 1832. Edinburgh, Scotland, weekly.
Continental Monthly. est. 1862. New York, New York, monthly.
The Eclectic Magazine of foreign literature, science, and art. est. 1844. New York, New York, weekly.
Every Saturday. est. 1866. Boston, Massachusetts, weekly.
The European Magazine. est. 1782. London, England, monthly.
Frank Leslie's Illustrated Newspaper. est. 1852. New York, New York, weekly.
Frank Leslie's Pleasant Hours for boys and girls. est. 1866. New York, New York, monthly.
Frank Leslie's Popular Monthly. est. 1876. New York, New York, monthly.
The Galaxy. est. 1866. New York, New York, monthly.
The Gift: A Christmas and New Year's Present. est. 1836. Philadelphia, Pennsylvania, yearly.
Gleason's Monthly Companion. est. 1872. Boston, Massachusetts, monthly.
Godey's Lady's Book. est. 1830. Philadelphia, Pennsylvania, monthly.
Graham's Magazine. est. 1841. Philadelphia, Pennsylvania, monthly.
Harper's New Monthly Magazine. est. 1850. New York, New York, monthly.
Harper's Weekly. est. 1857. New York, New York, weekly.
Holden's Dollar Magazine. est. 1848. New York, New York, monthly.
Household Words. est 1850. London, England, weekly.
The International Monthly. est. 1850. New York, New York, monthly.
The Knickerbocker. est. 1833. New York, New York, monthly.
The Ladies' Companion. est. 1834. Boston, Massachusetts, monthly.
The Locomotive Firemen's Magazine. est. 1876. Chicago, Illinois, monthly.
Massachusetts Ploughman and New England Journal of Agriculture. est. 1866. Boston, Massachusetts, weekly.
The New Monthly Magazine. est. 1814. London, England, monthly.
Overland Monthly. est. 1868. San Francisco, California, monthly.
Peterson's Magazine. est. 1842. Philadelphia, Pennsylvania, monthly.
Philadelphia Album and Ladies Literary Gazette. est. 1827. Philadelphia, Pennsylvania, weekly.
Potter's American Monthly. est. 1875. Philadelphia, Pennsylvania, monthly.
Robinson's Magazine: A Weekly Repository of Original Papers and Selections from English Magazines. est. 1818. Baltimore, Maryland, monthly.
The Southern Literary Messenger. est. 1834. Richmond, Virginia, monthly.
The Southern Magazine. est. 1871. Baltimore, Maryland, monthly.
The Strand. est. 1891. London, England, monthly.
Tit-Bits from All the Most Interesting Books, Periodicals and Newspapers in the World. est. 1881. Manchester, England, weekly.

Books Cited

Blackstone, William. *Commentaries on the Laws of England.* Oxford: Clarendon. 1765–1769.
Browne, Junius Henri. *The Great Metropolis: A Mirror of New York; a Complete History of Metropolitan Life and Society; with Sketches of Prominent Places, Persons, and Things in the City, as They Actually Exist.* Hartford: American, 1869.
Buntline, Ned. *The Mysteries and Miseries of New York.* New York: Berford, 1848.
Bynum, W.F. *Science and the Practice of Medicine in the Nineteenth Century.* Cambridge: Cambridge University Press, 1994.
Caulfield, James. *Portraits, Memoirs, and Characters, of Remarkable Persons.* London: Whitley, 1820.
Christie, Agatha. *Come, Tell Me How You Live.* London: Collins, 1946.
Collins, Wilkie. *The Moonstone.* London: Tinsley, 1868.
Comstock, Anthony. *Traps for the Young.* New York: Funk and Wagnalls, 1881.
Davis, Leopold. *Strange Occurrences.* Boston: Published for the author, 1877.
Davis, Sam. *Short Stories.* San Francisco: Golden Era, 1886.
Dickens, Charles. *Bleak House.* London: Bradbury & Evans, 1853.
Fielding, Henry. *An Enquiry into the Causes of the Increase of Robbers.* London: Miller, 1751.
Forrester, Andrew, Jr. *The Female Detective.* London: Ward and Lock, 1864.
_____. *The Revelations of a Private Detective.* London: Ward and Lock, 1863.
Gaboriau, Emile. *Le Petit Vieux des Batignolles.* Paris, Dentu, 1876.
Harris, Thomas. *The Silence of the Lambs.* New York: St. Martin's, 1988.
Hawkins, William. *A Treatise of the Pleas of the Crown: or, A System of the Principal Matters, Relating to That Subject, Digested Under Their Proper Heads.* Dublin: Lynch, 1721.
Hayward, William Stephens. *Revelations of a Lady Detective.* London: George Vickers, 1864.
Knapp, Andrew, and William Baldwin. *The Newgate Calendar: Comprising Interesting Memoirs of the Most Notorious Characters Who Have Been Convicted of Outrages on the Laws of England Since the Commencement of the Eighteenth Century; with Occasional Anecdotes and Observations, Speeches, Confessions, and Last Exclamations of Sufferers.* London: Robins, 1825.
Lippard, George. *The Quaker City, the Monks of Monk-Hall: a Romance of Philadelphia Life, Mystery, and Crime.* Philadelphia: G.B. Zieber, 1844.
Maitland, James. *Suppressed Sensations, or Leaves from the Note Book of a Chicago Reporter.* Chicago: Rand McNally, 1879.
THE MALEFACTOR'S REGISTER; OR, New NEWGATE and TYBURN CALENDAR. CONTAINING THE AUTHENTIC LIVES, TRIALS, ACCOUNTS OF EXECUTIONS, DYING SPEECHES, AND OTHER CURIOUS PARTICULARS. London: Cooke, 1780.
Martel, Charles. *The Detective's Note-Book.* London: Ward and Lock, 1860.
McWatters, George. *Detectives of Europe and America, or Life in the Secret Service, a Selection of Celebrated Cases.* Hartford: J. B. Burr, 1877.
Mitford, Mary R. (ed). *Stories of American Life by American Writers.* London: H. Colburn and R. Bentley, 1830.
The Newgate Calendar or MALEFACTORS' BLOODY REGISTER, London: Cooke, 1774.
Newnes, George. "The Reminiscences of an American Detective" *Tit-Bits from All the Most Interesting Books, Periodicals and Newspapers in the World.* 3.72 March 3, 1883. 316.
Pinkerton, Allan. *The Expressman and the Detective.* Chicago: Keen, Cooke, & Co. 1874.
Stevens, James Fitzjames. *The Criminal Law of England.* London: Macmillan, 1863.
Stories for the Home Circle, New York: Putnam, 1857.
Twain, Mark. *Life on the Mississippi.* Boston: Osgood, 1883.
_____. *The Tragedy of Pudd'nhead Wilson.* New York: Webster, 1894.
Vidocq, Eugène Henri. *Memoirs of Vidocq, Principal Agent of the French Police Until 1827.* Philadelphia: Carey and Hart. 1834.

Warren, Samuel. (pseud.?) *The Confessions of an Attorney; Which Are Added Several Papers on English Law and Lawyers by Charles Dickens.* New York: Cornish, Lamport, & Co. 1852.
_____. *Experiences of a Barrister.* New York: Cornish, Lamport, & Co. 1852.
Waters, Thomas. (William Russell). *The Autobiography of an English Detective.* New York: Dick & Fitzgerald, 1864.
_____. *The Diary of a Detective Police Officer.* New York: Dick & Fitzgerald, 1864.
_____. *The Experiences of a French Detective Officer, Adapted from the MSS of Theodore Duhamel.* London: Charles H. Clarke, 1861.
_____. *Leaves from the Diary of a Law-Clerk. By the Author of "Recollections of a Detective Police Officer," &c.* London: Brown, 1857.
_____. *Recollections of a Policeman*, New York: Cornish and Lamport, 1852. a.k.a. *Recollections of a Detective Police-Officer.* London: J. & C. Brown, 1856.
_____. *Strange Stories of a Detective; or, The Curiosities of Crime.* New York: Dick and Fitzgerald, 1863.
Williams, John B., M.D. *Leaves from the Note-Book of a New York Detective: The Private Record of J[ames]. B[rampton].* New York: Dick and Fitzgerald, 1865.
Wontner, Thomas. *Old Bailey Experience: Criminal Jurisprudence and the Actual Working of Our Penal Code of Laws.* London: Fraser, 1833.

Websites and Journal Articles

Chronicling America: Historic American Newspapers. *The Library of Congress.* chroniclingamerica.loc.gov.
Dunn, P. M. "Oliver Wendell Holmes (1809–1894) and His Essay on Puerperal Fever." *Archives of Disease in Child. Fetal and Neonatal Edition* 92.4 (2007): F325–F327. doi: 10.1136/adc.2005.077578.
Flexner, Abraham. "Medical Education in America." *The Atlantic Monthly.* June 1910. 797–814.
Harvey, Reed. "Waiver of the Criminal Defendant's Right to Testify: Constitutional Implications." *Fordham Law Review* 60.1 (1991): 175–197. FLASH: The Fordham Law Archive of Scholarship and History, http://ir.lawnet.fordham.edu/flr/vol60/iss1/5.
"History." *The Crown Prosecution Service.* www.cps.gov.uk.
Hughes, Michael F., Barbara D. Beck, Yu Chen, Ari S. Lewis, and David J. Thomas, "Arsenic Exposure and Toxicology: A Historical Perspective." *Toxicological Sciences.* 2011. doi: 10.1093/toxsci/kfr184.
Jones, Marian Moser, and Isidore Daniel Benrubi. "Poison Politics: A Contentious History of Consumer Protection Against Dangerous Household Chemicals in the United States." *American Journal of Public Health* 103.5 (2013): 801–812. doi: 10.2105/AJPH.2012.301066.
Langbein, John H. "Historical Foundations of the Law of Evidence: A View from the Ryder Sources." *Columbia Law Review* 96.5 (1996): 1168–1202. JSTOR, doi: 10.2307/1123403.
Papers Past. *The National Library of New Zealand.* https://paperspast.natlib.govt.nz.
"Prosecutors and Litigants." *London Lives, 1690 to 1800—Crime, Poverty and Social Policy in the Metropolis.* April 2012. www.londonlives.org.
Trove. The National Library of Australia. http://trove.nla.gov.au.
Westminster Detective Library. https://wdl.mcdaniel.edu

Index

"The Abducted Ward" 82
Abilene Reflector 110
Abilene Weekly Reflector 200
"The Accusing Leaves" 209
"Adroitly Foiled" 82
"An Adventure in Paris" 69
L'Affaire Lerouge 34
"After those Seven-Thirties, a Simple Job" 180
Ainsworth 137, 144
The Albion: A Journal of News, Politics and Literature 28, 29, 204
Alden, Henry Mills: "Crime Detected: an Anecdote of the Paris Police" 9, 99, 112
"An Alibi" 14, 23
"An Alibi, Being False It Could Not Withstand Investigation" 23
All the Year Round 9, 47, 133
The Allen County Democrat 91, 130, 214
Alpena Argus 2
"An Amateur Detective" 200
"An Amicable Agreement" 211
"Anastasie Jouvin" 134
The Anderson Intelligencer 49, 59
Angier, Frank H.: "Charming Madame Auvergne" 119; "The Diamond Cross" 135; "The Vital Point" 111
"The Apothecary's Compound, from a Physician's Notebook" 74, 80, 155, 161, 168, 216
Appleton's Journal of Literature, Science and Art 82, 84, 194
The Arizona Kicker 2
Armstong, J.B.: "A Police-Officer's Seven Thousand Mile Chase" 178
"Arresting a Murderer" 16, 190
"The Art Detective" 128
"Assassin of Castellane" 92, 180
"The Assassin's Track" 24, 196, 207
"An Assignment" 46, 52, 56, 60
"At the Right Time: A Lawyer's Story" 55
The Athens Messenger 16, 135
The Atlantic Monthly 28, 67, 180, 200, 202, 220
Aubrey, Eugene: "Not a Ghost Story" 140
Australia 2, 4, 20, 35, 64, 123, 143, 144, 209, 215

"Australian Detective Story or Murder Will Out" 35
The Autobiography of an English Detective 29–30, 66, 79, 90
Autopsy *see* post-mortem

B., J.M.: "Doctor D'Arsac" 129; "Jean Monette" 102; "Marie Laurent" 10; "The Strange Discovery" 10, 129
Baden, Frances Henshaw 113
Bakewell, George 44
Baldwin, Lola Greene 124
Baldwin, William 44
Ballistics 60, 62, 84–85
Ballou, Maturin Murray 19–20, 27, 31–32, 34, 72, 103, 180–181; *see also Ballou's Dollar Monthly Magazine*; *Ballou's Monthly Magazine*; *Flag of Our Union*
Ballou's Dollar Monthly Magazine 13, 17, 19, 22, 25, 27, 32, 72–73, 82, 117, 118, 145, 157, 180–181, 198, 203, 206, 209
Ballou's Monthly Magazine 3, 22, 33, 78, 81, 83, 103, 112, 119, 134, 135, 155, 159, 181, 195, 211
Baltimore 20, 25, 26, 45, 173, 174
Bangor Daily Whig and Courier 118
"A Bank Note in Two Halves" 9
"The Bank Vault" 150, 152, 180
"The Banker's Clerk" 152
banks 22, 143, 145, 149–152, 154, 163, 174
Barnstable Patriot 25, 91, 133
Baron Ludwig, or the Female Detective (play) 131
Batcheller, Irving 182
"The Bath of Blood" *see* "Mademoiselle Jabirouska"
Beadle, Erastus 181
"Beat the Brace Game: A Detective's Yarn of the Early Days of the Mississippi" 203
The Bee 16, 21, 144, 145
Belnheim, Belinda: "A Mormon Way" 133
The Berkshire County Eagle 195
Bennett, Emerson: "Arresting a Murderer" 16, 190; "Detecting a Murderer" 190, 211; "Hidden Crime Revealed" 118; "Murder Will Out"

162; "The Murderer's Ordeal: A California Story" 21, 157, 159–160
Bentham, Jeremy: *A Treatise on Evidence* 21, 45, 157, 160, 161
Bentley's Miscellany 9
"Betrayed by a Button" 108, 129
"Bigamy or Not Bigamy" 105
Bill of Rights 38, 45, 221
Binnacle: "The Detective" 123
The Bismarck Tribune 109, 114, 119
The Bismarck Weekly Tribune 8
"A Bit of Detective Business" 199
"A Bit of Mystery" 182
Bittersweet, Hester: "Our New Pupil" 159
"The Black Satin Gown" 118
Blackstone, William: *Commentaries on the Laws of England* 55
Blackwoods Magazine 47
"The Blasted Tree" 13, 51–52, 60, 69, 221
Bleak House 62, 72, 85, 137
blood 23–24, 34, 56–57, 66, 79–80, 85–86, 88, 89–90, 93, 95, 99, 108–109, 116, 120, 157, 188, 190, 195, 205, 209, 221
The Bloomfield Times 38, 50, 76, 78
"The Blue Diamond" 21
"Bob Cheriot, Esq.; or, the Tragedy at Chelmsford" 119, 213
"The Bohemian's Story of 'La Silhouette'" 134
"A Bold Stroke for a Wife" 107, 112
Bonner, Robert E. 28, 180; *see also* The New York Ledger
The Boon's Lick Times 71
"The Boorn Affair: A Strange Story of Circumstantial Evidence" 58
Booth, John Wilkes 136
Borden, Lizzie 154
Boston 16, 20, 25, 126, 138, 147, 173, 176, 205, 216
The Boston Daily Atlas 8
Boston Daily Globe 92
The Boston Weekly Globe 150
Bottchers, Emma 125
Boutelle, Clarence M.: "The Lost Lady" 132
Bow Street Runners 9, 28, 30, 178
Bowdler Thomas 217
"The Bowie Knife Sheath" 19, 22, 213
Braddon, Mary Elizabeth 137
Bradford, Jonathan 48
Bradford Reporter 14, 54
Brampton, James 19–20, 68–70, 73–74, 84, 181, 193–194, 198, 206, 212; "The Bowie Knife Sheath" 19, 22, 213; "The Defrauded Heir" 73–74, 82; "The Knotted Handkerchief" 73, 157, 181, 209; *Leaves from the Note-Book of a New York Detective* 20, 22, 24, 68, 70, 73–74, 141, 167, 181, 194, 213; "Masked Robbers: A Leaf from a Detective's Notebook" 19, 181; "Mr. Sterling's Confession" 181; "The Mysterious Advertisement" 19, 203, 206; "The Silver Pin" 69–70; "Stabbed in the Back" 19–20, 27, 209

"The Brand of Cain" 199
The Branding Iron 2
"Breaking up a Gang: A Detective's Story" 146–147, 192
"The Bride's Diamond" 153
"A Brilliant Confidence Swindle in High Life" 110
"The Broken Cent" 20
"Broken Evidence" 79
Brooklyn Eagle 28, 35, 148, 185
"The Brother's House" 46
"Brought to Justice" 132–133, 135, 169
"The Brown Mystery" 111
Browne, Junius Henri 170, 174, 196
Bucket, Mr. 62, 72, 85
The Buffalo News 104
"Bullet Marks, a Story of Love and Circumstantial Evidence" 62
Bulwer-Lytton 137, 144
Buntline, Ned: 137 "The Last Crime" 146, 167; *The Mysteries and Miseries of New York* 33
"The Buried Bullet: A Detective's Story" 147, 206
"The Burke Diamond Case, An Omaha Detective Story, Showing the Trails and Disappointment of Detective Work" 21
Burlington Free Press 170
Burlington Weekly Hawkeye 108
Burroughs, Adoniram/Andrew J. 120–121
Burton, William Edwin 7, 8, 10, 12, 98, 116, 175–176, 187; "The Cork Leg" 8, 10–11, 118, 175–176; "The Secret Cell" 8, 10, 28, 35, 97–98, 116, 128, 175, 176, 187; *see also* Burton's Gentleman's Magazine
Burton's Gentleman's Magazine 8, 10–11, 35, 48, 49, 52, 54, 97–98, 102, 116, 129, 175
"The Butcher's Story—A Detective Police Party" 8, 28, 35
The Butler Citizen 58
"The Button: An Experience of a New York Detective, Related by Himself" 18–19, 179
Bynum, W.F. 68–69
Byrnes, Thomas 126, 127, 173, 109; (character) "First Great Success" 109; *Professional Criminals of America* 158

Caleb Williams 138
The Cambria Freeman 56, 109
camera 89–90, 91, 211; *see also* photography
"Can Chloroform be used to Facilitate Robberies?" 82
"Cape Diamonds" 35, 153
capital punishment 14, 39–41, 44–45, 48, 55, 57, 83, 122, 144, 167–169, 221
"The Car Acquaintance: or, the Two Bits of Paper" 25, 117
Cary and Hart 7, 45, 171, 175
"A Case of Circumstantial Evidence" 60, 61, 141, 142
"A Case of Conscience—A Lawyer with Conscientious Scruples" 58

Index 235

"A Case of Mistaken Identity" 144
"The Case of the Widow Lerouge" 34
The Casket, or, Flowers of literature, wit & sentiment 13, 51, 222
"Catching a Ghost: A Philadelphia Detective's Story" 21
"Catching Counterfeiters" 84, 189
Catoctin Clarion 2
"Caught by a Thread" 186, 206
Caulfield, James 40
Cecil, John 44
The Cedar Valley Times 111, 205
Centre Democrat 86
Chaloner, William 145
Chambers' Edinburgh Journal 4, 8–9, 17–18, 31, 47, 53, 108, 128, 171, 177–178, 184–185, 197, 218
"A Chapter on Aristocracy" 48
"Chapters from the Note-Book of a Deceased Lawyer" 48
The Charleston Daily Supplement 135
"Charming Madame Auvergne" 119
Chaucer 39; "The Nun's Priest's Tale" 59
chemist 77–78, 81–83, 93, 194, 210, 216
"The Chemist's Story; or Science vs. Murder" 81, 216
The Cheyenne Daily Leader 166
Chicago 20, 25, 27, 36–7, 68, 125–126, 173–174, 191, 218
The Chicago Daily Tribune 82
Chicago Journal 92
Chicago Tribune 34, 95, 211, 213
The Chillicothe Constitution 186
Chitty, Joseph: *A Practical Treatise on Criminal Law Comprising the Practice, Pleadings, and Evidence* 45
Christie, Agatha 7
Chronicling America: Historic American Newspapers 1, 71
The Cincinnati Daily Star 86
The Cincinnati Enquirer 88, 115
circumstantial evidence (concept) 11–15, 17, 24, 30, 36, 43–45, 47–48, 52, 56–59, 64–65, 69, 71–73, 79, 84–85, 139–142, 152, 163, 169, 177–178, 187–189, 199, 210, 213, 221–222
"Circumstantial Evidence" (stories): (1832) 56; (1840) 13, 15, 56, 141; (1849) 70, 188; (1852) 47, 53, 57, 82; (1867) 56; (1879) 56; (1881) 115; (1883) 14, 57; (1886) 57
"Circumstantial Evidence, a Strange Instance of Its Uncertainty" 56
"Circumstantial Evidence: An Adventure in Western Virginia" 61
"Circumstantial Evidence, or The Fatal Resemblance" 59
cities 20–23
Clark, Judge: "A Bold Stroke for a Wife" 107, 112; A Curious Case 75; "A Legal Slip 'Twixt Cup and Lip" 63; "Mabel's Christmas Gift" 115
Claude, M.: *Mémoires de M. Claude, chef de la police de sûreté sous le second Empire* 34

"A Clever Capture" 30, 92
"The Clever Detective" 95
"A Clew in a Dream: A Detective Who Firmly Believes in the Truth of Visions" 211
"Clock Peddlers in the West: Scraps from the Notebook of a Missouri Lawyer" 49
"The Club" 198
"Clubnose" 108–109
Cobb, Sylvanus, Jr. 27, 74–76, 81, 87, 181; "The Apothecary's Compound" 74; "The Bank Vault: From a Lawyer's Notebook" 150, 152, 180; "Hunt on to Highway: From the Record of a Sheriff" 189; "The Left-Handed Thief" 87; "The Mad Philosopher: A Startling Adventure from the Diary of a Physician" 75, 93, 160, 166; "The Pen Knife Blade: From a Surgeon's Diary" 70, 75–76, 107, 157; "A Post-Mortem Discovery: A Scrap from a Physician's Diary" 75–76, 82, 155; "The Resurrectionists" 161; "The Sick Robber: and How Tim Cured Him" 118; "The Two-Fingered Assassin" 87, 103, 105
"Coiners and Forgers" 30
"The Coiners of Kansas" 4, 16, 135, 145
Coldwater Sentinel 70
Collins, Wilkie 137; "The Fourth Poor Traveller" 178; "A Marriage Tragedy" 28, 114; *The Moonstone* 30, 115, 153; *The Seven Poor Travellers* 178; "The Stolen Letter: A Lawyer's Story" 129, 178; "Who is the Thief?" 28, 180; *Woman in White* 106
The Columbia Spy 20, 82, 106, 114, 130
The Columbus Journal 89, 132
The Columbus Post 132, 153
Columbus Sunday Enquirer 81, 119
Come, Tell Me How You Live 7
"Coming out of Exile; or the Diamond Bracelet Found" 28, 114, 130, 137
Commentaries on the Laws of England 55
A Compendium of the Law of Evidence 45
Comstock, Anthony 104; *Traps for the Young* 117
Conan Doyle, Arthur 76, 172, 215, 220; "Scandal in Bohemia" 215; "A Study in Scarlet" 133
Confession 15, 50, 57–58, 60–61, 63, 75, 78, 83, 109, 112, 118, 120, 127, 149, 168–169, 192, 210
The Confessions of an Attorney; which are added Several Papers on English Law and Lawyers by Charles Dickens 47
"The Confidential Clerk" 22, 148, 160
"Conflict with Burglars, a Physician's Story" 76
Conrad, Caroline: "Eloise" 106
Continental Monthly 145
"Convicted but Innocent" 129, 141
Cooper's Clarksburg Register 57
copyright piracy 3–4, 7–9, 20, 28–31, 38, 47, 73, 95, 171, 178, 181–182; *see also* reprints
"The Cork Leg" 8, 10–11, 118, 175–176
The Cornhill Magazine 9
Cornish and Lamport 8, 47–48, 82, 171, 178
coroner 64, 67, 85, 93, 112, 138
The Corrector 190

236   Index

The Coshocton Democrat 88, 187
"The Costly Kiss" 18–19, 22, 100, 102, 148, 163, 179, 196, 202–203, 207
"The Counterfeit Bill" 146
"The Counterfeit Detective" 145
"The Counterfeiter" 48
counterfeiting 16, 19, 40, 66, 90, 118, 143–147, 151, 154, 164, 174, 185, 192, 211
courtroom 41, 45, 52, 61–62, 63, 64, 85, 209
crime: abduction 97; arson 94, 124; bank 149–152; blackmail 97, 117, 129, 143, 178; counterfeiting 16, 19, 40, 66, 90, 118, 143–147, 151, 154, 164, 174, 185, 192, 211; embezzlement 22, 100–101, 143, 148, 163, 177, 199, 212, 218; extortion 98, 143; forged wills 54–55, 107, 112; forgery 30, 54–55, 107, 112, 115, 118, 120, 123, 143, 151, 153, 182, 190, 192, 195; gambling 36, 143, 163, 177, 183; grave robbing 13, 51, 69–70, 74, 161; highway 16, 19, 30, 39–40, 92, 118, 143–145, 147, 159, 161, 189–190; infanticide 52; jewel robbery 9, 21, 30, 34, 91, 111, 113–115, 122, 128, 132, 148–149, 153–154, 159, 182, 210; kleptomania 124; moonshining 16, 124, 143; murder 4, 8, 11–12, 14–15, 19, 21–23, 25, 27, 35–36, 46, 48, 52, 54, 56–59, 66, 69–73, 75–85, 88, 90–91, 93–95, 98, 101–105, 107, 109–112, 114–122, 124, 129–130, 132–133, 137–140, 142–145, 154–158, 162–165, 167, 169, 172, 175–176, 180, 187–188, 193, 198, 201, 205–206, 208–210, 212–213, 215, 218–219, 221–222; murderer 16, 21, 24, 33–34, 46, 56, 72, 76, 79, 85–86, 88–89, 93, 101, 103–104, 109, 112, 118–120, 122, 125, 128, 135, 138, 141, 153–158, 160–161, 165, 167–169, 177, 199, 206, 209–211, 214, 217; murderess 48, 49, 52, 120, 123; perjury 43, 54, 60; pickpocket 29, 85, 111, 117, 122–124, 143, 147; robbery 17, 19, 58, 105, 111, 115–117, 120, 132, 143, 147–150, 152–153, 164, 185, 196, 204; shoplifting 40, 116, 123–124, 126, 143, 148–149; smuggling 118, 126, 143
"Crime Detected—An Anecdote of the Paris Police" 9, 99, 112
crime scene investigation (CSI) 23–25; *see also* forensics
The Criminal Law of England 42
Criminal Lunatics Act 165
Criminal Reminiscences and Detective Sketches 10
"The Criminal Witness, A Lawyer's Story" 62
Crosse, Marah: "The Withered Hand" 135
The Crown Prosecution Service 42
"The Culprit Judge, A Tale of Bench and Bar" 58
"A Curious Case" 75
"A Curious Stratagem" 31–32, 180, 209

Daily Alta Californian 111–112, 117, 149, 157, 186, 205
Daily Bulletin 149
The Daily Evening Bulletin 145
Daily Gazette 142

The Daily Independent 35, 89, 92
The Daily Intelligencer 56
The Daily Kennebec Journal 146
The Daily Press 61
Dallas, Mary Kyle: "Dr. Puffer's Lost Opportunity" 68, 75, 81–82, 216
The Darling Downs Gazette 4, 20
"A Dark Chapter from the Diary of a Law Clerk" 49, 75, 78
Davis, C.: "The Pigot Murder" 21, 82, 180, 198
Davis, Leopold 134; *Strange Occurrences* 132
Davis, Sam: "Miss Armstrong's Homicide" 94–95
The Dead Letter 26
"The Dead Man's Inn" 15
death penalty *see* capital punishment
The Decatur Daily Republican 20, 64
The Decatur Daily Review 197
"A Defence without Evidence" 158, 168
"The Defendant's Accomplice" 78
Defiance Democrat 151, 203, 205
"The Defrauded Heir" 73–74, 82
De Friese, A. Ehnenger: "A Sympathetic Link" 119
The Delta Herald 35, 186, 206
The Democratic Press 116
"A Den of Phantoms" 106, 146
Denton Journal 78, 129, 141, 213
"Detected by Peculiar Habits" 20
"Detecting a Murderer" 211
detective 1–2, 7–11, 13, 15, 17, 19, 23–26, 30, 34, 36, 48, 64–65, 84, 89–90, 92–93, 96, 99–101, 104, 106–107, 112, 114, 117–119, 123, 130, 132–135, 138–139, 142–144, 147–148, 151, 154–155, 157–161, 163–166, 169, 171–172, 174–177, 179–180, 182–184, 186, 188–202, 206–213, 219, 221; amateur 1, 29, 36, 96–97, 129–131, 135, 172, 191, 193–194, 199–202, 205, 210; American 15–17, 28, 178, 180, 191, 193–194, 216; animal 29, 191, 202; boy 200–201, 218; city 19, 25–28, 192, 206; English 8, 11–12, 28–31, 153, 159, 171–172, 177, 179, 189, 197; female 96–97, 108, 124–136, 199, 207; French 4, 7–8, 11–12, 20, 30–35, 109, 134, 171, 175, 181, 193; government 84, 104, 191–193, 221; hero 24, 27, 67, 142, 145, 179–180, 183, 186, 201–202, 206–208, 211, 214, 220, 222, 229; lawyer 1, 62–65, 96, 112, 129, 172, 181, 194, 205; narrator: 18–19, 26, 30, 36, 46, 49, 52, 59, 61, 63–64, 71, 73, 75, 78, 81, 83, 85, 98, 100, 103–104, 132, 150, 159, 166, 179, 182–183, 185, 195, 202–205, 218; New York 12, 18–24, 27, 34, 72, 74, 84, 125, 127, 141, 146, 172, 174, 178–179, 181, 192, 203, 206; nuisance 191; physician 1, 68, 70–73, 75–76, 84, 96, 194, 205; plainclothes 8, 25, 172–173, 175–176, 191; police 12, 26, 74, 127, 148, 171, 173–174, 191, 195–199, 205, 218, 222; private 65, 96, 125–126, 132–133, 174–175, 191–192, 195, 197, 208; professional 19, 36, 73, 96, 104, 115, 127–128, 131–136, 145, 151, 174–175, 191,

193, 199, 201, 210; robot 95; traits 63, 207–214; undercover 84, 92, 108, 122, 126–128, 132
"The Detective" (by Binnacle) 123
"The Detective" (1869) 204
"The Detective: A Story of New Orleans" 21, 108
detective agency 65, 125, 174–175, 190–192, 195, 197, 203
"The Detective as Forger" 195
"Detective in the Bud" 30
"A Detective Officer" 123
"A Detective Outwitted" 20
"Detective Pierson's Queer Dream" 189, 211
"Detective Police Party" 8, 35, 148, 171, 193, 171, 193, 216
"The Detective Quality" 20
"Detective Story" (poem) 82
"A Detective Story: Tracking a Burglar" 208
"A Detective Taken In" 145, 147
"A Detective's Experience" (stories) 182–183; (1858) 204; (1868) 99, 108, 168
"A Detective's Experience: A Female Forger" 118, 182
"A Detective's Experience: A Life of Crime" 165
"A Detective's Experience: The Missing Jewels" 30, 132, 153, 182
"A Detective's Experience: The Romance" 190
"A Detective's Great Feat" 118
The Detective's Note-Book 4, 9
Detectives of Europe and America, or Life in the Secret Service, a Selection of Celebrated Cases 34
"The Detective's Opinion of Crime" 104–105
"A Detective's Sketch" 155, 163, 168
"A Detective's Story" 183; (1862) 145; (1867) 202; (1868) 111, 205; (1869) 183, 208; (1870) 123, 148; (1876) 20; (1878) 203; (1880) 20, 159; (1887) 20, 192; (1889) 65
"The Detective's Story" (1864) 197; (1866) 36, 195, 203–204; (1871) 194, 196–197; (1872) 146; (1874) 140, 201; (1879) 22, 90, 147, 149; (1883) 105
"A Detective's Story: Hasheesh" 191
"A Detective's Story: How He was Convicted and Sent to State Prison" 64
"A Detective's Story of New York Life" 21
"A Detective's Story: The Convict Coachman" 119
"A Detective's Story: Tracing a Gang of Counterfeiters—A Close Call" 37
"A Detective's Story: Tragic End of a Brilliant Songstress" 182
"A Detective's Yarn" 21, 26, 158, 167, 203
The Detroit Free Press 20, 102, 105, 141
"The Devil and the Lawyers" 63
"The Devitt Will Case" 162
"The Diamond Bracelet" 28, 113
"The Diamond Cross" 135
"The Diamond Cross or, the Female Assassin" 119

"The Diamond Necklace" 153
"The Diamonds of the Duke de B." 34, 153
The Diary of a Detective Police Officer 29, 186
Diary Stories 29–30, 37, 48–52, 54, 59, 75, 105, 107, 117, 172, 178, 182, 185–186, 210
Dick and Fitzgerald 9, 20, 22, 24, 29–31, 34, 68, 73–74, 79, 81, 83, 90, 93, 100, 141, 145, 148, 159–160, 167, 181, 185–186, 194, 196, 207, 213
Dickens, Charles 3, 8–9, 17, 28–29, 47, 63, 140, 142, 148, 171, 173, 176–179, 191, 193, 230; Bleak House 62, 72, 85, 137; "The Butcher's Story—A Detective Police Party" 8, 28, 35; "A Detective Police Party" 148, 171, 216; "Hunted Down" 28, 82–83; Mr. Bucket 62, 72, 85; "The Modern Science of Thief-Taking" 171, 177; see also Household Words; All the Year Round
"The Difference Between English and French Detectives" 31
A Digest of the Law of Evidence in Criminal Cases 45
dime novels 180–181, 183, 200, 220
disguise 64, 87, 89, 108, 111, 115, 118, 134–135, 142, 147, 159, 170, 175, 179, 190, 199, 208; cross-dressing 118, 123, 134–135, 159, 190
"The Disguised Robbers; From a Lawyer's Notebook" 49
"The Disguised Servant" 78
dissection see post-mortem
Dix, John Ross: "The Black Satin Gown" 118
"Doctor D'Arsac" 129
"Dr. Puffer's Lost Opportunity" 68, 75, 81–82, 216
"The Doctor's Story" 74
"The Dog Detective" 29, 191, 202
"Dolly's Diamonds" 153
domestic abuse 97, 104–106
"A Double Crime" 182
"The Double Elopement" 117
"The Dramatic Author" 29
"The Dumb Countersign: A Deputy's Story" 36
The Dunkirk Observer-Journal 192
Dunn, P.M. 67
Dupin, C. Auguste 11, 23, 35, 64, 98, 172, 175, 193–194, 201, 208, 214
Dusseault, Edward: "The Bohemian's Story of 'La Silhouette'" 134
Dykman, Mrs. Mina 125

"'Earless Bill' the Detective" 145, 167
The Eaton Democrat 60–62, 142
Eau Claire Free Press 146, 167
"The Ebony Bedroom" 109
The Eclectic Magazine of foreign literature, science, and art 28–29, 114, 130
The Edgefield Advertiser 58, 60
Edison, Thomas 94–95
"Edward Drysdale" 178
The Edwardsville Intelligencer 35
"Eleven Thousand Pounds" 117
The Ellensburg Dawn 2

"Eloise" 106
"An Embarrassed Detective: A Story of the French Prefecture" 134
England 4, 7, 12, 18, 28–30, 32, 34, 38–39, 42–45, 47, 55, 62, 66–67, 80, 82, 101, 106, 122, 128, 131, 137, 142–144, 146–148, 170–173, 176, 180, 182, 186, 191, 207, 216, 218, 221
"The English Highwayman" 118
An Enquiry into the Causes of the Increase of Robbers 42–43
The European Magazine 46
Evening Star 85, 125
The Evening Telegraph 174
The Evening World 127
Every Saturday 35
evidence, rules of: circumstantial 11–15, 17, 24, 30, 36, 43–45, 47–48, 52, 56–59, 64–65, 69, 71–73, 79, 84–85, 139–142, 152, 163, 169, 177–178, 187–189, 199, 210, 213, 221–222; direct 43, 60, 80, 83, 210; eyewitness 12, 37, 39, 55
Experiences of a Barrister 47, 53, 177; "Circumstantial Evidence" 82; "Guilty or Not Guilty" 177
The Experiences of a French Detective Officer 31–32
The Expressman and the Detective 174
Extracts from a Lawyer's Port-Folio 46, 48, 51–52, 56
"Extracts from a Portfolio of a Man of Letters" 48
"Extracts from an Arctic Navigator's Journal" 48

"A Family Secret" 114
family story papers 1, 95–96, 215, 217; *see also Flag of Our Union; The New York Fireside Companion; The New York Ledger*
"Fanny Talbot: A Tale of Circumstantial Evidence" 58, 60
"The Fashionable Highwayman" 144
"The Fatal Cigar" 78
"The Fatal Liaison" 119
"The Fatal Potato" 22
"The Fatal Safe" 150
"The Fatal Woman" 109
The Fayette County Herald 3
The Fayetteville Observer 3, 21, 55, 71
"The Female Assassin" 122
The Female Detective 128, 131; *see also* Forrester, Andrew, Jr
The Female Detective, or The Boathouse on the Lake (play) 131
The Female Detective, or Women Against the World (play) 131
Féval, Paul: *Jean Diable* 34
"Fiacre No. 2525" 34
Fielding, Henry: *An Enquiry into the Causes of the Increase of Robbers* 42–43
"Finding a Criminal from the notes of an English Detective" 28–29, 189
"The Finger of Providence" 94, 182

firearms 62, 82, 84–85, 92–93, 130, 156–157, 209–210; air rifle 93; airgun 93; dartgun 93; gun 93; pistol 32, 62, 70, 84, 92, 99, 118, 128, 157, 168; revolver 15, 93; rifle 57, 84–8
"The First Case" 84, 194
"First Great Success" 109
Flag of Our Union 19, 31–32, 35–36, 72, 91, 94, 111, 117, 128, 146, 149, 150, 153, 180–181, 193, 201–204, 207, 212
"A Flash of Lightning" 81
Flexner, Abraham 67
"Flint Jackson" 128
"Foiled by a Woman" 109, 135
"A Foot-Light Flash. A Detective's Story" 4
forensics 46, 54, 56, 62, 66, 79, 86, 156, 189, 201; ballistics 84–85; bullet mark 62; dentistry 101; *see also* blood; prints
Forrester, Andrew, Jr. 131; *The Female Detective* 128; *The Revelations of a Private Detective* 128, 131; "Who Stole the Plate?" 153, 204
Forrester, John, and Daniel 30
The Fort Wayne Gazette 132
Fort Wayne Sentinel 34, 116, 159
Fort Wayne Weekly Democrat 107
Fort Worth Daily Gazette 119
"Found Out" 70
"The Fourfold Alibi" 23, 200
"The Fourth Poor Traveller" 178
The Fox Lake Gazette 119, 149, 157, 162
France 2, 4, 7–11, 28, 31–34, 66, 80, 111, 138, 141, 175–176, 180–181, 191, 201, 208, 222
Frank Leslie's Illustrated Newspaper 146
Frank Leslie's Pleasant Hours for boys and girls 21, 78, 83, 118, 165, 199, 207
Frank Leslie's Popular Monthly 20, 83, 132, 134, 201
Franklin, James F. 180; "A Curious Stratagem" 31–32, 180, 209; "The Guest-Chamber of the Inn of St. Ives" 31, 94, 155, 180
The Franklin Gazette 4, 22, 115
Freeborn County Standard 35, 124, 133
The Freeport Daily Bulletin 4
"The French Detective" 3
"The French Detective: The Little Affair" 3
The Fresno Republican 118
"From the Note Book of an Eminent Philadelphia Lawyer: Lately Deceased" 49
"From the Portfolio of a Lawyer: A Diseased Heart Cured" 49

Gaboriau, Émile 8, 34, 201; *L'Affaire Lerouge* 34; *Le Petit Vieux des Batignolles* 4
The Galaxy 144, 168, 191
The Galveston Daily News 109
"The Gambler's Revenge" 8
gang 16, 25, 36–37, 66, 69, 116, 123–124, 144–148, 151, 164, 192, 208
Garrett, Percy 74; "The Knotted Handkerchief" 157, 181, 209; "The Masked Robbers: A Leaf from a Detectives Note-book" 19, 181
The Gazette 126

Index 239

"A German Detective Story" 213
Germany 11, 34, 69, 160
The Gift: A Christmas and New Year's Present 90
Gilbert, Godfrey: *The Law of Evidence* 45
"The Girl Detective" 130
Gladden, Mrs. 131
"Gleanings from Dark Annals" 78
Gleason's Monthly Companion 22, 35, 91, 99, 102, 107, 119, 148–149
Godey's Lady's Book 12, 85
Godwin, William: *Caleb Williams* 138
"The Gold Bug" 172
The Golden Era 21, 26, 94, 158, 167, 203
"The Golden Haired Wig" 159
Gouveror Free Press 211
Graham's Magazine 35, 51, 215
"The Gramercy Park Mystery" 117
Grand Traverse Herald 110, 211
Grant County News 207
"The Great Diamond Robbery" 153
"A Great Jewel Robbery" 9
The Great Metropolis: A Mirror of New York; a Complete History of Metropolitan Life and Society; with Sketches of Prominent Places, Persons, and Things in the City, as They Actually Exist 170, 174, 196
"The Great Seymour Square Mystery" 149
The Green-Mountain Freeman 54, 62
"The Guest Chamber of the Inn at St. Ives, From the Journal of a Detective" 180
Guillot, M.: "A Curious Stratagem" 31–32, 180, 209; "The Guest Chamber of the Inn at St. Ives" 31, 94, 155, 180; "The Mysterious Deaths at Castellane" 31
"Guilty of Murder in the First Degree" 12
"Guilty or Not Guilty" (Eben E. Rexford) 119, 130, 166
"Guilty or Not Guilty" (*Experiences of a Barrister*) 177
"Gunning for Outlaws" 16

The Hamilton County Press 65
Harper Brothers 9, 17–18, 27, 154, 178, 180, 189, 191; *see also Harper's New Monthly Magazine*, *Harper's Weekly*
Harper's New Monthly Magazine 9, 14, 18–19, 21–23, 28–29, 49, 82, 91, 99, 100, 102, 110, 112, 114–115, 129, 148, 164, 167, 169, 178–180, 191, 196, 199, 202, 207, 210, 220
Harper's Weekly 17, 18, 26, 35, 117, 121–122, 145, 178–180, 189, 191, 204, 206
Harris, Mary 121–122
Harris, Thomas 137
Hartford Courant 110, 151
Harvey, Reed 43
"The Haunted Pool" 35
Hawkins, William 42
Hayward, William Stephens: *Revelations of a Lady Detective* 131
"Helen Montressor; Judge Remsen's First Client" 61, 114

"Her Clay Idol: A New York Detective Story" 26, 111
The Herald (Syracuse) 120
Herring, Miss 131
Herschel, Sir William 86–88, 91
"Hidden Crime Revealed" 118
Higgins, Ella: "Saved by a Telephone" 92
Highwaymen 16, 30, 39, 118, 143–144
"His First Case, How a Detective Found the Lost Money and a Wife" 186
"His Own Detective" 90
"Historical Foundations of the Law of Evidence: A View from the Ryder Sources" 40–41
Hodge, Hugh 67
Holcroft, Thomas: *A Tale of Mystery* 137
Holden's Dollar Magazine 116
Holmes, Oliver Wendell 66–67
Holmes, Sherlock 2, 4–5, 124, 157, 172, 182, 187, 214, 220, 222
Holmes County Farmer 71
The Holmes County Republican 195
"The Horse Detective" 162, 191
Household Words 8–9, 28, 148, 171, 177–178
"How Bob Bolter's Prisoner Escaped" 17–18, 178, 204
"How He Got a Start" 76
"How I Captured the Burglars" 186
"How I Got Promoted: A Detective's Story" 186, 197
"How I Wasn't Taken Down, from the Journal of a Detective" 208
"How I Won My Wife: A Doctor's Story" 71, 100, 102, 186
"How Linton Bank was Robbed" 186
"How the Burglars were Taken" 186
"How the Burglars were Trapped" 186
"How to Prove an Alibi" 186
"How We Caught Him" 186
Hughes, Jennie 125
Hughes, Michael F. 80
"Hunt on the Highway" 159, 161
"Hunt on the Highway; From the 'Record' of a Sheriff" 189
Hunter, Fred.: "Mag Dufries; or, The Lost Child" 128
Hunter, J.T.: "Brought to Justice" 132–133, 135, 169
Huntingdon Journal 81–82

The Illinois Free Trader 14–15, 56, 141
imported stories 3–4, 7–8, 28–30, 34–35, 144
"The Imprint of a Thumb, Which Caused the Confession of a Thief and Puzzled a Detective" 89
"In a Cellar" 35, 202
"In Answer to an Advertisement" 9
"In the Bush" 35, 144
"In the Cellar" 35
"In the Magurriwock" 167
"The Incendiary" 94, 178
The Indiana Democrat 30, 195, 197

240　Index

The Indiana Progress 79, 119, 189, 192, 210, 211
The Indiana Weekly Messenger 119
"An Infallible Test of Identity" 86–87
"infernal machines" 92–95, 156
"ingenious devices" 92–97; air syringe 93–94; booby-trapped bed 94; dartgun 93; spring-loaded rings 92
Ingram, John Henry 172
"An Innocent Man Hanged" 102
The International Monthly 128
"The Invisible Crime or Foot-Print Evidence" 110–111, 157
Iowa State Reporter 84, 189
The Isola Register 120

The Jackson Citizen 26
Jackson, Henry 87
James, G.P.R.: "The Mysterious Occurrence in Lambeth" 28–29, 115, 178
"The Jandidier Mystery" 4
"Jane Eccles" 117
The Janesville Gazette 25, 30, 205, 212
The Janesville Weekly Gazette 197
Jean Diable 34
"Jean Monette" 102
Jefferson, Thomas 122
The Jeffersonian Republican 50
Jennings, Thomas 87
"The Jersey Lawyer's First Case in Minnesota" 50
"The Jewel Thief" 159
Jewelry 22, 113–114, 149, 153–155, 210
J.M.B.: "Doctor D'Arsac" 129; "Jean Monette" 102; "Marie Laurent" 10; "The Strange Discovery" 10, 129
"John Taylor the Timon of the Backwoods Bar and Pulpit" 53
Johnson, Mrs. 125–126
Jonathan Bradford, or Murder on the Roadside 48, 137
"Jules Ingram, or a Race Down the St. Lawrence" 151
The Junction City Weekly Union 24
justice 59–63
"Justice vs. Mercy" 199

Kellogg, Ansel Nash 182
The Kenosha Telegraph 159, 161
Ker, David: "The Print of a Finger" 201
Kirby, Mrs. 125
Knapp, Andrew 44
Knapp and Baldwin 44
The Knickerbocker 48, 53
"The Knotted Handkerchief" 73, 157, 181, 209

The Ladies' Companion 28, 65
The Lady Detective (play) 131
"A Lady's Glove" 32
LaFarge, Marie 80
The Lake Village Times 93
Langbein, John H. 38, 40–41

Laromie, Eugene 31–32, 181, 207; "A Lady's Glove" 32; "A Little Affair" 32–33, 181; "An Official Blunder" 31, 33; "Seventy Miles an Hour" 31; "The Tell-Tale Eye" 31, 33, 181, 193
"The Last Crime" 146, 167
"The Laurieville Mystery" 76
"A Lawyer's Adventure" 14, 54
"A Lawyer's Story" 38, 50, 54, 61, 129, 141
"A Leaf from a Lawyer's Diary" 49, 59
"A Leaf from the Diary of a Detective" 186
Leaves from the Diary of a Law-Clerk: "Bigamy or Not Bigamy" 105; "A Dark Chapter from the Diary of a Law Clerk" 49, 75, 78; "Edward Drysdale" 178; "The Incendiary" 94, 178; "Jane Eccles" 117; "Malvern vs Malvern" 105, 107; "The Temptress" 58
Leaves from the Note-Book of a New York Detective: The Private Record of J(ames). B(rampton) 20, 68, 73–74, 181, 193–194, 212–213; "The Bowie Knife Sheath" 19, 22, 213; "The Broken Cent" 20; "My First Brief" 83, 141; "A Satanic Contract" 74; "The Silver Pin"; "The Walker Street Tragedy" 23–24, 167
"Leaves from the Portfolio of a Practicing Lawyer: The Bracelet" 49
The Lebanon Advertiser 140
Lecoq, M. 34, 201
The Ledger see *New York Ledger*
Lee, Marl: "Helen Montressor or, Judge Remsen's First Case" 61, 114
Leech, Harry Harewood: "The Robbery of Plate" 19, 111, 117, 153, 204
"The Left Hand" 25, 30, 205–206, 212
"The Left-Hand Glove: or Circumstantial Evidence" 105, 115
"The Left-Handed Assassin: A Detective's Story" 88, 187
"The Left-Handed Thief" 87
"Legal Metamorphoses" 178
"A Legal Slip 'Twixt Cup and Lip" 63
Leslie, Frank 34; see also *Frank Leslie's Illustrated Newspaper*; *Frank Leslie's Pleasant Hours for boys and girls*; *Frank Leslie's Popular Monthly*
Lewis, Monk 137
Lexow Committee 196
"The Libertine" 100
"The Librarian's Portfolio" 48
Life on the Mississippi 89
"A Life's Lesson" 99, 102, 119
The Lincoln County Herald 3
"Link by Link" 83
Lippard, George 137; *The Quaker City* 33
"A Little Affair" 3, 32–33, 181
"A Little Mistake" 115
Locard's Exchange Principle 24
locked-room mystery 11, 24–25, 93, 109
Logansport Daily Star 116
London 3–4, 8, 10, 12, 20–21, 28–31, 35, 40–42, 44, 46, 69, 71, 84, 94, 105, 107, 117, 131, 153, 179–180, 185, 187, 201, 204, 212, 218

The London Referee 9
The London Truth 9
The London World 9
The Long Island Traveler 152
Longfellow, Henry Wadsworth: "Retribution" 59
"The Lost Lady" 132
"Lost, Stolen or Strayed" 114, 129
"The Lost Will: An American Detective Story" 64
Lotta (Crabtree, Lotta) 131
"The Lottery Ticket" 22
"Lou Lispenard's Escape" 166
The Louisiana Capitolian 94, 109, 135
The Louisiana Democrat 30, 144
"Love and War: A Physician's Story" 71
The Lowell Sun 79, 115
"Lucky Larceny" 70, 81, 216
Lynch, Lawrence: *Shadowed by Three* 208

"Mabel's Christmas Gift" 115
Mabry, Luvena 125
MacDonald, Rufus Cyrene: "The Terrors of the Telephone: A Detective Story" 92
"The Mad Philosopher: A Startling Adventure from the Diary of a Physician" 75, 93, 160, 166
"Mademoiselle Jabirouska: The Modern Messalina" 69, 116, 122, 160
"Mag Dufries: or, The Lost Child" 128
Mahon, Mrs. 125
"The Maimed Hand" 130, 214
Maitland, James: "A Mysterious Murder" 36–37, 80, 112, 119
"Major Truslow's Mistake" 135
"The Major's Wife" 112
"Making a Fortune" 197
THE MALEFACTOR'S REGISTER; OR, New NEWGATE and TYBURN CALENDAR. CONTAINING THE AUTHENTIC LIVES, TRIALS, ACCOUNTS OF EXECUTIONS, DYING SPEECHES, AND OTHER CURIOUS PARTICULARS 44
"Malvern Versus Malvern" 105, 107
"Man or Demon" 166
"The Man with Big Whiskers" 23
The Manitowoc Pilot 118
"Maria Vassar" 119, 121
"Marie Laurent" 10
The Marion Daily Star 81, 83, 92
"A Marriage Tragedy" 28, 114
Married Woman's Property Act 106
Marsh, James 62, 80–81
The Marshall Statesman 25
Marten, Maria 137
"Mary Kingsford" 128
"The Masked Robbers: A Leaf from a Detectives Note-book" 19, 181
Mason, Miss Kale 125
Massachusetts Ploughman and New England Journal of Agriculture 191, 207

"The Matched Button" 148
Matthews, Brander 172
Maxim, Hiram Percy 93
Mayne, Sir Richard 30
M'Cabe, James D., Jr. 181; "A Lady's Glove" 32; "A Little Affair" 3, 32–33, 181; "An Official Blunder" 31–33, 207, 212; "Seventy Miles an Hour" 31, 33; "The Tell-Tale Eye" 31, 33, 91, 146, 181, 193
The McArthur Democrat 53
McCann, Mrs. 115, 125
McClure, S.S. 182, 220
The McCook Tribute 82
McDaniel, Stephen 40, 55, 170
The McKean Miner 30, 153
McMillen, James: "A Detective's Story: Hasheesh" 191
McPhearson, Nellie 125
McWatters, George 34
"Medical College Sketches: The Ex-Professor's Stories: The Skull" 35–36
medical education 66–70, 77
medical examiner *see* coroner
Meigs, Charles 67
melodramas 99, 103, 137, 183–184, 220–221
Mémoires de M. Claude, chef de la police de sûreté sous le second Empire 34
memoirs 7–8, 34, 37, 70–71, 175, 186–187
Memoirs of Vidocq, principal agent of the French police until 1827 7, 45, 171, 175
Memphis Daily Appeal 128–129
mental illness 46, 60, 74, 98, 107, 110–111, 117, 121–122, 139, 164–165, 176; Criminal Lunatics Act 165
Metropolitan Police 30, 42, 128, 172, 175, 177, 218
microscope 66, 80, 86, 89–91, 210–211
"The Microscope as a Detective" 90
The Middlebury Galaxy 49
Millheim Journal 127
Minister of Police and the Female Detective (play) 131
"Miriam: A Tale of Circumstantial Evidence" 60 61
"Miss Armstrong's Homicide" 94–95
"Miss Garnett's Tenant" 78
"The Missing Jewels" 132, 153, 182
"The Missing Picture" 89
"The Missing Ring" 111
"Mr. Buston's Eye: Amazing Detective Work Performed by that Organ" 200
"Mr. Furbush" 91, 169, 180, 202, 210
"Mr. Snicker's Misadventure" 13, 17, 180
"Mr. Sterling's Confession" 181
Mitford, Mary R. 71, 84
"The Modern Science of Thief-Taking" 171, 177
"Monday" 118
"Moneybags and Son" 101
The Monk 10
"The Monk Detective; or The Maniac's Release" 35, 107, 166

242   Index

The Monongalia Mirror 49
The Moonstone 30, 115, 153
"A Mormon Way" 134
Mott, Valentine 76
"A Mountain Adventure" 205
The Mountain Democrat 70, 100, 167, 181, 186
"A Moustache, and What Came of It" 20
Mower County Transcript 97
Munn, Cora 125
Munro, George 181, 229; see also *The New York Fireside Companion*
Munroe, N.T.: "A Mysterious Manifestation" 72, 117
"The Murder at Carew Court" 82–83
"The Murder at Cedar Glen" 78, 130, 140
"Murder Most Foul" 119
"The Murder of the Miser" 27, 155
"Murder Under the Microscope" 66, 90
"murder will out" (phrase and concept) 59, 76, 139, 162–163, 167, 169, 202, 221
"Murder Will Out" (titles) 59, 139, (1864) 162
"Murder Will Out: A Gold Digger's Adventure" 35
"Murdered Himself" 133
"A Murderer's Ordeal: A California Story" 21, 157, 159–161
"The Murderess" 133
"The Murders at Sunset Canyon" 145, 206
"The Murders in the Rue Morgue" 8, 11–12, 23, 25, 35, 98, 142, 154, 172, 175–176, 187–188, 208, 215, 219
"My First Brief" 83
"My First Case" 187, 205
"My First Trip Across the Atlantic" 30
"My German Tutor" 82
"My Own Peculiar, or Stray Leaves from the Port-Folio of a Georgia Lawyer" 48, 53
"My Uncle's Story: How a Murderer Was Discovered by Dreams" 211
"My Wife's Maid" 152
The Mysteries and Miseries of New York 33
The Mysteries of Paris 33
"The Mysterious Advertisement" 19, 203, 206
"The Mysterious Burglar: A Detective's Story" 166
"The Mysterious Deaths at Castellane" 31
"A Mysterious Disappearance" 94
"The Mysterious Highwayman" 30, 144
"A Mysterious Manifestation" 72, 117
"The Mysterious Mark" 216
"A Mysterious Murder" 36–37, 80, 112, 119
"The Mysterious Murder" 78, 82, 117, 119, 210
"The Mysterious Murder, Leaves from the Diary of a Detective" 210
"The Mysterious Occurrence in Lambeth" 28–29, 115
"Mysterious Robberies: A Detective's Story" 204
"A Mysterious Valise" 9
"The Mystery of Marie Roget" 8, 11, 64, 69, 98, 154, 188
"A Mystery of Paris" 33

The National Era 71
National Republican 127
The New Bloomfield, Pa., Times 127
The New Hampshire Statesman 35, 49
The New Monthly Magazine 48, 123
The New Orleans Picayune 165, 182–183
New York 4, 11–13, 17–27, 29, 34, 47, 68–69, 73–74, 90, 94, 122–123, 125–127, 138, 147–148, 166, 171–174, 176, 178–179, 192, 194, 196, 200–201, 203, 216, 218
New York Daily Tribune 171
The New York Fireside Companion 21, 30, 35, 76–77, 81, 104, 108, 123, 145, 155, 163, 166–168, 183, 186–187, 204–205, 208, 229
The New York Ledger 4, 13, 15–16, 21–22, 27–29, 32, 35–36, 49, 58, 61, 63, 68–70, 72, 74–76, 78, 80–83, 85, 87, 93, 103, 105–109, 112–115, 118–119, 129–130, 135, 140–141, 144–147, 150, 152, 155, 157–162, 166, 168, 180–181, 186, 189–192, 204, 210–211
The New York Star 35
New York Times 1, 34, 88, 121, 175, 194, 197, 210
New Zealand 4, 209
Newark Union 147
The Newgate Calendar: Comprising Interesting Memoirs of the Most Notorious Characters who Have Been Convicted of Outrages on the Laws of England Since the Commencement of the Eighteenth Century; with Occasional Anecdotes and Observations, Speeches, Confessions, and Last Exclamations of Sufferers 44
Newnes, George 222
News and Citizen 102
The News and Herald 14, 57
Newton, Sir Isaac 145
"A Night Adventure" 175
"A Night Adventure in New York" 103
"A Noble Sacrifice: A Tale of Washington, D.C." 37, 81, 83, 112
"Not a Ghost Story" 140
notebook stories 18, 20, 29, 31, 37, 48–49, 159, 172, 182, 184–186, 203, 218
"Number Eight" 93, 198
"Number Thirty-Nine" 110
"The Nun's Priest's Tale" 59

"An Observing Man: The Capture Made by a Private Detective" 25
Oconto Pioneer 181
"An Official Blunder" 31–33, 207, 212
The Ohio Democrat 27, 155
Old Bailey 41, 48
Old Bailey Experience: Criminal Jurisprudence and the Actual Working of our Penal Code of Laws 41
"The Old Doctor's Story" 71
"An Old Lawyer's Story" 63
"Oliver Wendell Holmes (1809–1894) and his essay on puerperal fever" 66–67
Omaha Daily Bee 57, 64, 89, 126
The Omaha World Herald 21

"On a Field of Azure a Silver Star" 150, 164
"On his Track, a Detective's Story" 207
Once a Week 9
"One Night in a Gaming House" 171
The Orleans County Monitor 90
Orleans Independent Standard 3, 53
"The O'Shaughnessy Diamonds" 153
The Oshkosh True Democrat 8
"Our Cabin Passenger" 161
"Our Cook's Revenge" 81, 216
"Our New Pupil" 159
Overland Monthly 101–102, 168

"Pages from the Diary of a Philadelphia Lawyer" (series) 48; "A Chapter on Aristocracy" 48; "The Counterfeiter" 48; "The Murderess" 49; "Unnatural Prosecution" 48–49; "The Will" 54
Palmer, Melvin Delmar [Del] 85
The Palo Alto Reporter 34, 94
The Parisian Detective or, A Desperate Deed 34
Paris 8, 10–12, 21, 31–35, 66, 89–90, 94, 101, 109, 113, 122, 129, 176, 181, 218
Parker, Kitty 125
Parkman-Webster case 78, 138
Paschal, Mrs. 131
Peake, Thomas: *A Compendium of the Law of Evidence* 45
Peck, Mrs. Ellen 125, 126
Peele, Robert 173
"The Pen Knife Blade: From a Surgeon's Diary" 70, 75–76, 107, 157
The Perrysburg Journal 54
"Personal to Mr. Gimblett" 132–133
"The Pet of the Law" 122
Peterson's Magazine 82, 92, 162
Le Petit Vieux des Batignolles 4
Philadelphia 11–12, 19–21, 25, 27, 34, 52, 137–138, 147, 173, 192, 198, 216
Philadelphia Album and Ladies Literary Gazette 7, 175
Phillipps, Samuel March: *A Treatise on the Law of Evidence* 45
photography 33, 56, 88–91, 146, 158, 210
phrenology 69, 116, 159–160, 162–163
physical evidence 54–55, 63–64, 79, 221; *see also* blood; prints
physicians 1, 65–68, 70–77, 81, 84–85, 96, 169, 172, 181, 185, 188, 194, 218, 222; heroes 71–78
physiognomy 161
"A Piece of Deception" 35
"The Pigot Murder" 21, 82, 180, 198
Pinkerton, Allan 28, 125, 151, 174, 190; "A Brilliant Confidence Swindle in High Life" 110; *Criminal Reminiscences and Detective Sketches* 110; *The Expressman and the Detective* 175; Pinkerton's Agency 125, 127, 174, 191; Pinkerton's Rogue's Gallery 26
"A Pinkerton Detective" 104
"The Pious Robber" 163
Pittsburg Dispatch 131, 208

plagiarism *see* copyright piracy
The Plain Dealer 23, 76, 92
"The Platinum Filling" 76, 101–102, 168
Plot and Passion; Or, The Female Detective (play) 131
plot types 187–190; capture-and-escape 183; cipher 179; circumstantial evidence 84, 142, 187–189, 199, 213; forensic 55; hunt-and-chase 22–23, 28, 189–190; innocent accused 60–61, 115–116, 119, 133, 140–142, 154, 163, 174, 188–189, 221–222; locked-room 11, 24–25; missing body 56; perjury 55; treasure hunt 55
The Plymouth Weekly Democrat 177
Poe, Edgar Allan: "The Gold Bug" 172; "The Murders in the Rue Morgue" 8, 11–12, 23, 25, 35, 98, 142, 154, 172, 175–176, 187–188, 208, 215, 219; "The Mystery of Marie Roget" 8, 11, 64, 69, 98, 154, 188; "The Purloined Letter" 8, 11, 90, 98, 208; "Thou Art the Man!" 11–14, 62, 85, 142, 188
poison 78, 80–85, 92–93, 117, 154, 156, 159, 210, 216–217, 221; aconite 72; antimony 76, 82; Aqua Toffana 78; arsenic 62, 70, 75, 78, 80–81, 143, 210, 216; atropia/atropine 82; belladonna 72, 82; chloroform 77, 82, 217; ergot 80; hydrogen cyanide 81; laudanum 101; potassium cyanide 80; Prussic acid 81–82; strychnine 80, 82
"The Poisoner" 81, 119, 182
police departments 8–9, 17–18, 25–28, 30, 32–34, 42, 64–65, 123–129, 134, 138, 171–176, 178–179, 184–185, 190–192, 195–197, 207, 218, 220
"A Police-Officer's Seven Thousand Miles' Chase" 17, 178, 189
"A Polish Princess' Appetite" *see* "Mademoiselle Jabirouska"
Pope, Alexander: "The Rape of the Lock" 41
"The Porcelain Button" 119, 149, 157, 162
The Portage Sentinel 52
Portraits, Memoirs, and Characters, of Remarkable Persons 40
"A Possible Case of Circumstantial Evidence" 146
post-mortem 69–70, 72, 75–76, 157, 165, 188, 210
"A Post-Mortem Discovery: A Scrap from a Physician's Diary" 75–76, 82, 155
Potter's American Monthly 119, 214
A Practical Treatise on Criminal Law Comprising the Practice, Pleadings, and Evidence 45
A Practical Treatise on the Law of Evidence 45
Prairie du Chien Patriot 122
Prairie Farmer 23, 119, 130, 166
"Pray, Sir, Are You a Gentleman?" 106
The Preble County Democrat 3
"The Price of Two Lives" 81–82
"The Print of a Finger" 201
prints 85–89; bootmark 24, 230; fingermarks 86–88, 91; fingerprints 56, 85–89, 91, 158,

244　Index

201; footprints 111, 130; thumbmark 86–88, 91; thumbprint 88–89
Prisoners' Counsel Act 43
"A Private Detective" 197, 200
"Prosecutors and Litigants" 40
The Puget Sound Herald 29, 145, 191
Pullman Herald 16, 28, 95, 125
"The Punched Kopeck" 35
"The Purloined Letter" 8, 11, 90, 98, 208
"The Pursuit" 177, 189

The Quaker City 33
"A Queer Clue" 9
"Quick Work: From the Diary of Hawkshaw the Detective" 30, 186

Racine Advocate 111
The Radical 56, 171
The Raftsman's Journal 2, 53, 62
Railroad 25, 33, 92, 126, 147, 174, 216
Randolph, Amy: "Major Truslow's Mistake" 135; "The Murder at Carew Court" 82–83; "The Murder at Cedar Glen" 78, 130, 140
rape 97, 102–104, 143
"The Rape of the Lock" 41
"Reaped What They Sowed" 81
Rexford, Eben E.: "Guilty or Not Guilty" 12
"The Robber's Revenge" 9, 110
"The Robber's Roost" 15, 145
Rocky Mountain News 20
Recollections of a Detective Police-Officer; see *Recollections of a Policeman*
Recollections of a Policeman (a.k.a. *Recollections of a Detective Police-Officer*): "The Gambler's Revenge" 8; "Guilty or Not Guilty" 177; "Legal Metamorphoses" 178; Mary Kingsford 128; "One Night in a Gaming House" 171; "The Pursuit" 177, 189; "The Revenge" 178; "The Robber's Revenge" 9, 110, 178; "The Twins" 177; "Villainy Outwitted" 9, 178
"Recollections of a Retired Lawyer" 48
The Red Barn 137
"The Red Chest: An Experience in the Life of a Russian Detective" 35, 124
"A Reminiscence of a Bow-Street Officer" 9, 28, 178
"The Reminiscences of an American Detective" 222
Reno Evening Gazette 23, 116
reprints 3, 8, 16–17, 30, 46–47, 56, 62, 91, 109, 116, 125–126, 178, 182, 192, 216
"Resting Powders" 80–81, 159, 216
"The Resurrectionist" 161
resurrectionists 13, 51, 69–70, 74, 157, 161
"Retired from the Force" 28
"Retribution" 59
Revelations of a Lady Detective 131
The Revelations of a Private Detective: "Who Stole the Plate?" 153; see also Forrester, Andrew, Jr.
"The Revenge" 178

rewards 39–40, 94, 104, 127, 131–132, 175, 196–198
Rexford, Eben E.: "Guilty or Not Guilty" 119, 130, 166
Reynolds, George W. M. 137
rhetoric 53–55
The Richwood Gazette 140, 201
"The Rifle" 71–72, 84
The River Press 127
The Riverine Grazier 64
"The Robber's Revenge" 9, 110, 178
"The Robbers' Roost" 15, 145
"Robbery at Osborne's Hotel" 185
"The Robbery of Plate" 19, 111, 117, 153, 204
Robinson, Sarah Jane 154
Robinson's Magazine: A Weekly Repository of Original Papers and Selections from English Magazines 45, 48, 56
The Rock Island Argus 87, 88
Rockland County Journal 151
The Rocky Mountain News 20
Rogers, Mary 154
Rogers, Stephen, M.D. 82
rogues gallery 18, 26–27, 89, 148, 179
"Romance of a Diamond" 153
"Romance of a Railway Carriage" 159
"The Romance of Cracker's Neck" 16, 144–145
"Romance of Making Wills" 54
Rommily, Samuel 55
Roscoe, Henry: *A Digest of the Law of Evidence in Criminal Cases* 45
Rulloff, John 138
Russell, William see Waters, Thomas
Russia 11, 34–35, 92, 124

Sacramento Daily Union 35, 90, 99, 108, 148, 168
Sacramento Sunday Union 126
safes 115, 143, 149–152, 166
St. Joseph Herald 3, 25, 212
St. Louis Globe-Democrat 20, 37, 83, 133–134, 211
Saint Mary's Beacon 90
St. Paul Daily Globe 119, 126, 203
St. Tammany Farmer 199
Salt Lake Evening Democrat 94
The Sandusky Daily Register 16–17, 20
Santa Fe Weekly Gazette 106, 146
"Sapphire Eyes" 83
"A Satanic Compact" 74
Saunders, Margaret 108–109
"Saved by a Detective" 160, 192
"Saved by a Dream" 211
"Saved by a Mark: A Detective Story" 4, 79, 192, 210
"Saved by a Telephone" 82, 92
"Scandal in Bohemia" 215
"The Scarlet Ribbon: A Detective Story" 22, 184, 195
Schenectady Reflector 82, 117, 119
science 78–95
Scotland Yard 20, 34–35, 108–109, 148, 159, 170, 173

"The Scourge of the Highway" 144
"Scraps from the Notebook of a Missouri Lawyer" 49, 53, 61
"The Scratch of a Pin" 22
"The Second Sight" 102, 105, 140
"The Secret Cell" 8, 10, 28, 35, 97–98, 116, 128, 175–176, 187
"The Secret Door" 25
The Sedalia Weekly Bazoo 2
"The Seducer" 98
Semi-Weekly Bourbon News 152
sensation novels 30, 52, 55, 60, 65, 72, 99, 114, 130, 137, 164, 183–184, 217–219
servants 72, 107, 114–115, 117–119, 123, 129–130, 133–134, 163, 210, 213
The Seven Poor Travellers 178
"Seven Up" 151
"Seventy Miles an Hour" 31, 33
Sevier, Sadie 125
"A Sewer Rat: A Leaf from a Detective's Life" 207
Shadowed by Three 208
Sherman, Lydia 154
Short Stories: "Miss Armstrong's Homicide" 94–95
"Shoving the Queer" 211
"Sibyl's Augury: From a Physician's Diary" 75
"The Sick Robber: and How Tim Cured Him" 118
"Signed with my Own Blood" 195
The Silence of the Lambs 137
"The Silver Arrow" 140
"The Silver Bullet" 16–17
"The Silver Pin" 20, 69–70
Sinclair: "A Noble Sacrifice: A Tale of Washington, D.C." 37, 81, 83, 112
Sinclair, Oliver: "The Diamond Cross or, the Female Assassin" 119
"A Singular Story" 110
Sioux County Herald 83, 128, 130, 205
"A Sister's Vengeance" 120
sleepwalking *see* somnambulism
small towns 12–15
Smith, Dr. S. Compton: "The Horse Detective" 162, 191; "The White Perfumery Bottle" 162
Le Solitaire 111–112
The Somerset Press 58
somnambulism 115, 166, 213, 217
The Southern Literary Messenger 48
Southern Watchman 113
Spence, George 44
spies 3, 32, 133, 143, 173
"Spirits Utilized: Two Thieves Captured Through Information Given by the Spirit of Vidocq" 8
The Spirit of Democracy 49, 53, 59, 61
The Spirit of Jefferson 50, 54, 58
Spofford, Harriet E. Prescott 91, 202; "In a Cellar" 35, 202; "In the Magurriwock" 167; "Mr. Furbush" 91, 169, 180, 202, 210
Spring-heeled Jack 137
"Stabbed in the Back" 19–20, 27, 209

The Star and Sentinel 111, 114, 118, 160
The Stark County Democrat 47
Starke, Thomas 45
"State's Evidence, A Detective Story" 195
The Staunton Spectator 63
"The Step Mother: Leaves from a Lawyer's Portfolio" 49
Sterling Standard 132, 135, 169
Stevens, James Fitzjames 42
Stevens Point Journal 92, 153
"The Stolen Diamond" 113–114
"Stolen Laces" 149
"The Stolen Letter: A Lawyer's Story" 129, 178
"The Stolen Silks: A Detective's Story" 149
stomach pump 76
Stories of American Life by American Writers: "The Rifle" 71–72, 84
Stories for the Home Circle: "The Left-Hand Glove: or Circumstantial Evidence" 105, 115
"Story of a London Bank Cashier" 212
"Story of a Thumb-Mark, Remarkable Detection of a Murder" 88, 91
"Story of an Australian Detective" 35
"A Story of Circumstantial Evidence" 130
"Story of Crime" 182
"A Story of Russia" 35
"Story Paper Literature" 200
story papers 1, 3–5, 19, 33, 80, 95–96, 180–182, 200–201, 215, 220, 229–230
The Strand 5, 215, 222
"The Strange Discovery" 10, 129
"A Strange Story from the French" *see* "Mademoiselle Jabirouska"
Strange Occurrences 132
Strange Stories of a Detective; or, The Curiosities of Crime 4, 8–9, 20, 31, 74, 100; "The Assassin's Track" 24, 196, 207; "The Confidential Clerk" 22, 148, 160; "The Golden Haired Wig" 159; *The Libertine* 100; "Moneybags and Son" 101; "The Torn Glove" 93; "The Trap" 145, 148, 185; "The Trial for Murder" 81
"A Strange Story Wonderful: Chain of Circumstantial Evidence" 56–57
"A Study In Scarlet" 133
Sue, Eugène 10, 137; *The Mysteries of Paris* 33
suicide 80, 82–83, 100–101, 112, 115, 117, 122, 135, 143, 168, 184
Sullivan Republican 199
Sumner Gazette 197, 200
The Sumter Watchman 119
The Sun 126, 179
The Sunday Herald 34, 201
The Sunny South 27, 111
Suppressed Sensations, or Leaves from the Note Book of a Chicago Reporter: "A Mysterious Murder" 36–37, 80, 112, 119
Sûreté Nationale 175
"A Sympathetic Link" 119

"T4FG2G: A Detective Experience" 18–19, 179
Tait's Edinburgh Magazine 47

246 Index

A Tale of Mystery (play) 137
"Tale of a Shadow, Many a Merry Chase After an Eccentric Young New Yorker. The Divorce Detective's Puzzle" 208
"Tardy Justice" 116
telegraph 3, 27, 91–92, 185, 216
"The Telegraph Detective" 25, 91–92
telephone 37, 92
"The Tell-Tale Eye" 31, 33, 91, 146, 181, 193
"A Tell-Tale Toothpick" 26
Temple, Charles: "Pray, Sir, Are You a Gentleman?" 106
"The Temptress" 58
"Ten Millions—An Extraordinary Story" 165
"The Terrors of the Telephone: A Detective Story" 92
Theodore Duhamel 31
Therman, Mrs. Clara 125
"Thief-Catching in Canada" 91–92
"The Thief in the Night" 115
thief-taker 31, 40, 105, 159, 170–171, 201
"Thou Art the Man!" 11–14, 62, 85, 142, 188
"A Thumb-print and What Came of It" 88
"The Ticket of Leave Man" 30
The Tiffin Weekly Tribune 71, 102
The Times-Picayune 165
The Tioga County Agitator 27
Tioga Eagle 8, 128
Tit-Bits from All the Most Interesting Books, Periodicals and Newspapers in the World 222
"Told by a Detective" 150
Tompkins, Mrs. Mary J. 125
"The Torn Bill" 27
"The Torn Glove" 93
"The Torn Newspaper" 72, 85
"Tracing a Murderer" 34
tracking 176–177, 207–208; *see also* prints
The Tragedy of Pudd'nhead Wilson 88
"Trailing a Thief. A Detective's Long Chase After a Fugitive Cashier. From Minnesota Through Canada, England, France, Spain and Italy to Switzerland—A Clever Ruse to Avoid Extradition Proceedings" 28
"The Trap" 145, 148, 185
Traps for the Young 217
"Treasure of Rampsinitus" 129
A Treatise on Evidence 45
A Treatise on the Law of Evidence 45
A Treatise of the Pleas of the Crown: or a system of the principal matters, relating to that subject, digested under their proper heads 42
"The Trial for Murder" 81
"Tried for Murder" 4, 76, 81
Trove 215
True American 129
The True Northerner 125
The Tuapeka Times 4
Turner, Johnson B. 182; "A Bit of Mystery" 182; "A Double Crime" 182; "The Finger of Providence" 94, 182; "The Poisoner" 81, 119, 182; "Story of Crime" 182

Turner County Herald 199
Turpin, Dick 137
Twain, Mark: *Life on the Mississippi* 89; "Making a Fortune" 197; "A Thumb-print and What Came of It" 88; *The Tragedy of Pudd'nhead Wilson* 88
"Twenty-Six Heads" *see* "Mademoiselle Jabirouska"
"The Twins" 177
"The Twisted Ring: Experience of a French Detective in Russia" 35, 92
"The Two Chiefs of the Detective Force" 34
"The Two-Fingered Assassin" 87, 103, 105
"The Two Nephews" 80, 216
Tyler, Tom "The Ticket of Leave Man" 30

"An Uninvited Guest" 151
The Union Democrat 116
"The Unknown Death" 93
"Unnatural Prosecution" 48–49
"Unpublished Passages in the Life of Vidocq, The French Minister of Police" 7–8, 10, 175; "Doctor D'Arsac" 129; "Jean Monette" 102; Marie Laurent 10; "The Seducer" 98; "The Strange Discovery" 10, 129
Urbana Union 50

Valley Herald 123, 210
Van Dine, S.S. 153–154
The Van Wert Republican 104
Varnoe, Detective 94, 182; "A Bit of Mystery" 182; "A Double Crime" 182; "The Finger of Providence" 94, 182; "The Poisoner" 81, 119, 182; "Story of Crime" 182
"A Verdant Juror" 58
Vermont Phœnix 3, 171
The Vermont Watchman and State Journal 208
"A Very Narrow Escape" 58
"The Victim of a Plot" 110
Victor, Metta Fuller: *The Dead Letter* 26–27
"The Victory; a Strange Crime and its Solution" 83, 128, 205
Vidocq, Eugène François (character) 7–11, 31, 64, 98–99, 126, 129, 175; (man) 7–8, 37, 45, 171, 175, 180, 186, 193; (term) 171; *see also* "Unpublished Passages in the Life of Vidocq, The French Minister of Police"
"Vidocq and the Sexton" 7, 9, 175
"Vidocq; or, The Charcoal Burners of France" 175
"The Vigilants' Mistake" 34
"Villainy Outwitted" 9, 178
"The Vital Point" 111
"The Volunteer Counsel" 53

"The Walker Street Tragedy" 23–24, 167
"Walnuts" 117
Walters, Warren: "Bob Cheriot, Esq.; or, the Tragedy at Chelmsford" 119, 213
Ward and Lock 4, 9, 128, 153
Warne, Kate 125, 131

Warner, Charles Dudley 149
Warren, Samuel: *The Confessions of an Attorney; which are added Several Papers on English Law and Lawyers by Charles Dickens* 47
Warren Ledger 81, 150, 164
Washington Intelligencer 121
Washington Post 1
"Watched and Watching: A Detective Story" 28–29, 204
The Waterloo Courier 93, 198
Waters, Inspector 128, 177, 194, 198
Waters, Thomas (William Russell): *The Autobiography of an English Detective* 29–30, 66, 79, 90; *The Diary of a Detective Police Officer* 29, 186; *The Experiences of a French Detective Officer, Adapted from the MSS of Theodore Duhamel* 31; *Leaves from the Diary of a Law-Clerk* 105, 107, 108; *Recollections of a Policeman* (a.k.a. *Recollections of a Detective Police-Officer*) 8–9, 17, 31, 37, 47–48, 128, 171, 177–178, 184, 189, 193–194; *Strange Stories of a Detective; or The Curiosities of Crime* 4, 8–9, 20, 31, 74, 100
Weekly Argus and Democrat 117
The Weekly Portage Sentinel 58
The Weekly Thibodaux Sentinel and Journal of the 8th Senatorial District 105
Weekly Wisconsin 69, 116, 122, 160
Wells, Alice Stebbin 124
Wells, L.H.: "A Story of Circumstantial Evidence" 130
Wellsboro Agitator 88, 91, 200
The Western Democrat 57
The Western Kansas World 83
The Western Rural and Illinois Stockman 25
Western Union 2
Westminster Detective Library 2, 5–6, 225
"What I Learned About Counterfeiting" 25
The Wheeling Daily Intelligencer 125
White Cloud Kansas Chief 15, 145
"The White Perfumery Bottle" 162
"Who is Guilty" 81
"Who is the Thief?" 28, 180
"Who Killed Him? Or, The Twisted Ring" 83
"Who Killed the Judge? a Mystery of Crime" 24
"Who Stole the Plate?" 153
"'Who was the Murderer!' from the German" 177

"Why I Became a Detective" 148–149, 186, 205
"Wicked Ah Hee" 20
"The Widow Reed" 118
"A Wife's Crime: A Mexican Murder which for a Time Defied Solution" 35
Wild, Jonathan 40, 55, 170
"A Wild Goose Chase" 199
wilderness 15–17
"The Will" 54
Williams, John B., M.D. 22, 141, 194; *Leaves from the Note-Book of a New York Detective: The Private Record of J(ames). B(rampton)* 20, 68, 73–74, 181, 193–194, 212–213; "The Bowie Knife Sheath" 19, 22, 213; "The Broken Cent" 20; "My First Brief" 83; "The Satanic Compact" 74; "The Silver Pin" 20, 69–70; "The Walker Street Tragedy" 23–24, 167; *see also* Brampton, James
Wilmington Journal 71
Winwood, Rhett: "The Scarlet Ribbon: A Detective's Story" 22, 184
Wisconsin Argus 189
Wisconsin Patriot 122, 187, 192
The Wisconsin State Register 112
"The Withered Hand" 135
Wolf, Phillip: "Who is Guilty" 81
Woman in White 106
Wontner, Thomas 41
Wood, Mrs. Henry (Helen/Ellen) 137; "Coming Out of Exile; or The Diamond Bracelet Found" 28, 114, 130
"A Work-Woman's Misfortune" 115–116
"Worked by Telephone" 92
The World: Saturday Evening 126
"Written in Blood" 120
"The Wronged Wife" 114, 119
wronged woman 98–102, 111, 114, 122, 168

"'X' AND 'H.' A Telegraph Operator's Story" 91–92

Yorkville Enquirer 105
Young, Mary C.: "Our Cabin Passenger" 161
"The Young Lawyer's First Case" 50
"The Young Widow" 122, 187, 192

"ZiZi the Little Detective" 168, 191

www.ingramcontent.com/pod-product-compliance
Lightning Source LLC
Chambersburg PA
CBHW051218300426
44116CB00006B/617